Praise for *World Christianity*

"It is becoming very difficult to figure out _____ Christianity and its almost infinite compositions and multifaceted forms of existences, we feel at loss. World Christianity and Interfaith Relations is a remarkable resource to help us get into those muddy waters. With voices from different parts of the world, this book engages vivid themes of our time such as nationalism, intolerance, race, gender, ecology, forms of resistance, religious dialogues, ecumenical efforts, and more. This book shows us how much we need to pause, learn, and change our views. It is indeed rich material for anyone who wants to understand the complexities of the Christian faiths across the globe."

—Cláudio Carvalhaes, associate professor of worship,
Union Theological Seminary, New York City

"In Asia, Africa, and Latin America, Christianity is recklessly entangled with matters relating to justice, poverty, race and ethnicity, nationalism, ecological destruction, and encounters with other religious traditions. Courageously and competently, the authors immerse themselves in what too often have been the 'touch-me-not' issues of those fixated on church growth. Representing wide-ranging disciplinary perspectives and cultural experiences, these scholars make highly original and indispensable contributions to the study of World Christianity. At a time when livelihoods are threatened by toxic nationalism, climate change, land displacement, and interreligious conflict, the rigorous engagement presented in this volume couldn't be timelier."

—Chandra Mallampalli, Fletcher Jones Chair of Social Sciences
and Professor of History, Westmont College, Santa Barbara, California

"Volume 4 of this ground-breaking series delivers a rich selection of multi-layered narratives and interpretations of interfaith realities within and beyond indigenous Christian communities in Myanmar, India, Canada, Brazil, Uganda, Nigeria, and Southern Africa. Interrogating the entanglements of religion and nationalism, race, gender, ecology, privilege, decolonization, violence, caste, spatiality, and theological normativity, this volume uniquely offers emic and etic perspectives of Christians and religious others. A nuanced, thought-provoking, and vital contribution to the field of World Christianity!"

—Thomas John Hastings, executive director, OMSC
at Princeton Theological Seminary, and editor,
International Bulletin of Mission Research (SAGE)

"In *World Christianity and Interfaith Relations*, Richard Fox Young has put together an excellent collection of essays from scholars representing an array of perspectives on World Christianity. Various regions of Asia, Latin America, and Africa receive attention in this book as categorized within provocative sub-themes. This illustrates how World Christianity is embedded within some of the most topical aspects concerning human existence today, both as a contributing factor to some of our most serious challenges but also, potentially, as crucial to their resolution. This is a great contribution on the wider series theme of World Christianity as a public religion."

—Retief Müller, VID Specialized University,
Stavanger, Norway

"In one volume, readers will find is a broad-based survey of the contemporary interface between Christian communities and other faith traditions across the globe. Writing from disparate perspectives and using tools from various disciplines, the authors critically and carefully analyze a wide range of issues, in particular interfaith and ecumenical relationships. A much-needed resource! I highly recommend it to scholars and students seeking to understand and appreciate World Christianity."

—James Taneti, assistant professor of World Christianity,
Union Presbyterian Seminary, Richmond, Virginia

"This book is a splendid achievement: it illustrates how Christians, as members of the world community, constantly relate to their contemporaries belonging to living religions and ideologies. This relationality is especially true for Asian, African, and Latin American Christians in the Global South. They understand and interpret their Christianity in relation to their non-Christian neighbors. Fourteen essayists of this volume capture the views of these Christians, as they engage with their neighbors on the ground. Their Christianity reflects their living contexts, experiences, challenges, and aspirations for themselves and their neighbors. Therefore, a healthy study of World Christianity necessarily considers interfaith relations and religious experiences.

"This volume contains four focal points and approaches them from multidisciplinary and transnational perspectives. Firstly, four essayists representing India, Myanmar, and Brazil discuss the impact of contemporary notions and practices of religious freedom, religious intolerance, and resurgent nationalism on fellow Christians, who often constitute minorities. Secondly, three Brazilian authors examine the place and role of gender and ecology in ethnographic imagination. Thirdly, an American and two Nigerian authors articulate the indispensable need for peace and reconciliation initiatives in troubled and peaceful times.

Finally, two Indian theologians, a Ghanian theologian, and a South African theologian, who had their early education in the Global South, but live and work in the Global North, reflect on the North-South and South-North relationship of Christianity both in the Global South and the Global North.

"I warmly recommend this book to all scholars and students who engage with studies in World Christianity, Theology, World Religions, Indigenous religions, philosophy, and the social sciences."

—P. Daniel Jeyaraj, professor of world Christianity
and director of Andrew F. Walls Centre
for the Study of African and Asian Christianity,
Liverpool Hope University, England

World Christianity and Public Religion Series, Vol. 4

Series Editor: Raimundo C. Barreto

WORLD CHRISTIANITY AND INTERFAITH RELATIONS

World Christianity and Public Religion Series, Vol. 4

Series Editor: Raimundo C. Barreto

WORLD CHRISTIANITY AND INTERFAITH RELATIONS

Richard F. Young

Editor

FORTRESS PRESS

MINNEAPOLIS

WORLD CHRISTIANITY AND INTERFAITH RELATIONS

Cover image: A close-up of multiple candles in a vigil by Tammy616 | iStock photo

Cover design: Kristin Miller (series design by Alisha Lofgren)

Print ISBN: 978-1-5064-4849-7

eBook ISBN: 978-1-5064-4850-3

CONTENTS

THE WORLD CHRISTIANITY AND PUBLIC RELIGION SERIES

During the latter half of the twentieth century, scholars began to pay closer attention to the polycentric and culturally diverse nature of Christianity worldwide. In particular, the rapid growth in the number of Christians living in the Global South caught the attention of Western scholars as a trend that would not be reversed in the near future.

A number of books have been written in an attempt to offer clues on how these drastic demographic changes are reshaping Christian identity and relations worldwide. Beyond the fascination with numbers, the rapid growth Global South Christianities and their respective diasporas have experienced in recent decades is giving birth to a new global Christian consciousness with profound cultural, social, and economic implications that demand further scholarly attention. World Christianity scholarship has demonstrated that Christianity can no longer be dismissed as a Western religion. We have stepped onto the threshold of a new era. New and creative theological insights have emerged, debunking a Eurocentric hegemonic understanding of Christianity that prevailed in the modern era. Contrary to some assumptions, conversion to Christianity in former Western colonies did not imply the westernization of converts. On the contrary, Indigenous cultures and spiritualities that were expected to disappear or be absorbed into the colonial civilizational project remain alive and well. In fact, the end of the twentieth century saw a revitalization of Indigenous traditions and spirituality. Such a resurfacing of Indigenous voices significantly contributed to renewed understandings of Christianity that are not at odds with traditional worldviews.

This series engages emerging voices from a variety of Indigenous Christianities around the world, focusing not only on particular histories and practices but also on their theological articulations and impact on the broader society. If in the modern/colonial world the study of Christianity was predominantly informed by Eurocentric perspectives and priorities, the study of world Christianity at the beginning of the twenty-first century is more representative of diverse contextual experiences, their interaction through the formation of multidirectional transnational networks, and the relationship between Christianity and other religions. Globalization and mass migration have contributed to deepened exchanges among peoples and cultures worldwide, creating a growing demand for making intercultural communication, intercultural theologies, and interfaith dialogue more central to the study of world Christianity. Likewise, questions about hybridity, liminality, border thinking, and cultural interweaving—particularly in the context of formerly colonized cultures—have also gained more attention.

While new tools have been added to the study of Christianity, particularly in response to the cultural turn in the social sciences, some long-existing problems nevertheless still linger and equally require attention. Scientific and technological progress has not mitigated existing injustices and economic asymmetries. Socioeconomic injustice remains as fiercely prevalent as when the first theologies of liberation emerged in the 1960s. As Indian theologian Felix Wilfred reminds us, the demographic shift of world Christianity is not simply a shift "from the West to the South, but a shift of Christianity from the rich and middle classes to the poor." According to him, more than half of all Christians in the world live with less than $500 of annual income.[1]

In a context marked by disparity and scarcity, standing in solidarity with the poor remains a priority. Yet a concern with economic justice is not enough. Christians living in contexts marked by widespread poverty and injustice in different parts of the world are asking challenging and complex questions about the reasons for such inequality. The inhuman treatment many migrants, refugees, asylum seekers, and stateless persons receive when crossing borders, for instance, helps increase awareness of the indivisibility of justice, demanding renewed moral commitments and creative responses to problems that are amounting to a global calamity. Unjust relations based on race, gender, and sexuality, along with land-related disputes and environmental concerns, are part of the public agenda Christians are called to engage in, in both the Global North and the Global South. The growing awareness of the impact of the colonial hegemonic project upon minoritized groups—especially the eclipsed non-European Other—has produced new identity claims of previously silenced voices who are now more vocal about the epistemic injustice they have experienced. On the other hand, their regained visibility is often used to justify the growing fear of difference and a relentless sense of insecurity that are at the heart of multiple forms of nationalist and xenophobic ideologies. Such ideologies are quickly poisoning societies across the world, increasing the risk of violence against those who, perceived as different, are feared and discriminated against.

---

[1] Felix Wilfred, "Christianity between Decline and Resurgence," in *Christianity in Crisis?*, ed. Jon Sobrino and Felix Wilfred, vol. 3, Concilium 2005 (London: SCM, 2005), 31.

Considering all these things, public reasoning has become an increasingly important dimension of the study of world Christianity. After all, Christians worldwide are key actors in what scholars commonly refer to as the public sphere. Their public living and thinking are important sources for the interrogation of the impact of religion on public life vis-à-vis themes such as citizenship, public witness, peace, justice, environmental relations, and contemporary migration, among others.

This series, which stems from a partnership between Princeton Theological Seminary and Faculdade Unida de Vitoria (Brazil), aims to provide a unique space for sustained dialogue on all these matters. It blends a number of methods and approaches in the burgeoning field of world Christianity, placing them in conversation with other fields of study and disciplines, including public theology, postcolonial/decolonial theory, intercultural studies, migration studies, critical gender theory, critical race theory, queer theory, and globalization studies. The series intentionally gathers religious scholars and theologians representative of diverse Christian traditions and continents into conversation with one another. At its root are two schools related to the Reformed tradition, one located in South America and the other in North America—one that is young (having existed for a little more than two decades) and another with a tradition spanning over two hundred years.

In the first half of the twentieth century, Princeton Seminary appointed John A. Mackay as president after his tenure of almost two decades as a missionary in Latin America. That cross-cultural experience deeply influenced him and impacted his ecumenical thinking. By turning ecumenics into a field of study for the church in the twentieth century, Mackay, in many ways, anticipated the rise of the field we know today as world Christianity: "A new reality has come to birth. For the first time in the life of mankind the Community of Christ, the Christian Church, can be found, albeit in nuclear form, in the remotest frontiers of human habitation. This community has thereby become 'ecumenical' in the primitive, geographical meaning of that term. History is thus confronted with a new fact."[2]

Faculdade Unida de Vitoria, in turn, has a history marked by a commitment to the retrieval of a particular memory. Such memory is linked to theologians such as Richard Shaull and Rubem Alves. Shaull was a pioneer in encouraging young Latin American Christians such as Alves himself, Jovelino Ramos, João Dias de Araújo, Joaquim Beato, Beatriz Melano, and others to take their own social and cultural locations as their theological and social loci. In other words,

---

[2] John Alexander Mackay, *Ecumenics: The Science of the Church Universal* (Englewood Cliffs, NJ: Prentice Hall, 1964), vii.

he called them to do theology as Latin Americans. By doing that, he inadvertently contributed to the rise of Latin American liberation theology. Alves, who studied under Shaull at both the Presbyterian Seminary of Campinas and Princeton, wrote the first book-length treatise on liberation theology[3] while living in the United States. He was one of the most creative thinkers of his day, having also contributed to other subfields such as theopoetics.

As an heir of these combined stories, this series is deeply rooted in a long tradition, which continues to be renewed to respond to the challenges and circumstances of a new era. It fosters a dialogue that places priority on voices from the Global South but also invites participants from the Global North to engage with their peers from the South.

Furthermore, the series is published in English and Portuguese. Its bilingual nature garners an inclusionary approach. The work of authors who originally wrote in Portuguese (some also in Spanish) and otherwise would not be available to a broader English readership are through this series brought to the attention of Anglophone scholars, seminarians, and religious leaders. Similarly, the work of authors who, despite being known in the English-speaking world, remain largely unknown in Latin America are through this series made available to Latin American scholars who can read Portuguese. Above all, this series shows that it is possible to advance transnational and transcultural scholarly dialogues without placing priority on one particular language as lingua franca.

The series has six volumes. The first one, published in Brazil in 2016 and in the United States in 2017, approaches world Christianity as a form of public religion, identifying areas for possible intercultural engagement. Each of the remaining five volumes focuses on specific topics deemed important for a public agenda for world Christianity scholarship in the twenty-first century. Volume 2, published in English in 2019, examines migration as an important concern in world Christianity's public discourses. Volume 3 discusses current approaches to urbanization and identity in world Christianity. Volume 4 focuses on interfaith relations. Volume 5 presents a variety of perspectives on race, ethnicity, gender, and sexuality in world Christianity as part of a broader reflection on the evasion of justice. Finally, volume 6 brings attention to pressing environmental concerns in world Christianity scholarship, engaging with Global South and Global North theological responses to the imminent planetary crisis.

---

[3] Rubem Alves, "Towards a Theology of Liberation: An Exploration of the Encounter between the Languages of Humanistic Messianism and Messianic Humanism" (PhD diss., Princeton Theological Seminary, 1968).

Finally, in the hope that this series becomes a platform for intercultural and intergenerational dialogue, the editors of all volumes have sought to increase the interaction between seasoned and emerging scholars from all parts of the world, creating a broad table that may contribute to and enlarge international, intercultural, and interdisciplinary conversations.

Raimundo C. Barreto

ACKNOWLEDGMENTS

The gestation period before a book is born can, I suppose, be quite short. In my experience, however, books start slowly and take their time. That was the case this time, and the two years it took to bring this one out were interrupted by the global Covid-19 public health crisis. More than most books perhaps, a book like this must be true to its purpose and enlist a globally diverse spectrum of contributors who truly reflect the diversity of world Christianity. This was definitely not the easiest of times to sit at the keyboard, with life unsettled globally, but we (by which I mean the fourteen contributors to this volume) brought the baby to term and rejoice at its birth.

The midwives were plenty, but just a few can be mentioned here: the ones most immediately involved in conceiving of the project in the first place (that would be the general editor, Raimundo Barreto of Princeton Theological Seminary); our Fortress Press editor (the ever-helpful Jesudas Athyal); our Portuguese-English translator for several chapters by Brazilian friends (the versatile Monika Ottermann); our conscientious team of editorial assistants (Shalon Park, Guilherme Brasil de Souza, and Stephen DiTrolio, all Princeton doctoral candidates); our colleague in Brazil at the Faculdade Unida de Vitoria who will oversee the eventual publication of this volume in Portuguese (Professor Wanderley Pereira da Rosa, president of that institution); and, of course, Professor Jacqueline Lapsley, the academic dean here at Princeton Theological Seminary, who provides a generous subvention for the bilingual publication of the Fortress Press series on World Christianity and Public Religion. Without their help, always cheerfully rendered, the birthing process would not have been as easy.

As I sit to compose these words of thanks, I have just heard the sad news of the passing of Andrew F. Walls, a figure revered by all in the field of world Christianity, whom I had the joy of knowing as a colleague for the first few years of my tenure here on the faculty of Princeton Theological Seminary. Whatever I have done in the years since would not have been possible without his vision for the field, including the study of Global South religions as integral to studies in world Christianity. It seems only fitting that Andrew was on my mind and that I quoted him twice when I was writing the introduction to this volume the other day, shortly before the news broke. May his memory be a blessing.

A special word of thanks goes to my colleague Raimundo C. Barreto, already singled out for his birthing of the series as a whole. Raimundo also deserves credit for his unstinting encouragement during the production of the current volume and especially for his deep insights into world Christianity *and* ecumenics. Coming late to theological education and from a background in the history of religions, I have had much to learn from you, my friend!

Richard Fox Young
Princeton Theological Seminary
August 12, 2021

CONTRIBUTORS

Amidu Elabo earned his PhD in 2022 at Princeton Theological Seminary with a dissertation in religion and society. His research interests include religion, space, and place; critical spatial theories; data science; remote sensing; GIS and cartography; African Indigenous religions, Indigeneity, and land; material religion; African religions in the diaspora; African urbanism, postcoloniality; and the spatiality of African ethics.

Babalawô Carlos Alberto Ivanir dos Santos holds a PhD in comparative history from the Federal University of Rio de Janeiro (PPGHC/UFRJ), where he also conducted postdoctoral research. A babalawô of the Ifá religion in Nigeria and a babalorixá of Candomblé in Brazil, he is the author of the book *Marchar Não é Caminhar: Interfaces políticas e sociais das religiões de matriz africana no Rio de Janeiro* (2020). He teaches comparative history at PPGHC/UFRJ and is also a research fellow and coordinator at UFRJ's Laboratory of History of Religious Experiences (LHER/UFRJ). A widely respected human rights activist, he serves as public interlocutor and convener of the Walk in Defense of Religious Freedom and is the strategy adviser at the Center for Articulation of Marginalized Populations (CEAP).

Casely Baiden Essamuah, secretary, Global Christian Forum, is an ordained Methodist minister from Ghana. With degrees from the University of Ghana, Harvard, and Boston University, he has worked for two decades in global missions at evangelical churches in the United States. A reflective practitioner of his faith, he is a bicultural bridge builder, straddling the spheres of the Global South and North while working in missions, ecumenism, the church, and the academy. His publications include *Genuinely Ghanaian: A History of the Methodist Church, Ghana, 1961–2000* (2010).

David A. Hoekema served as academic dean and professor of philosophy at Calvin University (Michigan, USA), following previous appointments at the University of Delaware and St. Olaf College. He directed Calvin's

Ghana study program four times and served as a Fulbright Teacher-Scholar in Kenya. In retirement, he divides his time between West Michigan and southern Arizona, where he is a visiting scholar in the Philosophy Department at the University of Arizona. His contribution to this volume draws on research conducted for his 2019 monograph *"We Are the Voice of the Grass": Interfaith Peace Activism in Northern Ghana.*

David Emmanuel Singh, PhD, is research tutor and PhD stage leader at the Oxford Centre for Mission Studies. His areas of interest are Sufism, Islam, and interfaith relations in South Asia. Dr. Singh is the author of numerous research articles, seven edited volumes, several encyclopedia entries, book chapters, and two research monographs: *Sainthood and Revelatory Discourse: An Examination of the Basis for the Authority of Bayan in Mahdawi Islam* (2003) and *Islamization in Modern South Asia: Deobandi Reform and the Gujjar Response* (2012).

Elisa Rodrigues is professor of the Department of Religious Studies at the Federal University of Juiz de Fora (Brazil). Her PhD in social sciences is from the Universidade Estadual de Campinas (Unicamp), and her PhD in religious studies is from the United Methodist University of São Paulo. Professor Rodrigues is chair of Religion and Education, dedicated to the study of the relationship between religion and education and the teaching of religion in Brazilian public schools. She researches topics related to religious studies (or, as it is called in Brazil, "Science of Religion"), epistemology and education, Pentecostalism, religion in the public sphere, religion and politics, secularism, and religion-identity-culture.

Felipe Fanuel Xavier Rodrigues is an assistant professor of English at the Universidade Federal de Roraima (UFRR). He holds a PhD in comparative literature from the Universidade do Estado do Rio de Janeiro (UERJ). During 2014–15, he was a Fulbright Visiting Scholar at Dartmouth College. Dr. Rodrigues was the 2016–17 FAPERJ Nota 10 Postdoctoral Fellow in Literature at UERJ. His work focuses on the intersections of race, gender, and religion in Anglophone and Lusophone Black literatures. He is an elected executive committee member of the Modern Language Association (MLA) Languages, Literatures, and Cultures Luso-Brazilian Forum (2022–27).

Frederico Pieper is professor of the Department of Religious Studies of Federal University of Juiz de Fora (Brazil). His PhD was earned in religious studies at the United Methodist University of São Paulo (UMESP) and his PhD in philosophy at the University of Sao Paulo (USP). Professor Pieper is chair of Theory of Religion for research on hermeneutics, phenomenology, and religion; epistemology of religious studies; and religion and film. He is the author of *Religion and Film* (2015) as well as numerous articles in specialized journals.

Henry Mbaya is an Anglican priest currently assisting in the Diocese of False Bay, Cape Town. He is associate professor in church history in the Faculty of Theology at the University of Stellenbosch. He is the author of *The Making of an African Clergy in the Anglican Church in Malawi: 1898–1996* (2004) and *Resistance to and Acquiescence in Apartheid: St. Paul's Theological College, Grahamstown: 1965–92* (2018). His research focus is on the interface of colonial missions and African cultures in southern Africa.

Peniel Jesudason Rufus Rajkumar currently serves as "Global Theologian" with United Society Partners in the Gospel (formerly known as Society for Propagation of the Gospel), the oldest Anglican mission agency. He is also on the staff of Ripon College, Cuddesdon, in the UK. Rev. Dr. Rajkumar was until recently program coordinator for interreligious dialogue and cooperation with the World Council of Churches and adjunct professor at the Ecumenical Institute at Bossey. He is also an Honorary Canon of Worcester Cathedral. His most recent publications include *Faith(s) Seeking Understanding: Dialogue and Liberation* (2021, as editor).

Pum Za Mang (MA, Princeton Theological Seminary; PhD, Luther Seminary) is associate professor of world Christianity at Myanmar Institute of Theology, Yangon. His articles have appeared in *Asia Journal of Theology, Church History and Religious Culture, Dialog: A Journal of Theology, International Journal of Public Theology, Journal of Church and State, Review of Faith & International Affairs,* and *Studies in World Christianity.* His special interests include religion, politics, and ethnicity in his native country of Burma.

Richard Fox Young holds the Timby Chair in the History of Religions at Princeton Theological Seminary (Princeton, New Jersey, USA). An Indologist by training with a PhD from the University of Pennsylvania, he works in mission studies, world Christianity, and contiguous areas. *Resistant Hinduism* (1981), *The Bible Trembled* (1995), and *Vain Debates* (1996) are several of his most widely cited monographs on the encounter of Hindus and Buddhists with Christian missions in South Asia. His research is diverse but usually revolves around theory and methodology for the study of conversion to and from Christianity.

Ruth Vida Amwe is a PhD candidate at Princeton Theological Seminary in the religion and society program. She is interested in the religious and social life of African women in precolonial, colonial, and postcolonial Africa within Africa and its diaspora. Her research traverses across African (Indigenous) religions; African precolonial, colonial, and postcolonial histories; world Christianity; and ethics, migration, and African diasporic studies.

Sandra Duarte de Souza, PhD, is professor of the graduate program in religion sciences of the Methodist University of São Paulo and coordinator of the Group of Studies on Gender and Religion—Mandrágora/Netmal. She currently develops research in the following areas: gender and religion, with an emphasis on the debate on violence against women; politics and religion, especially considering the Brazilian political scenario and the actions of Catholic and evangelical parliamentarians opposed to reproductive and sexual rights; and feminist theology, having as its starting point the decolonial feminist debate.

Sunder John Boopalan, assistant professor of biblical and theological studies at Canadian Mennonite University in Winnipeg, Canada, is the author of the book *Memory, Grief, and Agency* (2017). His most recent essay, "Religious Amnesias, Mythologies, and Apolitical Affects in Racist Landscapes," is freely available online on *Religions*. Boopalan serves on the steering committee of the Liberation Theologies Unit of the American Academy of Religion and is a columnist for *The Blueprint*, a digital publication that explores identity, society, culture, human rights, and freedom by centering marginalized voices with an emphasis on South Asia and its diaspora.

INTRODUCTION

Richard Fox Young

In the concluding paragraph of an essay at the conclusion of a major resource on world Christianity, Andrew Walls, a pioneering figure in this newly emergent field—a field barely half a century old in its current form and notable for its preferential focus on the Global South—wrote of its transformative potential for Christian scholarship in the Global North:

> Perhaps the most striking single feature of Christianity today is the fact that the church now—more than ever before in its history—looks more like that great multitude whom none can number, drawn from all tribes and kindreds, people and tongues (Rev. 5:9; 7:9). Its diversity and history leads [*sic*] to a great variety of starting points for its theology and reflects varied bodies of experience. The study of Christian history and theology will increasingly need to operate from the position where most Christians are, and that will increasingly be the lands and islands of Africa, Asia, Latin America, and the Pacific. *Shared reading of the Scriptures and shared theological reflection will be to the benefit of all, but the oxygen-starved Christianity of the West will have most to gain.*[1]

While the jury may be out on whether Christianity's need of life support in the Global North is really so dire as Walls seems to say, world Christianity as a new and energetic field of study stands ready with a fresh supply of oxygen to invigorate "theological reflection." It will do this in ways that take into creative account the global reality of Christian faith as a polyform, polycentric, and polyglot phenomenon in a world of many religions that are also polyform, polycentric, and polyglot.

Accordingly, and in tandem with its predecessor volumes in the Fortress Press World Christianity and Public Religion series, this collection of essays prioritizes a diversity of scholarly voices, mainly from the Global South, who come

---

[1] Andrew Walls, "The Transmission of Christian Faith: A Reflection," in *The Wiley Blackwell Companion to World Christianity*, ed. Lamin Sanneh and Michael J. McClymond (Chichester, UK: Wiley-Blackwell, 2016), 698 (emphasis added).

from all continents and regions (except Oceania), from multiple ecclesiological traditions (except the Orthodox), and (in one case) from another faith altogether (Candomblé, an Afro-Brazilian religion). Some are confessional scholars, some are not; some are theologians whose concerns are normative, some are more at home in religious studies and other nonconfessional fields and disciplines; and some straddle both sides of the academic divide. Congruent with the epistemological orientation of world Christianity, most probably subscribe to some kind of perspectivalism and hold that if you only know Christianity in terms of your own location, you probably lack an appreciation of its variety and complexity; that if you seek to plumb the depths of Christianity in all of its locations simultaneously, the attempt is doomed to fail; and that if you ignore your own particular location, the endeavor could turn out to be empty of meaning.[2] Global North Christians who cultivate a predisposition of openness to the many ways Christians can be differently Christian in the Global South will hopefully experience in the pages ahead a fresh infusion of oxygen from the study of world Christianity.

To highlight an astute observation made by the general editor of this series, Raimundo Barreto, in the preface to volume 1, I extract here a kernel of the insight he offered there: "While in the past five centuries, Christianity's most immediate surrounding environment was highly influenced by Western dominance and its priorities (like the long debate around secularization), *world Christianity exists primarily in a context of religious pluralism, which necessarily puts it in relationship with other world religions.* In fact, from its inception, Christianity has always been shaped by its encounter with other religions. No religion is hermetically sealed."[3]

Not only is no religion "hermetically sealed," siloed, or isolated antiseptically from other religions, but religions are, I submit, the primary matrix out of which Christianity in the Global South emerges. Just as early Christianity emerged among and was conditioned by the preexisting Greco-Roman religions of Mediterranean antiquity (culturally, socially, and in a myriad of other ways), so have they by the religions in their respective extra-European contexts.[4]

---

[2] Here, I borrow inspiration for my understanding of perspectivalism from anthropologist Richard A. Shweder in *Why Do Men Barbecue? Recipes for Cultural Psychology* (Cambridge, MA: Harvard University Press, 2003), 2.

[3] Raimundo C. Barreto, preface to *World Christianity as Public Religion*, ed. Raimundo C. Barreto, Ronaldo Cavalcante, and Wanderley Pereira da Rosa (Minneapolis: Fortress, 2017), xvi (emphasis added).

[4] Here, I adduce as a case in point (only one among many) the translation of the Bible into Burmese by the American missionary Adoniram Judson (1788–1850). Judson crafted his theological nomenclature almost solely out of terminology already conditioned for a millennium or more by Theravada Buddhism. See La Seng Dingrin, "Is Buddhism Indispensable in the Cross-Cultural Appropriation of Christianity in Burma?," *Buddhist-Christian Studies* 29, no. 1 (2009): 3–22.

Today, too, the lived reality of being a Global South Christian should of necessity be understood in relation to the lived reality of neighboring religious communities and populations. That is all the more evident in light of the fact that in the highly pluralized regions where Global South Christians live (and, increasingly, Global North Christians as well), the dominant religion could well be—and very likely is—another religion than Christianity itself. For scholarship in world Christianity, therefore, interreligious (or interfaith) relationality is an unavoidable past, present, and future reality. That is why this volume eschews the approach of abstracting religions from their lived contextual realities for comparative or normative purposes, applying extrinsic criteria to a preselected set of ostensibly timeless doctrines. Instead, the thematic coherence this volume aspires to exemplify will be its emphasis on interreligious relationality. Of particular interest are its case studies of grassroots initiatives—involving peace, justice, and reconciliation in a variety of forms—that transcend the ostensible boundaries between religions in the Global South, urban and rural. Ordinarily, such initiatives fail to elicit much attention in the Global North; the studies presented here will hopefully contribute to rectifying that unfortunate deficit.

First, though, some caveats and clarifications.

Even though the readers of this volume are unlikely to stand in need of being converted (as it were) to an antiessentialist approach to the study of religion, it does bear mention that the volume at hand by and large reflects a postmodernist skepticism of yesteryear's sine qua non definitional models premised upon dubiously universalized theories about the essence of religion (e.g., belief in "God") without which religion, so it was thought, would not be religion. Whether African Indigenous religions, Buddhism, Hinduism, or Islam, the chapters in which they are featured resist simplistic reductionism and afford them the same radical internal diversity that world Christianity itself exhibits. Likewise, nothing here could or should be suspected of prioritizing belief over the noncognitive dimensions of religious experience. As a predecessor of mine here at Princeton, the Lebanese Islamic scholar Edward Jurji, once wrote at the end of the 1960s when phenomenology was rare in theological education and Wilfred Cantwell Smith railed against "religion" as an ontological reification, "Religion is never adequately grasped through books [viz., sacred texts] alone. Persons and communities are the true repositories of faith."[5] As the phrasing reveals, Jurji had begun to echo Cantwell Smith, who preferred *faith* over *religion* as a more dynamic category for grasping what religious experience is all

---

[5] Edward J. Jurji, "Religious Convergence and the Course of Prejudice," *Journal of the American Academy of Religion* 37, no. 2 (1969): 121.

about. While today the tide has largely turned against Cantwell Smith, with many now agreeing with Talal Asad that the real issue has more to do with the privatization of "religion"—a modern development within European intellectual history associated with the rise of secularism—in ordinary speech, *faith* and *religion* are often interchangeable. On this, there seems to be a consensus that *faith* can be used as a stand-in for *religion* whenever it denominates "a system of beliefs" (cf. Merriam-Webster). Despite being saddled with complex baggage, an especially vexatious issue in extra-European contexts where the religious/secular binary remains largely alien, the relations this volume discusses will be called "interfaith" and not "interreligious" relations,[6] in consonance with current usage.

From here, one can now divine more easily why a volume on interfaith relations belongs in a series on World Christianity and Public Religion. First and foremost, of course, is that religion is not at all partitioned off from the secular in the Global South the way it is (or appears to be) in the Global North, notwithstanding the fact that "secularism" in South Asia denominates—confusingly for those who are unfamiliar with it—a political philosophy (enshrined in India's constitution) that requires the state to treat all religions equally.[7] That secularism so understood is now under siege in today's India highlights how hiving off religion from an imagined religionless public realm into the closeted private lives of its citizens simply seems wrong to many in this huge Global South population cohort where democracy often translates into majoritarianism. Not only that, but Global North societies are hardly so dereligionized as scholars once thought, and the secularization thesis has engendered a plausible counterthesis of deprivatization, undercutting the premature predictions about the death of religion above the equator. By and large, religion will be treated in these pages as itself socially constructed and, ipso facto, "inescapably public,"[8] whatever adjustments may be needed to fine-tune what any particular "public" might actually look like, locally or globally. Accordingly, the contributors to this volume speak from their diverse locations in a variety of (mainly) Global South settings on a wide range of concerns, from human rights violations (in Myanmar in one case) to endangered Indigenous rites and rituals (in Amazonia in another), voicing what I would characterize as a progressive Christian ethic. Naturally, the meanings of words such as *progressive* and *Christian* are

---

[6] On all such topics, see the magisterial work of Brent Nongbri, *Before Religion: A History of a Modern Concept* (New Haven, CT: Yale University Press, 2015), starting with 1–7.

[7] The classic study would be Donald E. Smith, *India as a Secular State* (Princeton, NJ: Princeton University Press, 1963).

[8] Raimundo C. Barreto, introduction to Barreto, Cavalcante, and Pereira da Rosa, *World Christianity*, 1. Here, Barreto draws insight from our Princeton colleague Mark L. Taylor, whose work illuminates the "inescapable sociality" of both religion and theology.

famously unstable; to find out more, reference should be made to each author's respective chapter.

As a concluding footnote before offering a synopsis of the several essays in this collection, I submit that, as a whole, they are inescapably ecumenical in terms congenial to what I call the Princeton school of world Christianity. Genealogically, this type of scholarship traces back to the era of John A. Mackay (1889–1983), president of the seminary from 1936 to 1959 after long years of missionary service in Latin America. Better known for his role in the birth of the World Council of Churches, Mackay was the underacknowledged founder of a new field of theological education that he denominated ecumenics. Named in 1937 to the first chair of its kind, Mackay opined that an awareness of what today would be called world Christianity had begun to crystalize and that this new reality should become the subject of multidisciplinary study. Important here is that Mackay recognized the indispensability of religion to ecumenics; as a theologian, he was hardly averse to normativity, but that was hardly all that ecumenics consisted of, and he was keenly aware, for instance, of the specter of religious nationalism in the Global South (Hindu and Buddhist nationalism were particularly worrisome to him). In fact, in *Ecumenics: The Science of the Church Universal*, published in 1964, the first subheading in the final chapter, "The Relations of the Church Universal," was "The Church and the Non-Christian Religions." Notably, ecumenics at Princeton was team taught from its inception, Mackay sharing the podium with the faculty's historian of religion, the aforementioned Edward Jurji.[9] By Mackay's definition, more than a few of the authors of this volume are engaged in ecumenics.

* * *

Part 1 of this collection tackles the prickly topic of ethno-religious nationalism, a concern of Mackay's in the 1960s and nowadays a fact of life for Christians and other minorities in South and Southeast Asia. Writing on Myanmar, Pum Za Mang (chapter 1) walks us down the years from independence (1948), documenting the travails Christians experienced because of the state-enforced policy of "Burmanization." Like the author, most Christians are non-Burmese (Karen, Kachin, Chin, etc.), and their very existence is deemed subversive of the linkage among race, religion, and nation. The good news the author highlights is that Aung San Suu Kyi having reined in the most militant elements of the sangha before the military coup of early 2021, a newfound streetwise

---

[9] Mackay, *Ecumenics*. On the unusually simpatico relationship between Mackay the theologian and Jurji the historian of religions, see Richard Fox Young, "Obliged by Grace: Edward Jurji's Legacy in the History of Religions at Princeton Theological Seminary, 1939–77," *Theology Today* 69, no. 3 (2012): 333–43.

Buddhist-Christian solidarity has emerged from the shared struggle for democracy. On India, David Emmanuel Singh (chapter 2) also adduces welcome evidence of intersectional solidarities—mainly Muslim, Sikh, and Christian but also Hindu—in nationwide protests catalyzed by the increasingly illiberal BJP Hindu nationalist party's thus far abortive attempt at theocratizing India as a "Hindu" nation by nefarious changes to its citizenship requirements. Such protests are notably interfaith, drawing on the Qur'an, Granth Sahib, Bible, and Gita, each recitation eliciting chants of divine names, including—to my surprise, though an India scholar—"Jai Jesus!" (Praise Jesus!).

By rounding off part 1 with paired essays from Brazil, one gets not only broader world Christianity coverage but also badly needed perspectives on the misguided belief prevalent in some corners of the erstwhile Christendom of the Global North that Christianity alone of all religions falls victim to intolerant "Others."[10] Going deep into Brazil's colonial past, Babalawô Carlos Alberto Ivanir dos Santos (chapter 3), himself a *Candomblécista*, diagnoses the hostility evinced toward Afro-Brazilian religions as "quotidian," "endemic," and overtly racial. As a stereotypical incident of violence, dos Santos adduces one involving a young girl of his own faith, bloodied by a stone hurled at her by an *Evangélico* (presumably) for being one of the agents of the devil. Despite rampant appropriation of Afro-Brazilian religious elements into Pentecostalism, which the author calls "religiophagy," the violence-prone stigmatization of "Black religion" persists and in today's Brazil often goes unchecked. Troubled by the same brutish intolerance of *Candomblécistas* as dos Santos, Felipe Fanuel Xavier Rodrigues (chapter 4), a Black pastor-theologian, tells in his essay how, after years of immersion in the canon of "white male" authors, he discovered the liberative power of self-(re)definition in the writings of Afro-Brazilian women, finding them to be "agents of transformation" offering "solace," "hope," and "purpose." Among the several women discussed is Carolina Maria de Jesus, author of *Junk Room* (*Quarto de Despejo*), a 1950s novel about growing up in a *favela* among *Candomblécistas*: "Here in the favela, there's a shed on B Street where believers come to pray three times a week. There's a tinplate covering one part of the shed and tiles covering the other one. There are days when they're praying, and the thugs throw stones at the shed and break the tiles. . . . Even after being insulted, the believers don't get discouraged. They advise *favela* dwellers not to steal, drink and love their neighbors as themselves."[11]

---

[10] For a masterful debunking of that persistent myth, see Jason Bruner, *Imagining Persecution: Why American Christians Believe There Is a Global War against Their Faith* (New Brunswick, NJ: Rutgers University Press, 2021).

[11] Translation by Felipe Fanuel Xavier Rodrigues in chapter 4.

Not being well read in the literature on Afro-Brazilian religions but wanting to know more *about* them, I am humbled by how much I might also learn *from* them, things that resonate with biblical teachings about turning one's cheek, returning good for evil, and not throwing stones.

For the right segue from part 1 to part 2, "Gender, Ecology, and Ethnographic Imagination," which highlights an all-Brazilian cadre of scholars, we start with an ecofeminist critique by Elisa Rodrigues (chapter 5) of the affinities of Christian conservatives—whether church leaders, politicians, or agribusiness CEOs—for a skewed biblical hermeneutic that authorizes, rationalizes, and justifies the twin evils of misogyny and ecological genocide in the Amazon. Offering a constructive counterhermeneutic of her own, Rodrigues draws on biblical and archaeological studies of Near Eastern antiquity to argue the case for recovery of long-dormant gynocentric imagery of the divine. Knowing, likewise, that androcentric imagery has real-world consequences, Frederico Pieper's essay (chapter 6) begins with a recollection of São Paulo on a day when smoke from the Amazon fires blotted out the sun. That memory evokes a somber analysis of Brazilian "necropolitics" but eventuates in a hope-filled proposal partly inspired by Brazilian theologian Leonardo Boff. Accordingly, Pieper envisions a soteriology that recognizes the need of the earth itself for liberation. With a view toward ecological interconnectedness, he succinctly states, "No salvation outside the relationship." And for opening a window onto an epistemologically autochthonous knowledge system sustainable—but for how long?—even in Brazil's urban jungles, we have Sandra Duarte de Souza (chapter 7) to thank for her ethnography of two Amerindian *raizeiras* (root herbalists). A mother-daughter transplant to São Paulo, Flora and Rosa are neighborhood healers whose medicinal arts are deemed superstitious by the churches (Catholic and Pentecostal) where they worship, despite popular demand for (as it were) their cure of city ills. De Souza's detheologized approach is sophisticatedly decolonial, a powerful solvent on the invidious image of the Amazon as "a forest inhabited by Indians waiting for progress."

Even though, as a public religion, Christianity's public agenda in any single locale varies widely, territorial conflicts, resource wars, and the displacement of the populations affected are often high on the list of the struggles affecting Christians and their fellow citizens of other faiths across the Global South. That includes Africa, on which part 3 provides a special focus. Zeroing in on northern Uganda, unsettled for years by Joseph Kony's Lord's Resistance Army, a cancerous aberration of Christianity, and by the Ugandan military's savage attempt at putting it down, David A. Hoekema (chapter 8) relates how Christian and Muslim leaders affected a rapprochement between the warring parties.

Invoking an Acholi proverb, "When elephants fight . . . it is the grass [viz., the people] that suffers," the two communities, though mutually suspicious, calculated that the gain from interfaith collaboration would be greater than the loss. Today, a decade after hostilities subsided, the gains are palpable, and Hoekema finds reason for "optimism." Unfortunately, grounds for optimism are harder to find in Amidu Elabo's essay (chapter 9) on Nigeria's Jos Plateau, a cauldron of ethno-religious tension exacerbated by clashing narratives about the first arrivals: Were they Christians or Hausa-Fulani Muslims? Enriched by insights from critical space theorists on the influence of religion on the construction of spatiality and employing satellite-based cartographic software, Elabo adduces evidence of long- and short-term demographic reconfiguration. The changes he finds result in no small part from a cycle of seemingly unstoppable communal violence. Elabo leaves us with an open question about the attainability in Jos of interfaith "spatial simultaneity" under present circumstances. Lastly, Ruth Vida Amwe (chapter 10) calls attention to an extraordinary instance of "naked agency" in 2020 in Kaduna State, northwestern Nigeria, where women of the Atyap ethnolinguistic group doffed their clothing to shame local authorities into action against the lawlessness afflicting their community. Such an upending of the gender-based power hierarchy—however temporary—was not unheard of in pre-Muslim, pre-Christian Kaduna but now involved both Muslims and Christians. Apart from the dauntingly complex semiotics she adroitly negotiates, Amwe exposes what she considers an unchecked bias in world Christianity studies against the agency of Black women in the Global South. Determined to effect a change in discourse about their agency, she reminds us that such women are now the largest cohort in the world Christian population. In short, their agency matters, and Kaduna ought to convince anyone who thinks differently.

Though durably seminal in its original scope, ecumenics as envisioned by Princeton's John A. Mackay has continued over the decades to evolve in ways that even he might not have anticipated. As Raimundo Barreto puts it, "Ecumenism is not only about church unity"—recall that Mackay was a pioneer of postwar institutional ecumenicalism—"but about the unity of humankind; even more, it is about the interconnectedness of all life."[12] Given the continuing struggle of Indian Christians to throw off the shackles of caste, a system of social organization that subverts the "interconnectedness" and "unity of humankind," it seems fitting that part 4 includes Peniel Jesudason Rufus Rajkumar's discussion (chapter 12) of recent ecumenical efforts to "combat" caste. First, though, comes a candid self-reflection by Sunder John Boopalan

---

[12] Raimundo C. Barreto, "Ecumenism in the Era of World Christianity," *Unbound: An Interactive Journal on Christian Social Justice*, Fall 2015, https://justiceunbound.org/ecumenism-in-the-era-of-world-christianity/.

(chapter 11), a Dalit ethicist teaching in Canada, on the complex situational logics of transnational interfaith solidarity. Though Christians and Muslims are both beleaguered minorities in India, Christians in Canada do enjoy the privileges of being identified with the dominant community. Without an awareness of this, Boopalan points out, any profession of interfaith solidarity would ring hollow, betrayed by an unacknowledged complicity in the minoritization of Islam in the Global North.

To round off part 4, Henry Mbaya (chapter 13) takes the baton and runs us through four centuries of the doomed-to-fail efforts of mission-initiated Christianity and its successors, the mainline churches, to replicate in South Africa a system of Eurocentric theology that was arguably Afrophobic. Having witnessed a hemorrhage of members into African-initiated Christianity and the Pentecostal churches, the older bodies, Mbaya believes, are nowadays more open toward and willing to learn from African ways of being differently theological. That said, faith-and-order ecumenical initiatives of the centralized kind designed to repair historic doctrinal rifts originating in, for example, the European Reformation have fared less well among the churches Mbaya discusses and others that now flourish in and beyond Africa. However, along with the burgeoning of Indigenous Christianity (here, the plural "Christianities" might be in order) and the diffusion of Pentecostalism in the Global South, fueled by the demographic decline of "mainline" churches in the Global North, a more decentralized, less creedally scrupulous form of ecumenicity has begun to coalesce around the Global Christian Forum (GCF). As the finale, its origins are reviewed by Casely Baiden Essamuah (chapter 14), the current director. Considering that ecumenics for Mackay included intrafaith as well as interfaith relations, it would surely be a story he would want to hear.

* * *

Here at the end, going back to where I began, I extract a snippet of dialogue from an African novel, a favorite of mine, called *Ethiopia Unbound* (1911),[13] by a Ghanaian Christian, Joseph Ephraïm Casely-Hayford (1866–1930). Believing, as Ethiopianists did, that Christianity was African in origin and essence, Casely-Hayford was an advocate for Christianity's de-Europeanization. As such, *Ethiopia Unbound*, subtitled "Studies in Race Emancipation," reads like a work of public-theology fiction, a precursor (as it were) of decoloniality in literary form. The snippet I extract involves a dialogue in London between Silas Whitely, a seminarian about to be ordained into the Anglican priesthood

---

[13] J. E. Casely-Hayford, *Ethiopia Unbound: Studies in Race Emancipation*, 2nd ed. (London: Frank Cass, 1969).

9

despite his doubts about the divinity of Jesus Christ, and Kwamankra, a student of law from the Gold Coast (as Ghana was called in Britain's imperial era). Bemused by Whitely's befuddlement and convinced that his uncertainty was due to "the feebleness of the idea of God in the Anglo-Saxon language," Kwamankra shares with him several of God's divine names in Fanti, his mother tongue, starting with "Nyankopon" and "Nyame," along with their deep meanings ("He who alone is great," "He who is I am"). How exactly this will help Whitely remains unclear, but not the philological fact that such words are derived from a pre-Christian matrix already conditioned by West African (Akan) religion. Then comes the kicker, a counterfactual:

> [KWAMANKRA] "Supposing Jesus Christ had been born of an Ethiopian woman instead of Mary of the line of David, do you think it would have made a difference in the way he influenced mankind?"
>
> [WHITELY] "What a strange question."
>
> [KWAMANKRA] "Yes, it is strange. . . . But, tell me, what is there extraordinary about the idea?"
>
> [WHITELY] "Oh, I don't know. Habits of thought, convention, and all that sort of thing, I suppose."[14]

Beclouded by his "habits of thought" and clearly hypoxic theologically, Whitely badly needed someone like Kwamankra as an interlocutor for an extra-European perspective, someone who could open his eyes to the difference a few degrees of latitude and longitude might make. To reiterate what Andrew Walls has rightly said,

> *Shared reading of the Scriptures and shared theological reflection will be to the benefit of all, but the oxygen-starved Christianity of the West will have most to gain.*

---

[14] For these dialogue snippets, see Casely-Hayford, 3–11, 19–21, 26–29. And for more on the novel, see Richard Fox Young, "Between Englishness and Ethiopianism: Making Space at Princeton for Intercultural Theology," *Ghana Bulletin of Theology* 4 (2012): 1–12.

PART I

RELIGIOUS FREEDOM, INTOLERANCE, AND RESURGENT NATIONALISM

CHAPTER 1

COUNTERACTING RESURGENT BUDDHIST NATIONALISM AND FOSTERING INTERRELIGIOUS COLLABORATION IN CONTEMPORARY BURMA

Pum Za Mang

Those who know the history of contemporary Burma should be familiar with the stomach-turning details of ethnic war, religious conflict, and political violence tearing ethnic and religious minority communities apart. The damage caused by religious bigotry and racial hatred to harmony and peace among diverse ethno-religious groups in the country is very real, if not irreversible. This chapter navigates the historical trajectory of ethnic exclusion and religious intolerance stemming from the distorted form of Buddhism and addresses how the Burmese have grappled with the grave ramifications of such profound division along the lines of race and religion. It is also claimed that Burma will see real peace and sustainable prosperity only when the Burmese are not divided along the lines of race and religion and instead accept and cherish their diversity.

Christianity

In reflecting on the rich diversity of the modern state of Burma, what stands out the most is that the Burmese consist of distinctive ethnic groups speaking numerous vernaculars, practicing diverse religious traditions, and perpetuating multiple cultures, which have various antecedents. Whereas the majority of ethnic Burman people and some minorities have adopted Buddhism as their religion, Christianity is enormously popular among other minorities, such as the Karen, Kachin, and Chin, who now represent the vast majority of the Christian population in the country.[1]

---

[1] Martin Smith, *Ethnic Groups in Burma: Development, Democracy, and Human Rights* (London: Anti-Slavery International, 1994), 32–62.

Renowned Burma expert Josef Silverstein illustrates our religious and racial diversity when he rightly states that Burma "is not and never has been a nation in the sense that all or nearly all of its people share a common set of values, beliefs, and goals and acknowledge a primary loyalty to a polity that transcends their loyalty to race, religion, or place of origin."[2]

Native to many parts of southern Burma, the Karen first came into close contact with Christian missionaries as early as 1828, and many of them enthusiastically adopted Christianity in the years since, thereby marking the beginning of Karen Christianity. The lasting contributions made by missionaries to the political, social, and cultural life of the Karen as a people include the Karen Bible, orthography, education, mission schools, hospitals, and modern literature that catalyzed a historically unprecedented national awareness, political awakening, social advancement, and economic affluence before and after independence.[3] It must be noted that they also immensely benefited from British rule and enjoyed notable progress and modernization in all areas of life after they effectively deepened all viable ties with the British politically, socially, and religiously.[4] The fact that these paternal Westerners had served them well partly explains why they firmly defended and supported British rule, whereas their Burman counterparts forcefully fought for independence from the British.

Living in the northern frontier of Burma, the Kachin practiced the cosmic religion of their ancestors for centuries but increasingly accepted Christianity as their new religion of power, seemingly to protect their identity against Burmanization after they positively responded to the evangelization effort of the American Baptists who started mission work among them in 1877. Although many Baptist missionaries worked with and for them, Ole Hanson (1864–1927) played the single most important role in the process of developing the collective life of the Kachin as a people, for he made an incredible contribution to Kachin orthography, lexicography, and Bible translation.[5] As a result, he has a special place in the hearts of the Kachin.

The first missionaries to the Chin in the western frontier of Burma arrived in Chinland in 1899 after being invited by the British colonial officers who had recently conquered what was then known as the Chin Hills. The Chin, not unlike

---

[2] Josef Silverstein, *Burma: Military Rule and the Politics of Stagnation*, Politics and International Relations of Southeast Asia (Ithaca, NY: Cornell University Press, 1977), 197.

[3] Ardeth Maung Thawnghmung, *The "Other" Karen in Myanmar: Ethnic Minorities and the Struggle without Arms* (New York: Lexington Books, 2013), 26–28.

[4] Bertil Lintner, *Burma in Revolt: Opium and Insurgency since 1948* (Boulder, CO: Westview, 1994), 44–45.

[5] Herman G. Tegenfeldt, *A Century of Growth: The Kachin Baptist Church of Burma* (South Pasadena, CA: William Carey Library, 1974), 117.

the Kachin, initially opposed what they previously called "alien religion," which could destabilize their traditional society, but they gradually accepted it as their new religion over the years. The fact that missionaries developed orthographies for Chin languages, began schools, translated the Bible, instilled Judeo-Christian values, and exposed the Chin people to technological modernization aroused them politically and socially. Chin historians underline the historical importance of Christian faith in the collective life of the Chin people, arguing that Christianity and Chin identity have become effectively intertwined.[6]

In what follows, I succinctly describe how Christianity has favorably impacted some aspects of the history of minorities and the wider Burmese society as a whole before and after independence. Peace for these minorities means little more than security and survival, primarily because they continuously face a campaign of what they call "Burmanization," which has posed a direct threat to their existence. Christians claim against this backdrop that their religion has made a significant contribution to protecting and enhancing minorities' ethnic identities in the politically and racially turbulent context of postcolonial Burma. The churches established private colleges, seminaries, and voluntary associations that gave minorities space to maneuver to protect their language, literature, and identity in the face of a flurry of stringent restrictions enforced by the military regime. Christian institutions have, for instance, published vernacular magazines, offered ethnic language classes, and contributed to the literature on minority cultures and history.[7] Despite the government policy of marginalizing and purging the history, language, culture, and literature of minorities, those religious institutions, associations, and even individual churches have, therefore, played a decisive role in preserving the ethnic identities of minority Christians.[8] It is therefore perhaps unsurprising that whereas Buddhist nationalists typically accused the colonialists and missionaries of systematically and intentionally dividing and separating minorities from the mainstream Burman culture and society,[9] Christians proudly characterize their new adopted religion as a source of power to protect their ethnic identity against Burman supremacy and repression.

---

[6] Lian H. Sakhong, *In Search of Chin Identity: A Study in Religion, Politics and Ethnic Identity in Burma* (Copenhagen: NIAS, 2003), 225–40; Vumson, *Zo History: With an Introduction to Zo Culture, Economy, Religion, and Their Status as an Ethnic Minority in India, Burma, and Bangladesh* (Aizawl: Published by the author, 1986), 142–45.

[7] Pum Za Mang, "Christianity and Ethnic Identity in Burma," *Journal of Church and State* 61, no. 1 (February 1, 2019): 87, 104.

[8] Thawnghmung, *"Other" Karen in Myanmar*, 66–70.

[9] Maung Htin Aung, *A History of Burma* (New York: Columbia University Press, 1967), 285, 312, 313.

There are also renowned Christians who helped shape the collective life of the country with special reference to Burmese scholarship. Educated at Oxford University, Pe Maung Tin, for instance, played a remarkable role in modern Burma by making enormous contributions to Burmese literature. In 1910, he, along with John S. Furnivall, U May Oung, Gordon Luce, and Charles Duroiselle, founded the Burma Research Society (BRS), devoted singularly to Burmese studies. BRS published the *Journal of Burma Research Society (JBRS)*, Burma's first ever academic journal, from 1911 until 1980. Serving as the nation's scholarly journal, *JBRS* deeply stirred academic interest in Burmese studies, published over thirteen thousand articles, and still remains a major source for all scholars focusing on Burma. Both a scholar of Pali literature and author of multiple classics on Buddhism, he served not just as editor but also as a prolific contributor, penning numerous articles. He was, moreover, the only Burmese member of a commission set up in 1918 to establish Rangoon University, the country's first university and still the most prestigious learning center in Burma, in 1920. It should be added that eminent Burmese scholars and authors such as Maung Sein Tin (Theik-pan Maung Wa), Maung Thein Han (Zawgyi), Maung Wun (Minthuwun), Maung E. Maung, and Maung To Aung were his former students.[10] In all, Pe Maung Tin made a place for himself in the history of Burmese literature, serving as its conscience and establishing himself as the patriarch of Burmese scholarship.

In trying to decimate the intelligentsia, drain the public of quality higher education, and form a pliable nation as part of his ambitious strategy of prolonging military rule and entrenching his reviled role in politics, General Ne Win systematically undermined a national education system that was once the envy of Southeast Asia. He was the one who closed down *JBRS* in 1980, presumably in the name of decolonization. A new generation of military dictators who came to power in 1988 virtually destroyed the already distressed education system, as if they perceived academics as dangerous enemies of the state. In 2000, in reaction to the overwhelming national educational crisis at the time, Myanmar Institute of Theology (MIT) started, after years of serious deliberation, social science and liberal arts programs for all students regardless of ethnicity or religion.[11] This much-needed program has been so popular among students truly hungry for higher education that MIT annually accepts only 250 out of over 1,000 applicants (an acceptance rate of 20 percent) for its

---

[10] Anna Allot, "Professor U Pe Maung Tin (1888–1973): The Life & Work of an Outstanding Burmese Scholar," *Journal of Burma Studies* 9 (2004): 12–26.

[11] Samuel Ngun Ling, "Revisiting Theological Education in Myanmar: With a Special Reference to Myanmar Institute of Theology as a Model," in *Ministerial Challenges in Contemporary World: Toward a Transformative Theological Education*, ed. Limuel Equina and Wati Longchar (Serampore: PTCA, 2019), 101.

various nontheological degree programs, making it "one of the most prestigious and respected higher educational institutions in the country."[12]

Education historically served as a bridge between Christians and Buddhists during British rule and even after independence for the practical reason that local Christians and middle- to upper-class Burman Buddhists gladly sent their children to Christian mission schools, which provided a modern and professional education. Education that practically offered the essential requirements for social progress in the modern world was so popular among the Burman that numerous Burman politicians, historians, artists, traders, and scholars, including legendary Buddhist monk Ledi Sayadaw Rajinda, actually received their education from mission schools.[13] Christians fertilized Burma with their schools and education—so much so that the Burmese history of literature, ideology, art, and many other accomplishments cannot be fully understood without them.

Taken together, it is clear that not only has ethnic diversity defined the young state, but religious variety has characterized the religious landscape of Burma ever since 1948, when it declared independence. This suggests that the Burmese should accept and cherish ethno-religious diversity as an underpinning source of strength for the country. In a perfect world, state leaders would treat all citizens equally regardless of race and religion, but that is rarely the case in the real world of Burman nationalist rule. In the name of protecting ethnicity, religion, and the country, successive regimes dictated by the majority Burman have consistently perpetrated a campaign of undermining and eliminating the presence of religious, ethnic, and cultural Others from the face of the country as part of what is now infamously called "Burmanization."[14]

BURMANIZATION

British colonization (1824–1948) struck ghastly fear into the heart of every Burman, and all rulers of Burma after 1948 have been prisoners of political paranoia. This has contributed to a persistent fear of losing their religion and ethnicity, a fear that remains in the collective national memory of the contemporary

---

[12] Benedict Rogers, "The Contribution of Christianity to Myanmar's Social and Political Development," *Review of Faith & International Affairs* 13, no. 4 (October 2, 2015): 68.

[13] Tun Aung Chain, "The Christian-Buddhist Encounter in Myanmar," *Engagement: Judson Research Center Bulletin* 1 (December 2003): 9; Wei Yan Aung, "The Missionary School That Educated Many of 20th-Century Myanmar's Most Prominent Figures," *Irrawaddy*, May 26, 2020, https://www.irrawaddy.com/specials/places-in-history/missionary-school-educated-many-20th-century-myanmars-prominent-figures.html.

[14] Richard Cockett, *Blood, Dreams and Gold: The Changing Face of Burma* (New Haven, CT: Yale University Press, 2015), 64–108.

Burman.[15] The Burman, of course, argued not only for the necessity of a state policy to undercut and eliminate the ethnic identities of minorities to Burmanize the entire country but that they should begin a process of reducing foreign influence while at the same time reviving native values and cultures in order to decolonize Burma once they took power back from the colonialists.[16] However, the enduring political ramifications of their racially and religiously exclusive nationalism are nowadays severely damaging and devastating for ethnic minorities, particularly Christians, as we will see later in this chapter.

The plight of contemporary Christians can hardly be fully understood without understanding how the staunch Buddhist Burman typically perceived Christianity during the colonial era. In the eyes of a typical Burman, Christianity, which was historically the religion of the colonizing power, subverted the revered role of the sangha as mission schools rapidly overtook monastic schools in education. It was thus not unexpected that political monks famously played a leading role in resisting foreign domination and fighting for native rule.[17] In underscoring the collective reaction of the Burman to Christianity at that time, Pe Maung Tin precisely states, "Burmans had lost their country to the politicians but they were determined not to lose their religion and culture to the missionaries."[18] Overall, they vowed to protect Buddhism, which was central to their national identity after the king, traditionally entrusted with the solemn responsibility to protect religion, was dethroned and removed.

When the British finally withdrew their colonial administration from Burma, the Burman and ethnic minorities voluntarily founded the state of modern Burma in 1948 after they negotiated and signed the historic Panglong Agreement in 1947 that guaranteed ethnic equality, religious freedom, and full political autonomy in minority states. Aung San, who negotiated for the Burman, was, however, assassinated, and all Burman who came after him refused to respect the terms of that agreement, thereby eroding the sacred trust ethnic minorities placed in their Burman counterparts. In departing from the founding fathers, U Nu, the first prime minister, for instance, instantly amended the constitution that claimed that the union shall observe neutrality in religious

---

[15] Mikael Gravers, *Nationalism as Political Paranoia in Burma: An Essay on the Historical Practice of Power* (Richmond, VA: Curzon, 1993).

[16] Robert A. Holmes, "Burmese Domestic Policy: Politics of Burmanization," *Asian Survey* 7, no. 3 (1967): 188–97.

[17] Matthew J. Walton, *Buddhism, Politics and Political Thought in Myanmar* (New York: Cambridge University Press, 2018), 107–8.

[18] Pe Maung Tin, "Certain Factors in the Buddhist-Christian Encounter," in *Called to Be a Community: Myanmar's in Search of New Pedagogies of Encounter*, ed. Samuel Ngun Ling, Than Win, and Peter Joseph (Yangon: Association for Theological Education in Myanmar, 2003), 95.

matters. The revised bill asserted that the state recognized the special position of Buddhism as the faith professed by the great majority of the citizens of the union.[19] This politically reckless amendment has been a deadly source of religious exclusion and political violence all around the country ever since, as both religious nationalists and xenophobic politicians have repeatedly and adeptly manipulated religious sentiments for their own ends.

U Nu made no secret of the fact that he was determined to protect and promote Buddhism, much like the monarchs, considering that he started the controversial ministry of religious affairs, built new pagodas, renovated old pagodas, held an international Buddhist conference, and finally declared Buddhism the official state religion as part of his policy of protecting and promoting Buddhism.[20] Despite his political rhetoric on national unity, his divisive acts, accordingly, effectively sealed the ethno-religious division between Buddhists and Christians, given that the Kachin and Chin withdrew their previously undisputed political loyalty to the state by starting an armed revolution against the government in the aftermath of Buddhism being named as the state religion.[21] In all, ethnic minorities trusted the Burman, but the latter broke that hallowed trust, thereby crossing the Rubicon.

Ne Win then took control of political power in 1962 and started his egregious campaign of Burmanization, which proved so disastrous for minorities—including the Karen, Kachin, and Chin—that a deep sense of fear pervaded the minority communities. Christians genuinely feared that the Burman intended not merely to dictate to them but eventually to assimilate them into mainstream Burman. Historically, they had been deprived of opportunities to teach and learn their distinct languages and history, thus reinforcing distrust and division between different ethno-religious groups. Specifically, executive orders had been issued that Burmese would be the sole language used and taught in the entire country. Moreover, all members of the regime were racially Burman and religiously Buddhists, whereas many Kachin, Karen, and Chin were Christians, and this intensified their resentment and trepidation.[22] That minorities were denied the legitimate right to use their mother tongues to the extent that their languages would disappear forever lies at the heart of forced assimilation.

---

[19] Maung Maung, *Burma's Constitution* (The Hague, Netherlands: Martinus Nijhoff, 1959), 247, 260.

[20] Michael W. Charney, *A History of Modern Burma* (Cambridge: Cambridge University Press, 2009), 88–90.

[21] Pum Za Mang, "Buddhist Nationalism and Burmese Christianity," *Studies in World Christianity* 22, no. 2 (August 1, 2016): 156.

[22] Ian Holliday, *Burma Redux: Global Justice and the Quest for Political Reform in Myanmar* (New York: Columbia University Press, 2011), 75.

What is more, the junta not only expelled missionaries, banned native Christians from leaving the country, and nationalized mission schools and hospitals; it also prohibited Christians from constructing new churches and renovating old church buildings, restricted religious publishing, and repeatedly interrupted other activities.[23] Describing how Christians struggled under military rule, Benedict Rogers writes, "Obtaining permission to build new churches, or renovate or extend existing churches, or hold church gatherings other than a Sunday service became extremely dangerous."[24] What especially strikes at the heart of Christians in minority areas is the sight of the so-called national armed forces desecrating and destroying places of worship, which understandably worsens the growing division among different religious groups in the country. Lacking any of the decencies of humanity, the Burma army, entirely conscious of the centrality of the church in Christian society, intentionally not only forced Christians to build military camps on Sundays but even used some of their churches as military bases.[25]

Further, the military regime was accused of forcing Christians to convert to Buddhism, building pagodas within church compounds, replacing Christian crosses on mountaintops in Christian-majority areas with white pagodas, destroying church buildings, weaponizing sexual violence against minorities, and torturing and even murdering some Christians.[26] That the tyrannical military regimes have a history of abusing, torturing, and killing innocent men and women in upland Burma surprises no one, for a culture of violence with impunity against minorities has become virtually normalized.[27] Though Ne Win apparently withdrew from politics in 1988, his power continued, and in 1989, his loyalists unilaterally changed the names of places, races, and even the country itself and replaced them with Burman names as part of the process of Burmanization.[28] In sum, Ne Win, the chief architect of Burmanization, was so central to nearly every national event over a four-decade period (1950–90) that even some of those who hated him couldn't believe he would ever die.

---

[23] Herman G. Tegenfeldt, *Through Deep Waters* (Valley Forge, PA: American Baptist Foreign Mission Society, 1968), 39–41.

[24] Benedict Rogers, *Burma: A Nation at the Crossroads* (London: Rider Books, 2012), 95.

[25] Rogers, 94.

[26] Salai Za Uk Ling and Salai Bawi Lian Mang, *Religious Persecution: A Campaign of Ethnocide against Chin Christians in Burma* (Ottawa: Chin Human Rights Organization, 2004), 1–2; Kachin Women's Association in Thailand and Legal Aid Network, *Justice Delayed, Justice Denied: Seeking Truth about Sexual Violence and War Crime Case in Burma* (n.p.: KWAT & LAN, 2016), 1–6; Chin Human Rights Organization, *Threats to Our Existence: Persecution of Ethnic Chin Christians in Burma* (Nepean, Canada: Chin Human Rights Organization, 2012), 43–70.

[27] "'Untold Miseries': Wartime Abuses and Forced Displacement in Burma's Kachin State," Human Rights Watch, March 20, 2012, 43–50, https://www.hrw.org/report/2012/03/20/untold-miseries/wartime-abuses-and-forced-displacement-burmas-kachin-state.

[28] Cockett, *Blood, Dreams and Gold*, 82.

Due to religious persecution and restriction under military rule, many Christians left Burma and resettled in various Western countries after languishing for years in refugee camps in neighboring countries like Thailand, Malaysia, and India. To display the dynamic of this Christian immigration, recent US refugee admissions statistics show that between 2007 and 2016, about 25 percent of all refugees entering the United States for permanent resettlement were largely Burmese Christians.[29] Chin community leaders in the United States recently told me that according to their survey, the Karen and Chin who immigrated to the United States alone are estimated to number 73,626 and 62,147, respectively, making the entire number of Chin Americans, both foreign and native born, around 100,000.

This Christian exodus may tempt us to assume that the church in Burma has dramatically declined, but the latest national census of 2014, according to which Christians accounted for 6.2 percent of the national population of 53.26 million, revealed that that was not the case.[30] To put this statistical account in context, Burma is currently home to over three million Christians, despite the pathetic fact that the central government is chronically accused of underestimating the actual strength of religious and ethnic minorities in the country for various political reasons.

SECTARIAN VIOLENCE

In order to better understand the resurgence of violence against Muslims after 2011, it is important to understand the historical development of religious nationalism in colonial Burma. In stressing an intimate and reciprocal relationship between religion and politics before the British occupation, Melford E. Spiro contends that whereas the sangha usually gave political legitimacy to the government and defended the public from repression, the kings traditionally supported the monks, protected Buddhism, and sometimes even intervened to purify the faith.[31] The king was, in historical terms, essentially a protector of the national religion, Buddhism, and the Burman appeared unable to think of nationality without Buddhism. The monarchs and monks, therefore, thought colonialism presented a serious threat to nationality and religion, and monks started a series of armed rebellions during the British annexation of the kingdom

---

[29] Patrick Winn, "The Biggest Group of Current Refugees in the US? Christians from Myanmar," World from PRX, May 4, 2017, https://www.pri.org/stories/2017-05-04/biggest-group-refugees-us -christians-myanmar.

[30] "The 2014 Myanmar Population and Housing Census—The Union Report: Religion—Census Report Volume 2-C," ReliefWeb, accessed October 3, 2021, https://reliefweb.int/report/myanmar/ 2014-myanmar-population-and-housing-census-union-report-religion-census-report-volume.

[31] Melford E. Spiro, *Buddhism and Society: A Great Tradition and Its Burmese Vicissitudes* (Berkeley: University of California Press, 1982), 382.

between 1852 and 1886, thus illuminating the close ties between Buddhism and the state in Burman history. Historical evidence confirms that the Burman perceived the decline of their religion and culture with deep dismay in the aftermath of the exile of the king and the royal court, which had normally appointed the *thathanabaing* (the primate).[32]

Encouraged and supported by the British authorities, hundreds of thousands of cheap laborers emigrated from British India to then British Burma annually, and they effectively dominated the bureaucratic services, industries, and commerce, which in turn resulted in the Burman intensely resenting these mostly Indian migrants. Immigration from India continued unabated, and by 1937, Indians made up more than half of the entire population in Rangoon, the capital of Burma at that time.[33] In terms of statistics, the total number of Indians in Burma dramatically increased from less than 8,000 in 1921 to 1,017,825 in 1931,[34] which naturally led to the growing incidence of interreligious marriage between Indian men and Burman women during and even after colonial rule. In graphically articulating the commercial disadvantage of the Burman and the downgrading of their language in their native country during British rule, J. S. Furnivall pertinently claims that whereas English was used as the common language in education and government, the Indians solidly controlled local trade.[35]

The bitterness and widespread resentment the Burman almost universally harbored against the British and Indians alike fueled the religious nationalism that emerged and continued to characterize the Burman political struggle for independence during the early twentieth century. It should not therefore be surprising that even though renowned nationalists fighting for freedom in the late 1930s appear to have accepted Western political ideologies like socialism and Marxism, they portrayed Buddhism as the foundation of Burman national identity.[36] On the eve of the Second World War, which would cost the lives of hundreds of thousands of Burmese, change the destiny of alien immigrants forever, and reshape the ethno-religious landscapes of Burmese cities and towns, Burma saw the first Indian-Burman riots in 1938, stemming from a small book by a Muslim author alleged to have insulted Buddhism.[37]

---

[32] John F. Cady, *A History of Modern Burma* (Ithaca, NY: Cornell University Press, 1969), 168–73.

[33] Charney, *History of Modern Burma*, 22.

[34] Fred R. von der Mehden, *Religion and Nationalism in Southeast Asia* (Madison: University of Wisconsin Press, 1963), 6.

[35] J. S. Furnivall, *Colonial Policy and Practice: A Comparative Study of Burma and Netherlands India* (New York: New York University Press, 1956), 205.

[36] Niklas Foxeus, "The Buddha Was a Devoted Nationalist: Buddhist Nationalism, *Ressentiment*, and Defending Buddhism in Myanmar," *Religion* 49, no. 4 (October 2, 2019): 666.

[37] Von der Mehden, *Religion and Nationalism*, 167.

Ne Win, perhaps not surprisingly, was accused of not treating all citizens of Burma equally, as a cycle of violence against Indians periodically broke out after his coup, revealing a deep national sentiment against foreigners, especially Indians, as colonial rule was still fresh in the memory of the Burman. Ne Win drove over five hundred thousand people to leave Burma for India and Bangladesh when he nationalized all businesses (1965) and launched an operation in Rakhine State to stop what he called "unlawful immigrants" (1978).[38] The generals who came to power after 1988, when thousands of innocent civilians, including students and monks, were massacred for protesting against his tyranny, were clearly aware of the historical importance of Buddhism for the much-needed legitimacy of their authority. They romantically portrayed themselves as the guardians of Burman ethnicity and religion by repairing pagodas, giving alms to senior monks, supporting religious studies on Buddhism, restoring ancient palaces, and building Naypyitaw, a new national capital.[39] Their desperate attempt to appear religious hardly mattered, however, as they, in 1991–92, continued a violent crusade that saw an exodus of over 250,000 Rohingya.[40]

The religious nationalism that profoundly confused the international community, brutally rocked religious minorities, and damaged the fabric of multiple communities across Burma in recent years started with religious violence between Rakhine Buddhists and Rohingya Muslims in June 2012. This bloody conflict occurred when Burma saw the rise of religious nationalist organizations and movements (the 969 movement, for example) calling for the protection of race, religion, and the nation.[41] In rationalizing the underpinning ideology of nationalism, nationalist monks even claim that the Buddha actually was a nationalist defending his religion and ethnicity.[42] Whereas the military, nationalist monks, and the Union Solidarity and Development Party (USDP) mostly favor the ideology of nationalism, progressive monks and the National League for Democracy (NLD) seemingly accept modern democratic values such as equality, diversity, human rights, and the rule of law. These different stances, however, become blurred and somewhat overlap if and when people refer to the grave danger of losing national identity. What this signifies is that though

---

[38] Jacques Leider, "Rohingya: The History of a Muslim Identity in Myanmar," in *Oxford Research Encyclopedia of Asian History*, ed. David Ludden (New York: Oxford University Press, 2018), 160–61.

[39] Niklas Foxeus, *Contemporary Burmese Buddhism*, ed. Michael Jerryson, vol. 1 (New York: Oxford University Press, 2017), 225.

[40] Martin Smith, "The Muslim Rohingya of Burma" (unpublished manuscript, December 11, 1995), http://netipr.org/policy/downloads/19951211-Rohingyas-of-Burma-by-Martin-Smith.pdf.

[41] Matthew J. Walton, "Monks in Politics, Monks in the World: Buddhist Activism in Contemporary Myanmar," *Social Research* 82, no. 2 (2015): 507, 518.

[42] Foxeus, "Buddha Was a Devoted," 663.

they demur against brutality, some of the politically activist monks who once intrepidly stood for individual freedom, human rights, and democracy in 2007 actually "share the fear of Muslim dominion."[43]

In 2013, the Sangha Nayaka Committee (SNC), the highest sangha authority sanctioned by the state, accused the 969 movement of breaching the state constitution, which ideally forbids the use of religion for political ends, and finally banned the group, illuminating the fraught relations between the SNC and nationalist monks at the time. In reaction to that move, nationalist monks, in early 2014, called for a major sangha conference in Mandalay to take necessary steps to protect Buddhist women. Tens of thousands of monks reportedly attended that meeting, pledging to propose a new and restrictive law on marriage between different faiths. In order to continue the promotion of nationalist ideology, they formed a new organization, the association for the protection of race, religion, and nation (locally known as MaBaTha).[44] In 2015, the parliament passed and the president signed laws that seek to "regulate marriages between Buddhist women and non-Buddhist men, to prevent forced conversions, to abolish polygamy and extra-marital affairs, and to promote birth control and family planning."[45] Christian leaders sent a formal letter of protest against this constitutional move to the Thein Sein regime, citing the possible potent ramifications for religious freedom in the future, but their concerns went unmet.[46] They were worried, among other things, about legal hurdles for marriage between Buddhist women and Christian men and were proved right in the years that followed.[47]

The year 2016 saw the apparent decline of the once unquestioned influence of nationalist monks across the country, less because they withdrew from politics but more because they increasingly faced a series of legal restrictions from the new government that came to power in 2016, as the NLD-led regime seldom allows them to preach in public. Instead of delivering openly xenophobic speeches to huge audiences, they began community services and Sunday schools for children.[48] As a sign of troubled relations between the government

---

[43] Mikael Gravers, "Anti-Muslim Buddhist Nationalism in Burma and Sri Lanka: Religious Violence and Globalized Imaginaries of Endangered Identities," *Contemporary Buddhism* 16, no. 1 (January 2, 2015): 3.

[44] Gravers, 14.

[45] Iselin Frydenlund, "The Birth of Buddhist Politics of Religious Freedom in Myanmar," *Journal of Religious and Political Practice* 4, no. 1 (2017): 2.

[46] Personal information, Pum Za Mang, Kaythi Min Din, Associate General Secretary of the Myanmar Council of Churches, January 2020.

[47] Ye Mon, "'Fees' and Frustration: Myanmar's Mixed-Marriage Law, in Practice," *Frontier Myanmar* (blog), May 30, 2019, https://www.frontiermyanmar.net/en/fees-and-frustration -myanmars-mixed-marriage-law-in-practice/.

[48] Foxeus, "Buddha Was a Devoted," 662.

and MaBaTha, in 2017, the SNC banned U Wirathu from speaking in public for a year after he was accused of abusive demagoguery and hate speech against Muslims. Tensions between the two organizations continued to escalate as time went on, and the SNC, in July 2017, directly accused MaBaTha of violating the 1990 law regulating Buddhist religious orders and finally banned the entire organization, revealing the vulnerable position of nationalist monks under the NLD government.[49] In May 2019, the government eventually issued a warrant to arrest U Wirathu under article 124 (a) of the penal code, and he vanished from the scene, meaning that the government has eradicated MaBaTha and other nationalist groups. However, it should not be forgotten that such radical religious groups could come back in different forms because of Buddhist identity politics.

How could it be that the once unquestioned and unchallenged power of ultranationalist monks abandoning the peaceful tenets of Buddhism by preaching and justifying hatred and violence against religious minorities with legal impunity was swiftly suppressed? Well, when we think of what happened to religious nationalists, especially MaBaTha, we must recall the policy of the new government, with Aung San Suu Kyi determining to rein in radical monks. In recognizing the existence of ethno-religious diversity and so seeking peaceful coexistence, she directly calls upon the public to foster and cherish the progressive idea of mutual respect and constructive collaboration among various religions. In May 2016, not long after she became state chancellor and accordingly the leader of the NLD government, she met with the SNC and made it clear that her government would adopt a policy of treating all religions equally, adding that such a policy would "promote the image of Buddhism."[50] She also apparently thinks the violent acts of monks disgraced Buddhism, a religion known for pacifism, according to a well-placed source asking for anonymity, underscoring tense relations between her party and nationalist monks in the recent past. Therefore, it has been observed that with the active support of the SNC, her regime aptly and effectively restrained and removed MaBaTha.

RELIGIOUS COLLABORATION

The presence of pagodas, temples, mosques, spirit houses, and churches clearly defines the diverse religious landscape of Burma. The Burmese themselves, however, appear to pay inadequate attention to the importance of maintaining

---

[49] Susan Hayward and Iselin Frydenlund, "Religion, Secularism, and the Pursuit of Peace in Myanmar," Transatlantic Policy Network on Religion & Diplomacy, 2019, 5, https://www.tandfonline.com/doi/abs/10.1080/15570274.2019.1681765.

[50] Nyi Nyi Kyaw, *Interreligious Conflict and the Politics of Interfaith Dialogue in Myanmar* (Singapore: ISEAS, 2019), 16.

peace and harmony among religions because there was no religious collaboration between religious leaders exercising moral authority in society. In this particular respect, Samuel Ngun Ling, a pioneer of interfaith dialogue, remarks, "There has never been a real interfaith encounter or inter-religious dialogue between Buddhists and non-Buddhists in Myanmar."[51] He once told me that interreligious dialogue will be indispensable to peace and prosperity in a religiously diverse country like Burma in the future, as peace among religions is essential in diverse societies anywhere, adding that religious collaboration would allow different peoples to work together to address common societal problems.

In stressing the urgency of interreligious dialogue for tolerance, understanding, and cooperation between religions for any viability of enduring peace and prosperity among religious communities, MIT scholars accordingly introduced the core idea of interfaith dialogue among Christians as early as the 1990s. In justifying why they feel urged to call for interfaith dialogue in order to advance a deep sense of tolerance, understanding, respect, and enrichment among religions, they strongly argue that the Burmese need to accept and cherish diversity as a source of strength.[52] When they began discussing such new concepts as religious pluralism and dialogue, they initially understandably encountered considerable opposition from the fairly conservative Baptist church. However, they persistently pushed ahead, earnestly believing it to be not only important but essential for better religious relations. Gradually, they managed to popularize their ideas, more because people increasingly understand the importance of productive religious collaboration among multiple religious communities than because church leaders easily relented from their earlier resistance.

As part of a broader long-term policy of promoting such a crucial program of religious collaboration across the nation for peace, in 2003, MIT established the Judson Research Center (JRC) to serve as a research platform where scholars from all major religions could come together, share, and discuss their beliefs, experiences, and visions for the nation. In articulating the underlying rationale of the center, Ling states, "The center's primary purpose is to help bring about interfaith dialogue and cooperation among the major religions practiced by people of different races and languages in this country."[53] JRC regularly conducts seminars twice every year and publishes all papers presented by scholars from all religions on key issues facing the country in *Engagement: Judson*

---

[51] Samuel Ngun Ling, *Theological Themes for Our Times: Reflections on Selected Themes of the Myanmar Institute of Theology* (Yangon: Judson Research Center, 2007), 157.

[52] Samuel Ngun Ling, *Communicating Christ in Myanmar: Issues, Interactions, and Perspectives* (Yangon: Judson Research Center, 2010), 220–21; Saw Hlaing Bwa, "Why Interfaith Dialogue Is Essential for Myanmar's Future," *Review of Faith & International Affairs* 13, no. 4 (October 2015): 75.

[53] Samuel Ngun Ling, "Foreword," *Engagement: Judson Research Center Bulletin* 1 (2003): 1.

Research Center Bulletin.[54] If reducing sectarian tension and bloody conflict requires transcending the growing barriers among religious groups, then it is certainly constructive to foster collaboration among the religious groups for tolerance, understanding, and peace.

The practical impact of the interfaith dialogue MIT scholars long promoted under the repressive military rule of Burmese society seemed rather limited until after 2011, when the primary notion of dialogue among religions for conflict resolution began to enchant the general public. The immediate reasons behind the emergence of public interest in dialogue are the rise of religious conflict between Buddhists and Muslims and a new political openness that enabled interfaith advocates to bolster their primary argument in underscoring the immense gravity of improving religious relations.[55] In seeking interreligious harmony and peace, progressive groups and individuals began engaging in dialogue and collaboration among religious communities. Beginning in 2012, the Religion for Peace-Myanmar, consisting of the Sitagu International Buddhist Academy (SIBA), the Ratana Metta Organization (Buddhist), the Myanmar Council of Churches (MCC), the Catholic Church, the Sanatan Hindu Organization in Myanmar, and the Islamic Center of Myanmar, started working together to mitigate sectarian tensions and address humanitarian challenges.[56]

In 2012 and the years that followed, Burma sadly saw the dangerous intensification of sectarian tensions and an upsurge of violent conflicts between Buddhists and Muslims shaking the foundation of Burmese communities. In reaction to a series of such deadly religious incidents, those backing the idea of engaging with other religious groups positively for mutual understanding and trust held an interfaith gathering at Pann Pyo Let, Pegu, in January 2012 and appealed for religious tolerance, friendship, and cooperation among religions. Despite many challenges, its participants, who came from all faiths, vowed to continue promoting the notion of interfaith dialogue in their respective regions.[57]

Religious leaders from four major religions attended a national interfaith conference, organized by the Myanmar Peace Center in 2013, in order to

---

[54] This is the first and perhaps the only ecumenical magazine in Burma where different scholars from different religions share and publish their views together.

[55] Frydenlund, "Birth of Buddhist Politics," 3.

[56] Cherry Thien, "Religions for Peace Launched," *Myanmar Times*, September 1, 2012, https://www.mmtimes.com/national-news/1998-religions-for-peace-launched.html.

[57] San Yamin Aung, "Amid Religious Tensions, Interfaith Advocates Work for Harmony," *Irrawaddy*, January 17, 2017, https://www.irrawaddy.com/news/amid-religious-tensions-interfaith-advocates-work-for-harmony.html.

improve relations among religions. Being well cognizant of religious bigotry impeding the recent experiment of democracy in the country, they pledged to work together for peaceful coexistence and also appealed to the government to hold accountable individuals or groups perpetrating racial and religious prejudice.[58] Painfully witnessing the disastrous consequences of hate speech and religious bigotry deriving from nationalism, the Metta Setwaing Organization (Circle of Love), seeking any possible way to reduce sectarian tension to build a more peaceful society, similarly organized a national forum on interfaith understanding and peace advocacy in 2016. Underscoring the urgent need for religious tolerance among them, community leaders from all religious traditions attended that meeting and denounced the alleged abuse of religion for political ends; urged religious, political, and community leaders to condemn any sort of religious intolerance; and appealed to the government to take legal action against hate speech.[59]

In order to promote interreligious peace across Burma, eminent religious leaders (Buddhism, Islam, and Christianity), leaders of civil organizations, and activists likewise formed Peaceful Myanmar Initiatives (PMI) in December 2016 and, in partnership with the Vienna-based International Dialogue Centre (KAICIID), held many interfaith teachings, gatherings, and other related events in cities and towns all around Burma.[60] In October 2017, less than a month after the outbreak of brutal conflicts between Buddhists and Muslims in western Burma that led to the forced departure of about 750,000 Rohingya Muslims to Bangladesh, the new government organized a public interfaith gathering for better relations among religious communities, implying that the NLD was serious about checking religious bigotry and deterring sectarian clashes among religious communities. In response, thousands of Buddhists, Muslims, Christians, and Hindus assembled in Yangon, and religious leaders appealed for tolerance, collaboration, and peace among religions as the audience lit candles and prayed for peace.[61] In stressing the necessity of restoring unity among diverse racial groups, accepting religious diversity, empowering women, and furthering education for youths, the NLD and religious leaders from all traditions held another conference in Naypyitaw in May 2019.[62]

---

[58] Saw Augurlion, *Christian Existence: And Issues Related to Nationalism and Religious Identity in Post-colonial Myanmar* (Yangon: Judson Research Center, 2017), 205.

[59] Lawi Weng, "Interfaith Leaders Call for Legal Action against Hate Speech," *Irrawaddy*, April 29, 2016, https://www.irrawaddy.com/news/burma/interfaith-leaders-call-for-legal-action -against-hate-speech.html.

[60] Kyaw, *Interreligious Conflict*, 25.

[61] Mann Zarni, "Thousands Gather for Interfaith Rallies," *Irrawaddy*, October 11, 2017, https://www.irrawaddy.com/news/burma/thousands-gather-interfaith-rallies.html.

[62] Nyein Nyein, "State Counsellor, Interfaith Leaders Offer Message of Unity and Understanding," *Irrawaddy*, May 8, 2019, https://www.irrawaddy.com/news/burma/state-counsellor-interfaith-leaders -offer-message-unity-understanding.html.

When we discuss ongoing religious collaboration in recent years, we should not lose sight of the fact that prominent monks such as Sitagu Sayadaw (SIBA), Bhaddanta Iddhibala (SNC), Bhamo Sayadaw (SNC), and Khammai Dhammasami (also known as Oxford Sayadaw) have played key roles in endeavoring to improve relations among religions. Highly educated and experienced, they use their high social status and influence for the prospect of better relations among religions. Known for his philanthropic works, Sitagu Sayadaw is, for instance, arguably the most influential living monk in the country, and Pope Francis and President Barack Obama met with him when they visited Burma. It is, at the same time, good to remember that he is also accused of implicitly justifying the killing of the Rohingya in western Burma.[63]

Looking back at the complicated interplay between religion and politics in the 2010s, it has been observed that whereas the NLD administration directly plays a pivotal role in interfaith dialogue and promotes religious collaboration, the former USDP government (2011–16) never played any direct role in the important work of interreligious dialogue in seeking to defuse the rise of sectarian tensions and violence, which suggests that the USDP most likely lacks the political will to accept diversity. One can, indeed, argue here that some USDP leaders seemingly encouraged such religious dialogue following religious conflicts between Buddhists and Muslims, but the fact is that they entirely failed to back up their words with real actions.[64] If they actually cared about maintaining harmony and peace among religious groups, they could have taken their heads out of the sand and stood up to racial hatred and religious bigotry arising from nationalism.

What ought not to be overlooked while describing religious collaboration is that there was a notable history of Buddhists, Christians, Muslims, and Hindus working together for the common good. Bertil Linter recounts the fascinating solidarity among religions during Burma's struggle for democracy in 1988, stating, "Among the millions who marched in the capital were lawyers in their court robes, doctors and nurses in hospital white, bankers, businessmen, labourers, writers, artists, film actors, civil servants from various ministries, . . . Buddhist monks in saffron robes, Muslims brandishing green banners, Christian clergymen chanting 'Jesus loves democracy.'"[65] It is also good to remember that at a grassroots level, religion appears to pose no barrier to communities affected by natural disasters. In 2008, for example, Cyclone Nargis tore the southern coastal areas of the country apart; destroyed

---

[63] "Sitagu Sayadaw and Justifiable Evils in Buddhism," New Mandala, November 13, 2017, https://www.newmandala.org/sitagu-sayadaw-justifiable-evils-buddhism/.

[64] Kyaw, *Interreligious Conflict*, 15.

[65] Lintner, *Burma in Revolt*, 282.

infrastructure in towns, smashing schools, hospitals, monasteries, pagodas, churches, and mosques; left hundreds of thousands of people homeless; and took about 140,000 lives.[66] That natural tragedy left a gaping wound in the hearts of the Burmese forever, and all religious communities came together and helped those who were affected, regardless of religion and ethnicity.[67]

CONCLUSION

Nationalism, which exclusively centers on ethnicity (the Burman) and religion (Buddhism), has been a historical source of deadly violence against ethnic and religious minorities for the regrettable reason that in the name of protecting race, religion, and the nation, Buddhist nationalists and politicians distorted and manipulated the profound sacred and spiritual value and meaning of religion for many different ends. It is hard to exaggerate that the denial of diversity has devoured the soul of the Burmese, and there is little chance that Burma will see real peace as long as its people remain divided along the lines of religion and ethnicity. The core of the problem has been "Burmanization," which has shattered the racial and religious unity of Burmese society. It is clear that Burma will flourish only so long as people from different ethno-religious backgrounds do not divide themselves based on race and religion. Progressives from ethno-religious backgrounds should accept and cherish such diversity as an underpinning source of strength while working together for the possibility of interreligious harmony and peace. The future belongs to tolerance and diversity, not exclusion and hatred, and with love and peace, Burma could be so much better.

ADDENDUM

The always paranoid and self-serving generals seized power, toppled a democratically elected civilian government, and arrested top government officials on February 1, 2021, marking an end to a decade of limited liberalization and democracy. In justifying its coup, the military claimed that last November's election was heavily rigged, an accusation entirely debunked by independent election observers. To eliminate and obliterate Aung San Suu Kyi and her popular party, the National League for Democracy (NLD), from Burma's political landscape forever, the new junta charged her with many politically

---

[66] Robert H. Taylor, "Responding to Nargis: Political Storm or Humanitarian Rage?," *Sojourn: Journal of Social Issues in Southeast Asia* 30, no. 3 (2015): 914.

[67] Carine Jaquet and Matthew J. Walton, "Buddhism and Relief in Myanmar: Reflections on Relief as Dana," in *Buddhism, International Relief Work, and Civil Society*, ed. Hiroko Kawanami and Geoffrey Samuel (Basingstoke, UK: Palgrave Macmillan, 2013), 56.

motivated and bogus offenses.[68] Stunned and outraged, people from all walks of life took to the streets in cities, towns, and villages across the country in reject-ing military rule, demanding the immediate release of Aung San Suu Kyi and all political detainees, and calling for a return to democracy. Demonstrating unprecedented solidarity among numerous ethnic, religious, and social groups in the country against the takeover, street demonstrators included the Chinese, Burman, Karen, Rohingya, Buddhists, Christians, Muslims, medics, teachers, artists, poets, and trishaw drivers.[69]

The military, which has a long history of repression of prodemocracy movements and minorities, nonetheless sought to remain in power at any cost. When UN envoy Christine Schraner Burgener warned them of impending sanctions and isolation over arrests and killings, she got the answer, "We are used to sanctions and we survived. . . . We have to learn to walk with only few friends."[70] In order to subdue any opposition to them, their security forces use deadly weapons such as snipers, machine guns, and rocket-propelled grenades against unarmed protesters and bystanders. In the face of extreme brutality and bloodshed, the public, particularly women and the younger generation, continue resisting military rule for freedom and democracy, primarily because they just can't think of being sent back to the dark era of atrocious military dictatorship. Burma has been under military rule for the better part of the past seventy years.

The first question scholars and students of Burmese studies grapple with following this devastating political turmoil is the rationale for the coup. There are some fundamental factors influencing the calculations and decisions of the generals. By controlling the state bureaucracy and monopolizing key national economic sectors for decades, they have amassed wealth, enriched themselves, and live like kings; therefore, they absolutely want to protect their business interests.[71] Despite the undemocratic 2008 constitution being laced with

---

[68] AFP, "Myanmar's Suu Kyi Hit with New Criminal Charge," *Bangkok Post*, March 12, 2021, https://www.bangkokpost.com/world/2098863/myanmars-suu-kyi-hit-with-new-criminal-charge.

[69] Thin Lei Win, "How Myanmar's Post-coup Violence Is Transforming a Generation," Nikkei Asia, April 7, 2021, https://asia.nikkei.com/Life-Arts/Life/How-Myanmar-s-post-coup-violence-is-transforming-a-generation; Helene Kyed, "Hopes for a New Democracy in Myanmar: Multiethnic Unity against Military Power," Tea Circle Oxford, March 19, 2021, https://teacircleoxford.com/2021/03/19/hopes-for-a-new-democracy-in-myanmar-multiethnic-unity-against-military-power/.

[70] Michelle Nichols, "Myanmar Army Tells U.N. It Is Ready to Weather Sanctions, Isolation, Envoy Says," Reuters, March 3, 2021, sec. Emerging Markets, https://www.reuters.com/article/us-myanmar-politics-un-idUSKCN2AV2CJ.

[71] Kate Mayberry, "Follow the Money: Myanmar Coup Puts Pressure on Army Businesses," Al Jazeera, accessed October 3, 2021, https://www.aljazeera.com/news/2021/2/26/follow-the-money-myanmar-coup-puts-pressure-on-army-businesses.

constitutional roadblocks for greater reform, Aung San Suu Kyi managed to make some consequential changes in the past five years and vowed to do more in the next term, which threatened to undermine the supremacy of the military in politics.[72] Moreover, the coup leader, Min Aung Hlaing, openly expressed his desire to become president during an interview with a Russian media outlet months before the election.[73] His ambitious dream disappeared into the distance, however, after a party his military backed was badly defeated at the polls. We must remember that politics in Burma in the past thirty years has been basically a rivalry between the military and the NLD.[74]

The military, under the watch of the coup leader, terrorized and savaged the Rohingya in northern Rakhine in 2017, which led to allegations of crimes against humanity and possible genocide. A persistent fear of being held accountable for these atrocities and ending up in jail contributes to his strategic calculations. What is more, the generals failed to fully understand how much the public loathed them considering that the coup leader later said he didn't expect much resistance from the public while taking control of the country and overthrowing the elected government.[75] These dynamics must be understood in the particular context that he was required to retire from the military within months, and he just could not think of leaving power. In sum, this takeover has nothing to do with nationalism—outdated propaganda fostered by earlier dictators.

In reaction to the appalling return of direct military rule, hundreds of thousands of public civil servants left their desks and joined what would become a nationwide peaceful movement blocking the military from consolidating power. Refusing to work under military rule, medics started the civil disobedience movement (CDM), and academics, lawyers, engineers, railroad workers, nurses, schoolteachers, bankers, and many others joined that movement in rejecting the putsch, demanding the release of political detainees, and calling for democracy.[76] The unflinching bravery of these civil servants is remarkable, for many of them are arrested and remain behind bars instead of

---

[72] Zoltan Barany, "Burma: The Generals Strike Back," *Journal of Democracy* 32, no. 2 (2021): 34.

[73] San Yamin Aung, "Myanmar Military Chief Hints at Political Role in Interview with Russian Media," *Irrawaddy*, June 30, 2020, https://www.irrawaddy.com/elections/myanmar-military-chief-hints-political-role-interview-russian-media.html.

[74] The NLD defeated the military-backed parties in 1990, 2015, and 2020, which means the military has always been bad at politics.

[75] "Myanmar Coup Leader Admits Not in Full Control of Country," *Irrawaddy*, June 4, 2021, https://www.irrawaddy.com/news/burma/myanmar-coup-leader-admits-not-in-full-control-of-country.html.

[76] "Policy Position on the Rohingya in Rakhine State," Online Burma/Myanmar Library, June 3, 2021, https://www.burmalibrary.org/en/policy-position-on-the-rohingya-in-rakhine-state.

working under the military regime.[77] Their nonviolent movement for freedom and democracy has been so effective that the public and private sectors, such as banks, hospitals, and schools, are barely functioning.

Meanwhile, people continue street protests and security forces continue arrests, torture, and killings, corroborating the ruthlessness of the coup leader and proving the fullest extent of brutal violence displayed by the military toward the public. One of the bloodiest days, for instance, came on March 14, 2021, when soldiers cracked down on and killed fifty-eight protestors in Hlaing Tharyar, Yangon.[78] Night raids, arrests, and killings continued, and the cruelest day came on March 27, when security forces shot to death over one hundred protesters and bystanders nationwide, indicating that the coup leader would stop at nothing to remain in power. Being unable to think of living another day under military rule, the people, however, continue their protests, and as of May 10, 2021, 860 were killed, according to a monitoring group.[79] In the face of extreme brutality and bloodshed perpetrated and perpetuated by the military, people have finally started arming themselves with whatever weapons are available and begun fighting back, as illustrated by deadly fighting between the military and the civilian resistance.[80]

Furthermore, the economic and humanitarian consequences of this calamity have devastated communities across the country, especially the poorest and most vulnerable in urban centers, farmers in the uplands, and internally displaced persons in the borderlands. Stressing the gravity of economic ruin, the security crisis, and humanitarian disaster, Richard Horsey warns that Burma is on the brink of state failure.[81] A failed state in the heart of Asia would be costly for the region and beyond because illicit narcotics syndicates will flourish, and

---

[77] "Myanmar Junta Charges and Arrests Striking Doctors and Senior Medical Staff," *Irrawaddy*, April 14, 2021, https://www.irrawaddy.com/news/burma/myanmar-junta-charges-arrests-striking -doctors-senior-medical-staff.html.

[78] "A Day of Tragedy and Terror in Hlaing Tharyar," *Frontier Myanmar* (blog), March 17, 2021, https://www.frontiermyanmar.net/en/a-day-of-tragedy-and-terror-in-hlaing-tharyar/. I live in Insein, next to Hlaing Tharyar, and on that day, this industrial township was more like a war zone than a protest site.

[79] Assistance Association for Political Prisoners (@aapp_burma), "AAPP daily update (10/06)," Twitter, June 10, 2021, https://twitter.com/aapp_burma/status/1403013484422393862.

[80] "Resistance Fighters Inflict Heavy Losses on Junta Forces in Myanmar's Chin State," *Irrawaddy*, June 7, 2021, https://www.irrawaddy.com/news/burma/resistance-fighters-inflict-heavy-losses-on -junta-forces-in-myanmars-chin-state.html; Thawnghmung, *"Other" Karen in Myanmar*; "Myanmar Military Launches Airstrikes against Karenni Resistance," *Myanmar Now*, May 31, 2021, https:// www.myanmar-now.org/en/news/myanmar-military-launches-airstrikes-against-karenni-resistance.

[81] "The Cost of the Coup: Myanmar Edges toward State Collapse," International Crisis Group, April 1, 2021, https://www.crisisgroup.org/asia/south-east-asia/myanmar/b167-cost-coup-myanmar -edges-toward-state-collapse.

the world will have to deal with the deadly consequences of this situation.[82] Remember, Burma has been the world's second-largest opium producer after Afghanistan. Instead of helping to fix the quickly worsening crisis, ASEAN leaders are unsurprisingly undertaking chaotic diplomacy, and the Chinese are busy plundering Burma's rich natural resources.[83] Though China cultivated very good relations with Aung San Suu Kyi, Beijing is and always has been ready to work with anyone in power in Naypyitaw. Ironically, the military started political reform in 2011 in order to reduce the alarming level of China's influence on Burma, and the same military now returns to China for economic and diplomatic assistance.[84] Democratic countries in the West, especially the United States and the European Union, use arrows in their quiver against the coup makers, but their effectiveness on the ground is limited.

Meanwhile, hundreds of thousands of people flee their homes and hide in the jungles as escalating fighting between the military and the civilian resistance in many parts of the country causes a catastrophic humanitarian crisis.[85] The military will seemingly fight for years, if not decades, considering the historically unprecedented level of public hatred for them. In the midst of this suffering and the near collapse of the health care system after the takeover, the third wave of Covid-19 continues upsetting cities and towns in western Burma with a rising death toll.[86] Without a well-functioning health care system, along with medics on strike, most Burmese remain unvaccinated, and this reality will perhaps complicate the potential success of governments in the region to control the pandemic.

Vowing to remove military dictatorship from Burma once and for all, the adversaries of the military, in the meantime, formed the parallel National Unity

---

[82] Rachel E. Harding, *A Refuge in Thunder. Candomblé and Alternative Spaces of Blackness* (Bloomington: Indiana University Press, 2000); "With Conflict Escalating, Karen BGF Gets Back to Business," *Frontier Myanmar* (blog), May 13, 2021, https://www.frontiermyanmar.net/en/with -conflict-escalating-karen-bgf-gets-back-to-business/.

[83] "Illegal Rare Earth Mines on China Border Multiply since Myanmar's Coup," *Irrawaddy*, April 26, 2021, https://www.irrawaddy.com/news/burma/illegal-rare-earth-mines-china-border -multiply-since-myanmars-coup.html.

[84] "Chinese Foreign Minister Assures Myanmar Junta It Has Beijing's Support," *Irrawaddy*, June 10, 2021, https://www.irrawaddy.com/news/burma/chinese-foreign-minister-assures-myanmar -junta-it-has-beijings-support.html.

[85] "U.N. Says 100,000 Flee Fighting in Myanmar Border State | Reuters," Reuters, June 8, 2021, https://www.reuters.com/world/china/myanmar-junta-defends-response-crisis-amid-southeast -asian-criticism-2021-06-08/; "Civilians Forced to Flee Again as Myanmar Junta Shells IDP Camps in Chin State," *Irrawaddy*, June 9, 2021, https://www.irrawaddy.com/news/burma/civilians-forced-to -flee-again-as-myanmar-junta-shells-idp-camps-in-chin-state.html.

[86] "Myanmar Regime Orders Schools in Seven Townships Closed Due to COVID-19," *Irrawaddy*, June 8, 2021, https://www.irrawaddy.com/news/burma/myanmar-regime-orders-schools-in-seven -townships-closed-due-to-covid-19.html.

Government (NUG) in April 2021 to challenge the authority of the new junta. Envisioning a more diverse, equal, and progressive future, the NUG drafted a federal democracy charter assuring ethnic equality, self-determination, and civilian control over the military. To avoid using religion for identity politics or political ends, article 16 of the charter states, "The Federal Union shall practice a political system that has separation between politics and religion and that is secular, not based on religion."[87] In a policy statement released on June 3, 2021, the NUG promised to rescind the controversial 1982 citizenship law, which in effect made the Rohingya stateless, and replace it with a new citizenship law that must "base citizenship on birth in Myanmar or birth anywhere as a child of Myanmar Citizens."[88] The same policy pledges to abolish the use of National Verification Cards (NVC), which has been exploited by the military against minorities, including the Rohingya, adding, "The Rohingyas are entitled to citizenship by laws that will accord with fundamental human rights norms and democratic federal principles."[89]

In departing from the exclusive and discriminatory policy of all previous civilian and military governments, the NUG intends to respect and serve the legitimate interests and aspirations of ethnic and religious minorities, including the Rohingya. This is a watershed change crucial to a freer and fairer Burma. A master plan of building a modern state of Burma deeply rooted in religion (Buddhism) and ethnicity (Burman) in the past seventy years has failed, and ideally the Burmese need to imagine a different future, one more diverse, progressive, and equal. Exclusion and isolation stemming from religious nationalism and tribal loyalty have failed and will continue to fail. Taken together, the only way toward the enduring peace and prosperity desired by everyone is for the Burmese to imagine a different future—one more plural, inclusive, and equal—and work together for that brighter future.

---

[87] "Federal Democracy Charter Part I: Declaration of Federal Democracy Union 2021," National Unity Government (NUG), n.d., https://crphmyanmar.org/wp-content/uploads/2021/04/Federal-Democracy-Charter-English.pdf. As of July 2021, parts 1 and 2 of the Federal Democracy Charter were accessible through the internet (but only outside of Myanmar).

[88] "NUG Releases Statement Recognizing Rohingyas' Right to Citizenship," *Myanmar Now*, accessed May 4, 2022, https://www.myanmar-now.org/en/news/nug-releases-statement-recognising-rohingyas-right-to-citizenship.

[89] "NUG Releases Statement."

CHAPTER 2

EMERGING COOPERATION AMONG MINORITIES IN DEFENSE OF INDIAN SECULARISM SINCE THE ADOPTION OF THE CITIZENSHIP AMENDMENT ACT (CAA) UNDER THE BJP

David Emmanuel Singh

This chapter offers a review of the countrywide protests beginning in late 2019 following the controversial Citizenship Amendment Act (CAA) and the discourse on the National Register of Citizens (NRC) in India. It highlights key reasons why protests led me to review the diverse interfaith expressions of dissent against the CAA/NRC. The underlying argument here is that the protests point toward emerging grassroots cooperation among minorities supported by many fair-minded Hindus. The sources for this chapter have been diverse, ranging from my own observations in India in early 2020, to the social media records of "public protests," to reports, interviews, and discussions from the increasingly shrinking free media. This shows not just that there is a battle being fought by and for Muslims (indeed, all minorities) but that across the religious divide, many, including some who voted the Bharatiya Janata Party (BJP) into power, are fearful of the changing nature of the idea of India. That change is manifestly antisecular in overtly defining citizenship, for the first time since independence, along religious lines. It also arguably adopts an idiosyncratic idea of India from Hindutva thinkers—that is, right-wing religious nationalists—who played little or no role in India's independence as a secular democracy.

PROTESTS

Dissent

In a democracy, people often express dissent through public expressions of protest, especially when they feel a lack of power or agency to change a decision or action of the government impacting them. Kenneth Jones, a social historian, attributes dissent mainly to "uneven development."[1] "Census enumeration" begun under the British included the question of religion for the first time in Indian history.[2] The creation of religious identities was thus partly a product of the colonial enterprise. Despite an increasing perception of distinctions, a sense of the British as a common "enemy" enabled Indians to fight for freedom. A common objective not only enabled alliances to form but also enabled "the makers of modern India" to imagine secular-democratic nation-states despite inherent fault lines. Jones offers a detailed view of the dissent movements he calls "transitional" and "acculturative." The former consciously saw its roots in the precolonial milieu and thought of its origins as "Indigenous";[3] it denied any overt influence from the colonial context, lacked evidence of English-speaking reformers, and exhibited little hybridity.

In contrast, acculturative movements arose out of the colonial context and were led by those who benefited directly from its culture and education. One can find in the acculturative camp examples of those who endorsed the idea of India as a Hindu *rashtra* (nation), such as V. D. Savarkar (1883–1966), a rationalist and a member of the Hindu Mahasabha; and K. B. Hedgewar (1889–1940), a medical doctor and the founder of Rashtriya Swayamsevak Sangh (RSS). On the opposing end, we find M. K. Gandhi (1869–1948), a practicing Hindu and a member of the Inner Temple, who opposed India's partition along religious lines and argued for Indian unity amid diversity. Gandhi was not only an uncontested leader of Congress and an ecumenical political organization but also, along with Jawaharlal Nehru (1889–1964), an architect of the new India. Acculturative movements such as the ones these leaders represented exhibited hybridity but were informed by the "high cultures of South Asia and specific subcultures of a given region,"[4] and in this sense, they were authentically grassroots.

Those engaged in protests in India since December 2019 appear to see a disconnect between the BJP's Hindutva (a political ideology not to be confused

---

[1] Kenneth W. Jones, *Socio-religious Reform Movements in British India*, New Cambridge History of India, vol. 3, pt. 1 (Cambridge: Cambridge University Press, 1989), 3.

[2] See R. B. Bhagat, "Census Enumeration, Religious Identity and Communal Polarization in India," *Asian Ethnicity* 14, no. 4 (September 2013): 434–48.

[3] Jones, *Socio-religious Reform Movements*, 3–4.

[4] Jones, 3–4.

with Hinduism) and constitutionally mandated secularism. The slogans of *azadi* (freedom) point toward similarities in protestors' minds between British colonization and the signs of a new colonial regime under the BJP's Hindu nationalism. The expressed aim in protests since December 2019 seems to be to preserve secularism, but it appears there are also other underlying aims among the protestors, such as, for example, to offer a publicly performed critique of (1) the daily harassment of minorities, (2) the looming threat of detention camps and eventual statelessness, and (3) state-sponsored distraction from the real issues facing India, where any critique or disapproval of the government or the ruling party is perceived as being antinational.

Leading Factors

The BJP's rise has been gradual, but since 2014, it has continuously been in power. Its ideology is linked to the aforementioned Savarkar and Hedgewar. Unsurprisingly, therefore, it has been focused on realizing its vision for Hindu nationalism or Hindutva. Since 2019, observers have become familiar with the evolution of the Citizenship Amendment Bill (CAB) into the Citizenship Amendment Act (CAA); such moves by the government have clearly exposed deeper fault lines. The BJP had, in 2003, introduced a finer adjustment in the law governing citizenship when it stated that one acquires citizenship not simply by birth but by proving that either both parents are citizens or one parent is and the other is "not an illegal immigrant" at the time of one's birth.[5] The specific condition relating to the legality of one parent's immigration status was introduced as part of a BJP policy that has echoes both in the recent amendment and in the discourse on the controversial National Register of Citizens (NRC).

The BJP's 2019 election manifesto was unapologetically nationalistic. It expressed a commitment to the enactment of CAB purportedly for the protection of "Hindus, Jains, Buddhists and Sikhs escaping persecution from India's neighbouring countries," declaring that they would "be given citizenship in India."[6] The proposed CAB was passed as the CAA on December 12, 2019. The CAA exceeded the manifesto in two respects: (1) it added Parsis and Christians to the list, and (2) it identified "the neighbouring countries" as Afghanistan, Bangladesh, and Pakistan (significantly excluding non-Muslim neighbors). What it showed was that religious minorities other than Muslims who may have illegally entered India to escape persecution (impossible to prove apart from qualitative autobiographies) on or before December 31, 2014 (when

---

[5] The Constitution of India, accessed December 9, 2020, https://web.archive.org/web/20210126094642/http://legislative.gov.in/sites/default/files/COI_1.pdf.

[6] "Sankalpit Bharat—Sashakt Bharat [Determined and Strong India]," *Sankalp Patra*, April 12, 2019.

the BJP returned to power), would qualify for naturalization.[7] The adoption of the CAA, however, led to unprecedented countrywide protests stopped only by the arrival of Covid-19. Below, I offer four interrelated reasons for these protests.

First, there is an undeniable linkage between the CAA and the NRC. The BJP sources have largely denied there was a link between the CAA and the NRC. Harsh Mander, a highly respected commentator-activist, called it a "lie."[8] We know that Home Minister Amit Shah clearly noted this no fewer than five times, including in the recorded sessions of parliament. One of Shah's Twitter handles said, "First we will pass the Citizenship Amendment bill and ensure that all the refugees from the neighbouring nations get the Indian citizenship. After that NRC will be made and we will detect and deport every infiltrator from our motherland."[9] It is evident that the intent was to introduce religious criteria to India's citizenship laws: "We will ensure implementation of NRC in the entire country. We will remove every single infiltrator from the country, except Buddha [*sic*], Hindus and Sikhs."[10]

Second, the CAA excludes Muslims. The CAA specified three countries, which are all Muslim. The fundamental assumptions were that (1) only Muslim countries in India's neighborhood persecute minorities; and (2) Muslims or Muslims as minorities are not persecuted either in these three countries or in other countries in India's neighborhood. Arguably, it highlights the BJP's aspiration for a "Hindu Pakistan," a majority Hindu state. This stands at odds with clauses 6 and 7 of the COI concerning the "rights of citizenship" (COI.II.7).

Third, the CAA has a precedent in the history of the partition.[11] Following the partition, there were two waves of migration from West Pakistan: Hindus and Sikhs and Indian Muslims who had migrated to Pakistan but then chose to return to independent India. Significantly, even then, the Hindu and Sikh refugees were described as "displaced" persons, whereas the Muslim returnees were

---

[7] Bharat ka Rajpatr, "The Gazette of India: The Citizenship (Amendment) Act, 2019, Extraordinary; Part II (New Delhi: Ministry of Law and Justice)," *Gazette of India*, 2–3, accessed July 17, 2021, https://egazette.nic.in/WriteReadData/2019/214646.pdf.

[8] Akhil Kadidal, "BJP Claim over NRC-CAA Linkage Is a Lie," *Deccan Herald*, December 23, 2019, https://www.deccanherald.com/city/bengaluru-politics/bjp-claim-over-nrc-caa-linkage-is -a-lie-787919.html.

[9] Amit Shah (@amitshah), "First we will pass the citizenship amendment bill and ensure that all the refugees from the neighbouring nations get the Indian citizenship," Twitter, May 1, 2019, https:// twitter.com/AmitShah/status/1123581776415399937.

[10] Rafi Syed (@syedrafi), "We will ensure implementation of NRC in the entire country," Twitter, January 7, 2020, https://twitter.com/syedrafi/status/1214478875587043329.

[11] See Satyen K. Bordoloi, "History of CAA Lies in the History of 1948: Abhinav Chandrachud [Mumbai Collective 2020]," YouTube video, February 11, 2020, https://www.youtube.com/watch?v =gifeGicNLfI.

called "evacuees."[12] The properties of Muslims who had left India for Pakistan were used to rehabilitate Hindu and Sikh refugees from Pakistan. The returning Muslims, therefore, presented Indian politicians and administrators with a problem: it meant displacing Hindu or Sikh refugees a second time to make way for the returning Muslims. This they felt could easily fuel the communal passion of fringe groups such as the Hindu Mahasabha and the RSS and hence had to be carefully managed. The permit system was invented in this context to decrease the flow of Muslim evacuees returning to India.[13] This shows that the bias against Muslims, therefore, is rooted in history and somewhat tarnishes the secular credentials of Congress-led India; India's constitution, however, was and largely remains secular.

Fourth, the NRC is about a comprehensive register of citizens. The first and the only nationwide NRC happened after the partition on the date when the COI became effective in 1950. The NRC thus took place as part of the census of 1951 of a new secular India. The CAA/NRC under the BJP is therefore seen as an attempt to make a new start of a Hindu state. The countrywide NRC is still in the works, but we already have the results of the NRC conducted in Assam in northeastern India. These results are horrifying. There were mistakes and discrepancies in the NRC mechanism that resulted in some persons being included and others being excluded from the citizenship register. Women from other regions of Assam or outside the state who married in the state or in a district were excluded, whereas their families were included.[14] The result showed that 1.9 million Assamese did not make it to the final list. They have the right to appeal, but most if not all are desperately poor and simply unable to complete the complex appeals process on their own. By far the most contentious issue

---

[12] See more in Joya Chatterji and David A. Washbrook, eds., *Routledge Handbook of the South Asian Diaspora*, Routledge Handbooks (London: Routledge, 2014), 184.

[13] See Vazira Fazila-Yacoobali Zamindar, *The Long Partition and the Making of Modern South Asia: Refugees, Boundaries, Histories*, Cultures of History (New York: Columbia University Press, 2010).

[14] A case in point is that of Abeda Begum (fifty) in Baksa district, about one hundred kilometers from Guwahati (the state capital). Her husband has been ill for some time, and she is the only member of the family who earns a living. They have three daughters. Most of her money goes toward legal fees. She has by now already sold part of her land to survive. She was identified as being "doubtful" in the NRC. In 2018, her case went to the tribunal, where she went to the High Court, which ruled that the "land revenue receipt, bank document, PAN card—were not conclusive proof of citizenship." Even the voter lists of 1966, '70, and '71 of her father did not help, as the court noted she "produced no satisfactory proof of linkage with her father." She remains "disenfranchised by the government" and faces an uncertain future, possibly at a detention camp. Ratnadip Choudhury, "15 Official Documents Can't Prove She's Indian: Assam Woman's Ordeal," NDTV, accessed July 17, 2021, https://www.ndtv.com/india-news/declared-foreigner-assam-womans-story-predicts-citizenship-list-effect-2182212.

this exercise brought to light was the existence of the detention camps, which for most, especially Muslims or poor migrants, could easily be a prison for life.[15]

EVIDENCE OF COOPERATION

It is impossible to cover all aspects of the evidence of cooperation in expressing dissent across India. The attempt to review this here is, therefore, selective, but the aim is to address two interrelated objectives: (1) How is dissent expressed? and (2) What evidence of intra/interfaith cooperation can one see in these cases?

Shaheen Bagh

The Shaheen Bagh (SB) protest in Delhi began on December 15, 2019. It has since been evolving into a bold civil disobedience movement with spin-offs in other states and cities. Against the backdrop of the Delhi election (the BJP lost), BJP politicians have attempted to discredit it as "a global conspiracy of Muslim countries";[16] they have spoken of the protestors as "traitors" and have warned that "if left unchecked, they would 'rape and kill.'" BJP leaders have also accused SB protestors of being "terrorists" and "Pakistani sympathisers."[17] It is true that SB and its spin-offs have been led by Muslims and mainly women, but the evidence shows that their protest has been permitted by the spirit of Indian secularism. It is no surprise that SB has attracted broader interfaith backing.

SB's goals (among others) have been to roll back the CAA and cancel plans for the NPR-NRC. As this is a twenty-four-hour sit-in *dharna* (peaceful demonstration), its methods of dissent have been varied compared to the student protests. Most if not all of the means of expressing dissent are also characteristic of acculturative movements, which draw inspiration from both the high and subcultures of India and are evidently connected to the legacy of Indian independence. Thus, for example, the movement draws on the Gandhian strategy of civil disobedience as in the great Salt March[18] by blocking a main road around the clock; the protestors are also conscious that they are breaking the law. The protesters expect some sort of state-sanctioned violence and arrest

---

[15] Prabhash K. Dutta, "NRC and Story of How Assam Got Detention Centres for Foreigners," *India Today,* December 27, 2019, https://www.indiatoday.in/india/story/nrc-story-how-assam-got-detention-centres-for-foreigners-1631835-2019-12-27.

[16] "Shaheen Bagh Dharna a Global Conspiracy by Muslim Countries against India: BJP MLA | India News," *Times of India,* February 22, 2020, https://timesofindia.indiatimes.com/india/shaheen-bagh-dharna-a-global-conspiracy-by-muslim-countries-against-india-bjp-mla/articleshow/74256796.cms.

[17] "Shaheen Bagh: Anurag Thakur, Paresh Varma Penalised for Comments," BBC, January 29, 2020, https://www.bbc.com/news/world-asia-india-51276867.

[18] See Thomas Weber, *On the Salt March: The Historiography of Gandhi's March to Dandi* (New Delhi: HarperCollins India, 1997).

or detention from government agencies. They have learned from the Jamia Millia Islamia (a federally funded Muslim university) case that the state authorities are culturally conditioned to not be seen publically as harsh or violent against women and children, so SB has been ingeniously composed largely of Muslim women and often children. There is also a large number of people present at the location, making it difficult or impossible for the police to use force to arrest or detain. It also involves the Gandhian strategy of hunger strikes, sloganeering, speeches, and artistic expression and performances. Despite it being seemingly Muslim-women led, it has been ecumenical in terms of ages represented (toddlers to age ninety-plus), gender, and religion.

I referred above to the method of civil disobedience drawn from India's independence. This is evident from the use of drawings of independence heroes such as M. K. Gandhi, Bhagat Singh (1907–31), Maulana Azad (1888–1958), and B. R. Ambedkar (1891–1956); it is also evident in some children dressing in a style reminiscent of the independence movement, the use of the Indian flag as a symbol of resistance to the BJP's lotus, and so on. Theoretically, this can be explained in terms of the notions of "aestheticisation of politics" or "aesthetic revolt."[19] In what follows, I present some evidence of SB as an "aestheticized" civil disobedience movement—a movement that has so far remained within the boundaries of India's secular constitution.

Protest/Performative Art

SB is a thriving "art gallery." One of the walls of a dilapidated building depicts two *dadis*[20] (grandmothers) of "the fearless Shaheen Bagh" in partial hijab and among a number of significant symbols. Above their heads are the well-known words of the preamble of the constitution: "We the people of India—Sovereign Socialist Secular Democratic Republic . . ." with what seems like artistic license: "forever and ever and ever"[21] is juxtaposed with the crescent (a common symbol of Islam). One of the *dadis* is adorned with a "shaheen falcon" (a nonmigratory Indian falcon) holding on to a copy of the constitution of India and crying *Ishq inquilab* (Love the revolution) and the other says *Mohabbat jindabad* (May love last forever) as the three colors of the Indian flag partially form the background.

---

[19] See Esther Leslie, *Walter Benjamin: Overpowering Conformism* (London: Pluto, 2000); and Nina Gurianova, *The Aesthetics of Anarchy: Art and Ideology in the Early Russian Avant-Garde* (Berkeley: University of California Press, 2012).

[20] The two were made famous by their interview on a private national channel—in fact, there are three, the oldest of whom is the most articulate!

[21] In the constitution, the more complete wording is as follows: "Having solemnly resolved to constitute India into a sovereign Socialist Secular democratic Republic and to secure all its citizens Justice . . . Liberty . . . Equality . . . Fraternity . . . in our constituent assembly this 26th day of November 1949, do hereby adopt, enact and give ourselves this constitution."

It is clear that the protest this artwork symbolizes is peaceful, as three doves fly in the vicinity. The picture is made complete by a number of slogans, including some drawn from protest songs and poetry, such as *ham honge kamyab* (we shall overcome),[22] *ham dekhenge* (we shall see), *bebak buland azad auratein* (brave, proud, and free women), *azadi, ham ek the—ham ek hain—ham ek rehenge* (we were one, we are one, and we shall remain one), and *nafrat ki is deewar utha denge* (we shall remove the wall of hatred).[23]

As SB is happening on a main road, one of the road signs for a national highway has been blocked by a painting of what appears to be a woman addressing a gathering. The caption accompanying this picture says, "Everywhere, you encounter strong women. Whether silent or speaking." There is a picture of a woman in partial hijab who has a mild smile on her face as she walks the busy road with men around her; her handbag has the following slogan pasted on it: "Ham desh nahi tutne denge" (We will not allow the country to be divided [again]—NO CAA NO NRC NO NPR). The anonymous writer of a Scroll.in article says, "With the women come children. Many are drawn to the detention camp."[24] The article also has a picture of four children performing a scene from one of many detention camps (the existence of which Prime Minister Narendra Modi denied in his speech from Ramlila Maidan). The children are seen caged in a tiny shell made of angled iron. They peer out into the freedom they hope for while one of them has his hands spread out for help.[25] A picture shows a large map with lights representing all of India (including undivided Kashmir); within it are words from the preamble of the constitution: "Bharat ke log CAA NPR NRC nahi manenge" (We the people of India will not accept CAA, NPR, and NRC).[26] A poster showing Gandhi with his followers (presumably on the Salt March) says, "Citizenship is not religious membership."[27] There are also boards and makeshift spaces for works of art from children: one of them shows Modi and Shah watching the burning of the constitution of India with the wooden logs of CAA, NRC, and so on, and another shows Shah holding a police officer in one hand and a media person in another—a picture of how

---

[22] The original "anthem" of the civil rights movement in America, attributed to Charles Albert Tindley. Published in 1947 in *People's Songs Bulletin*, it was translated into Hindi by Girja Kumar Mathur and was sung in the 1970s and 1980s in Indian schools as a patriotic song: "We shall overcome (repeated thrice)—one day; yes we have faith in our hearts, complete faith—we shall overcome one day."

[23] Two famous opening lines of an Urdu *nazm* by Fai Ahmad Faiz, a Marxist poet from Pakistan, written to protest Zia-ul-Haq's fundamentalist regime (1977–88; my translation).

[24] "The Art of Resistance: Delhi's Shaheen Bagh Has Turned into an Open Air Gallery," Scroll.in, January 23, 2020, https://scroll.in/article/950720/the-art-of-resistance-delhis-shaheen-bagh-has-turned-into-an-open-air-art-gallery.

[25] "Art of Resistance."

[26] "Art of Resistance."

[27] "Art of Resistance."

the BJP is believed to be controlling private and public institutions. The police officer is shooting at the crowd, and the media person is shooting with a camera.[28] Both the police and the media are distrusted for good reasons.

Participation of Non-Muslims

SB is becoming a new symbol for secular and democratic India; it is led principally by Muslim women but is attracting people from all walks of life and religious affiliations. Visitors and speakers have included two veteran members of Congress, M. S. Aiyar and S. Tharoor, and C. S. Azad, a Dalit social activist who was also jailed for his protest with Muslim worshippers at the Jama Masjid, the grand mosque in Delhi. Visitors have also included a social activist and lawyer from Gujarat, J. Mevani, and a well-known filmmaker, A. Kashyap. They could all be loosely categorized as Hindus. In their own right, each of them represents a large constituency across India. However, by far the most significant and sustained alliance has been between ordinary Sikhs (mostly men) and Muslim women protestors.

A delegation of five hundred Sikh farmers (men and women) was reportedly "greeted with warm hugs and smiles" at SB. An SB Twitter handle (@shaheenbaghoff1) says, "We are overjoyed to welcome our sisters and brothers from Punjab amongst us! Our fight for the Indian constitution grows stronger with your solidarities [*sic*]." One can see Muslim women hugging Sikh women bearing their farmer union flags; the pictures also show Sikh men lounging on carpets and some of them engaged in deep conversation with an old Muslim gentleman.[29] Unlike the Sikh political leadership in Punjab (the Akali Dal, a BJP ally), ordinary Sikhs are openly showing their solidarity with Muslims on the issue of CAA/NRC. The Hindu narrative has represented the Sikhs as a martial force in defense of the Hindus. In his article, H. S. Singh includes a picture by Sania Ahmad of an odd pair, a Sikh and a Muslim woman jointly claiming, "Hamari ladayi jindabad; hamari ekta zindabad" (Long live the revolution; may our unity last forever). The Sikhs here are not making speeches; their intellectual counterparts in Punjab are (despite occasional critique) still in political partnership with the BJP.[30]

Unlike the religiously justified social hierarchy of caste among many Hindus, Sikhism is essentially egalitarian, and nowhere is this as apparent as at a *langar* (free meal) at SB. The Sikh visitors at SB are expressing solidarity with Muslims in

---

[28] "Art of Resistance."

[29] "CAA-NRC: Video of Sikhs Arrival at Shaheen Bagh Going Viral," *Siasat Daily*, February 6, 2020, https://www.siasat.com/caa-nrc-video-sikhs-arrival-shaheen-bagh-going-viral-1817207/.

[30] Harmeet Shah Singh, "Why Are Ordinary Sikhs Serving Langar at Shaheen Bagh?," *India Today*, February 4, 2020, https://www.indiatoday.in/india/story/why-are-ordinary-sikhs-serving-langar-at-shaheen-bagh-1643256-2020-02-04.

a very concrete way by feeding the protestors. The local community helped in setting up the *langar*.[31] Singh's article includes a beautiful picture of women (mostly
Muslim) helping with the *langar* preparation.[32] Preparing, serving, and eating
food together with strangers who differ in gender, religious, linguistic, and cultural senses is a powerful symbol of collaboration and unity, which is essentially
what the preamble of India's constitution expresses. It is a dream or an idea of
India that the makers of modern India saw, and one can see it in these pictures at
SB—a microcosm of India. Ameen in his report includes the statement of a local
Sikh lawyer: "The Sikh community understands what the Muslim community
is going through. . . . This [*langar*] is just an excuse to show that we stand with
you." The lawyer, according to this report, also said, "It is going to be a long fight
and all brothers—Hindu, Muslim, Sikh, Isai [Christians]—should come out and
unite."[33] Ahmad's video report shows Sikhs lounging at SB, where it appears one
has suddenly entered a gurudwara and not a protest site with Muslim women in
the majority. A Sikh leader is heard saying, "We have come to offer our support
against CAA/NRC. We want it taken back and will remain here until it is rolled
back. We laud the efforts of SB. We have never experienced this level of closeness
and had no idea we had people like this [Muslims] who honour us. We have now
decided to carry the light lit by SB to all corners of India. . . . SB is the edge [i.e.,
tip of the iceberg] and a symbol of resistance rising in whole of India."[34]

SB has also been getting support from Hindus. A selection of excerpts from
interviews with some of them should suffice. Trilokinath *ji*, a colorful visitor to
SB, is one of many examples:

> My message is that all the women here are the daughters of mother India and my
> daughters. We have come to reassure them [Muslim protesters]. We represent
> India and we are in support of the path [of resistance] they have chosen. This
> [resistance] is not for one person or one community. It is to save the constitu-
> tion of India. This is to protect the *akhandta* [unity] and *bhaichara* [brother-
> hood] that has characterised this land for centuries. . . . There is no traitor here.
> Bharat has four *sipahi* [policemen], Hindu, Muslim, Sikh, Isai [Christian]—
> who then is the traitor; no one we are all insiders seeking to protect Indians [as
> *sipahis*]. *Gaddar sadak par nahi, modi ke bagal me baithe hain* [traitors are not
> on the streets but are seated next to Modi].[35]

[31] Furquan Ameen, "Hot Food for Protesters at Shaheen Bagh," *Telegraph*, January 17, 2020,
https://www.telegraphindia.com/india/hot-food-for-anti-citizenship-amendment-act-protesters
-at-shaheen-bagh/cid/1736665.

[32] Singh, "Why Are Ordinary Sikhs."

[33] Ameen, "Hot Food for Protesters."

[34] A. Ahmad, "Shaheen Bagh Ko Sikhon Ka Support Lagatar Hasil," *Millat Times*, February 10,
2020.

[35] "Gaddar sadak par nahi Modi ke bagal par baithe hain," Newsmx.tv (URL invalid), February
13, 2020.

In a recent outreach by two Hindu supreme court lawyers, one of the issues raised by the locals was that not once has the government tried to engage with them since their struggle began. This interlocution brought to light a little-known fact that even Hindu women are joining the protest in support of SB. This is what one of them said (as an insider) to the lawyers: "This fight is for my *wujud* [existence], my *pahchan* [identity]. We are not here for biryani [food] or money, we are here to fight from our heart. We have here Hindus, Muslims Sikhs and Isai [Christian]. They [government] should understand that this [SB] is not a 'mini Pakistan' but Hindustan. Come and see how Hindustan looks like. Those who rule us have tried to poison our hearts. We thank Modi for bringing CAA-NRC because it has demonstrated Indians [despite belonging to different religions] remain undivided."[36]

Jignesh Mewani, an MLA (Member of the Legislative Assembly) from Gujarat who was at SB, is known also as a leader of Dalit protests. He said in an interview, "Shaheen Bagh *jayenge par kagaz nahin dikhainge* [We will go to SA but will not show our papers as required by the infamous plan for NRC]. Modi and Amit Shah *ayenge aur jaeinge* [come and go] but the idea of India will survive; the Indian constitution will survive. Fight on! Struggle on! We will win one day."[37]

Beyond Shaheen Bagh

One of the spin-offs of SB is the Shaheen Bagh Square (SBS) in Kozhikode in South India. Organized by the Muslim Youth League, this protest has been going on for some time now. The state BJP president called this an event "organised by extremists" and a "band of anti-nationals," an accusation that has been rebutted by the organizers: "It is Surendran [president of BJP] who is heading the largest extremist organisation."[38] This mutual squabble aside, SBS itself has similarities with SB, since apart from speeches by adults, even children are known to have given speeches against the CAA/NRC.[39] While Muslim youths are the organizers of SBS, they collaborate with people of other faiths, including Christians; indeed, we know many non-Muslims show solidarity with Muslims

---

[36] Rawish News World, @abhisarfans, Facebook, February 20, 2020, https://www.facebook.com/110601667015192/posts/196120558463302/?sfnsn=scwspmo&extid=Gfu1aWbVLo2arY41&d=n&vh=e.

[37] "Jignesh Mewani Exclusive Interview with Noor Zahira about CAA-NRC-NPR, Shahin Bagh, Bilal Bagh," Gohash.in, February 16, 2020, https://www.facebook.com/gohash.tv/videos/143325623457336/.

[38] See "'Shaheen Bagh Square' Run by Extremists: Surendran," *Times of India*, February 17, 2020.

[39] Mayyil Movies, "Kid's Speech against NRC and CAA, Shaheen Bagh Square Kozhikode, Part 07, Mayyil Movies 0401," YouTube video, February 22, 2020, https://www.youtube.com/watch?v=ATkT8Fs-O-w.

through their presence at such gatherings. The non-BJP constituency in Kerala may not all have the well-being of Muslims uppermost in their hearts, but most are interested in preserving the secular democratic constitution of India. This is the basis for collaboration between Muslims and other faiths. This point is best illustrated by a multilingual speech by a Muslim woman:

> My life is the prophet, the Qur'an and the Constitution—this is my life. If Islam is in my heart, I breathe India. I am the son and the daughter of this soil and you cannot question me whether I am an Indian or not. For me both are equal [the Qur'an and the Constitution]. . . . As much as we love Islam we love India. . . . We will live here [our home] . . . We are standing here not with the intension of going back home. . . . We have two ways, we will win India or we will die for India. This is not a war for CAA-NRC but a war for India; a war between India and fascism, against RSS . . . this is a war with those who want to divide us based on religious identities, languages, caste, creed and gender. This India is not easy—do you think you can bring a law and our Hindu or Christian brother will just leave? I know in this crowd how many from other faith communities are sitting here. I salute all of you who are here to show to our prime minister and our home minister that we cannot be divided. *Sare jahan se accha, Hindustan hamara* [Hindustan is better than the whole world]. . . . No one can throw us out [of this Hindustan]. If you do not take back your CAA, SB will become a *shahid bagh* [martyrs' paradise].[40]

The resolve to keep secular India alive is so strong that demonstrators from different faith backgrounds even participated in interfaith prayer events. A Hindu priest sits in front of a fire with people from different faiths surrounding it, including Muslim women. Those sitting here feel united by the need to "save the constitution"; they can be heard raising the slogan "People's unity, long live!" Sister Daphne from All Saints' Church, Faridabad (near Delhi) reads the Bible at this ceremony and hopes for "peace in the country"; she says, "We want to follow the policy of live and let live." Sikhs sing a religious song from the Granth Sahib, and a Muslim leads a prayer. The crowd erupts in chants of "Jai shri ram" (Praise Sri Ram), "Allahu akbar" (God is the greatest), "Jo bole so nihal, sat sri akal" (Join in the ecstatic shout, the eternal is holy), and "Jai Jesus" (Praise Jesus).[41]

On the seventy-first Republic Day, as the movement against CAA/NRC was growing, people gathered to form a "human chain in Kolkata" in order "to

---

[40] Mayyil Movies.

[41] Sumaira Rizvi, "Indian Protesters Hold Interfaith Prayers at Shaheen Bagh," Al Jazeera, February 7, 2020, https://www.aljazeera.com/news/2020/2/7/indian-protesters-hold-interfaith-prayers-at-shaheen-bagh.

uphold unity and protect the Constitution."[42] The chain was eleven kilometers long from the north to the south of the city; this happened at noon for ten minutes, and it included people from different faith communities. The event was organized by the United Interfaith Foundation of India (UIFI), which consists of people from different faith communities in the state of West Bengal. Many of those participating had the national flag; they read from the preamble of the constitution ("We the people . . .") and sang the national anthem and other patriotic songs, like *Sare jahan se accha, Hindustan hamara*; they repledged "to safeguard the tenets of the Constitution" and reaffirmed commitment to secularism. UIFI said in a statement, "We have decided to form a human chain . . . as we drive home the message that we—Hindus, Muslims, Sikhs, Christians, Buddhists, Jains—are one. Everyone stands united as an Indian citizen and we will never allow anyone to sow the seeds of discord among us."[43] The passersby spontaneously joined in; even children were part of this. A woman with her son said, "I . . . decided to come with my family. We are Indian and remain united despite attempts to divide us."[44]

It was Kerala, however, that arguably led "the way in anti-CAA protests on Republic Day" with an unbelievably long human chain. The ruling Left Democratic Front (a coalition of left-wing parties in Kerala) was the organizer of the event. The chief minister, Pinarayi Vijayan, and the Communist Party of India state secretary, K. Rajendran, were present at this event, as were many religious leaders. According to a reliable news report, the state *wakf* (Muslim endowment) board-owned mosques and churches under the Kerala Regional Latin Catholic Council (KRLCC) took part in the flag hoisting, where, significantly in the background of the CAA/NRC, the preamble of the constitution was read to mark the day. According to the circular sent out by KRLCC, all its churches pledged to protect the Indian constitution. An estimate of the number of people who participated suggests six to seven million. This collaborative event ended with an oath to "protect the Constitution from the attempts of the Central government to destroy it."[45]

While many Christians participated in joint events against the CAA, their voices have not always been united. For example, the National Commission

---

[42] "Kerala Leads the Way in Anti-CAA Protests on Republic Day," *The Week*, January 26, 2020, https://www.theweek.in/news/india/2020/01/26/Kerala-leads-the-way-in-anti-CAA-protests-on-Republic-Day.html.

[43] "Kerala Leads the Way."

[44] "Thousands Form Human Chain in City against CAA, NRC on 71st Republic Day," *Economic Times*, January 26, 2020, https://economictimes.indiatimes.com/news/politics-and-nation/thousands-form-human-chain-in-city-against-caa-nrc-on-71st-republic-day/articleshow/73639324.cms?from=mdr.

[45] "Kerala Leads the Way."

for Minorities (NCM) vice chair, George Kurian, said the CAA "is good for Christians and should be welcomed by all."[46] Clearly, the provision in the CAA makes way for Christians persecuted in the three neighboring Muslim countries to find a home in India, and some Christians see this as "justice" being "done to Christians." One needs, however, to note that Kurian has been a leader of the BJP in Kerala, and his view unsurprisingly also reflects the party line. The NCM has not just been content with expressing its pro-CAA (and, by implication, NRC) position. A panel representing the NCM was tasked to travel to seven states[47] and union territories to persuade no fewer than "100 church leaders" to support the NCM line.[48] Following this outreach, many reporters contacted the church leaders who had met the pro-CAA panel. All of these "church leaders requested anonymity," many had concerns about the linkage between the CAA and NRC, and some felt the CAA was unacceptable because it was "against the secular ethos of the Constitution." The Catholic church to which the panel went maintained their original position as well because they believed the "CAA cannot be looked at in isolation and has to be seen with NRC. The citizenship law is seemingly favourable to Christians but we told him [Kurian] that we are not selfish and we want justice for all communities. The Indian population is certainly not prepared for NRC and we (church leaders) told him that the nationwide NRC is going to be catastrophic."[49]

The Church of South India also "expressed concerns about CAA and exclusion of Muslims." They believe also that "the law is discriminatory," and they "oppose it."[50] According to a report, many "churches in Kerala, Kolkata, Telangana, and Assam gave sermon calls to people on Christmas-eve and morning mass to oppose" the CAA. This was altruistic, since the CAA does not exclude Christians; what these Christians opposed was the attempt to divide and play the "politics of hate."[51] The Catholic Bishops' Conference of India, the Church of North India, and the National Council of Churches in India (NCCI) have "expressed concerns over CAA."[52] The NCCI, which

---

[46] "Citizenship Amendment Act Is Good for Christians, Says National Commission for Minorities Vice-Chairman," *Hindu*, December 17, 2019, sec. National, https://www.thehindu.com/news/national/citizenship-amendment-act-is-good-for-christians-says-national-commission-for-minorities-vice-chairman/article30332028.ece.

[47] The seven states are Maharashtra, Odisha, Kerala, Karnataka, Jharkhand, Tamil Nadu, and Delhi.

[48] "Thousands Form Human Chain."

[49] "Thousands Form Human Chain."

[50] "Thousands Form Human Chain."

[51] "While CAA Seeks to Give Citizenship to Persecuted Christians from Neighbouring Islamic Nations, Churches on Christmas Oppose Act," *OpIndia*, December 26, 2019, https://www.opindia.com/2019/12/church-caa-opposes-citizenship-to-persecuted-christians-islamic-nations/.

[52] "Thousands Form Human Chain."

represents most mainline churches, has issued a statement clarifying that "the Act polarised communities and contravened the fundamental principles of the constitution."[53] The Evangelical Fellowship of India (EFI) came out boldly to declare both the CAA and the NRC as "unnecessary"; they saw this as a distraction from other "burning issues" India faces and advised that the "government should focus on restoring peace and taking urgent steps to stabilise the economy, reduce prices and revive employment."[54] A report suggested that in Kolkata, a non-BJP state, "more than 8000 people from the Christian community took to the streets"; they believed that the CAA "discriminates against Muslims."[55] As many Christians walked from St. Paul's Cathedral, they showed placards and shouted slogans: "Don't be silent, don't be violent!" "We are all citizens!" "No NRC, no CAA!"[56]

Post-Delhi Violence

Block B in Yamuna Vihar in Delhi has two sides—one is dominated by Muslims and another by Hindus. In a bold show of solidarity, against the backdrop of Shaheen Bagh, "Hindu, Muslim and Sikh residents of the colony came together and stood guard against the frenzied mobs which ran riot . . . vandalising homes, shops and torching cars." The local residents' strategy was simple. As the mobs were a motley crowd possibly paid to terrorize Muslims, the Hindu residents, despite risks, assured Muslim neighbors that they would face the mobs. This included sitting outside homes for night vigils, unarmed in the way of Gandhi (since such resistance could fuel violence instead of quelling it). Many reportedly said, "Violence begets violence; crowd begets crowd. . . . There are good people who outnumber the handful involved in violence."[57]

This is just one example of altruism from the Hindus, but there are also examples of local Sikhs and Muslims expressing their gratitude to each of the other faith communities by standing with them in the face of violence. One

---

[53] "Christian Member of Minorities Commission Says Community Welcomes CAA, 2 Bodies Disagree—the Wire English," Dailyhunt, December 18, 2019, https://m.dailyhunt.in/news/india/english/the+wire+english-epaper-wireng/christian+member+of+minorities+commission+says+community+welcomes+caa+2+bodies+disagree-newsid-n154073308.

[54] "Christian Member."

[55] "Indian Christian Protest against 'Anti-Muslim Law,'" AFP, January 20, 2020, https://news.yahoo.com/indian-christians-protest-against-anti-muslim-law-145240433.html; see also AFP news Agency@AFP tweet on 20 January 2020.

[56] "Christian Community Takes Out Protest against CAA," *Deccan Herald*, December 26, 2019, https://www.deccanherald.com/national/christian-community-takes-out-protest-against-caa-788920.html.

[57] "Hindu, Muslim, Sikh Residents Unite to Fend Off Mobs in Northeast Delhi Colony," *New Indian Express*, accessed July 17, 2021, https://www.newindianexpress.com/cities/delhi/2020/feb/28/hindu-muslim-sikh-residents-unite-to-fend-off-mobs-in-northeast-delhi-colony-2109887.html.

example comes from the town of Saharanpur (majority Muslim) near Delhi. The controversy there centered on a gurudwara situated next to a historic building (a *pili kothi*) with a mosque on its property. In 1948, when this land was sold, the mutation papers showed that the mosque would continue in its place. In 2001, the whole property was bought by the Sikhs. When the Sikhs tried to expand the gurudwara in 2010–11, there was resistance from Muslims. This case then went to court, leading to local riots in 2014 and the loss of many lives and property. The court's decision was that the land should have both the mosque and the gurudwara. The decision was never fully accepted by the communities involved. In the face of the CAA/NRC protests, however, in an unexpected move, the Muslim leaders got together and decided not just to withdraw their claim but also to donate some money and *karseva* (free labor) for the expansion of the gurudwara: "We were deeply touched by the Sikhs in Delhi who helped Muslims [during the recent attacks in Shaheen Bagh]. . . . Because the Sikhs are helping us, our people said we will not be in their debt. The Muslims of Saharanpur sent me to Delhi in order to assure the Sikhs. We then returned not just the money but all claims to the land. . . . We are in your debt and we will repay it whenever you ask."[58]

Incidents of violence, often with police support, were overshadowed by the evidence of altruism—for example, in the case of a Sikh man and his son who saved eighty Muslims during the Delhi violence as CAA/NRC protests raged: "In the 1984 [violence against the Sikhs after Indira Gandhi's assassination] my *nana* (grandfather) had to remove his turban when travelling on a bus in India so the mobs outside wouldn't kill him for being Sikh." But the report says that in "2020 Inderjit Singh (the Sikh from the bus) and Mohinder Singh were putting *paghs* (turbans) on men so the mobs [would not] kill them for being Muslim," and they transported Muslim "neighbors to safe locations." They had to make about twenty trips to move women and children, boys and men, often placing turbans on their heads to keep them safe in transit.[59]

As an insider, it is hard for me to imagine any other period in the history of India (except, of course, the era of the independence movement) when people of faith formed a closer bond to express dissent. As British India deliberated the partition in a deal for independence, a Hindu Gandhi led a diverse political

---

[58] Punjab Kesari UP, "*Muslimon ne gurudware ken am ki masjid ki zamin salon se zamin ko le kar chal rah tha vivad*," Facebook, March 3, 2020, https://www.facebook.com/upkesari/videos/499991767612625/.

[59] K. C. Archana, "Here's How a Brave Sikh Man and His Son Rescued Nearly 80 Muslims during the Delhi Riots," *India Times*, February 29, 2020; see also "Sikh Man Saves 80 Muslims by Transporting to Save [*sic*] Location," Daily Sikh Updates, February 28, 2020.

movement toward religious unity and prevention of violence. We now appear to have few such statesmen.

Maulana Arshad Madani is the current amir (head) of Jamiat Ulema-e-Hind (the Indian Muslim council of Deobandi theologians who fought for independence and opposed the partition of India based on religion). He was at a press conference organized in Hyderabad by the Jamiat, also attended by people of other faiths, including Hindus. He spoke passionately about Hindu-Muslim riots since independence (including the one in Gujarat under Narendra Modi's watch as then chief minister of the state, where about two thousand Muslims lost their lives). Compared to previous riots, the number of Muslims who have lost their lives is minuscule, but there is something different today. It is as if the soul of India has been awakened; people of faith, and especially Hindus, are rising in support of Muslims as never before. One can see in the video recording of this press conference that the dais is shared also by non-Muslims.[60] At the conference, Madani spoke of the NRC in Assam and the possibility of a large number of Indian Muslims being excluded from citizenship. The Jamiat, he said, was therefore playing a role in resisting the NRC, but Muslims were not alone in this, and he said he was encouraged by witnessing something unprecedented:

> What was absent before in terms of *hindu-muslim ittehad* [unity] [is evident now]. Thank God that there is evidence of love [*pyar awe mohabbat*] and [evidence of] participation in each other's struggles. What we see today, we have never seen before since independence [*mulk ki azadi*]. This is a great *niamat* [gift] of God and if this resolve [to work collaboratively] grows from strength to strength then God will intervene and the BJP will eventually be unsuccessful [*nakam*] and [will not be able to] realise its aims [*namurad*]. . . . If [the BJP] does not abandon its three-pronged strategy for disenfranchising Indians [through CAA-NPR-NRC], then we will call for an *am ijlas* [common movement] of Muslims and Hindus in huge numbers so we can maintain our commitment [to the cause]. And we hope in God you all [sitting here] will support us. This is our country and we have always been here. The ancestors [*bap-dada*] of our Hindu brothers and ours were all one. We are not different. It is a different matter that some chose to remain [Hindu], others chose to be Christian, Sikh or Muslim. But we had such a level of flexibility that enabled us to live together for centuries without any sense of real distinction [*bhed bhao*]. Muslims go to masjid, Christians go to church, Hindus go to *mandirs*, and Sikhs to Gurudwaras. There is/was no reason for quarrels among them. These

---

60 Azad reporter Abu Aimal, "Maulana Arshad Madani Sahib: Press Conference in Hyderabad," Facebook, March 3, 2020, https://www.facebook.com/AZADREPORTERABUAIMAL/videos/505357100179022/.

[viz. the BJP cadres] have initiated the conflict. We think this conflict is like poison.... We need to rid our country of this.[61]

CONCLUSION

Covid-19 has globally been a challenge to deal with. Although it brought the street protests to a halt all over the country, neither the resolve of the government nor that of the dissenters has waned (concerning CAA/NRC). The recent federally controlled ceremony at the proposed Ram Temple (in place of the demolished sixteenth-century Babri Mosque) demonstrates the BJP's determination not to let Covid-19 dampen the spirit of Hindu nationalism. The recently reported arrest of critics of the BJP government offers another piece of evidence for this.[62]

In this chapter, I outlined selected cases of the countrywide protests following the controversial CAA and the discourse on the NRC in India. Protests are commonplace in India, where, after electing a government, citizens often have few effective means to express dissent between elections. Today's India is moving in the direction of becoming an "illiberal democracy."[63] Here, increasingly, apart from voting, the citizens have little power and few civil liberties; state institutions, including the police, the courts, and the media, lack full independence; and a high-minded secular constitution is barely recognized as a nominal framework.

I have reserved the investigation of the themes of moral sabotage, physical violence, and the strategy of distraction that the government of a receding democracy employs to suppress dissent voiced by its citizens. The focus here was on highlighting cases of protests, which, as I see it, offer evidence of emerging grassroots cooperation among religious minorities; this is hearteningly also supported by many fair-minded Hindus. Many in the BJP have already declared India to be a "Hindu rashtra" (Hindu nation), but what these protests show is that the idea of a secular India, which the constitution promises and which was envisioned by the makers of India, is still alive and kicking. This highlights the battle for the idea of India: a battle between those whose ideologues and institutions played no role in India's independence as a secular democracy and those whose heroes/institutions laid down their lives to build modern India.

---

[61] Aimal, "Maulana Arshad Madani Sahib."

[62] Kai Schultz and Sameer Yasir, "India Rounds Up Critics under Shadow of Virus Crisis, Activists Say," *New York Times*, July 19, 2020, https://www.nytimes.com/2020/07/19/world/asia/india-activists-arrests-riots-coronavirus.html.

[63] See Fareed Zakaria, "The Rise of Illiberal Democracy," *Foreign Affairs* 76, no. 6 (May 26, 2021): 22–43.

ABBREVIATIONS

BJP = Bharatiya Janata Party (Indian People's Party)
CAA = Citizenship Amendment Act
CAB = Citizenship Amendment Bill
NCCI = National Council of Churches in India
NPR = National Population Register
NRC = National Register of Citizens
RSS = Rashtriya Swayamsevak Sangh (National Volunteer Organization)
SB = Shaheen Bagh

CHAPTER 3

RELIGIOUS INTOLERANCE IN BRAZIL

THE CASE OF THE GIRL AND THE STONE

Babalawô Carlos Alberto Ivanir dos Santos

No one is born hating another person because of the color of his skin, or his background, or his religion. People must learn to hate, and if they can learn to hate, they can be taught to love, for love comes more naturally to the human heart than its opposite. Man's goodness is a flame that can be hidden but never extinguished.

—Nelson Mandela, *Long Walk to Freedom*

For decades, Black communities, which have their origins in Black sub-Saharan Africa, were confined to objectifying research in various scientific fields, at best as a statistical substrate for research databases.[1] Getting out of this social marginality to which they were conditioned and promoting studies focused on the resistance of religions of African origins as historical subjects was, and still is, one of the greatest challenges for Brazilian academia. Although I have worked in the education field for more than thirty years, until now, I have not written anything about academic biases, analyzing the historical processes of religious intolerance. Also, in years of research, I have not found many studies focusing

---

[1] Translated from the Portuguese by Monika Ottermann. This chapter offers a brief review of the history of religious intolerance in Brazil, in conversation with the case of Kayllane, a young victim of religious intolerance in 2015. A previous version of this text was published in Babalawô Ivanir dos Santos et al., eds., *Intolerância Religiosa No Brasil: Relatório e Balanço/Religious Intolerance in Brazil: Report and Balances*, bilingual ed. (Rio de Janeiro: Klíne/CEAP, 2016). The book chapter was developed with the collaboration of Professor Mariana Gino. While I am the sole author of this new version, this text is the result of continuous analysis and exchange of ideas with the aforementioned professor, to whom I am very grateful.

on the resistance of religions of African origins in Brazil vis-à-vis the growth of religious intolerance and the struggles of these particular religions for freedom of belief and worship.

In the course of lecturing, teaching, researching, and monitoring several cases of religious intolerance reported to the Commission to Combat Religious Intolerance (Comissão de Combate à Intolerância Religiosa; CCIR), my ideas on the subject gradually matured. It was precisely during that process of analysis and research that the "Kayllane Case" (as it became known) took place and several other cases began to emerge and receive attention in the media. The Kayllane Case is not unique in the history of the persecution that adherents of religions of African origin have experienced. However, it became a symbolic case in the struggle against religious intolerance in Brazil.

THE KAYLLANE CASE

June 14, 2015, will remain for a long time in our memory as one of the symbolic dates in the struggle against religious intolerance in Brazil. The image of Kayllane Campos, only eleven years old, dressed in her white religious robes all stained with blood, shocked the entire country. The bleeding was caused by a stone—thrown by whom? Even today, we do not know for certain, but along with the stone, the insults "Go burn in hell!" and "Macumbeira!" were heard.[2] Shouted by whom? Likewise, to this day, we do not know. The "Kayllane Case," as this fateful episode of religious intolerance came to be known, is not unique in the history of the persecution of religious[3] minorities[4] in Brazil. On the contrary, it is an example of new manifestations of such phenomena in recent history. As Ari Pedro Oro and Daniel Francisco Bem state, "Attacks on the Afro-Brazilian religions, which had previously occurred only on the premises of their temples and were carried out by evangelicals, have become more widespread throughout society due to media coverage. The impact of these new discursive strategies, therefore, reinforces the historical distrust and the disrespect for the symbols of religiosity of African origin, leading to intolerance and confrontation with these 'agents of the devil.'"[5]

It is already known to us that Brazilian society, governed by a system where church and state constituted one single body, for a long time had Catholicism

---

[2] *Editor's note: Macumbeira* is a derogatory way to identify a practitioner of Macumba, a word that refers both to specific Afro-Brazilian religious practices and to the religions of the orishas in general.

[3] In most cases, Afro-Brazilian religions and religiosities.

[4] "Minority" in the sense of political representation.

[5] Ari Pedro Oro and Daniel Francisco Bem, "A Discriminação Contra as Religiões Afro-Brasileiras: Ontem e Hoje," *Ciências e Letras*, no. 44 (2008): 314.

as the official state religion. At that point in history, "the State regulated with an iron fist any religious expression that diverged from the official religion . . . ; it repressed the religious beliefs and practices of Indians and black slaves and prevented the entry of competing religions, especially Protestantism, and their free exercise in the country."[6] Kayllane Campos, like her grandmother Kátia Marinho, who accompanied her at the time she was assaulted, is a Candomblé initiate. On the day of the aggression, both were returning from a religious ceremony in Vila da Penha, a neighborhood located in the northern zone of the city of Rio de Janeiro.

Looking back in history in the attempt to understand the triggering of this process, we realize that with the advent of the 1824 constitution—which stated that no one could be persecuted for religious reasons as long as they respected the state religion, Catholic Christianity—religious persecution began to happen in a veiled and sometimes indirect way. Subsequently, in 1891, with the end of the patronage regime, the constitution,[7] in addition to legally separating the temporal power from the spiritual one, ensured the constitutional right of religious freedom, extending freedom of worship to other religions.[8]

However, Afro-Brazilian religions (in their most diverse resignifications) continued to be discriminated against and persecuted as a problem of criminality, as shown in article 157, on the practice of Spiritism (which, in addition to Kardecism, also includes Candomblé and Macumba), and article 158, on the practice of "healerism." It is important to highlight that article 156, on the illegal practice of medicine, was also invoked in lawsuits against priests of Afro-Brazilian religions. This fact refers to the context of the officialization of medical discourse in Brazil as, for instance, in the Sanitarist Movement.[9] During the period known as Estado Novo (New State; 1930–45), such repression intensified with the creation of a committee for the suppression of Afro-Brazilian religions, denominated then as *baixo espiritismo* (low spiritism).

According to Norton F. Correa, direct persecution was further intensified with the creation of the first Auxiliary Police Unit (Delegacia Auxiliar) directly responsible for combating the practices of Calundu and Candomblé in 1934,

---

[6] Ricardo Mariano, "Análise Sociológica Do Crescimento Pentecostal No Brasil" (PhD diss., Universidade de São Paulo, 2001), 127–28.

[7] *Editor's note:* Brazil has seen seven constitutions since independence from Portugal in 1822. The founding constitution of Brazil (1824) is known as the Imperial Constitution. The 1891 constitution, known as the Old Republican Constitution, is the constitution of the first Brazilian republic, following the deposition of Emperor Pedro II.

[8] *Editor's note:* Article 72, paragraph 3 of the 1891 constitution stated, "All individuals and religious confessions may publicly and freely exercise their worship, associating for this purpose and acquiring goods, subject to the provisions of common law."

[9] Oro and Bem, "Discriminação Contra as Religiões," 308.

with chief Mattos Mendes having the mandate of forming and chairing a committee for the suppression of "low spiritism."[10] Around the same period, General Manoel de Cerqueira Daltro Filtro, appointed by President Getúlio Vargas as a federal intervener in the state of Rio Grande do Sul, enforced a religious hygienist policy against non-Christian religions, which impacted, in particular, orisha religions such as Batuque.[11] As Correa states, "In the collective memory of the Batuque members [Batuque being an Afro-Brazilian religion], the beginning of the Intervener's term coincides with the beginning of a dark period, with the systematic closing of many of the temples by the police, with arrests and violence carried out by policemen."[12]

In the period known as the "Years of Lead" in Brazilian political and social history, the military dictatorship, the raids—persecution and apprehensions—in the *terreiros* (as the meeting places of the Afro-Brazilian religions are called in Brazil) intensified at the initiative of political commissions that had the prerogative to declare that such religious sites were sheltering communists. In such a context, it is not difficult to conclude that "there was no religious freedom when facing the 'National Security Doctrine,'[13] nor freedom of speech, association, assembly, dissemination, press, etc."[14] By contrast, in recent decades, we have seen various dynamics and practices of reconstruction and symbolic appropriation of Afro-Brazilian religious elements by evangelicals, especially in the Pentecostal and Neo-Pentecostal sectors, as examples of what Emerson

---

[10] See Norton F. Correa, "Sob o Signo Da Ameaça: Conflito, Poder e Feitiço Nas Religiões Afro-Brasileiras" (PhD diss., Pontifícia Universidade Católica de São Paulo, 1998).

[11] *Editor's note:* For an overview of the variety of Afro-Brazilian religions in Rio Grande do Sul and the internal diversity of Batuque, see Ari Oro, "Religiões Afro-Brasileiras do Rio Grande do Sul: Passado e Presente," *Estudos Afro-Asiáticos* 24, no. 2 (2002): 345–84.

[12] Correa, "Sob o Signo," 224.

[13] *Editor's note:* A doctrine developed by the United States and spread throughout Latin American states through the US schools for Latin American military. It disseminated the view that Latin American countries were threatened by "international communism," and unless the military in those countries acted preemptively to combat the communist takeover, the Cuban Revolution would spread throughout the continent. This doctrine provided the impetus for military coups and repressive regimes throughout the region between the 1960s and the late 1980s. In Brazil, this doctrine is associated with the 1964 coup d'etat and the twenty-one years of military dictatorship that followed. On top of being anticommunist, the national security doctrine embodied an ideological view of morality, which was unabashedly Christian and Western. Under the banner of this doctrine, for instance, sexual minorities and non-Christian religions were often targeted. It favored conservative Christianity and its family model. In light of the association of liberation theology with Marxism, the military regime in Brazil privileged conservative Catholic and evangelical churches, which, in response, sought to show their allegiance to the regime. José Comblin provides a helpful perspective on the relationship between Christianity and the doctrine of national security in Latin America. See José Comblin, *The Church and the National Security State* (Maryknoll, NY: Orbis Books, 1979).

[14] Antônio Flávio de Oliveira Pierucci and J. Reginaldo Prandi, *A Realidade Social Das Religiões No Brasil: Religião, Sociedade e Política* (São Paulo: Editora Hucitec, 1996), 247.

Giumbelli has called "redefinitions of the religious in Brazil."[15] As Oro and Bem have shown, this religious sector experienced significant growth during the last two decades of the twentieth century and the first decade of the twenty-first century, mainly due to its ritual and syncretic particularities, which combine Christian elements with elements of the mediumistic religions, mediated by conversion strategies and by their growing presence in politics, media, and social philanthropy.[16]

Ari Pedro Oro points out that one of the most striking characteristics of this syncretic process is what he calls "religiophagy"—that is, "the extent to which a religion appropriates and reworks elements of beliefs from other churches and religions, especially Afro-Brazilian ones (e.g., Candomblé, Umbanda, Quimbanda, Macumba); as well as the 'exacerbation of these elements of belief and ritualistic practice taken from these religious organizations.'"[17] This development is accompanied by a major resignification of the syncretism of popular religions in Brazil. As a manifestation of popular syncretism, these religions are situated in a field of cultural forces woven by hegemonies and hybridizations, a continuous flow of exchanges, and the assimilation of disproportionate and multiple elements in time and space.[18]

Vagner G. da Silva highlights five forms of attacks against religions of African origin in Brazil: "1) attacks made within the realm of worship services in Neo-Pentecostal churches and their means of dissemination and proselytism; 2) physical attacks *in loco* against *terreiros* and their members; 3) attacks on Afro-Brazilian religious ceremonies held in public places or on existing symbols of these religions in such spaces; 4) attacks on other symbols of the African heritage in Brazil that are related to the Afro-Brazilian religions; 5) attacks stemming from alliances between evangelical churches and politicians."[19]

The Kayllane Case fits with da Silva's typology. Even with the enactment of Law No. 7716—known as *Lei Caó*—of January 5, 1989, which defined crimes of racial prejudice, persecution of and attacks against adherents of

---

[15] Emerson Giumbelli, "Um Projeto de Cristianismo Hegemônico," in *Intolerância Religiosa: Impactos Do Neopentecostalismo No Campo Religioso Afro-Brasileiro*, ed. Vagner Gonçalves da Silva (São Paulo: EDUSP, 2007), 150.

[16] Oro and Bem, "Discriminação Contra as Religiões."

[17] Ari Pedro Oro, "O 'Neopentecostalismo Macumbeiro,'" *Revista USP*, no. 68 (February 1, 2006): 320, https://doi.org/10.11606/issn.2316-9036.v0i68p319-332.

[18] Peter Ludwig Berger, *Dossel sagrado: Elementos para uma Teoria Sociológica da Religião* (São Paulo: Paulinas, 1985); Pierre Bourdieu, *A Economia das Trocas Simbólicas* (São Paulo: Perspectiva, 1974).

[19] Vagner Gonçalves da Silva, "Neopentecostalismo e Religiões Afro-Brasileiras: Significados Do Ataque Aos Símbolos Da Herança Religiosa Africana No Brasil Contemporâneo," *Mana* 13, no. 1 (April 2007): 216.

Afro-Brazilian religions have persisted. The aforementioned law declares the following in articles 1 and 3:

> Art. 1. In accordance with this Law, crimes resulting from discrimination or prejudice based on race, color, ethnicity, religion, or national origin will be punished.

> Art. 3. To prevent or impede the access of any duly qualified individual to any position of the Direct or Indirect Administration, as well as to public service concessionaires. Penalty: two to five years of imprisonment.

> The same penalty applies to those who, due to discrimination based on race, color, ethnicity, religion, or national origin, impede functional promotion.

The vast majority of victims of attacks of religious intolerance in Brazil are followers of religions of African origin.[20] Referring to this segment, Jose Geraldo da Rocha asserts, "When speaking of religions of African origin, there is no distinction in belonging to any tradition, whether Ketu, Jeje, Nagô or Angola. Nor between Candomblé, Batuque and Umbanda. This is because intolerance is widespread, extended to all those who profess the religions of the Orixás, whose label or stigma becomes naturalized in social relations such as the *macumbeiros*."[21]

This persecution fortifies an induced mentality concerning the adherents of Afro-Brazilian religions and religiosities and their religious practices, as seen in the latest updated data from the 2016 Report on Cases of Religious Intolerance in Brazil (Relatório Sobre os Casos de Intolerância Religiosa no Brasil).[22] These data reveal that the vast majority of cases of religious intolerance are related to adherents of Afro-Brazilian religions and religiosities. According to the Center for the Promotion of Religious Freedom and Human Rights (Centro de Promoção da Liberdade Religiosa e Direitos Humanos; CEPLIR), between July 2012 and August 2015, it offered support to a total of 1,014 cases reported by 582 individuals. Complaints of attacks against Afro-Brazilian religions represented 71.15 percent of them.

---

[20] According to Verger, religions of African origin (*religiões de matrizes africanas*) is a term originally used to designate the religious practices developed by Black Brazilians. The first mentions of African religions in Brazil date back to 1650, during research carried out by the strong arm of the Catholic Church, the Holy Office of the Inquisition, when Sebastião Barreto denounced the customs of Black people in Bahia. See Pierre Verger, *Orixás: Deuses Iorubás Na Africa e No Novo Mundo* (Salvador: Corrupio Edições e Promoção Cultural, 1981).

[21] Jose Geraldo da Rocha, "A Intolerância Religiosa e Religiões de Matriz Africanas No Rio de Janeiro," *Revista África e Africanidades* 4, nos. 14/15 (2011): 14.

[22] Santos et al., *Intolerância Religiosa No Brasil*.

Kind of support	Total
Cases supported	1,014
Individuals requesting legal or psychological support	582
Details	
Against Afro-Brazilian religions	71.15%
Against evangelicals, Protestants, or Neo-Pentecostals	7.7%
Against Catholics	3.8%
Against Jews or people without religious affiliation	3.8%
Attacks against religious freedom	3.8%

Source: Centro de Promoção da Liberdade Religiosa e Direitos Humanos (CEPLIR)

We also highlight the data provided by the Commission for Combating Religious Intolerance (Comissão de Combate à Intolerância Religiosa; CCIR), which demonstrate that the vast majority of the fifty-seven cases of religious intolerance reported and documented between 2010 and 2014 refer to Afro-Brazilian religions.[23]

Period	Religion	Complaint filed		
		Total	*Yes*	*No*
2008–9		32	28	4
2010–14		25	11	14
	Afro-Brazilian	15	7	8
	Spiritism	9	2	7
	Wicca	1	1	—
	Total	57	39	18

Source: Comissão de Combate à Intolerância Religiosa (CCIR) in the 2008–14 period

When analyzing the quantitative data of the growing cases of religious intolerance in Brazil, we realized that little or nothing was being done in favor of representative minorities as called for in the Durban Declaration, which reaffirms "the principles of equality and non-discrimination in the Universal Declaration of Human Rights and encourages respect for human rights and fundamental freedoms for all without distinction of any kind such as race,

---

[23] Cases related to the year 2015 were not included in this table.

colour, sex, language, religion, political or other opinion, national or social origin, property, birth or other status."[24]

Religious intolerance has been one of the causes of social disintegration and conflict in the world, and this fact is not new. However, this is not a problem that would be limited to differences in religious belief. It is linked to a much greater evil, that of ethno-racial intolerance, which is directly correlated to individual and collective identity markers displayed in concepts such as ethnicity, "race," "color," gender, beliefs, appearance, and origin, among others.[25]

Thus, as an authoritarian attitude linked to ethno-racial prejudice, intolerance confines specific human individuals or groups in relation to other individuals or groups to a situation of cultural inferiority manifested in the forms of racism, machismo, homophobia, elitism, xenophobia, political intolerance, and religious intolerance. The disguised intolerance on the part of those who claim to be the defenders of "good customs" and "good taste" brings with it disregard and contempt for Others. It can develop into physical violence when a certain individual or group is unable to impose their "reasons" through discursive persuasion and other nonviolent means.

Religious Intolerance and Racism in Brazil

Africa is a rich and diverse continent, but it is often seen as a homogeneous space associated with poverty, not only in the representations of textbooks, but also in the social imagery that created condescending stereotypes about Africans. Over the centuries, the concepts of "Black people," "Black continent," and "Black persons" began to appear in the travel accounts of missionaries and merchants in Africa. In these, it appears that the idea of "race" was clearly related to the culture and religion of different African peoples—their religious practices, eating habits, clothing, social manners—which appeared as identifying elements of the particularity of each race.

During the seventeenth century, the concept of race began to be scientifically explained in two strands—namely, monogenism, or the hypothesis according to which humanity is a single species, descended from a common ancestor,[26]

---

[24] This declaration came out of a world conference organized by the General Assembly of the UN, *Against Racism, Racial Discrimination, Xenophobia e Related Intolerance* from August 31 to September 8, 2001, in Durban, South Africa. See "Durban Declaration—A/CONF.189/12 Chapter I—UN Documents: Gathering a Body of Global Agreements," UN Documents: World Conference against Racism, Racial Discrimination, Xenophobia and Related Intolerance, accessed September 21, 2021, http://www.un-documents.net/durban-d.htm.

[25] Rocha, "Intolerância Religiosa."

[26] As a scientific theory or hypothesis, monogenism became widely accepted from the mid-nineteenth century onward as a result of the Darwinian evolution theory. It is also a nearly unquestioned principle of social and cultural anthropology today.

and polygenism, the hypothesis according to which humanity does not have a common origin, as the various prehistoric human groups or the supposed races of present-day humanity descend from distinct species.[27] Thus, in the second half of the eighteenth century, racialized scientific perspectives consisted of a set of preconceived views based on poorly justified intuitions and European aesthetic models. The construction of those models led to the hierarchization and characterization of peoples in a frenetic rush to understand how physical characteristics influenced the moral and rational behavior of each individual. These theories opened spaces for the ideas of evolution and hierarchization of races.

In the following century, the appearance of different scientific currents led to the formation of theories that sought to prove the racial superiority of European elites through objective methods, placing the Europeans at the top of the hierarchy of humanity with regard to cultural, religious, moral, artistic, political, technical, military, and industrial aspects. Industry, science, and technology became indicators of the European superior civilization. Gradually, these theories began to increasingly influence the social imagination through public education, media, and various artistic manifestations.

In the mid-nineteenth century, the publication of fierce discussions about the concept of evolution made it possible to put an end to the disputes between polygenists and monogenites. Charles Darwin's famous work *On the Origin of Species* (1859) was one of the main disseminators of the theory of evolution. This theory held that biological diversity was the result of changes in the hereditary characteristics of groups over time so that living organisms gradually adapted through natural selection.

Following the evolutionary mainstay, Herbert Spencer (1820–1903) adapted these scientific reflections to the study of social relations. For Spencer, everything that was good for living organisms could be applied to human beings and their actions. Accordingly, he founded the school of social Darwinism, a theoretical framework for scientific discussions about human difference. From this perspective, society was seen as governed by rigid, linear, and unbreakable laws, just as nature was believed to be. Supporters of social Darwinism such as Arthur de Gobineau (1816–82) and Gustave Le Bon (1841–1931) even revived the polygenist hypothesis, theorizing that race was immutable and that interracial crossbreeding was a mistake. Thus, their proposal was to exalt the existence of pure racial types by virtue of believing that miscegenation would lead to socioracial degeneration.

---

[27] Polygenism, a current spread mainly in the nineteenth century, became obsolete with the acceptance of the Darwinian evolution theory, having as its main theorists Enlightenment philosophers.

On the other hand, there were those who believed that most human races could never civilize on their own unless there was a process of miscegenation with other races considered superior. De Gobineau argued that the yellow and Black races were condemned to eternal bestiality and that the Black race belonged to the group of "humans unable to civilize themselves."[28] At the same time, the social evolutionist school conceived human development on the basis of fixed and predetermined stages, where humanity was constituted by an immense pyramid divided into distinct stages: savagery, barbarism, and civilization. Such an image put Europe at the top of the pyramid. In order to reach this civilizational level, other societies would have to follow the same paths until reaching evolution.

Throughout the nineteenth century and, subsequently, into the twentieth century, intellectuals created and justified scientifically racialist and hierarchical ideas of humanity, according to which physical attributes were used to understand sociocultural behaviors and actions. Other peoples and groups were subjugated, humiliated, and massacred in the face of such racialized scientific theories and justifications[29] that served as the basis for criminal anthropology. Subsequently, these social representations and hierarchies were also identified in African individuals of the diasporas in Europe and the Americas. Racial stereotypes, based on an individual's skin color and other physical traits, have fiercely driven not only the process of enslavement and the social stratification of Blacks but also the dissemination of religious prejudice.[30] This has been the case in Brazil, where conflict around the right to freedom of religious expression is associated with "prejudices in relation to the faith expressions of black people in Brazilian society."[31]

FINAL CONSIDERATIONS

Six years after the incident of religious intolerance experienced by Kayllane Campos, questions about the impetus of religious intolerance and its extremes still permeate the Brazilian social imagination. Religious intolerance is a

---

[28] See Lilia K. Moritz Schwarcz, "Usos e Abusos Da Mestiçagem e Da Raça No Brasil: Uma História Das Teorias Raciais Em Finais Do Século XIX," *Revista Afro-Ásia*, no. 18 (January 24, 1996): 77–101.

[29] Cesare Lombroso, an Italian, argued that criminality was a physical and hereditary phenomenon. From this perspective, it was believed that it was possible to carry out a crime prevention policy, making it capable of capturing criminals before they committed any crime, due to the physical characteristics that allegedly made them susceptible to crime. Francis Galton, on the other hand, based on the perspective of social Darwinism, created the theory of eugenics, believing it was possible to intervene in the reproduction of populations. According to Galton, human capacity was exclusively linked to heredity; as a result, education would accomplish very little.

[30] Rocha, "Intolerância Religiosa."

[31] Rocha.

phenomenon that deserves attention in the course of analyzing and explaining cases of religious violence in the field of human relations. We have to point out that religious intolerance—as well as racism—is not a social phenomenon that happens exclusively in Brazil. But on Brazilian soil, it has become a quotidian and endemic issue in our country. As we well know, even though religious freedom is guaranteed by law, it is not a reality for all religions on Brazilian soil.

Behind the actions of intolerance and racism—and at their very core—there is the binary of superiority versus inferiority and constructions relating to the identity of the Other. However, by underscoring "religious racism"—as identified in Brazil, based on skin color—we are stressing the existence of a religious identity that is related to people's skin color. In making such a point, however, we are neither eliminating the possibility of choice nor creating religious conditioning based on people's skin color.

Of course, one must point out that for a long time, the practices of Black men and women who arrived in Brazil as slaves were equated with the practices of "Black religions." However, this identification had to do with the identity that the Other, the Christian colonizer, attributed to religious practices that differed from their own beliefs and liturgies. Such identification does not exclude the initiation of non-Black people and their participation in the religions of African origin. Hence I understand that "religious racism" does not have an ontological dimension in the interpretation of cases of physical, psychological, and property aggression motivated by religious hate.

In fact, it is obvious that religious intolerance against adherents of African-derived religions is closely linked to scientific racism, which still persists in the collective Brazilian social imagination. However, in debates about racial issues in Brazil, racism cannot be the only vector for identifying cases of religious hate. In any event, one can say that (1) intolerance against religions of African origin derives from the culture it represents, and (2) intolerance is associated with Africanities that disqualify the religious identity of Afro-Brazilians as a possible match for the only valid Brazilian religiosity, which, of course, happens to be Christian.

Thus, in Brazil, when we highlight and analyze actions of religious hatred based on the idea of religious racism, we would also need to connect such an analysis to the idea of cultural racism. In relation to this dissonant religious identity, we need to understand that in Africa, the individual exists in his or her socioreligious-cultural totality; that is, it is impossible to separate the social being from the religious being. We also know that during the periods of forced diasporas of Black Africans, these individuals arrived in America embodying their religiosities, as the world in which they lived was not based on a Cartesian model in which it is possible to separate the religious individual from the social individual.

Prejudice, discrimination, and religious intolerance have always been, from the beginning of the colonial period down to the present, a recurrent factor in the history of religions in Brazilian society, dating to the arrival of the first enslaved Blacks with their African cultures and religiosities. The attacks on religions of African origin are calculatedly aggressive and overlooked by the government. It is true that many narratives in journalistic, literary, and scientific circles helped fabricate the distorted image of the religions of African origin and strengthened the idea of "religious war." At the present moment in Brazil, when we are experiencing an intense and extreme social and human rights setback, religious intolerance and racism have been significantly spreading in the country. That said, I still believe that knowledge and information about Brazilian religious diversity can contribute to tolerance building.

CHAPTER 4

THE POWER OF REWRITING HISTORY

LITERATURE, RACE, AND RELIGION IN CONTEMPORARY BRAZIL

Felipe Fanuel Xavier Rodrigues

Sou uma preta, muito negra brilhante cintilante, faço verso com requinte para o deleite das pessoas que amam a vida e fazem das tripas coração, para prosseguir ampliando a estética do mundo que, sabe Deus ou "Olorum," pela perfeição de sua criação.

[I am a very brilliant and bright Black woman; I write verses with refinement for the delight of people who love life and bend over backward to continue expanding the aesthetics of the world that God or "Olorum" knows for the perfection of their creation.][1]

—Ana Cruz, *Guardados Da Memória*

In her definition of Afro-Brazilian literature, Miriam Alves identifies this body of work as "an existential practice" that Black people utilize to express "self-recognition of their identity and ethnic-racial belonging."[2] Careful examination of Black women's literary existential practice reveals personal insights into the collective traumas and regeneration associated with slavery's legacy and prevalent racism. In producing creative discourses of individual and social histories, Black women writers provide antiracist critiques of identities and cultural heritage while struggling to survive in Brazil's contradictory sociopolitical context.

---

[1] All translations are mine unless otherwise indicated.
[2] Miriam Alves, *BrasilAfro Autorrevelado: Literatura Brasileira Contemporânea* (Belo Horizonte: Nandyala Livraria Editora, 2010), 42.

Central to the understanding of African diasporic life in the country that has birthed the second largest Black population globally is the interrelation of race and religion, particularly through the lens of those at the bottom of the social structure.

My interest in the articulations of race and religion in literary narratives that counteract the historical racist episteme had its beginnings in my undergraduate work at the State University of Rio de Janeiro under Professor Cida Salgueiro. Her courses in American literature directed attention to the poetry and prose of authors such as Phillis Wheatley, Harriet Jacobs, Zora Neale Hurston, Alice Walker, and Toni Morrison. After receiving a research grant, I explored the literary representation of race and religion in the United States and Brazil, culminating in a PhD dissertation analyzing contemporary Black women writers' religious discourses.

This story started in 2005 when I was a Black student of English at the first university to establish affirmative action on Brazilian soil dealing with the contradictory educational effects of a lack of diversity in its curriculum, which primarily focused on the canonical white male voices of Anglophone literary traditions. After reading Salgueiro's *Escritoras Negras Contemporâneas: Estudo de Narrativas—Estados Unidos e Brasil*,[3] I discovered new texts and contexts as well as innovative critical approaches to literature and culture, including discussions of race, class, and gender. Salgueiro's pioneering research into the marginalized written art of women of African descent resonated with my mother's axiomatic answer to my question during childhood about our family's racial identity: "We all have come from Africa."

That maternal wisdom offered an alternative to the negative connotations that the word *Africa* had in the mind of a child raised in a Baptist church, where pictures of African men, women, and children would be displayed during annual missionary campaigns to convey spiritual degradation, extreme poverty, and terrible diseases. Nevertheless, the personal experience that betrayed my Blackness came through an episode in my adolescence when I had to undo my overalls' straps to convince the white owner of a small grocery store that I had not stolen a pack of cookies. Unless his unspoken assumptions were the result of the visual markers of a lanky young Black male body, there were no grounds for suspicion, as I was a regular customer in that local store in my hometown in the state of Minas Gerais. The knot in my stomach led me to share the incident with my uncle, who immediately recognized racism. By the time I did theology years later, I knew that being Black in Brazil is an inversion

---

[3] Maria Aparecida Andrade Salgueiro, *Escritoras Negras Contemporâneas: Estudo de Narrativas—Estados Unidos e Brasil* (Rio de Janeiro: Caetés, 2004).

of Martin Luther King Jr.'s dream of a country where somebody is judged by their character, not by their complexion.[4]

Racist judgment can be violent when involving religious intolerance. As valedictorian of the Baptist Theological Seminary of Southern Brazil's class of 2006, I was about to start my ministry as an associate pastor at a church located in a working-class neighborhood of Rio with a dilemma: How would I work to bridge the gap between my liberal theological education and the spiritual needs of a quasi-fundamentalist community? Though the practice of evangelical proselytism could be understood sociologically, the acts of iconoclasm[5] of religious criminals destroying Afro-Brazilian religions' temples in the name of Jesus were too disturbing for an ecumenical Black minister wrestling with parochial anti-intellectualist tendencies. New perspectives on life in literature brought spiritual solace, hope, and a sense of purpose to my scholarship and academic career.

ANTIRACIST AND SURVIVAL LITERATURE

As black people we exist metaphorically and literally as the underside, the underclass. We are the unconscious of the entire Western world. If this is in fact true, then where do we go? Where are our dreams? Where is our pain? Where do we heal?

—Ntozake Shange

In Afro-Brazilian women's literary discourse, religion signifies the African-derived heritage that liberates personal identities from racist imagery and narratives. While gender, class, and race discriminatory practices affect their full citizenship status, Black women writers emerge as self-determined persons endowed with the power to rewrite trauma and survival. Through personal representations of the sacred in prose and poetry, they enter into a historical revision of the ideology of racial democracy.

Canonized in Gilberto Freyre's work *Casa Grande e Senzala*,[6] the notion of racial democracy has become a national historical narrative of peaceful coexistence between slaveholders and enslaved people in colonization. Such a

---

[4] "I have a dream that my four children will one day live in a nation where they will not be judged by the color of their skin but by the content of their character." See Martin Luther King Jr., *The Words of Martin Luther King, Jr.*, ed. Coretta Scott King (New York: William Morrow, 2014), 95.

[5] On recent iconoclasm targeting Afro-Brazilian religions, see Arthur Valle, "Religiões Afrobrasileiras, Cultura Visual e Iconoclastia," *Revista Concinnitas* 21, no. 37 (May 25, 2020): 140–62.

[6] See Gilberto Freyre, *Casa Grande e Senzala*, 48th ed. (São Paulo: Global Editora, 2003).

foundational myth created an ahistorical ideology of a racial paradise founded in Brazil through miscegenation. Although Freyre's interpretive essay's emergence contributed to challenging the belief hitherto in vogue that the mixture of races explained the country's backwardness, the narrative of a nondiscriminatory society avoids confrontation with Brazilian social contradictions because it retains the structures of injustice that affect Black people. As Abdias do Nascimento denounced decades later, the historical phenomenon of miscegenation occurred through the rape of African women and their descendants.[7] These racist wounds are still raw in a formally democratic society where Black women are the primary victims of different types of physical violence.[8] The promise of racial equality has never been fulfilled; it veritably grants unwritten permission to violate and discriminate against nonwhite people.

I could go on regarding the history of sophisticated racism in Brazil to demonstrate how the white elite has succeeded in devising stable power structures to prevent Afro-Brazilians' upward social mobility. However, as this essay focuses on Black women, I shall describe my mother's profile: born in Brazil, she is a Black retired housecleaner who raised her children alone. This brief description of Ms. Janet Xavier is a synecdoche of the majority of Black Brazilian women's socioeconomic conditions: namely, deprived of educational opportunities, they tend to occupy lowly social positions such as housecleaning while at the same time being breadwinners in their families. Despite being one of the most permanent legacies of slavery, domestic labor in Brazil was regulated

---

[7] See Abdias do Nascimento, *Jornada Negro-Libertária* (Rio de Janeiro: IPEAFRO, 1984).

[8] Data collected in 2011 shows that 88 percent of rape victims in Brazil were female, and 51 percent were Afro-Brazilian. Daniel Cerqueira and Danilo Santa Cruz Coelho, "Estupro no Brasil: Uma Radiografia segundo os Dados da Saúde," *Nota Técnica, IPEA*, no. 11 (March 2014): 7. In 2018, in the state of Rio de Janeiro, black women were the primary female victims of rape (55.8 percent) as well as intentional homicide (59.1 percent) and attempted murder (55 percent). Vanessa Campagnac and Flávia Vastano Manso, eds., *Dossiê Mulher 2019* (Rio de Janeiro: RioSegurança, 2019), 12. Besides, women of African descent are among the main targets of other violent crimes: for example, in Belo Horizonte, 62 percent of women who reported domestic violence between 1997 and 2003 were Black. Benilda Regina Paiva de Brito, "Violência e Solidão: Territórios Dominados por Mulheres Negras," in *Violência Contra a Mulher Adolescente/Jovem*, ed. Stella R. Taquette (Seminário Nacional sobre Violência contra a Mulher Adolescente e Jovem, Rio de Janeiro: EdUERJ, 2007), 68. Despite these statistics, it should be taken into account that in Brazil, historically, violence against women is protected by impunity for the crimes committed, which increases the suspicion that the number of crimes is higher than the official figures. Although law 11.340/2006 prohibits domestic and family violence against women, there are still many victims who do not register a complaint because they know or are close to their aggressors. Jefferson Drezzet, "Violência Sexual como Problema de Saúde Pública," in Taquette, *Violência*, 83. Another reason is that police institutions are not prepared to act on this kind of complaint, as security agents tend to air prejudices against assaulted women. Bárbara Musumeci Soares, "Enfrentamento da Violência contra Mulheres: Impasses e Desafios," in Taquette, *Violência*, 79.

only in 2015. However, the employers' conspicuous and continued lack of compliance with the law infringes on female and Black domestic workers' rights.[9]

Lélia Gonzalez traces the roots of domestic labor to the servitude of enslaved women (*mucamas*) in the colonial Big House, where in addition to cooking, doing the laundry, ironing, housecleaning, housekeeping, babysitting, and so on, their duties also included the provision of sexual services to their masters, hence the etymological meaning of *mucama* as an enslaved lover.[10] Gonzalez captures the ambivalence of this social representation of Black women when she asserts that "the domestic servant reveals the white culpability because she is seen as a veritable *mucama*. That is why she is violently and concretely repressed."[11] Such historical disenfranchisement of Black women speaks to the structural racism that undermines the integrity of Black personhood.

Although contemporary Black women writers live in societies that profess democratic ideals, their personal experiences are affected by the continuum of racism that deprives African descendants of their stature as persons. For Charles Mills, the concept of subpersonhood explains the condition of Black subjects living in a world structured by white racism. While the limited human status of subpersons includes having a soul, their dehumanization is the consequence of being treated as material possessions. Mills states, "The peculiar status of a subperson is that it is an entity which, because of phenotype, seems (from, of course, the perspective of the categorizer) human in some respects but not in others. It is a human (or, if this word already seems normatively loaded, a humanoid) who, though adult, is not fully a person."[12] As Mills notes in his essays on philosophy and race, such downgraded humanity reveals that the ideal Enlightenment ontology of equal individuals deserving respect was tarnished by a racialized social reality where respect was an exclusive privilege of white persons. From this unacknowledged dark side of the Enlightenment idealized world, Black persons had to fight for their personhood and self-respect while having to show deference to whites. Unlike the ideal of raceless respect, the actual racial disrespect to nonwhites materializes what Mills describes as the Enlightenment's "dark ontology"—that is to say, "the social ontology of the world

---

[9] Luana Pinheiro et al., *Os Desafios do Passado no Trabalho Doméstico do Século XXI: Reflexões para o Caso Brasileiro a partir dos Dados da PNAD Contínua* (Rio de Janeiro: IPEA, 2019), 12.

[10] See Lélia Gonzalez, "Racismo e Sexismo na Cultura Brasileira," in *Pensamento Feminista Brasileiro: Formação e Contexto*, ed. Heloisa Buarque de Hollanda (Rio de Janeiro: Bazar do Tempo, 2019), 237–56.

[11] Gonzalez, 247.

[12] Charles W. Mills, *Blackness Visible: Essays on Philosophy and Race* (Ithaca, NY: Cornell University Press, 1998), 6.

of slavery, colonialism, and segregation, where concrete individuals are seen as raced and colored and treated accordingly."[13]

Afro-Brazilian women writers have employed their creative talent to rewrite this history of dehumanization from their perspective. In fighting the legacies of slavery, colonialism, and institutional racism, these artists of the word have built what Dawn Duke distinguishes as a "legacy of black writing," which has its roots in the work of previous authors.[14] However, in the canons of literary criticism, Black women's writing receives less recognition and critical attention than that of their male and white counterparts.

Such can be said to be the case of Rosa Maria Egipcíaca da Vera Cruz (1719–78), an enslaved African woman who arrived in Brazil at the age of six. After being forced to be a prostitute in Minas Gerais, her spiritual gifts were recognized by the community, including part of the clergy. In Rio de Janeiro, where Franciscans called her a flower because of her piety and name (*Rosa* means "rose"), she founded the convent Nossa Senhora do Parto (Our Lady of Childbirth) to welcome Black women and former prostitutes. Due to the spiritual influence of her prophetic visions, deep devotion, and healing powers, she faced persecution by the Portuguese Inquisition, which arrested her in Lisbon, where she would eventually die.

Named after Saint Mary of Egypt, who was also involved in prostitution, Rosa Egipcíaca was the author of a theological work that is probably one of the oldest books written by a Black author in the Americas. Entitled *Sagrada Teologia do Amor de Deus, Luz Brilhante das Almas Peregrinas* (ca. 1752), her work was burned by the inquisitors, who considered it heresy. Her biographer Luiz Mott refers to "some original residual leaves" and other written materials, including letters, that can be found in the volumes of her inquisitional interrogations, apparently the lengthiest existing ecclesiastical documents about a single Black woman in the eighteenth century.[15] It is telling that this woman's considerable accomplishments and life were ignored and unacknowledged by literary critics and theologians alike until the moment an anthropologist published her biography in 1993.

In her last inquisitorial sessions, Rosa Egipcíaca narrated a vision of a spiritual voice that she heard when she was about to take communion, saying, "Tu serás a abelha-mestra recolhida no cortiço do amor. Fabricareis o doce favo de

---

[13] Mills, 71.

[14] Dawn Duke, "How She Strikes Back: Images of Female Strength in Esmeralda Ribeiro's Writing," in *The Afro-Brazilian Mind: Contemporary Afro-Brazilian Literary and Cultural Criticism*, ed. Niyi Afolabi, Marcio Barbosa, and Esmeralda Ribeiro (Trenton, NJ: Africa World, 2007), 101.

[15] Luiz Mott, *Rosa Egipcíaca: Uma Santa Africana no Brasil* (Rio de Janeiro: Bertrand Brasil, 1993), 8.

mel para pores na mesa dos celestiais banqueteados, para o sustento e alimento dos seus amigos convidados."[16] (You will be the queen bee gathered in the tenement of love. You will make the sweet honeycomb to put on the table of celestial banquets, for the sustenance and food of your invited friends.)

By harnessing the power of writing as a Black woman theologian during slavery, Rosa Egipcíaca became that symbolic queen bee who paved the way for Black women's literary tradition of writing and thought in the New World.

In 1859, Maria Firmina dos Reis published *Úrsula*, the first antislavery novel and one of the first novels written by a woman in Brazil. Her fictional narrative protests against racism by displaying racial discrimination as a social problem, depicting Black characters as human beings, and unveiling a slave master's villainy. In so doing, Reis subverts racial stereotypes, condemns the dehumanization of enslaved Blacks, and affirms and reinvents the creative legitimacy of African memories. As her narrator prays, "Senhor Deus! Quando calará no peito do homem a tua sublime máxima—ama a teu próximo como a ti mesmo—, e deixará de oprimir com tão repreensível injustiça ao seu semelhante" (Lord God! When will your highest command—"Thou shalt love thy neighbor as thyself"—get into men's hearts so that they stop oppressing their fellow men with such reprehensible injustice?).[17] This short prayer exposes slavery and racism as mortal sins that offend the highest divine command. It also criticizes Christianity's institutionalized involvement in racist practices by pointing out that there is no justification in the Christian faith for racial oppression.

In the 1950s, Carolina Maria de Jesus wrote *Quarto de Despejo* (junk room, translated as *Child of the Dark: The Diary of Carolina Maria de Jesus*), an autobiography exploring her condition as a Black woman living in a favela. De Jesus's writing is a powerful strategy to denounce the subhuman situation of Afro-Brazilians living on cities' fringes. Within the memoirs, there is a reference to Pentecostal Christians (*os crentes*) with their musical instruments praising God in the slum. While these characters offer external ascetic practices as a religious portal to transcend extreme poverty, they cannot escape from that harsh reality or confront the state of chaos and violence:

> Aqui na favela tem um barracão na rua B onde os crentes vem rezar tres vezes por semana. Uma parte do barracão é coberto com folha de flandres e a outra de telha. Tem dia que eles estão rezando e os vagabundos da favela jogam pedras no barracão e quebram as telhas. As que cai em cima das folhas faz barulho. Mesmo sendo insultados eles não desanimam. Aconselha os favelados para não

---

[16] Luiz Mott, "Rosa Egipcíaca: Uma Santa Africana no Brasil Colonial," *Cadernos IHU* 3, no. 38 (2005): 17.

[17] Maria Firmina dos Reis, *Úrsula* (Porto Alegre: Zouk, 2018), 101.

roubar, não beber e amar ao próximo como a si mesmo. Os crentes não permite a entrada das mulheres que usa calças e nem vestidos decotados. Os favelados zombam dos conselhos. . . .

A favela é uma cidade esquisita e o prefeito daqui é o Diabo.[18]

[Here in the favela, there's a shed on B Street where believers come to pray three times a week. There's tinplate covering one part of the shed and tiles covering the other one. There are days when they're praying, and the thugs throw stones at the shed and break the tiles. The ones that fall on the leaves make noise. Even after being insulted, the believers don't get discouraged. They advise favela dwellers not to steal, drink and love their neighbors as themselves. Believers don't allow women wearing pants or low-cut dresses to enter. The favela dwellers scoff at the counseling. . . .

The favela's a strange city, and the mayor here is the Devil.]

In underdeveloped urban spaces, where social injustices prevail, the Pentecostal practices of prayers, counseling, and strict dress codes have limitations. As the narrative voice reports, this form of Christianity does not include an ethic of service to community that shakes the very foundations of that neglected section of society. De Jesus's autobiographical social commentary went beyond national borders and became an international bestseller published in 1960, and it is still probably one of the most successful books authored by a Brazilian to date.

From the eighteenth to the twentieth century, Egipcíaca, Reis, and de Jesus provided the basis of Afro-Brazilian women's letters. With their significant autonomous existence and literary achievements, these paradigmatic writers, with their unpredictable mastery of theology, fiction, and autobiography, established literature as an antiracist survival strategy. In this sense, creative writing has opened new interpretive possibilities of addressing cultural and sociopolitical issues pertaining to Black Brazilians' lives. Contemporary Black women's poetry expands on these antiessentialist critiques of race and religion.

POETIC EXPRESSIONS OF BLACK SPIRITUALITY

Olha aí, eu sou do candomblé, eu amo a minha visão do mundo iorubano, amo e cultuo meus ancestrais, mas também fui batizada, crismada, fiz primeira comunhão e sempre fui à missa. . . . São duas raízes que coexistem dentro de mim.

[Look, I'm a Candomblé practitioner, I love my Yoruba worldview, I love and worship my ancestors, but I was also baptized and

---

18. Carolina Maria de Jesus, *Quarto de Despejo: Diário de Uma Favelada*, 10th ed. (São Paulo: Ática, 2018), 91.

confirmed, I took the first communion, and I have always attended mass. . . . These two roots coexist within me.]

—Mãe Beata de Yemonjá, "Quem Respeita, Tolera"

In her seminal essay "Escrevivências da Afro-brasilidade: História e Memória" ("Lived Experiences: Writings on Afro-Brazilians: History and Memory"), Conceição Evaristo evokes oral memory as a powerful resource that Africans brought to the diaspora while assembling a creative survival arsenal.[19] The productive use of storytelling allowed enslaved subjects and their descendants to preserve traditions, chronicle life experiences, and reinterpret the physical and spiritual worlds. Most importantly, by building up these living archives of collective memory, people of African descent continue their quest for freedom and dignity despite the threat of racist practices: "A luta de um povo para conservar, para retomar a sua memória confunde-se com a luta pela sua emancipação, pela sua auto-determinação."[20] (The struggle of a people to preserve and retrieve their memory intertwines with the struggle for their emancipation and self-determination.)

Drawing on the African-derived concept of the word as a vector of vital power (*axé*),[21] Afro-Brazilian literature emerges as an unexpected artistic expression of Black survival in Brazil. That is to say, as Evaristo argues, Afro-Brazilian writers produce a literary version of historical narratives that foreground Black heroes and their historicity. At the margins of the official racist history as colonized beings, Black subjects embody the possibility of new humanity when they appropriate artistic imagination to rewrite history from the survivors' standpoint. For Black women, this writing based on their lived experiences—in Evaristo's coinage, *escrevivência*—implies the self-representation of bodies living a double condition of race and gender that a racist society has historically made inferior.

The heroic poem "Cabeça Feita" (Head done) by Cristiane Sobral captures the survival experience of a subject who struggles for personal autonomy while at the same time confronting the heteronomous forces that mentally oppress Black people:

> *Resolvi fazer a cabeça*
> *Ocupar páginas em branco*

---

[19] Conceição Evaristo, "Escrevivências da Afro-Brasilidade: História e Memória," *Revista Releitura*, no. 23 (November 2008): 1–17.

[20] Evaristo, 8.

[21] For Afro-Brazilian religions, *axé* means a spiritual power that can be used in every aspect of life. This philosophical perception of the world comes from the Yoruba liturgical concept of *àsé*, which denotes a divine vital force.

Com palavras negras
Para refletir a nossa luz

No meu espelho negro
Meu reflexo brilha no escuro
Preto no preto!
A iluminar caminhos
Com escurecimentos necessários

Podem me prender
Podem me privar
Não vou negar
Encontrei outro jeito de me enxergar

Podem me prender
Podem me privar
Minha dignidade ninguém vai levar
Minha identidade ninguém vai comprar

Já programei meus neurônios
Enchi minha cabeça de sonhos
Cabeça feita, cabeça feita . . .
Caminhos, ideias, desenhos na fronte

Desafiam o horizonte.[22]

[I've decided to have my head done
Occupy blank pages
With black words
To reflect our light

In my black mirror
My reflection glows in the dark
Black on black!
Lighting paths
With necessary blackouts

You may arrest me
You may deprive me
I won't deny it
I found another way to see myself

You may arrest me
You may deprive me

---

[22] Cristiane Sobral, *Só por Hoje Vou Deixar o Meu Cabelo em Paz* (Brasília: Ed. Teixeira, 2016), 60.

78

My dignity no one will take
My identity no one will buy

I've programmed my neurons
I've filled my head with dreams
I've had my head done, head done . . .
Paths, ideas, drawings on the forehead

Defy the horizon.]

Beyond its apparent aesthetic significance, the expression "have my head done" (fazer a cabeça) conveys a spiritual meaning that empowers the poetic voice to re-create history heroically. In Afro-Brazilian religions such as Candomblé, having one's head done means an initiation into ancestral wisdom and power. In Sobral's poem, the ritual derives from a personal decision to affirm Black identity through the creative writing that occupies blank pages (páginas em branco) with black words (palavras negras). Crucial to the initiatory act is the word as a symbol of lives and experiences that have been unrecorded or erased from history.

When the initiate finds light, she reconciles her self-image with the collective Black traditions that provide alternative paths toward liberation. Endowed with her revived human dignity and personal identity, she is ready to fight by refusing to deny her African ancestry at any cost: "You may arrest me / You may deprive me / I won't deny it" (Podem me prender / Podem me privar / Não vou negar). Additionally, the epiphany of having her head done triggers transformation in her mind, including her capacity to dream, live, think, and create. As Afro-Brazilians rediscover relics of their heritage, they write new historical pages defying the horizons of institutionalized racism.

In her lyric poem "Voto" (Vow), Lívia Natália breaks through racist barriers when exploring the nuances of Black spirituality from the perspective of a liberated Black woman who comes to terms with the sacredness of her body. Hers is the power of representing, revising, and re-creating notions of intimacy pertaining to Black womanhood:

As senhas do meu corpo
Falo nenhum devassa.
Algo da borboleta que trago
Voa
transmutada em asas.

Não há alçapão confuso
ou isca de odores mudos

que arrebate esta minha alma
de ave-fêmea delicada.

Sem santidades
me anuncio em boas-novas:
mordo com dentes brutos
o fruto que era meu,
bendito,
e esfarelo seu sumo.[23]

[The access to my body
Cannot be violated by any phallus.
I carry a butterfly that
Flies
with transmuted wings.

There is no confusing trap
or bait of dumb odors
that take this delicate
female bird soul.

No sanctity
I announce my good news:
I bite with rough teeth
the blessed fruit that was
mine,
and I drink its juice.]

Introduced in the first stanza is the autonomy of a self-determined Black woman using intimate resources to avow her existence's wholeness. The lyric reference to a body that cannot be violated by a phallus reveals Black femininity's self-representation as a powerful tactic against racially motivated sexual violence.

As the symbol of her freedom, the butterfly's wings indicate the potentiality of a woman who rediscovers her immanent capacity to go beyond the violent limits of repressive social traps and baits. Freed from the demonic threats to her body and mind, the self perceives human individuality's sacredness. Within this healed soul of a female bird, there is a delicate sense of peace, pride, and purpose.

---

[23] Lívia Natália, *Água Negra e Outras Águas*, 2nd enlarged ed., 2nd printing (Salvador: EPP Publicações e Publicidade, 2017), 59.

Finally, the verse "I announce my good news" (me anuncio em boas-novas) expounds the ultimate message of a reborn subject whose body rediscovers the taste of her blessed fruit and juice. In these poetic images, the creative appropriation of the gospel and the Eucharist as metaphors of crucified and resurrected bodies provides the symbolic material where Blackness and transcendence intersect. In addition to the underlying assumption of Black corporal and spiritual integrity, there exists an image of liberation as a human gesture of piety. As proposed in the title (*voto* means "vow"), redefining female Black bodies' narratives implies making a vow to recognize the legitimacy of personal life experiences.

The strategic use of religious symbols as a poetic device enables Black subjects to merge their personal experiences and African people's collective history in the diaspora. In Conceição Evaristo's poem "Meu Rosário" ("My Rosary"), Christian rites of prayers collide with rituals of memory and self-knowledge to provide a litany calling for cognizance of Black women's creative genius. The first verses activate a form of spirituality that centralizes both the person and her community to bring back vivid recollections:

> *Meu rosário é feito de contas negras e mágicas.*
> *Nas contas de meu rosário eu canto Mamãe Oxum e falo*
> *padres-nossos, ave-marias.*
> *Do meu rosário eu ouço os longínquos batuques do*
> *meu povo*
> *e encontro na memória mal adormecida*
> *as rezas dos meses de maio de minha infância.*[24]

> *[My rosary is made of black and magical beads.*
> *In the beads of my rosary, I sing Momma Oshun and say*
> *Our Fathers and Hail Marys.*
> *From my rosary, I hear the distant drumming of*
> *my people*
> *and I find in the fading memory*
> *my childhood's prayers of May.]*

Having described her rosary as black and magical, having invoked the freshwater goddess Oshun, and having said Our Father and Hail Mary prayers, the poetic voice performs a celebratory ritual of collective and individual memories. As she counts prayers, she hears her people's spiritual dances and rekindles her

---

[24] Conceição Evaristo, *Poemas da Recordação e Outros Movimentos* (Belo Horizonte: Nandyala, 2008), 16.

formative years as a Catholic Christian. However, the poem goes on to lament the devastating consequences of racism for Black people:

> *As coroações da Senhora, em que as meninas negras,*
> *apesar do desejo de coroar a Rainha,*
> *tinham de se contentar em ficar ao pé do altar*
> *lançando flores.*[25]

> *[The coronations of Our Lady, when Black girls,*
> *despite their desire to crown the Queen,*
> *had to content themselves with standing at the foot of the altar*
> *throwing flowers.]*

In a racist Catholic liturgy, Black girls are not allowed to fully participate in the coronation of Our Lady. Ironically, that prohibition does not prevent them from worshipping the saint at the altar. They express their veneration by throwing flowers, which may also be a salutation to Oshun. Indeed, in Brazil, Oshun's initiates wear glass-bead necklaces, which look like Africanized rosaries. As the cult of African gods and goddesses was criminalized until the beginning of the twentieth century in Brazil, Black Catholics have traditionally associated their devotion to Our Lady of Light with Oshun, the deity of love, beauty, and motherhood. Here is another variation in Black Catholicism for a Yoruba-affiliated goddess: Our Lady of Fatima's feast day is May 13, the same date when Princess Isabel abolished slavery in 1888. Instead of commemorating the day, Afro-Brazilians have historically criticized the tardy abolition act, which not only was the last one in the Western Hemisphere but did not produce any structural changes to integrate formerly enslaved people into society.

Furthermore, Evaristo's poetic rendition of Oshun and Mary underscores the subject's autonomy to internally re-create her spirituality, which diverges from an essentialist notion of syncretism. In his study of Afro-Brazilians' attitudes when fusing orishas with Catholic saints, Roger Bastide operates within the anthropological discourse that categorizes Black religious expressions as part of acculturation processes known as syncretism.[26] Bastide centralizes his analyses in a comparative framework of equivalents based on external observations and generalized conclusions to decode variations in a phenomenon understood a priori as syncretic. However, in articulating religious symbols imaginatively, the lyric self attributes meanings to the orisha and the saint according to Evaristo's perception, which differs from institutionalized religious views. Therefore, I argue that Evaristo and her peers produce transformative versions of

---

[25] Evaristo, 16.

[26] Roger Bastide, *Estudos Afro-Brasileiros* (São Paulo: Perspectiva, 1973).

African-derived and Christian symbols by tapping into their intimate memory and artistic creativity.

As the prayer-like poem continues, the supplicant's hands carry the visible marks of suffering from discrimination in every sphere of life—work, home, school, the streets, and the world. As if each bead is representative of lived experiences, the poetic voice expresses hope despite police repression (visíveis e invisíveis grades), lost fights (luta perdida), and physical, emotional, and intellectual hunger (fome no estômago, no coração e nas cabeças vazias).

As contas do meu rosário fizeram calos
nas minhas mãos,
pois são contas do trabalho na terra, nas fábricas,
nas casas, nas escolas, nas ruas, no mundo.
As contas do meu rosário são contas vivas.
(Alguém disse um dia que a vida é uma oração,
eu diria, porém, que há vidas-blasfemas.)
Nas contas de meu rosário eu teço intumescidos
sonhos de esperanças.
Nas contas do meu rosário eu vejo rostos escondidos
por visíveis e invisíveis grades
e embalo a dor da luta perdida nas contas
de meu rosário.
Nas contas de meu rosário eu canto, eu grito, eu calo.
Do meu rosário eu sinto o borbulhar da fome
no estômago, no coração e nas cabeças vazias.
Quando debulho as contas de meu rosário,
eu falo de mim mesma um outro nome.[27]

[The beads of my rosary are living beads.
(Someone said one day that life is a prayer,
I would say, however, that there are sinful lives.)
In the beads of my rosary, I weave swollen
dreams of hopes.
In the beads of my rosary, I see faces hidden
by visible and invisible bars,
and I lull the pain of lost fights into my rosary's beads.
In the beads of my rosary, I sing, I scream, I silence.
From my rosary, I feel the growling of hunger
in the stomach, the heart, and the empty heads.

---

[27] Evaristo, "Escrevivências da Afro-Brasilidade," 16.

> *When I tell my rosary beads,*
> *I speak of myself with another name.]*

From the poetic perspective, the discerning reader looks at the intersection of the self and the collective dramas of Black people. Implicit in the repetition of "the beads of my rosary" (contas do meu rosário) is a declaration of spiritual power by a Black woman poet weaving dreams of hope, seeing injustices, and singing, screaming, and silencing. Her senses and speech regard other experiences with sympathetic identification, as the poetic voice declares, "I speak of myself with another name" (eu falo de mim mesma um outro nome). In the last verses, Evaristo exposes the purpose of her prayers and conceives her creative project:

> *E sonho nas contas de meu rosário lugares, pessoas,*
> *vidas que pouco a pouco descubro reais.*
> *Vou e volto por entre as contas de meu rosário,*
> *que são pedras marcando-me o corpo-caminho.*
> *E neste andar de contas-pedras,*
> *o meu rosário se transmuta em tinta,*
> *me guia o dedo,*
> *me insinua a poesia.*
> *E depois de macerar conta por conto do meu rosário,*
> *me acho aqui eu mesma*
> *e descubro que ainda me chamo Maria.*[28]

> *[And in the beads of my rosary, I dream of places, people,*
> *and lives that I little by little find out are real.*
> *I go and come back through the beads of my rosary,*
> *which are stones marking my body as a path.*
> *And on this journey of stone beads,*
> *my rosary is transformed into ink,*
> *it guides my fingers,*
> *insinuating poetry.*
> *And after fingering each bead of my rosary,*
> *I find myself here*
> *and I discover that my name is still Maria.]*

Rendered as a symbol of spiritual self-understanding and communion, the rosary functions as a prelude to the act of writing about real and imaginary places and people whom the poet meets on her journey. By communing with others

---

[28] Evaristo, 17.

with similar life stories, the (meta)poetic voice rediscovers the writer's identity while at the same time reconfiguring religious narratives so that they grant Blacks the full status of persons. Not only does the last verse convey that Evaristo's first name is Maria, but it also enshrines the sacredness of Black motherhood, womanhood, and ultimately, personhood.

CONCLUSION

If literature is a testament to human life, including its complex variables of persons and peoples, then the chapter on surviving under threat of extermination is a work in progress. By the time a white police officer's knee asphyxiated George Floyd to death in Minneapolis on May 25, 2020, a year had passed since Brazilian soldiers fired more than eighty bullets into a car carrying a family and killed Evaldo Rosa in Rio de Janeiro, on April 7, 2019. What did Floyd and Rosa have in common? They were Black men whose lives were ended by the brutality of armed forces responsible for protecting people. In the 1970s, decades before the Black Lives Matter movement protested against racial violence toward Black people, Abdias do Nascimento unveiled the social strategies of institutionalized "genocide of Brazilian blacks," a phenomenon that appears in official statistics indicating that a Black person is 2.7 times more likely to be murdered in Brazil.[29] With the Covid-19 pandemic, the death toll among Black populations is three times higher than that of white people in both Brazil and the United States.[30] It can be argued that these contemporary facts speak to what Achille Mbembe identified as "necropolitics" to decipher how the power of death has historically subjugated life.[31]

When Afro-Brazilian women writers creatively examine individual and collective expressions of their existence, they refuse the subjugation of death and assert Black humanity's value. Living in a world that produces new forms of racism to destroy human bodies and minds demands more than intellect or talent; it is a matter of survival. Following in a literary tradition of survivors' symbolic writing that has its roots in the audacity of an eighteenth-century

---

[29] Daniel Cerqueira and Samira Bueno, eds., *Atlas da Violência 2020* (Rio de Janeiro: IPEA, 2020), https://www.ipea.gov.br/portal/images/stories/PDFs/relatorio_institucional/200826_ri_atlas_da_violencia.pdf.

[30] According to the Color of Coronavirus project, African Americans have experienced the highest mortality rates in the United States. In Brazil, figures released by the health ministry show that Black people represent 61 percent of those victimized by the virus. See Mario Sergio Lima, Shannon Sims, and Patricia Xavier, "For Black Brazilians, Covid-19 Is Deepening Painful Inequalities," BloombergQuint, accessed June 5, 2021, https://www.bloombergquint.com/global-economics/for-black-brazilians-covid-19-is-deepening-painful-inequalities.

[31] See J.-A. Mbembé and Libby Meintjes, "Necropolitics," *Public Culture* 15, no. 1 (2003): 11–40.

Black theologian, contemporary Afro-Brazilian women writers reconfigure history with self-understanding, self-representation, and self-determination.

Woven into such a body of work is the intersection where African-derived religions and Christianity encounter each other. By rendering the symbology of the Afro-Brazilian system of belief from personal perspectives, the poetic texts challenge religious intolerance toward African heritage in a nation with the largest community of Roman Catholics. When conjured, Christian symbols are renegotiated and reinterpreted by multivalent expressions of Black experiences and identities that complicate essentialist notions of religious syncretism.

In the history of African-derived and Christian religious expressions, agents of transformation have emerged to oppose the destructive powers of deadly injustices with messages of ethical living. In the canon of Black women's survival writing, death can never bring an end to a long struggle for liberation. That is to say, life always regenerates itself, and as such, it gives birth to (re)new(ed) ways of thinking, believing, and being.

PART II

GENDER, ECOLOGY, AND
ETHNOGRAPHIC IMAGINATION

CHAPTER 5

FROM THE AMAZON TOWARD WOMEN'S BODIES

THE INFLUENCE OF CONSERVATIVE RELIGIOUS DISCOURSE IN THE DISMANTLING OF BRAZILIAN SOCIAL POLICIES

Elisa Rodrigues

For us women, more than ever, the invitation to move patriarchal waters at all levels of knowledge is imposed as a demand for justice in relation to ourselves and humanity.

—Ivone Gebara, *Teologia Ecofeminista*

In Brazil at the time I am writing, two news stories have ranked among the top trends in social media. The first is about the man-made fires burning the Amazon Rainforest. The second is related to the violation of women's rights. But what do those two topics have in common? To understand their possible relations, I focus on some religious references that would legitimize the dismantling of social policies and authorize violence against the Amazon and against female bodies. My hypothesis is that there is a type of exclusivistic and misogynistic terminology in biblical literature that is used to justify these modern destructive policies. By using sociological analysis and biblical-archeological methods, I seek to understand how a certain set of religious images of Christianity was (mis)appropriated by conservative political discourse. At the end, I analyze how these religious references are present, how they influence the current political structure of Brazilian society, and what their practical consequences are for social lives.

WHY THE ECOSYSTEM AND WOMEN'S BODIES MATTER

One way of thinking about the relationship between ecosystem destruction and violence against women is to think that both are important concerns for an agenda of grassroots resistance. But this answer seems too simplistic. From the point of view of preserving the ecosystem, this is indeed an important concern for popular movements that challenge the predatory exploitation of the nation's natural resources to serve the interests of agribusiness. Such an agenda, however, definitely does not contribute to liberal economic goals. The Brazilian agribusiness sector is made up of elites and is conducted by commercial principles that serve international interests, for which they use advanced technology. For Brazilian economic liberalism, the preservation of the Amazon and the Indigenous communities is an obstacle to Brazilian progress and development. That is why there are deep political forces working to change Brazilian laws to open up the national territory and subsidize agribusiness to deforest large territories for genetically engineered grain plantations.

In this sense, liberating land for sale to foreigners becomes a central issue. For more than four decades, special-interest groups have been interested in the relaxation of the laws that regulate foreign exploitation of Brazilian lands. Recently, legislation that focuses on the sale of national territories to foreigners was presented to the Brazilian parliament. This parliamentary act (LP 2.963/2019) resulted in benefits for agribusiness and in the weakening of agroecological practices that produce healthy foods using technologies that do not harm the ecosystem.[1]

Unfortunately, this particular legislation facilitates the surrender of Brazilian land to agribusiness and hinders businesses that focus on sustainable agricultural production of healthy and pesticide-free foods, such as organic coffee, grains, and vegetables, which are the basis of the economy of native populations such as Indigenous and Brazilian quilombola communities.[2] In other words, native peoples and workers who deal with land according to agricultural and

---

[1] "The Commissions for Economic Issues and Agriculture approved, with amendments, this Wednesday (August 11, 2020), a project that facilitates the acquisition of land by foreign individuals and legal foreigners. Parliamentary act 2.963/2019, which regulates article 190 of the Federal Constitution, now goes for the analysis of the Constitution and Justice Commission, which will have the final decision, that is, the final decision in the Senate." Alexandre Aprá, "Comissões aprovam projeto que facilita venda de terras para estrangeiros," Isso É Notícia, accessed May 20, 2020, https://www.issoenoticia.com.br/noticia/24491/comissoes-aprovam-projeto-que-facilita-venda -de-terras-para-estrangeiros.

[2] "Parliamentary act 2,963 / 2019 revokes the law that regulates the acquisition of rural property by foreigners (parliamentary act 5.709 / 1971), which provides for a series of restrictions so that they can acquire land in Brazil, such as limiting the dimensions of areas that can be purchased and the requirement for prior authorization from the National Institute of Colonization and Agrarian Reform to implement agricultural projects." Aprá.

ecological principles have been systematically attacked by the federal and state governments, which are aligned with a liberal economic policy that progressively privileges international capital and destroys national sovereignty. In effect, this is a political and economic movement for the recolonization of Brazil, an action against sustainable agriculture and one that disrespects our ecosystems and native peoples. It is a liberal economic policy that allows the advancement of a numerically small sector of Brazilian society that is more interested in surrendering our wealth and promoting an unhealthy lifestyle than in valuing our native communities and respecting our local cultures.

The political parties that support these economic policies and advocate for changing the law are aligned with deeply conservative politicians and certain religious groups. The special feature of these religious groups is that they have their origins in Christianity—or at least claim that they do. In general, they claim to believe in God and in his only son, Jesus Christ, who died and was crucified for the redemption of all humanity. They are Catholics, Protestants, and evangelical Pentecostals, and for them, a healthy family consisting of men, women, and children is God's desire. To support this view and support the idea of the nuclear family, there are more and more of both religious politicians and secular politicians that defend the Christian moral agenda.

At this point, the boundaries between the political field, the religious agenda, and theological constructions are blurred. For a large part of the Brazilian people, it is difficult to understand how it is possible that Christian groups could support the current type of liberal politics that operate in the Brazilian public sphere based on the Bible. It seems that something is wrong. Are solidarity, equality, and justice not intrinsic to the nature of Christianity? Wouldn't Christian theology be a kind of epistemology about God that aims to promote love and respect for all people? How is it possible to justify biblically so much destruction, violence, and aggression against the Brazilian poor, Indigenous social groups, and women?

In order to answer these questions and to identify connections between these issues, I think it is relevant to consider the conservative perspective that has permeated the social imaginary of Brazilian culture since the colonization period. That is the key. Basically, in this perspective, both the Amazon Rainforest (our natural resources) and women's bodies are objects of consumption. But there are deeper underground notions that constitute this destructive and violent discourse.

The base of this conservative perspective of Brazilian economic liberalism has constructed alliances with some conservative religious groups and appropriated their religious language and literalist hermeneutics of sacred texts.

Mainly, they do this by selecting Old Testament pericopes, which contain laws, moral prescriptions, and narratives of violence and conflict with countries from the ancient Mediterranean. From this set of religious references emerges a type of exclusivism and misogynistic biblical terminology that are used to justify modern destructive policies in Brazil. These references and religious language make it possible for women's bodies, in addition to natural resources, to be understood as sources of consumption to be exploited by civilized, white, and masculine societies.

Here, I draw a comprehensive framework to understand how and why the religious grammar of the underground social basis of Brazilian society has real, practical consequences in our political and social lives. As Talal Asad has said, secularity is a "concept that brings together certain behaviors, knowledge and sensibilities of modern life."[3] Similarly, religious concepts and notions affect our social practices. Thus, it seems necessary to problematize how these religious references produce certain behaviors, knowledge, and sensitivities in our modern lives.

SOME SOCIO-THEOLOGICAL ISSUES ABOUT THE NOTION OF USE

To approach this topic, there is a broad range of disciplinary methodologies for the study of Brazilian social and political thought that reveals that since the time of Portuguese colonization, the land of Brazil and its natural beauties attracted European greed, which was unconcerned with taking care of the natural patrimony of invaded land. In these terms, Brazil is to be nothing more and nothing less than a source of wealth to be explored. An important thinker in this regard is Sérgio Buarque de Holanda, author of *Raízes do Brasil* (1936) and *Visão do Paraíso* (1959). For Holanda, there are two ways to understand more about the colonization process of the Americas. The first proposes that the biblical image of Eden and paradise, interpreted theologically, in particular by Protestants, imagined North America as a type of "promised land" that could not be given for free. The territory discovered would need to be dominated and cultivated using rationality and technology. The second concerns the Brazilian case (or, more broadly, Latin America during European colonization), which, according to Catholic theological understanding, imagined Brazil as a splendid, rich, and seductive land, a natural paradise to be possessed and abused as a "garden of delights" given to men to enjoy in the name of God.

What both visions about nature have in common is that the land, its natural elements and beauties, should be dominated and used by civilized, elite

---

[3] Talal Asad, *Formations of the Secular: Christianity, Islam, Modernity*, Cultural Memory in the Present (Stanford, CA: Stanford University Press, 2003), 25.

white men. To me, it is remarkable that both visions are based on Christian biblical hermeneutics, in which "man" is the subject that undertakes and the land appears as a passive element that suffers the man's action. In other words, the male dominates *the female*, whether natural or human. And because of this obligation, both have to allow themselves to be dominated.

This kind of predatory logic is justified because of the understanding that God, the Creator, gave the whole world to Adam himself to control (Gen 1:26–28). Thus, it is the land and everything that exists in her that is owned by man, but not the wild man. We are talking about the man created by God who has dominion over the earth and subdues it. We are talking about the man created by God, who gave man Eve. In other words, according to biblical terms, the task of "dominating" and "subduing" the promised land belongs to man. Even more interesting is that women and land are simply properties in this literature. They are just objects, neither natural resources nor people.

A kind of patriarchal religious semantics emerges here. Ivone Gebara calls this *epistemological monotheism*. For Gebara, when in Genesis 1:26 the biblical text affirms that "he [man] dominates," it can be interpreted that man is given the power by the Transcendent to name all things. This radical Otherness, the absolute Other, becomes the foundation of all creation and everything that exists. Man receives from God the authority even to name God; at that point, man becomes the center of history. Here, anthropocentrism and monotheism are seen to be interdependent. As Gebara says, "For this reason, male Western monotheism had a chance to assume an imperialist stance capable of destroying the expressions of the divine considered inferior and excluding women from the 'sacred power.'"[4]

The understanding that man is the center that organizes the world corresponds to the sociological approach to "man" as a paradigm on which Western societies were able to organize themselves socially, culturally, and economically, marginalizing women, people of color, Indigenous peoples, LGBTQI+ communities, and other social groups. According to epistemological monotheism, "Domination is rooted in a common ideology based on the control of reason over nature, and on the separation of the spiritual from the material world, an idea based in turn on the division of our beings into soul and body."[5]

Epistemological monotheism is guided by an ideology based on male control over nature that can be identified in our social lives, as José Murilo

---

[4] Ivone Gebara, *Teologia Ecofeminista: Ensaio para Repensar o Conhecimento e a Religião* (São Paulo: Olho d'Água, 1997), 44. All translations from the Portuguese of Ivone Gebara are by the author.

[5] Ioanna Sahinidou, "Ecofeminist Theologies Challenge Domination," *Open Journal of Philosophy* 7, no. 3 (2017): 249.

de Carvalho shows us. In summary, his work, drawing upon research by institutes such as Vox Populi/CPDPC (Centro de Pesquisa e Documentação de História Contemporânea do Brasil) and Iser (Instituo de Estudos da Religião), demonstrates that the imaginary of many Brazilians about Brazil's national identity has been formed by images of natural beauty, soil fertility, cordiality of the people, and so on. Among other expressions, when Brazilians were interviewed about the reasons why they are proud to be Brazilians, some spoke of things like "wonderful nature," "landscape," "sacred land," "Amazon Forest," "fauna and flora," "physical beauty," "blessed country," "territorial extension," "beauty of the people," and "beautiful women."[6] Likewise, commonplace were expressions invoking the "beauty of the people" and "beautiful women." Such expressions were placed side by side with "wonderful nature," which seems to indicate that in the Brazilian cultural imaginary, *nature* and *women* possess similar meanings. Both are beautiful; both serve man.

What does this mean? What are the meanings behind the comparison between women's bodies and wild nature? One possible way to understand this is to highlight the substratum of religious images of a certain Christian theology based on epistemological monotheism. This substratum of religious images underlies a cultural mentality about Brazil and—for that matter—the earth, which accepts, authorizes, and justifies the abusive use of national territory and women's bodies. The link between nature and woman seems natural because it can be located in the Bible.[7] My point is that this is a set of biblical references mobilized to support a perverse theological discourse that denies women's rights and authorizes the abusive use of the environment by the public political sphere.

As John Collins writes, "There is much in the Bible that is undeniably patriarchal, [and] scholars with such commitments find themselves faced with a dilemma."[8] Biblical material of this kind serves the purposes of a certain type of perverse theological discourse that has its fundamental basis in the male experience, which erases female figures from history, as shown by Phyllis Trible.[9] For her, the hero of the exodus is Moses, and there is insufficient attention to the fact that it was three women—Moses's mother, Miriam, and Pharaoh's daughter—who prepared him. Exegesis in general does not discuss female protagonists in the Bible, which is the reason why some feminist theologians have used terminology from the hermeneutics of recuperation. Such a hermeneutics

---

[6] José Murilo de Carvalho, "O Motivo Edênico No Imaginário Social Brasileiro," *Revista Brasileira de Ciências Sociais* 13, no. 38 (1998): 6–7.

[7] Sahinidou, "Ecofeminist Theologies Challenge Domination," 250.

[8] John J. Collins, *The Bible after Babel: Historical Criticism in a Postmodern Age* (Grand Rapids, MI: W. B. Eerdmans, 2005), 78.

[9] See Phyllis Trible, *God and the Rhetoric of Sexuality* (Philadelphia: Fortress, 1978).

opens up the possibility for interpretation to counteract the patriarchal structure of biblical narratives and highlight women's actions in the Bible in a way that restores the centrality of the female role in history. Collins synthesizes this thought when he affirms that this is not a denial of the Bible, quoting Trible: "'The nature of the God of Israel defies sexism,' and 'depatriarchalizing' is a 'hermeneutic operating within Scripture itself.'"[10]

In short, in monotheistic epistemology, important social and political decisions, as well as acts of justice, come from the male sex. When women act, they are blamed and classified as rebels. They are to be in charge of the house and household chores and are to stay out of the public domain. In our modern Brazilian patriarchal culture, this is repeated. Women and their bodies, as well as natural resources, are merely objects, and their well-being matters less than the Brazilian economy and its progress—or, for that matter, than maintaining the male paradigm as a center of the world's interpretation. This leads us to the movement to depatriarchalize our Christian religions, politics, and daily culture.

THE EFFACED HISTORY OF THE GODDESS AND THE FEMALE SACRED IN THE BACKGROUND

As mentioned, the association between the Amazon Rainforest and physical beauty allows us to consider that for the average Brazilian, the female body is like a natural resource, ready to be explored and dominated by Adam, according to the archetypal meaning of the civilized Western white man.

In this sense, the question of women's rights, and especially the right to decide about their bodies, is central. When the female figure was expunged from the history of Christian reception, so were their bodies and social identities. Women lost the right to decide how they wanted to use their bodies, and men took over instead, building doctrinal systems that defined what would be right and what would be wrong for women to do. These doctrines have social implications, as, for example, in the recent case of a ten-year-old Brazilian girl who was sexually abused by her uncle. She became pregnant, and the Brazilian court gave her the right to an abortion. The decision was contested, however, by religious people on the far right who protested in front of the hospital and called her a "murderer."[11] Some people shouted against the violence of the man who raped her; some people asked what she wanted; but most people were concerned with imposing a regulation on the young mother for her infantile female

---

10   Collins, *Bible after Babel*, 79.
11   Tom Phillips and Caio Barretto Briso, "Brazil: Outcry as Religious Extremists Harass Child Seeking Abortion," *Guardian*, August 17, 2020, sec. World News, https://www.theguardian.com/world/2020/aug/17/brazil-protest-abortion-recife-hospital.

body—religious extremists and conservative evangelicals in particular. They simply wanted to prevent an abortion without taking the girl's life and her decision into account. Unfortunately, this is one of many similar cases that happen in Brazil.[12] Even so, this one story shows us the importance of broadening the effect of epistemological monotheism on our daily lives. This is central in order to understand (1) the process of the erasure of women, (2) violence against women's bodies, and (3) the social need for access to women's reproductive health care.

About the process of women's erasure, it almost goes without saying that the far-right religious group protesting at the hospital paid no attention to the girl herself. And if violence against women's bodies had been a concern, then, in fact, the girl suffered more than one act of violence. She had been raped multiple times from the age of six, became pregnant, and was accused of murder by these religious extremists. Finally, the need for access to women's reproductive health care in Brazil is highlighted by the fact that the girl had to fly to another state because the hospital in her home state refused to treat her.[13] There are different reasons for this, but the case discussed here is enough to show that religious motives were the main ones. And in Brazil, politicians know that.

The denial of public health resources for women's reproductive health is due to mentalities strongly marked by a conservative interpretation of the Bible, which results in pedagogies of sexuality. Under these conservative interpretations, far-right religious forces claim male control over female bodies, thinking of women's bodies as territories to be occupied by male desires and authority because they believe there is a basis for that in the Bible. Symbolically, in their religious universe, the woman needs to be dominated because her nature is dangerous and has been inclined toward sin ever since paradise. The biblical symbolic universe interests us specifically because from it emerge myths, rites, images, and references that prevail in our own day, introduced by the European colonizer project, whether Catholic-Portuguese or Protestant-English. Both projects were guided by the notions that women and nature could be exploited and, more than that, that both must be passive and accepting of exploitation.

---

[12] A higher prevalence of unsafe abortions in Brazil was observed in more socially vulnerable populations. See Rosa Maria Soares Madeira Domingues et al., "Aborto Inseguro No Brasil: Revisão Sistemática Da Produção Científica, 2008–2018," *Cadernos de Saúde Pública* 36, no. 1 (2020): e00190418.

[13] According to the World Health Organization (WHO), from 2010 to 2014, there were around fifty-five million abortions worldwide, 45 percent of which were unsafe, of which Africa, Asia, and Latin America account for 97 percent. In Brazil, data on abortion are incomplete, although it is possible to confirm that Black women had the highest levels from 2006 to 2012, and the next highest were Indigenous women. Bruno Baptista Cardoso, Fernanda Morena dos Santos Barbeiro Vieira, and Valeria Saraceni, "Aborto No Brasil: O Que Dizem Os Dados Oficiais?," *Cadernos de Saúde Pública* 36, no. 1 (2020): e00188718.

The erasure of female agency resembles what happened in the ancient Near East when the goddess Asherah (אֲשֵׁרָה) was venerated among Canaanites. She was the consort of a Semitic God called Baal, a word that primarily signifies "lord" or "owner." In accordance with the Semitic religions, this name was used to illustrate the relation of a husband to his wife or the deity to his worshipper. Within biblical literature, Baal is broadly mentioned as an opponent deity to the Israelite God, Yahweh. Baal was a god-king who died and was afterward resurrected by the power of the goddess.

According to William G. Dever,[14] during the eighth and ninth centuries BCE, terra-cotta representations of Asherah were commonplace in the ancient Near East.[15] Sometimes she was represented naked with snakes and flowers, sometimes standing on a lion. Baal, lord of the heavens—sun god—would be the male principle within Canaanite religions and was worshipped in association with Asherah, the female principle of nature. In 1975–76, scholars from Tel Aviv University discovered some curious inscriptions at Kuntillet 'Ajrud in the Sinai Desert dating to the eighth century BCE. The inscriptions found in the Israelite territory mentioned "Yahweh and his Asherah" in addition to other biblical references to Asherah. This inscription triggered a vigorous debate about the marital status of Yahweh, God of Israel, and whether God was married to the Goddess and divided the creation. Although the biblical texts reveal some evidence of goddess worship among the Judeans,[16] the set of biblical references that pertain to a strong and savior-like female divinity was smothered by Judaism's subsequent history. That the two—Yahweh and Asherah—were in earlier times connected can be seen in 2 Chronicles 31:1: "Now when all this was finished, all Israel that were present went out to the cities of Judah, and brake the *images in pieces*, and cut down the *groves*, and threw down the

---

[14] Dever is an American archaeologist specializing in the history of Israel and the Near East in biblical times. He was professor of Near Eastern archaeology and anthropology at the University of Arizona in Tucson from 1975 to 2002. Dever was director of the Harvard Semitic Museum—Hebrew Union College excavations at Gezer from 1966 to 1971, 1984, and 1990; director of the dig at Khirbet el-Kôm and Jebel Qacaqir (West Bank) from 1967 to 1971; principal investigator at the Tell el-Hayyat excavations (Jordan) from 1981 to 1985; and assistant director of the University of Arizona expedition to Idalion, Cyprus, in 1991, among other excavations. In retirement, Dever has become a frequent author on questions relating to the historicity of the Bible. See "William G. Dever," Arizona Center for Judaic Studies, accessed May 21, 2021, https://judaic.arizona.edu/user/william-g-dever.

[15] For a splendid example, often reproduced, see "Understanding Asherah—Exploring Semitic Iconography, Ruth Hestrin, BAR 17:05, Sep-Oct 1991," *Center for Online Judaic Studies* (blog), January 7, 2009, http://cojs.org/understanding_asherah-exploring_semitic_iconography-_ruth_hestrin-_bar_17-05-_sep-oct_1991/.

[16] Other biblical references to Asherah include 1 Kgs 16:33 (874–853 BCE); 2 Kgs 21:7 (696–641 BCE); 2 Kgs 23:6 (639–608 BCE); Judg 6:25; and described as a grove beside "the altar of the LORD thy God" in Deut 16:21 (KJV).

high places and the altars out of all Judah and Benjamin, in Ephraim also and Manasseh, until they had utterly destroyed them all. Then all the children of Israel returned, every man to his possession, into their own cities" (KJV; italics added).

The term *groves*, understood in English as a wood, a small wood, a group of trees, or a forest, indicates that the representation of the goddess was used in a Babylonian worship cult devoted to the Canaanite goddess of fortune and happiness. Other terms used in this text are *pole* or *pillars* to indicate *Asherim* (derived from a Hebraic root). In another version of the same Chronicles passage, the American Standard Version of 1901, the destruction of the goddess can be seen more clearly: "Now when all this was finished, all Israel that were present went out to the cities of Judah, and brake in pieces the pillars, and hewed down the Asherim, and brake down the high places and the altars out of all Judah and Benjamin, in Ephraim also and Manasseh, until they had destroyed them all. Then all the children of Israel returned, every man to his possession, into their own cities."

The biblical text's representation of the goddess as a tree, pole, or grove was indicative of fertility, usually associated with nature. However, what is crucial here is to understand that the destruction of the sacred poles—that is, the representations of the goddess—was part of a religious reform that aimed to exterminate the female divinity and give centrality only to the male God, Yahweh.[17] Actions against the goddess can also be interpreted as actions against noninstitutionalized religiosity—that is, popular religion. It is not the purpose of this chapter to define or discuss what popular religions are, but it is important to highlight that popular religions go back to a type of religiosity not guided by ecclesiastical discourse. It is possible, however, to affirm that popular religiosity was rejected by the priestly male elite.

Thus, *Asherim* referred to Jewish cult objects that were used in the worship of the goddess. She was represented by carved figurines, wooden posts, living trees, emblems, or small shrines. Within this tradition, other meanings were preserved: great goddess, mother, and goddess of fertility, represented with wide hips and large breasts, which was symbolically linked to the vitality of the goddess represented by vegetation, poles, and groves. According to this symbolism, the goddess cares about humanity. Despite ecclesiastical attacks against the goddess, she is still an important figure in Christian religiosity, especially in Brazilian popular Catholicism, even though Asherah has become a docile divinity in the Judeo-Christian tradition. She lives in the figure of a mother who welcomes and takes care of the domestic realm. In fact, she was

---

[17] See Judg 3:7 and 1 Kgs 18:19.

put backstage behind her husband and became associated with the wise woman of Proverbs 14:1.[18] After that, the New Testament affirms this new social construction about the role of women in Colossians 3:18 and Ephesians 5:22. Both verses reinforce submission and obedience as appropriate behaviors for women, and then they contribute to the understanding that women are inferior to men in the social hierarchy, even today.

THE LOGIC OF ABUSE IN PATRIARCHAL EPISTEMOLOGY

In Brazil, the patriarchal monotheistic epistemology that provides the basis for structural misogynist culture can be seen in daily speech and actions. The basis of this epistemology is anthropocentric and androcentric, constituted by the Western tradition and philosophical epistemologies that described human knowledge from the experience of a part of humanity as if that part represented the whole. Although this description is not false, it fails to consider the woman's experience and gives more attention to the phallus. Even though it is said that knowledge has no sex, it is also true that it is the prerogative of the anthropos (human); feminist scholarship has, moreover, found that while scientific knowledge was developed on a larger scale by male human beings, that knowledge was universalized on the basis of "his experience of wisdom and power."[19] Hence it can be said that the knowledge shared in the West and, consequently, in Latin America is phallocentric. Without the same centrality, the knowledge produced by women, people of color, Indigenous populations, and Others was excluded.

Thus, it can be said that in Latin America and Brazil, nonphallocentric knowledge has been devalued and the people who produce it undervalued. For feminist theologian Gebara, "moving these patriarchal waters" requires dealing with the issue of power and the hierarchy of genders subordinated to the interests of politics and the liberal market.[20] For politicians as well as for liberal market corporations, both Indigenous peoples and women are not legitimate producers, nor do they constitute a consumer public that deserves attention. And it is in this devaluation of both that I find a similarity: the destructive effect of patriarchal epistemology.

Patriarchal epistemology authorizes war and the destruction of natural resources in the name of economic development and progress, or what it considers progress to be. People die, forests are burned, and sustainable crops for the survival of Indigenous peoples and communities of workers are destroyed.

---

[18] According to Dever's premise, the biblical text as we know it today was produced by the male, priestly elite. William G. Dever, *Did God Have a Wife? Archaeology and Folk Religion in Ancient Israel* (Grand Rapids, MI: W. B. Eerdmans, 2005).

[19] Gebara, *Teologia Ecofeminista*, 33.

[20] Gebara, 26.

Native peoples, forests, and plantations are not included in the data for assessing the success of economic growth. The same is true of women. Women and their bodies become war targets: "Violated and beaten violently, they serve as bait to provoke hate in resistance groups, which become more vulnerable to being trapped. Women who are beaten to death, reveal the aggressor's strength in their body."[21]

Even more astonishing is that the evidence of this sexism finds reinforcement in the words of a Brazilian congressman. In December 2014, then congressman Jair Bolsonaro (affiliated with the Social Christian Party from Rio de Janeiro) stated in an interview that he would not rape congresswoman Maria do Rosário because she "didn't deserve [it]."[22] The statement was made again the next day, when Bolsonaro in an interview with the newspaper *Zero Hora* ironically said, "She doesn't deserve [to be raped] because she is very bad, because she is very ugly. She's not my type. I would never rape her." Faced with this sexist and vulgar statement, the congresswoman, known for being part of the Workers' Party (from Rio Grande do Sul) went to court, and on August 15, 2017, the Supreme Federal Court condemned Bolsonaro for "defending rape." According to the judges, his statements went beyond parliamentary immunity and constituted a personal offense.[23] Among other aspects that can be analyzed based on this episode, there is a culture favorable to the violation of women's bodies. According to this culture, the female body is a domain that can be occupied as long as one wants—more precisely, as long as any man might want, whether or not the woman consents. In these terms, women are seen as possessions. A second aspect, no less important, is that if the woman is understood as beautiful and sensual, men may naturally feel authorized to make advances, even with violence. Beautiful women, according to the logic of patriarchal epistemology, exist for the pleasure of men, whether they are husbands, religious people, or politicians.

After the incident involving him as a congressman, in August 2019, Bolsonaro, now president of Brazil, was classified by the international media as a far-right politician and protagonist of the worst diplomatic clash with France in the last forty years. After receiving criticism from French president Emmanuel Macron due to forest fires that swept the Amazon, Bolsonaro returned the criticism with rude and sexist comments about the French president's wife, Brigitte

---

[21] Gebara, 35–36.

[22] Bolsonaro's verbal tirade was recorded. See Brazilian Monarchy Movement, "(Eng Subs) This Is the Future President of Brazil—Maria Do Rosário and Bolsonaro Arguing," YouTube video, April 13, 2018, https://www.youtube.com/watch?v=MFb49slZtLc.

[23] See Marcelo Galli, "Bolsonaro deve indenizar Maria do Rosário por dizer que não a estupraria, decide STJ," Consultor Jurídico, accessed May 22, 2020, http://www.conjur.com.br/2017-ago-15/bolsonaro-indenizara-maria-rosario-dizer-nao-estupraria-decide-stj.

Macron. The president of France deplored what happened publicly: "What can I say? It's sad. It's sad for him firstly, and for Brazilians."[24]

The grotesque quality of recent Brazilian politics is inspired by religious structures of thought that feed discourses and practices of violence against women. According to these structures, women are objects. This objectification of women corresponds to the concept of gendered identity, according to which the traits of biological sex not only define her place and social role but also determine the way women are represented, in particular the fragile and submissive ideal type who presides over domestic life. This social construction derives from the desire of men to dominate women. As Joan Scott says, "Theorists of patriarchy have directed their attention to the subordination of women and found their explanation for it in the male 'need' to dominate the female."[25] This need for domination, then, justified by religious rhetoric, may be what predisposes some men to attack and rape women.

The other unfortunate case that empirically represents what I am trying to discuss theoretically is that of the Brazilian girl mentioned earlier who was sexually abused from the time she was six. This shocking episode shows that the victim-girl was turned into the aggressor at the same time that the immorality of the religious discourse that interprets abortion as sin was denied. In other words, abortion is not allowed, but violating a woman or a girl's body would be acceptable. In this sad example, it is possible to observe in action religious rhetoric that produces discourse and the practice of power by which they genderize the identity of women.

As an alternative to this paradigm, I argue that ecofeminism and feminist exegesis are paths forward that have the potential to highlight the visibility of women and open up epistemological possibilities for women's emancipation. In this sense, ecofeminist epistemology represents an analytical and political instrument for the transformation of religious and political awareness, which in turn provides support for social movements. As Guaciara Lopes Louro says, this kind of epistemology is no ordinary epistemology but one that has "pretensions to change."[26] In ecofeminism as a political epistemology that promotes academic practices that problematize, subvert, and transgress routine academic practice, I find the face of the fertile, strong, and self-possessed goddess, who, above all,

---

[24] Angelique Chrisafis, "Macron Rebukes Bolsonaro for 'Extraordinarily Rude' Comments about Wife," *Guardian*, August 26, 2019, sec. World News, https://www.theguardian.com/world/2019/aug/26/macron-rebukes-bolsonaro-over-extraordinarily-rude-comments-about-wife.

[25] Joan W. Scott, "Gender: A Useful Category of Historical Analysis," *American Historical Review* 91, no. 5 (1986): 1058, https://doi.org/10.2307/1864376.

[26] Guacira Lopes Louro, *Gênero, sexualidade e educação: Uma perspectiva pós-estruturalista*, 16th ed., Coleção Educação pós-crítica (Rio de Janeiro: Editora Vozes, 2014), 23.

strives to deconstruct the ideology of gender conventionally constructed and imposed on women.

FINAL CONSIDERATIONS

The erasure of the goddess from the Judeo-Christian tradition results in deep consequences for gender relations in the West, including regulations and taboos of both female and male bodies. It can be said that religions derived from the Judeo-Christian axis, constituting themselves around the one and only male God, symbolically legitimized patriarchal societies and gender inequalities. And this divinity, imagined as the only male Creator-Father-God, affects social and political relations in modern societies with its epistemological monotheism. The effect of this epistemology produces an abusive way of treating both nature and women's rights.

From this epistemological monotheism emerges the masculine imperative of domination by force, oppression, and the hierarchization of human relations and ecosystems. The effaced female element of the Judeo-Christian tradition and the conservative hermeneutics scholars of biblical literature employ, which confirm the domain of male authority, also allow the destruction of forests that demarcate Indigenous territories, rainforest fires, and finally, the development of public social policies to protect our ecosystems and vulnerable people. In this connection, it is worth highlighting another point. In the imagination of many Brazilians, there is a terrible culture of depredation and undemocratic behavior fed by the influence of conservative religious discourse, a kind of discourse that allows men the right to decide what is important for women and their bodies. The same culture of depredation and undemocratic behavior that allows the deforestation of our national territory grants privileges to agribusiness and hinders sustainable development policies.

In the face of the devastation and surrender of national sovereignty to foreign capital, in the face of disrespect for the rights of women and native peoples, another epistemology is badly needed, one with an epistemological openness that implies a different way of interpreting and relating to the world, human beings, and the notion of divinity. This would be an ecofeminist epistemology, which destabilizes "eternal truths" and "questions its partial and purely universal character."[27]

I would like to conclude by affirming that there is a need to recover an ecofeminist epistemology in order to push back against the new wave of political

---

[27] Gebara, *Teologia Ecofeminista*, 52.

and religious conservatism that could easily flood the world with exclusive privileges reserved for the elites. As indicated in the epigraph of this text, "more than ever, the invitation to move patriarchal waters at all levels of knowledge is imposed as a demand for justice in relation to ourselves and humanity." More than ever the world needs Asherah, the great goddess. To reinvest her with power and value is necessary for all varieties of Christianity, biblical research, and systems of education in contemporary societies.

Thus, rethinking the sacred as goddess is another way of reinventing the relations of power. It is not about trying to overcome the presence of Yahweh but about providing space for the female sacred, and this is hugely significant given today's context of violence against women. Although both men and women can experience violence daily, women are more likely to be abused.[28] And thus, to recover images of the female sacred would be to breathe new life into Christian theology and political and educational action by making them more aware of the critical importance of acknowledging and empowering cultural, ethnic-racial, and gender diversity. Christian theologies would then be better positioned to engage contemporary social policies in the context of our daily lives in our societies.

If Christian theologies do not open themselves to this kind of reconceptualization of divinity, a few decades from now, they will again be held accountable by future generations. And again, they will have to apologize for their current faults. To avoid that, I pray:

> *Our Goddess, who art in our streets and*
> *whorehouses, family homes and factories;*
> *Hallowed is the freedom of our own bodies;*
> *Come to us with your brave words;*
> *Thy kingdom be free of sexist husbands,*
> *fathers, or corrupt politicians;*
> *Our will be done against all conservatives,*
> *inside or outside our home;*
> *Give us our daily bread without rape or domestic violence;*
> *Forgive the offenses of Pussy Riot who hit the nail on the*
> *head and suffered unjustly also on our behalf,*
> *as we forgive those who have offended us by*
> *trying to silence our feminist dignity;*

---

[28] Shannan M. Catalano, "Intimate Partner Violence, 1993–2010," Bureau of Justice Statistics, accessed May 21, 2021, https://bjs.ojp.gov/library/publications/intimate-partner-violence-1993-2010.

And lead us not into the temptation of thinking
    that men want our well-being;
And, above all, deliver us and Pussy Riot from all evil.
Amen.[29]

---

[29] Originally, this prayer was made to Madonna (the singer) by the Brazilian philosopher Márcia Tiburi because Madonna claimed freedom for Protestant feminists in 2012 against the Russian government and the church, which were both responsible for arresting the members of the Russian rock group Pussy Riot. Note that in lines 7–10 of the prayer, the English translation used here differs slightly from the online version. Márcia Tiburi, "Oração Pela Liberdade Das Pussy Riot—Prayer for Free Pussy Riot," Revista Cult, accessed May 21, 2021, https://revistacult .uol.com.br/home/oracao-pela-liberdade-das-pussy-riot-prayer-for-free-pussy-riot/.

CHAPTER 6

FROM THE RUINS OF THE END OF THE WORLD

NECROPOLITICS, RELIGION, AND THE ECOLOGICAL CRISIS IN BRAZIL

Frederico Pieper

I am thinking of the possibility of the world civilization
which is just now beginning one day might overcome
the technical-scientific-industrial character as the
only measure of human dwelling in the world.

—Martin Heidegger, *Zur Sache Des Denkens* (translation mine)

How can we find a point of contact between these two worlds,
which have the same origin but have drifted so far apart that
today we have, at one extreme, those who need a river to live,
and, at the other, those who consume rivers as mere resources?

—Ailton Krenak, *Ideas to Postpone the End of the World*

It felt like it was the end of the world. But it was just another Monday afternoon in the city of São Paulo. People were busy with their tasks and activities. The traffic was, as usual, chaotic, with motorcycles passing dangerously between the cars to accomplish delivery deadlines. But August 19, 2019, would not go unnoticed. Around 3 p.m., the day turned into night. In a landscape reminiscent of apocalyptic prophecies, the sun was struck with darkness. In its place, a dense cloud of smoke appeared. Many rushed to social media with their selfies and photos to show the world the unlikely thing that had happened; suddenly, the day had turned into night. Everything was dark. But what was the reason for this strange phenomenon, which had never been seen before?

The explanation was neither in the city nor in the stars. It could only be found over two thousand miles away. In 2019, the northern region of Brazil, where the Amazon Basin is located, had a surge of 82 percent in the number of fires compared to the previous year.[1] Because of the rainforest, the biome is quite humid. Therefore, fires do not happen accidentally or by natural causes; rather, they are set by someone. These fires have been intentionally lit in order to guarantee that the richest ecosystem in the world (i.e., the Amazon Rainforest) does not hinder cattle ranching, soy planting, and mining extraction. These predatory economic activities are aimed at the export of commodities to Europe, the United States, and China. The smoke that charred the animals and the forest and destroyed the homeland of many peoples rose to the skies. Then the smoke found the currents that, in regular times, take the rain to the southeast of Brazil. These flying rivers have become flooded with this agonizing smoke, carrying the groans of creation to the metropolis. The forest's cry for help was momentarily heard. Government officials have tried to smother it. Although the groans of creation can no longer be ignored, for many people, they are just a nuisance to the ears.

When we talk about necropolitics, we think of the exposure of certain populations to conditions of mortality more than others: namely, deliberate political actions and decisions in which the sovereign power takes death as a project. Sovereignty is no longer a matter of discipline and punishment but of killing and letting die.[2] Moreover, necropolitics, as a contemporary version of colonialism, spreads the shadow of death beyond human beings. It affects our terrestrial condition. All life agonizes in the face of the irrepressible desire for accumulation and the unlimited production of wealth. The first records of human beings in the Amazon Basin date back to eleven thousand years ago. And by 1970, about 0.5 percent of the forest was deforested. This would be understandable for the establishment of villages, cities, and houses and the planting of what is necessary for life. But from 1970, an upsurge began: almost 20 percent of the forest is already destroyed. And the forecast is catastrophic; if the current pace of destruction is maintained, 40 percent of the Amazon

---

[1] In Brazil, the National Institute of Spatial Research (INPE) uses high-tech resources to monitor this area and has very accurate and varied records on the progress of deforestation over the years. See "Geographic Data Platform," Terrabrasilis, accessed June 25, 2021, http://terrabrasilis .dpi.inpe.br/en/home-page/.

[2] Achille Mbembe, *Necropolitics*, trans. Steve Corcoran, Theory in Forms (Durham, NC: Duke University Press, 2019), 34.

could be completely devastated by 2030.[3] As if this disaster in itself was not enough, one should also take into account its impact on the rain cycle and the planet's climate. Necropolitics has become an exercise of death on a global scale that knows no boundaries. Looking at it in the long term, this is a kind of collective suicide.

And what does Christianity have to do with all of this? What is the role of Brazilian Christianity in the face of these disastrous necropolitical/colonialistic outcomes? Assuming that the ecological crisis is not just an environmental issue, this chapter offers an understanding of how the evangelical sectors in Brazil have allied with authoritarian and destructive projects of power, leading them to support new forms of necropolitics. Understanding the paradigm is a first step in grasping the purposes of other epistemologies that, instead of segregating and exploiting, afford new ways of dwelling in the world by recognizing the interdependence of all beings.

THE ECOLOGICAL CRISIS, PROJECTS OF POWER, AND BRAZIL'S EVANGELICALS

The colony was the first place where necropolitics and its technologies were tested.[4] The conquest of the peoples and exploitation of the land have characterized the tight link between necropolitics and coloniality. Hence the understanding of our terrestrial condition implies an assumption that ecological crises surpass environmental issues. They are not disconnected from cultural, social, economic, and political subjects. In fact, *The Earth Charter* has already drawn attention to the fact that the ecological crisis is also a result of unfair socioeconomic conditions and authoritarian political regimes.[5] Since the causes of and possibilities for solving the ecological crisis must not be reduced to purely technical and biological matters, it is also important to consider the religious dimension of this necropolitical neocolonialism.[6] I use the phrase *religious dimension* but do not restrict it to the institutional aspect. Religious institutions

---

[3] See Kathryn R. Kirby et al., "The Future of Deforestation in the Brazilian Amazon," *Futures* 38, no. 4 (May 2006): 432–53.

[4] Mbembe, *Necropolitics*, 26–27.

[5] See Laura Westra and Mirian Vilela, eds., *The Earth Charter, Ecological Integrity and Social Movements* (London: Routledge, 2014).

[6] Achille Mbembe, while proposing the notion of necropolitics, has embedded religion into it as a justification for necropolitics. However, I think we should go further and investigate whether some forms of religion are more than just a justification. One possibility is to investigate the religious dimensions of necropolitics itself. How, for example, is it appropriate to use some religious practices (such as sacrifice) and make a symbolic use of them? With this, I am not arguing that necropolitics is religion but suggesting that it has less obvious religious dimensions. And as Mark C. Taylor warns us, "Religion is most effective where it is least obvious." Mark C. Taylor, ed., *Critical Terms for Religious Studies* (Chicago: University of Chicago Press, 1998), 4.

are important and have their role. However, in the Latin American context, religious experience often cuts across a variety of social spheres. Informed criticism of colonial and necropolitical practices must therefore also consider the presence of religion in this process.[7]

Even though religion and politics are intertwined, some interpretations of modernity attempt to relegate religion to a well-defined place. Religion should be confined to the private sphere, it is argued, and not intrude on other social spheres and the public space.[8] As much as this reduction of religion to the intimacy of the subject and its conscience has been tried, religious beliefs have affected the public debate even more. The rigid separation between religion and politics, however, was merely an abstraction. In concrete life, religious beliefs determine political behavior.[9] The emphasis of liberation theology on praxis was constructed on this principle. To be a Christian in a context of inequality implies engagement in political struggle.[10]

The trouble happens when religious beliefs are combined with projects of power, finding in some political projects the means to recover or establish hegemony in a national context. In turn, the projects of power find the necessary capillarity in religious groups to obtain popular support. This is necessary for their implementation and maintenance. This is no longer about religion and politics but about church and state. This alliance gives rise to conditions in which religion shows its wicked side. In the monotheistic religions in particular, and especially the ones with monarchical views of God, the theocratic inclination is most evident. Due to the entire colonization process, Catholicism has always kept very close relations with the state in Latin America. Brazilian historiography even has a name for it: patrimonialism. However, in recent years, the relationship between projects of power and religion and their presence in the

---

[7] In my view, the lack of emphasis on the religious dimension when decolonial theorists discuss epistemology is quite symptomatic. Walter Mignolo, for example, in dealing with the constitutive dimensions of colonial logic, does not mention religion. Instead, he refers to the economic, the political, the social, and the epistemological dimensions. More recently, he pays more attention to religion, although he does not evince much interest in deepening the theme. Walter D. Mignolo, *La idea de América Latina: La herida Colonial y la Opción Decolonial*, Biblioteca Iberoamericana de pensamiento (Barcelona: Gedisa Editorial, 2007), 36. See Walter D. Mignolo, "Enduring Enchantment: Secularism and the Epistemic Privileges of Modernity," in *Postcolonial Philosophy of Religion*, ed. Puruṣottama Bilimoria and Andrew B. Irvine (Dordrecht: Springer Netherlands, 2009), 273–93; and Walter Mignolo and Catherine E. Walsh, *On Decoloniality: Concepts, Analytics, Praxis*, On Decoloniality (Durham, NC: Duke University Press, 2018), 153.

[8] Talal Asad, *Genealogies of Religion: Discipline and Reasons of Power in Christianity and Islam* (Baltimore: Johns Hopkins University Press, 1993), 28.

[9] See Jose Casanova, *Public Religions in the Modern World* (Chicago: University of Chicago Press, 1994).

[10] See Edward A. Lynch, *Religion and Politics in Latin America: Liberation Theology and Christian Democracy* (New York: Praeger, 1991).

public arena has gained more attention from academia. All of this takes place in a historical moment in which evangelicals have begun to have more visibility. And we do not understand what happened on that Monday in August in São Paulo specifically or the ecological crisis in Brazil generally if we do not consider the affinity of these churches with some authoritarian projects of power.

In recent years, religious people have correctly defended their right to speak in the public sphere.[11] However, in the Brazilian context, some of these churches confuse the right to speak with hegemony of speech. They want to have a voice, but they have not learned how to listen. When they are a minority, they raise the flag of freedom. When they align with the projects in power, they begin to speak of truth. In that case, their truth must be imposed on everyone else.

In the last few decades, there has been rapid and exponential growth of evangelical groups (mostly Pentecostal and prosperity gospel churches) in Brazil. If in the 1980s, 89 percent of the population identified themselves as Catholics, today that number has fallen to 64 percent, with an indication of continued contraction in the years ahead. On the other hand, evangelicals have risen from 6.6 percent in 1980 to 22.2 percent in 2010.[12] If the statistical trend is maintained, it is expected that Catholics will cease to be the majority population in 2030 and that Brazil will become predominantly evangelical in 2040. In the Amazon region, the number of people who identify themselves as evangelicals has already surpassed the number of Catholics. This growth was not only numerical; the media—initially radio and television and, more recently, the social media—gave great visibility to these groups and their agendas. Thus, the question now is not whether religion has a right to speak in the public sphere but what its role in the public sphere should be. In more clear-cut terms, How does Brazil create instruments to guarantee all forms of religion a voice in the public space while keeping religion's totalitarian and hegemonic impulses under control? This question has become even more urgent in the context of the rise of far-right governments.

This growth in numbers and visibility has affected change in the development of the bonds between conservative evangelical groups and political projects of power. Many types of Protestantism that came to Brazil were characterized by

---

[11] See Jürgen Habermas and Joseph Ratzinger, *The Dialectics of Secularization: On Reason and Religion* (San Francisco: Ignatius, 2007).

[12] Leonildo Silveira Campos, "Os Mapas, Atores e Números da Diversidade Religiosa Cristã Brasileira: Católicos e Evangélicos entre 1940 e 2007," *Revista de Estudos da Religião*, December 2008, 9–47; Marcelo Camurça, "O Brasil religioso que emerge do Censo de 2010: Consolidações, tendências e perplexidades," in *Religiões em movimento: O censo de 2010*, ed. Fautino Teixeira and Renata Menezes (Petrópolis: Editora Vozes, 2013), 63–88.

their sharply ascetic worldview.[13] As a result, for many decades, the concept that took hold among conservative evangelical groups can be summarized in the phrase "Christians do not mess with politics." This denial of the world is ambiguous. On the one hand, many of these religious groups have conformed to some strict moral rules, avoiding as much as possible letting themselves be stained by the advances of modernity. On the other hand, they did not balk at adopting modern values such as a positive view of capitalism, the use of mass media, and an individualistic ethics. This ambiguity still has repercussions today, and it helps explain some religious attitudes and the approach of some religious groups to the ecological crisis.

After a long period under a dictatorial regime, Brazil in 1986 was living in the midst of a democratic reopening. In this new context, several evangelical religious denominations have organized themselves with the intention of electing their own representatives. The catchphrase was no longer "Christians do not mess with politics" but "brother votes for brother."[14] Belonging to a church would be a sign of the candidate's suitability as well as their alignment with Christian projects and values. Instead of voting for candidates who do not identify themselves with any Christian-evangelical institution, the faithful were expected to use their vote to elect a candidate recommended by the church. Religious institutions wished to have representatives when the political decisions being made had some influence on them. The elected candidate, in return for the votes received, had the obligation of defending the interests of the churches in legislative and executive decision-making. It was, for example, at this point that many of these denominations took control of various mass media across the country.

All these different phases have built-in aspects that allow us to understand the current situation, even though it was in the 2000s that the foundations were laid that more definitively explain the adjustment of these religious groups to the necropolitical projects of power. The first crucial change was the covenant, which included more than denominational concerns, that was established among the various religious representatives. Under the center-left government, agendas with moral concerns (especially linked to sexuality) began to receive more attention. The evangelical deputies in Brazil's parliament have assumed the role of the sponsors of morality, of "good customs" and of good citizens. They imagine themselves as the ones who resist the implementation of decisions that

---

[13] See Antônio Gouvêa Mendonça, *O Celeste Porvir: A Inserção Do Protestantismo No Brasil*, 3rd ed. (São Paulo: EDUSP, 2008).

[14] See Magali Do Nascimento Cunha, "Os Processos de Midiatização Das Religiões No Brasil e o Ativismo Político Digital Evangélico," *Revista FAMECOS* 26, no. 1 (August 19, 2019): 1–20, https://doi.org/10.15448/1980-3729.2019.1.30691.

threaten to destroy families and traditions. The slogan that sums up this new moment is no longer "brother votes for brother" but "the true Christian does not vote for so-and-so." The name in the blank is easily replaced by groups with center-left platforms, who are seen as a threat and must therefore be eliminated. For example, Silas Malafaia, a well-known pastor in Brazil and passionate supporter of the current far-right government, says that a believer should not vote for a communist because all of them are atheists who would defend values opposed to Christian ones. In the 2018 elections, in which Jair Bolsonaro was elected, this pastor said along the same lines, "The true believer does not vote for Haddad," the candidate of the Labor Party.[15]

There is a shift from a more denominational concern to a fictional construction of the enemy: Brazil suffers from a communist threat that must be stopped. Most of these accusations sound so absurd that it is difficult to see how anyone would actually consider them to be true. But in any case, they have a clear function: creating an atmosphere of conflict and fear by disqualifying progressive agendas. This enemy is responsible for all the disorders, their opponents allege, using the logic of scapegoatism. In this context, the label "communist" has become something of a curse. All those who are part of "them" are thus named, even if they do not subscribe to communist convictions themselves.

Some of those values of modernity, which have long been absorbed by conservative evangelical groups, are employed in the fictional construction of the enemy. Individualism in ethics and a positive view of capitalism have their theological counterparts in the prosperity gospel. And the cultural war is translated into spiritual warfare. These values are assumed as inalienable Christian values that must be defended against the threat of enemies. In some cases, the discourses are convergent. The patriarchal conception that women must take care of the home is coupled with neoliberal interests of allocating some responsibilities of the state to the family.

In some way, this confluence indicates that Wendy Brown's analysis is partially valid also for the Brazilian situation. There is a gradual dismantling of the idea of society and the state. Neoliberalism is not just an economic business but also a project of society and culture that has created room for antidemocratic programs when it provides freedom without society or without the state.[16] However, in the case of Brazil, it is necessary to consider a complement to this thesis. With the revival of neoliberalism after the 2008 crisis, authoritarianism

---

[15] Silas Malafaia Official, "Pastor Silas Malafaia Comenta: Por Que Um Verdadeiro Cristão Não Vota Em Haddad?," YouTube video, October 15, 2018, https://www.youtube.com/watch?v=QskGBZmNGxQ.

[16] Wendy Brown, *In the Ruins of Neoliberalism: The Rise of Antidemocratic Politics in the West* (New York: Columbia University Press, 2019), 44.

is not only a consequence of neoliberal discourse but also a condition for its realization. The plot is always the same. The progressivist president is forced out, and the vice president or someone else takes office. And the new president is an ally of the United States and puts forward a neoliberal project with the support of the conservative evangelical churches. These coups were intended to create the appropriate conditions for those economic policies, even against the people's will. This process began in 2008 in Honduras and spread throughout Latin America. In this whole process, the role and strength of the conservative evangelical groups cannot be minimized. The identification that is established among the fictional creation of the enemy, traditional values, and economic policies has received the consent of these groups. This was also the case in Brazil.

What does this have to do with ecological issues in Brazil? To understand the position that evangelical groups and leaders have taken in relation to the ecological crisis, we should consider these interconnected factors: a necropolitics and authoritarian project of power mixed with a neoliberal worldview. The fire in the Amazon Rainforest is only the tip of the iceberg. As we can see, it is not sufficient to argue with these religious groups that the normative texts of Christianity give rise to a responsible attitude toward other living beings. In order to understand this plot, it is also mandatory to consider how the interests of power make up the religious attitudes.

The fires in the Amazon Rainforest in 2019, which were reported all over the world, made it possible to identify the concrete nexus of this conjunction of factors. Important evangelical leaders followed the line of defense of the far-right president, Bolsonaro. There is a cynical discursive oscillation that moves back and forth between denialism, conspiracy theories, and indifference. This happens not only in relation to the forest as such but also in relation to the peoples of that region.

Cynicism is one of the hallmarks of contemporary far-right politics. Even in the face of indisputable facts, scientifically proven, they are simply denied. If reality questions the theory that is believed, then all the worse for reality. The data on deforestation and the fires were being monitored by NASA satellites and in Brazil by the National Institute of Spatial Research (INPE). Even in the face of such evidence, the position adopted by Brazil's president and his allies was (and still is) to deny that there was an increase in deforestation. As recently as July 2020, Bolsonaro stated that the forest was not burning very much and that if anyone could be blamed for this, it is the Indigenous people. In 2019, he also accused the nongovernmental organizations. In a strategy typical of conspiracy theories, when asked if he had any proof of his statement, he said that the evidence for his accusation was that there was no evidence.

We cannot minimize the impact that the fictional construction of the enemy has on all of this. After all, the adoption of denialism, conspiracy theories, and indifference by many evangelicals is based on this construction. Demonstrating ecological concern and care for Indigenous people and being critical of capitalism are associated with leftist behavior because—so the argument goes—all of this is opposed to "true" Christian values. Due to this positive view of neoliberalism, nature is something available for exploitation by human beings. Land, instead of being occupied by "primitive" peoples and staying idle, must be made productive. With this, it can become a source of wealth capable of raising Brazil to the status of a developed country. For those groups and leaders, forest wealth would justify the interest of other countries in dominating this Brazilian resource. Europe is accused of having destroyed its forests in the name of industrialization. Therefore, Brazil should also enjoy the same right. Some statements by Pastor Silas Malafaia on Twitter during the 2019 fires are an example of this.[17]

The association of the fictional enemy with neoliberalism is also directed at the Indigenous peoples. They are the target of evangelization, and their "primitive" way of dwelling on the land does not make it sufficiently productive. The forest only has value when it is exploited economically. And this exploitation takes place through the extraction that destroys it. The Indigenous people, instead of being regarded as populations that can help us understand other ways of dwelling in the world, are treated as populations that are unjustly protected by the benefits of the state. For this colonialist mentality, the Indigenous people are a numerically small population, but one that leaves large tracts of land idle.

THE MODERN PARADIGM: A WORLD IN DISARRAY

How can we create ways of "reexistence" against this necropolitics that advances the end of the world, destroys, and kills all living beings? How can we start from the end? Are there alternatives to this neocolonialism also derived from the link between Christianity and projects of power? What forms of dwelling in the world can we imagine/think/cultivate from the contaminated and polluted, from the vulnerability to which the doom of the end of the world has exposed us? To broaden the horizon, alternative proposals should attempt to understand what the structural features actually are of inhabiting the world.

---

[17] With his notoriously aggressive tone on August 23, 2019, Pastor Silas Malafaia tweeted, "NAUGHTY ABOUT THE AMAZON 3 The Amazon is invaded by Chinese, Norwegians, Canadians, and so on. The Norwegian government is a shareholder in a company that exploits wealth in the Amazon. The leftist press for ideological reasons opposed to the current government, hides these truths." Silas Malafaia (@PastorMalafaia), "A SAFADEZA SOBRE A AMAZÔNIA 3 a Amazônia está invadida por chineses, noruegueses, canadenses e, and so on," Twitter, August 23, 2019, https://twitter.com/PastorMalafaia/status/1164943661358092290.

In other words, what are the contours of the paradigm or epistemology[18] that underlie these destructive practices and policies? The importance of this is to avoid proposals of overcoming the crisis with merely palliative and reformist solutions. They should be able not only to reduce the destruction but to interrupt it and bring it to a stop.

The anthropocentrism of this model, of which the alliance between evangelicals and the power project is a sample, is its main feature.[19] It credits human subjectivity as a centralized and separated place, as if this subjectivity were given the possibility of constituting itself as a being outside and beyond the world. This subject becomes the place of significance for everything else, making itself the center that establishes Being. In this conception, knowledge is constituted from the representation of the object and its insertion into a conceptual system of the subject, which enacts the meaning of the object. In modern philosophy, this subject is thought of as gradually disconnected from objects, and this subjectivity then finds itself everywhere. Thus, the subject is configured as the foundation of representational knowledge that aims at exact knowledge. This self-conscious subject has knowledge of one's self. The subjectivity's certainty can therefore be a foundation because it has the certainty of one's self. Subjectivity is, therefore, what is most present to one's self.[20]

This subjectivity, elaborated by philosophy, constitutes the same citizen of modernity/coloniality.[21] At the same time, modernity/coloniality is also an experience of uprooting, which leads to a disconnect between "him" (subjectivity

---

[18] The word *paradigm* was adopted by Leonardo Boff in 1993 when he pointed out the need to move from an anthropocentric to an ecocentric paradigm (see Leonardo Boff, *Ecologia, Mundialização, Espiritualidade* [São Paulo: Editora Record, 2008], 35). More recently, with the development of decolonial theories, the term *epistemology* is more usual (see Walter D. Mignolo, *Local Histories/Global Designs: Coloniality, Subaltern Knowledges, and Border Thinking* [Princeton, NJ: Princeton University Press, 2000], 95; and Boaventura de Sousa Santos, *The End of the Cognitive Empire: The Coming of Age of Epistemologies of the South* [Durham, NC: Duke University Press, 2018]). Enrique Dussel summarizes the issue by stating, "The epistemological decolonization of theology begins by situating ourselves in a *new space* from which, as *locus enuntiationis* and original hermeneutic, it will be necessary to redo theology as a whole." Enrique Dussel, "Epistemological Decolonization of Theology," in *Decolonial Christianities: Latinx and Latin American Perspectives*, ed. Raimundo Barreto and Roberto Sirvent (New York: Palgrave Macmillan, 2019), 36. Although there are differences between them, both point to the need to reconsider rationality—that is, the way things are thought of and their relationships. Boff's contribution to this debate is to consider how ecology can be a kind of foundation for this new paradigm or epistemology.

[19] Leonardo Boff, "El Cristo Cósmico: La Superación Del Antropocentrismo," *Numen* 2, no. 1 (1999): 125–39; Ailton Krenak, *Ideias Para Adiar o Fim Do Mundo* (São Paulo: Companhia das Letras, 2019), 72.

[20] See Martin Heidegger, "Hegels Begriff der Erfahrung," in *Gesamtausgabe: Holzwege (1935–1946)* (Frankfurt: Vittorio Klostermann, 2003), 115.

[21] Drawing on insights from Mignolo and Walsh, *On Decoloniality*.

is ordinarily thought of as masculine) and other living beings. This disconnect can also be called alienation. The deep bonds that put all beings into relationship with one another are no longer recognized. It also establishes, as Boff argues, a kind of dualism, "such as the division of the world into the material and the spiritual, the separation between nature and culture, human being and world, reason and emotion, female and male, God and world, and atomization of scientific knowledge."[22] This dualistic view is organized by a hierarchy, and the poles are placed in conflictual interaction, with the result that if there are any kind of bonds at all, they are more of opposition, segregation, and competition. Let us not forget that segregation is one of the tools of necropolitics. Perhaps this understanding derives from a possible reading of the Christian concept that sin brings the world into conflict with human beings, human beings into conflict with God, and God into conflict with the world. This hierarchical and conflicting dualism generates the understanding of knowledge as conquest. Since nature is a threat that opposes human beings, their concern is to establish dominion over it. That was the hope at the beginning of modernity: by knowing the eternal laws that govern the universe, this subjectivity could gain control over it, and to this end, scientific knowledge tends to reduce the complexity of reality to simple causes. There exist only beings that can be handled and are susceptible to exploitation. Accordingly, human beings and other beings are reduced to instruments for production and consumption. Life is no longer the goal but rather the means by which instrumental reason is established. Life begins to be measured by its exchange value; living beings and nature have no intrinsic value and are evaluated by the possibility of being transformed into profitable commodities.

The Brazilian theologian Leonardo Boff points out that the theological concept that governs this understanding of the world is that of a monarchical God.[23] The term is quite appropriate. *Monarchy* refers to the idea of hierarchy. This God stands far from his creation. The distinction between creator and creature becomes separation. With that, the world loses its sacred aspect and becomes susceptible to unlimited exploitation. For this reason, the paradigm privileges the first narrative of creation in Genesis (Gen 1:26). In this reading, to exercise dominion over nature means to have the right and the duty to exploit it. It is a matter not of being responsible for creation but of seeking to extract infinite resources from it.

---

[22] Leonardo Boff, *Cry of the Earth, Cry of the Poor*, trans. Phillip Berryman (New York: Orbis Books, 1997), 25.

[23] Boff, *Ecologia, Mundialização, Espiritualidade*, 32.

No Salvation outside the Relationship:
An Epistemology to Postpone the End of the World

As was already made clear, we are not restricted only to environmental aspects when dealing with the ecological crisis. This crisis is so deep that it has awakened in some Brazilian theologians the perception that it requires a paradigm change. Some particular actions will not be enough; rather, a profound reorganization of epistemology must occur in the way that we realize again the bonds between all beings. It implies that we reconsider that everything is interconnected. Boff was the first in theology of liberation to call attention to this. His definition of ecology highlights aspects that are still great challenges today: "Ecology is the relationship, inter*action* and dialogue of all existing things (living or not) with each other and with everything that exists, real or potential. Ecology is not just about nature (natural ecology), but mainly about the society and culture (human, social ecology, etc.). In an ecological view, everything that exists coexists. Everything that coexists preexists. And everything that coexists and preexists subsists through an infinite web of omnipresent relationships. Nothing exists outside of the relationship. Everything is related to everything at all points."[24]

The alternative to the necropolitics resulting from the alliance among projects of power, neocolonialism, and religious views must go beyond a developmental solution. This solution would merely be an attempt to maintain progress while mitigating its side effects. The change, to use philosophical jargon, must affect the way in which the "totality of the entity" is conceived. In the face of separation and opposition, the interrelationship of everything must be affirmed. It is not a totality in the sense of a sum of the parts; it is not just placing one being next to another and jumping into the totality. Rather, what is affirmed is the deep link that unites each part to the other to form the whole in a chain of mutual interdependence. A being does not occur in isolation; it happens only in relationship with the other and with that totality. As a piece of this whole, one part affects and is affected by another. It is illusory to accept that there is an "outside" of the relationship.

In this paradigm, the relation between the whole and the parts assumes another dynamic. The whole is one, but it is not the negation of diversity. There is room for what is specific and particular, but its identity is shaped by the participation in that totality. The whole is in the parts, and the parts are recognized as such from the set of relationships that fall within that totality. For there to be a relationship, differences must be recognized as differences. On the other hand, there can only be differences from within a common ground. Hence "there

---

[24] Boff, 21.

116

is nothing outside the relationship." Or, risking another more religious paraphrase, "there is no salvation outside the relationship."

Human beings do not exist outside of or beyond this set of relationships; they are also involved in it. Modernity created the industrial model that separates beings from one another. In this cosmology, human beings are conceived as something apart from the earth. But paradoxically, we place ourselves as the ultimate end of all beings. The origin of this model, which coincides with the emerging ecological crisis, has a creative side; it lies in the possibility of deeply rethinking the foundations on which our way of living and dwelling in the world are constructed. It is a proposal that rescues the sense of religion as a *re-ligare*. It is this reconnecting of the human being to this totality through the recognition of interrelation that comes to us through the revelation of our fragility and mortality. This paradigm change affects our understanding of science. Can a model of science that divides disciplines be taken as absolute? Is it still feasible to absolutize a model of disciplinary science (with the separation of knowledge) that aims at the domination of nature?

In opposition to this paradigm, the Indigenous Brazilian leader Ailton Krenak, in a book with the suggestive title *Ideas to Postpone the End of the World*, says, "My challenge about postponing the end of the world is exactly that I can always tell one more story."[25] It means that narrating or telling stories is a way to postpone the end of the world. But how can storytelling have such power? To narrate is to create other possible worlds. Thus, each time a story is told, other worlds are created. The importance of these worlds is to show that there are other possibilities besides the modern mononarrative. There are other ways to dwell in the world and other forms of knowledge.

This way of dwelling in the world is also based on a conception of God. If the modern paradigm is placed in a reading of the first narrative of creation, Genesis 2:15 offers other theological symbols. In this account, the human being comes from clay. In addition, humans are called to care for a garden.[26] If Christianity opens a horizon of references capable of legitimizing a predatory paradigm, there are also symbols suggestive of another approach.

God's ecological face is even more evident in another Christian symbol: the Trinity. It points to the communion, the interrelationship, and the interdependence among the three persons. This God is one. But this oneness of God is not a denial of diversity, since God is three persons in ceaseless relationship. These three persons are not mere manifestations of a single being. They are distinct

---

[25] Krenak, *Ideias Para Adiar*, 27. This sentence is missing from the English translation.
[26] Leonardo Boff, *Essential Care: An Ethics of Human Nature*, trans. Alexandre Guilherme (Waco, TX: Baylor University Press, 2008), 33.

but not separate. Thus, "from this divine game of relationships, the entire universe is derived, made in the image and likeness of the Trinity."[27] Colonialism, with its monarchical God, simply fails to comprehend life as relationship, communion, and dialogue.

The paradigm change (in effect, a new epistemology) entails some aftereffects, one of which would be to lead to the sacramentalization of nature. Boff expresses this by reintroducing the term *panentheism*. This word should not be confused with *pantheism*, according to which beings are divine. In Boff's proposal, everything is not God, but God is in everything, and everything is in God. As a consequence, the gap between creator and creature, which results from the monarchical concept, is overcome by the approximation between them. For this reason, the mystic way presents itself as a path for articulating a spirituality consistent with this paradigm. Mystics recognize and want to promote this interrelation, this union with the Other. Furthermore, it is a form of experience that points to a sense of wholeness. In doing so, it highlights the deep codependence between all things.

The interconnection between all beings recognized by mystical spirituality takes ordinary thought beyond the walls of Judeo-Christian symbols and myths into an interreligious dialogue. In Boff's thinking, there is a gradual recognition that this mystical spirituality is present in oriental and Indigenous forms of religiosity, such as Indigenous and Afro-Brazilian traditions. In fact, this path, pointed out by Boff, has been explored by decolonial scholars. The potential contribution of Indigenous and non-Western religiosities to overcoming the modern paradigm is increasingly unchallenged.[28]

I understand that the unfolding of this new paradigm affects both a rupture with and, at the same time, a deepening of the assumptions of Latin American liberation theology. This theology was born as a critique of an unfair socioeconomic system. This was the reason why in its beginning the most urgent political, social, and economic issues occupied the forefront. The ecological dimension did not receive immediate attention. However, the recognition of the interdependence of both beings and knowledge has led the theology of liberation to revise some of its assumptions, especially the primacy of the political over other spheres. If life is about relationship and integration, should one dimension of life be privileged over others? It is not a matter of erasing distinctions among different social spheres; they are and should remain distinct, but they are not separate. Thus, it is a case not of singling out a singular cause as the

---

[27] Boff, *Ecologia, Mundialização, Espiritualidade*, 28.
[28] See, for example, Sylvia Marcos, "Mesoamerican Women's Indigenous Spirituality: Decolonizing Religious Belief," in Barreto and Sirvent, *Decolonial Christianities*, 63–87.

first in relation to the others but of understanding how they are integrated into a totality of relationships.

This paradigm change would also affect an important expansion of who the subject of liberation would be. In Boff's words, "It is not only the poor and oppressed who must be liberated but all human beings, rich and poor, because all are oppressed by a paradigm—abuse of the Earth, the consumerism, the denial of otherness, and of the inherent value of each being—that enslaves us all."[29] The preference for the weakest and poorest is not abandoned.[30] Rather, an expansion occurs due to the recognition that the ecological crisis places us all under threat. This insight is also shared by Krenak: "What I have learned over these decades is that we all need to wake up, because whereas before it was just us, the indigenous peoples, who were facing a loss of meaning in our lives, today everyone is at risk, without exception. As our planet Earth teeters on the verge of collapse beneath our impossible weight, none of us can ignore this reality."[31] So another outcome of this paradigm change is the challenge of thinking about liberation beyond the sociopolitical frame, conceiving of it at the cosmological level.

And it was up to the pope from the end of the world to bring that agenda into the official discourse of religious institutions. Pope Francis's encyclical *Laudato Si'* expresses this concern for the care of our common home, adopting the perspective that everything is interconnected and, therefore, of an integral ecology.[32] Adopting the same viewpoint, some important statements stand out on the occasion of the Amazon Synod, held in the heat of the fires that devastated the forest in 2019. Quite bluntly, the pope has linked the destruction of ecosystems with new forms of colonialism that eliminate diversity. In his words, "May God preserve us from the greed of new forms of colonialism. . . . The fire that destroys, on the other hand, blazes up when people want to promote only their own ideas, form their own group, wipe out differences in the attempt to make everyone and everything uniform."[33]

---

[29] Boff, *Cry of the Earth*, 103.

[30] Leonardo Boff, *Ética & Eco-espiritualidade* (Campinas: Verus Ed., 2003), 51.

[31] Ailton Krenak, *Ideas to Postpone the End of the World*, trans. Anthony Doyle (Toronto: House of Anansi Press, 2020), loc. 23 of 38, Kindle.

[32] Pope Francis, *Laudato Si'* (New York: Paulist, 2015), 137–62; Vincent J. Miller, *The Theological and Ecological Vision of Laudato Si': Everything Is Connected* (London: Bloomsbury T&T Clark, 2017).

[33] "Pope Opens Synod for the Amazon, Calling for Fidelity to the Newness of the Spirit," Vatican News, October 6, 2019, https://www.vaticannews.va/en/pope/news/2019-10/pope-at-mass-for-opening-of-synod-rekindle-fire-of-the-spirit.html.

Conclusion

The ecological crisis, which worsens each year, forces constraints upon us. In this sense, the crisis has something of a destiny. It is the result of past decisions and actions, of a world that we inherit but for which we are also responsible. Paradoxically, this borderline situation demands decisions and acts of freedom. It is precisely when we find ourselves at a dead end that freedom can be most strongly asserted. This freedom is guided to another rationality. Instead of an epistemology that starts from separation and segregation, we can affirm the recognition of the interdependence of all beings. We can move from a monarchical and separated God to recognize God in nature through the sacramentalization of it. Yet perhaps we have barely begun to understand the deep difference that this paradigm change in epistemology makes to our dwelling in the world.

In this way, ecological issues, once they lead us to other epistemologies, can also contribute to other ways of dwelling in the world. They can also show us ways to decolonize Christianity. After all, those forms of Christianity that are allied with and justify the authoritarian projects of power foster an exploitive relation to nature that is merely an extension of the colonial paradigm. These other rationalities may be some of the few remaining possibilities we still have to dwell in the world for a while longer or to postpone the end of the world.

CHAPTER 7

BETWEEN TEAS AND PRAYERS

DISOBEDIENT NARRATIVES OF TWO AMAZONIAN ROOT HERBALISTS IN SÃO PAULO

Sandra Duarte de Souza

THE INVENTION OF THE AMAZON: "THEY DIDN'T UNDERSTAND ANYTHING"

"It was very difficult! When I arrived here [in São Paulo], I was a girl. The school kids laughed at my accent, and even the teacher laughed at some words I used. One day I came home crying and told my mom everything. She said that they didn't understand anything.... She gave me some tea and put me to sleep."[1]

Flora was born in Manaus, in the Amazon.[2] Her brief time at school in São Paulo was anything but friendly.[3] The treatment received from her classmates

---

[1] All excerpts from the interview with Flora contained in this text are highlighted by quotation marks. The interview was held on June 5 and 7, 2020.

[2] Presently, the Brazilian Amazon consists of the federal states of Amazonas, Acre, Pará, Amapá, Roraima, Rondônia, and Tocantins.

[3] Originally, my field research would be carried out in Belém, in the state of Pará. However, all I had was a first reconnaissance trip in 2019 and access to a midwife and healer, the mother of a Pentecostal pastor, who established in her healing practices important dialogues with religious systems formally considered different from each other. The trip to the interview that I intended to conduct was scheduled precisely for the period when the Covid-19 pandemic caused by the new coronavirus affected the world severely, and I was forced to cancel the project indefinitely, since my contact had no access to the internet for long-distance conversation. For this reason, it was necessary to refocus the research. Through a personal contact, I knew Flora (a fictitious name), an Amazonian root herbalist who has lived in the city of São Paulo since she was ten years old. The interview was conducted in two phases, according to the interviewee's availability, and at her request we used the WhatsApp video call feature. Flora authorized the publication of the material as long as her identity was kept confidential. The distance did not allow the sensory experiences that only physical presence would allow, but I am grateful to Flora for telling her story and that of her mother, Rosa. It was a great learning experience and was essential for redesigning my initial proposal.

and her teacher was repeated a few times. As Flora's mother wisely said, "They didn't understand anything."

The understanding of the Amazon was produced on a colonialist basis. The self-referent Eurocentric vision invented an Amazon that was to be replicated by colonizers and colonized. One narrative stood out and, with small variations, was installed in people's minds and bodies. It was a unique story objectified to the point that it proved to be credible and indisputable. In her TED Global talk "The Danger of a Single Story," Chimamanda Adichie alerts us to the fact that the way stories "are told, who tells them, when they're told, how many stories are told, are really dependent on power. Power is the ability not just to tell the story of another person, but to make it the definitive story of that person."[4]

The agents of colonization produced one single story about the Amazon. This immense territory that shelters diverse people and is still far from being known for its cultural wealth inhabits the imagination found in the literature and art of travelers since the colonial period. The description of an almost virgin, exuberant, and sparsely inhabited continent that hides mysteries and riches appears in the letters written by colonial agents. In the middle of the sixteenth century, the Dominican Frei Gaspar de Carbajal, chronicler of the first European expedition along the entire length of the known Amazon River, reports that the encounter of then lieutenant Francisco Orellana with the Indigenous peoples of the region in 1542 involved continuous clashes. The description of such clashes appeals to fantastic narratives like that of the Amazons. Carbajal refers to warrior women, "very white and tall, with long hair, braided and curled around their heads. They have very strong arms and legs, walk naked, covering their shame, with their bows and arrows in their hands, making as much war as ten Indians."[5] The history of the Amazons and the region's riches is also recorded by Captain Gonzalo Hernandez de Oviedo y Valdés in a 1543 letter to Cardinal Pietro Bembo. After hearing the narrative from Orellana's own mouth, the captain did not hesitate to give written form to that account. A century later, in 1639, the Jesuit Cristóbal Acuña mentions these women warriors. These and many other expeditionaries were active in the production of the imaginary about the Amazon and the peoples who inhabited it.[6]

---

[4] Chimamanda Ngozi Adichie, "The Danger of a Single Story," TED global, 2009, https://www.ted.com/talks/chimamanda_ngozi_adichie_the_danger_of_a_single_story/transcript.

[5] Synezio Sampaio Goes Filho, *Navegantes, Bandeirantes, Diplomatas: Um Ensaio Sobre a Formação Das Fronteiras Do Brasil* (Brasília: FUNAG, 2015), 169.

[6] In addition to the chronicles about the Amazons, other "findings" were also reported. In the mid-eighteenth century, the Carmelite Frei José de S. Thereza Ribeiro mentions in a letter dated 1768 the existence of "a nation of Indians with a tail." F. J. de Santa Anna Nery, *Land of the Amazons* [Le Pays des Amazones], trans. George Humphery (London: Sands, 1901), 303–4.

Such narratives, fed by this and many other quasi-mythical sources, acquired among Europeans the status of fact. The act of naming people, waters, and lands based on European references, as occurs with the Amazon,[7] is an expression of the colonizing agency in Latin America, an affirmation of its territorial and cultural domain. The self-representation of the colonizer demands the translation of the colonized, and this occurs based on self-referenced knowledge. The other would be, in Shalini Randeria's words, "the pre-stage of the European self,"[8] or, as Talal Asad translates it so well, "ever since the Renaissance the West has sought both to subordinate and devalue other societies, and at the same time to find in them clues to their own humanity."[9]

The notions of heaven and hell, constitutive of the European Christian cosmovision, produced fabulous narratives about the existence of monstrous beings, a fountain of youth, and inexhaustible mineral wealth. Neide Gondim, referring to the imaginary of traveling chroniclers, demonstrates that "the sacred places of biblical stories were also constitutive of the construction of the imaginary. The miraculous water that prevented aging and the abundance of gold and precious stones cherished the dream of generations longing for having wealth without physical wear and living forever. Corporal monstrosities—men or beasts and even lonely women, the Amazons and the race of giants—were recurrent themes in this imaginary framework which does not end with the discovery of America."[10]

The discourses that invented the Amazon resorted to this imaginary and called for the exoticization of difference. The measure for the classification of the difference was Europe itself. The assumption that what was found overseas was something to be domesticated, since it did not correspond to the self-referring expectations of the colonizers, marked the colonial enterprise.

Based on the records of the expeditions and their publication, the conflicts among colonizers from different parts of Europe over the domain of the region intensified as they aimed to explore and appropriate the wealth described by the Spaniards. The Iberian domain was struggling with attempts by the Dutch, French, and English to explore the Amazon, and this extended from the mid-sixteenth century to the mid-seventeenth century. The authorization of the

---

[7] The term *Amazons*, which will later name the region, recalls Greek mythology and refers to seductive and fascinating women warriors who lived in Asia near the shores of the Black Sea.

[8] Shalini Randeria, "Jenseits von Soziologie Und Soziokultureller Anthropologie: Zur Ortbestimmung Der Nichtwestlichen Welt in Einer Zukünftigen Sozialtheorie," in *Ortsbestimmung Der Soziologie: Wie Die Kommenden Generation Gesellschaftswissenschaften Betreiben Will,* ed. Ulrich Beck and André Kieserling (Baden-Baden: Nomos, 2000), 45.

[9] Talal Asad, "Two European Images of Non-European Rule," in *Anthropology & the Colonial Encounter,* ed. Talal Asad (London: Ithaca, 1973), 104.

[10] Neide Gondim, *Invenção da Amazônia* (São Paulo: Marco Zero, 1994), 34.

Iberian alliance for Portugal to dedicate itself to the expulsion of competitors who tried to settle in the Lower Amazon ended up favoring the Portuguese government in expanding its dominion over the Amazon from the beginning of the seventeenth century to the middle of the eighteenth century.[11] The objectives of the Portuguese crown for the affirmation and expansion of its overseas territorial empire were consolidated in this dispute over the Amazon territory. Portuguese domination in the region was ensured with the establishment of the Jesuit missions, and the Jesuits were the main chroniclers of the Amazon in that period.

The first records about the Amazonian peoples, their social organization, their habits, and their belief systems were produced especially by missionaries. The Amazon was told by them. Just as the first expedition to the full length of what would come to be known as the Amazon River was attended by a religious, Frei Carbajal, who constructed the narrative of Orellana's expedition, the other expeditions were always accompanied by a church representative. It is not without reason that the colonization of the Amazon had the religious as its narrators. In the service of the crowns of Spain and Portugal, the religious orders, in addition to making efforts to guarantee the colonial political-economic order, understood that they had a civilizing mission that involved the conversion of Indigenous peoples, which meant the imposition of Christian cosmology.

Referring to representations of the devil in the writings of the missionaries working in the Spanish Amazon between the seventeenth and eighteenth centuries, Francismar Carvalho explains the civilizing intention through the idea of a spiritual conquest of the hellish Amazonian paradise. The missionaries would be the saviors of the Indigenous peoples, "who were chained to the worship of the devil who used the shamans to promote all sorts of conflicts and damage."[12] The explorers added yet other characteristics to this imagery about the native population. Reporting on his trip on the Amazon River in the 1740s, Charles Marie de La Condamine, a French botanist, characterizes the Indigenous peoples as insensitive, stupid, fearful, and "enemies of work," among other

---

[11] On this issue, see Tadeu Valdir Freitas de Rezende, "A Conquista e a Ocupação Da Amazônia Brasileira No Período Colonial: A Definição Das Fronteiras" (PhD diss., University of São Paulo, 2006).

[12] Francismar Alex Lopes de Carvalho, "Imagens Do Demônio Nas Missões Jesuíticas Da Amazônia Espanhola," *Varia Historia* 31, no. 57 (December 2015): 751. Here the emphasis is on the construction of missionary narratives about the Amazon in the colonial period, but it is important to point out the mediating place of the missions in this context. Cristina Pompa refers to the missions as cultural mediators, the place of intercultural translation, demonstrating the complexity of the colonial "encounter" and the multiple agencies and symbolic recompositions involving this phenomenon. See Cristina Pompa, *Religião Como Tradução: Missionários, Tupi e "Tapuia" No Brasil Colonial* (Bauru: Edusc, 2005).

aspects.[13] This imaginary about the native population, despite not being a consensus among the travelers, missionaries, and explorers of the time, perpetuated itself through the centuries. Albert Memmi shows how the colonial construction of the colonized as "lazy" proves useful to the colonizer, who builds his self-portrait as a worker while disqualifying the natives as enemies of work.[14]

From the middle of the eighteenth century and especially the beginning of the nineteenth, with the opening of Brazil to "friendly nations" and the liberation of navigation on the Amazon River, the region began to receive an increasing number of naturalists from Europe and the United States. In addition, some Brazilians also studied ethnography, such as the professor and poet Gonçalves Dias (1823–64), an Indianist who developed research in the region. At the service of the Historical and Geographic Institute, Dias traveled on the Rio Solimões and Rio Negro Rivers between 1858 and 1861. But it was not until the end of the nineteenth century, with the emergence of ethnology and anthropology as disciplinary fields, that more systematic information was made available about geography, fluviography, and Amazonian cultural expressions. It was under the reign of Dom Pedro II (1840–89), aiming to interiorize the nation-state in the north, that research by foreigners on Brazilian soil received incentives and economic support. His government was marked by nationalist romanticism. According to Erik Petschelies, in order to legitimize and consolidate his still young empire before the traditional monarchies of Europe and respond to the demands of the Brazilian middle class for a national identity, Dom Pedro II built the symbolism of the country based on the exaltation of nature and the Brazilian Amerindians.[15] Such a construction, however, did not prevent the empire from decimating the Indigenous population, in both physical and heritage terms, as well as culturally. The ethnographers of this period developed their studies by responding to his personal demands and those of the research institutions to which they belonged as well as responding to the political, economic, and symbolic interests of the empire.

Physician Karl von den Steinen (1855–1929) experienced this very situation. Steinen made his first expedition in the Amazon region in 1884 and published his studies in German in 1886.[16] He returned to Brazil in 1887 and followed the path of the waters of the Xingu River. Upon returning to

---

[13] Charles-Marie de La Condamine, *Viagem na América Meridional Descendo o Rio das Amazonas* (Brasília: Senado Federal, Conselho Editorial, 2000), 60.

[14] Albert Memmi, *Retrato Do Colonizado Precedido Do Retrato Do Colonizador*, trans. Marcelo Jacques de Moraes (Rio de Janeiro: Civilização Brasileira, 2007).

[15] Erik Petschelies, "Karl von den Steinen's Ethnography in the Context of the Brazilian Empire," *Sociologia & Antropologia* 8, no. 2 (August 2018): 543–69.

[16] Steinen published *Durch Central-Brasilien: Expedition zur Erforschung des Schingú* (1886).

Europe in 1888, he elaborated on two works that resulted from this expedition: "Die Bakaïrísprache" (1892) and "Unter den Naturvölkern Zentralbrasiliens" (1897). Steinen's two expeditions took place during the Brazilian imperial period (1822–89), and the empire had an important role in their financing, as it wished to cover and map the Amazon's territorial extension and have greater control over the region and its inhabitants, among other interests. Foreign scientists obtained permission to make their expedition because there was a "clear political motivation for seeking future territorial expropriation and control of indigenous populations" on the part of the empire.[17] Hence it also provided supplies, soldiers, and technical personnel to accompany the travels of Steinen and his retinue.[18] Once again, the act of naming asserted colonial power. To show deference to his imperial supporters, Steinen gave the name of the governor of the Province of Mato Grosso, Barão de Batovy, to a tributary of the Xingu River: Rio Batovy. He also dedicated his field notes in "Durch Central-Brasilien" to Dom Pedro II.

Karl and Wilhelm von den Steinen, Otto Clauss, Peter Vogel, and Paul Ehrenreich, among others, would influence the conceptualization of forms of knowledge and knowledge itself about the Amazonian population. The imaginary about the Amazon would be assimilated by anthropology, since the origins of this discipline were shaped by the European paradigm of civilization. Eurocentric anthropological readings treated the Amazon as exotic and strange, a land of primitives, of the good savage, of the uncivilized. Its population was the "Other" to be studied and civilized. The beginning of the twentieth century brought to the Amazon more scholars interested in knowing and describing the ways of life of the people of this vast and diverse region. Now the region's story was no longer told by missionaries—at least not mainly. The emerging anthropology took the place of (re)production of narratives about the Amazon; however, the view was still influenced by the colonialist perspective, which affected the very way it produced its objects of study. As Asad demonstrates when referring to the objectification of anthropological knowledge, it is generated in an unequal power relationship between the dominant and the dominated culture.[19]

---

[17] Petschelies, "Karl von den Steinen's Ethnography," 553.

[18] The first group of scholars who accompanied Karl von den Steinen was composed of Wilhelm von den Steinen, his cousin, who was a draftsman, and Otto Clauss, a physician and cartographer. In his second expedition, Steinen again counted on Wilhelm, in addition to Peter Vogel, who was a mathematician, and the physician Paul Ehrenreich, who made anthropological surveys and took body measurements of the populations they met and photographs of the studied field.

[19] Talal Asad, introduction to Asad, *Anthropology & the Colonial Encounter*, 9–19.

A Look at the Amazon: Learning to Unlearn

"They thought that in Manaus it was all jungle and that we all were Indians."

Anthropology was forged by its relationship with colonialism, and this cannot be ignored in the way it constructed its descriptions and produced its conclusions about the societies studied. The historical conditions that favored the emergence of anthropology constituted it as a discipline that occupied a comfortable and reproductive place in Western power structures, and this has been an impediment to the very transformation of anthropological knowledge. Divesting oneself from colonialist clothing implies questioning hegemonic thinking and the forces that maintain it.

In the 1970s, Asad had already raised this debate: "It is because the powerful who support research expect the kind of understanding which will ultimately confirm them in their world that anthropology has not very easily turned to the production of radically subversive forms of understanding."[20]

The detachment of the main narratives that support hierarchical systems based on ethnic-racial, class, and gender criteria has been the tonic of postcolonial theorists and, since the 1990s, of *decolonial*[21] theorists who question the epistemic basis upon which postcolonial studies itself is based. The expression *giro decolonial*, or "decolonial turn," coined by Nelson Maldonado Torres and added to the decolonial vocabulary, refers to "the openness and freedom of thought and forms of life-other (economies-other, political theories-other), the cleaning of the coloniality of being and knowing, the detachment from the rhetoric of modernity and its imperial imaginary."[22] The critique of the coloniality of power is the critique of colonialist epistemic universalism that defines ways of thinking, knowing, being, and believing, perpetuating itself beyond colonialism. Decolonial thinking explains the geopolitics of knowledge built by colonial difference and insists on the location of knowledge and the authenticity of the epistemic agency of all peoples.

Decolonizing thought means going beyond the single history of hegemonic narratives, overcoming homogenizing discourses, and—fundamentally—understanding that the coloniality of power, knowledge, and being crosses the lives of colonized peoples and settles in their bodies and subjectivities. Coloniality is

---

[20] Asad, introduction, 17.

[21] In Portuguese, we find two spelling forms: *descolonial* and *decolonial*. For some, the suppression of the "s" would be a way to differentiate the proposal to break with coloniality from that related to the decolonization process.

[22] Walter D. Mignolo, "El Pensamiento Decolonial: Desprendimiento y Apertura. Un Manifiesto," in *El Giro Decolonial: Reflexiones Para Una Diversidad Epistémica Más Allá Del Capitalismo Global*, ed. Santiago Castro-Gómez and Ramón Grosfoguel, Biblioteca Universitaria (Bogotá: Siglo del Hombre Editores, 2007), 31.

verified in the materiality of life and in subjective structures, distorting the image that is visualized by the Eurocentric mirror.[23] In it, multiple forms of domination intersect, hence Mignolo's affirmation that the decolonial option demands "learning to unlearn . . . , since our (a vast number of people around the planet) brains have been programmed by the imperial/colonial reason."[24]

The contemporary self-criticism of anthropology has made it possible to criticize the very representations and self-representations that produced anthropological subjects and "objects" from an invention and hierarchy of the Western and the non-Western. Unlearning what has been learned has been the challenge of studies on the Amazon, since the main sources of knowledge about the region were for a long time the writings of European colonizing expeditionaries, missionaries, and researchers or those trained and influenced by European references.[25] As indicated by Cristina Pompa,[26] the ethnological and anthropological knowledge about colonial Brazil was built on the basis of a conceptual framework external to this context, such as the notion of religion, and drew on religious sources produced during the colonial expansion in the sixteenth and seventeenth centuries in an effort to translate the native population for the Europeans.[27] This translation process, referenced in codes unrelated to the translated, tends to essentialize colonial knowledge. The decentralization movement of anthropological thought allows a better understanding of the translation processes. This decentralization, however, is not simple, as it is not a mere movement to change sources. It is about detachment from the colonialist imagination.

As we saw earlier, the imaginary about the Amazon is referenced in a historical construction of this region and its people. Representations of the Amazon generate familiarity in people as if they had already been there, to a place remembered for its natural wealth, its biodiversity, and its inhabitants. Perhaps the feeling of familiarity that one has with the Amazon, even if most people have

---

[23] Anibal Quijano, "Colonialidade Do Poder, Eurocentrismo e América Latina," in *A Colonialidade Do Saber: Eurocentrismo e Ciências Sociais. Perspectivas Latinoamericanas*, ed. Edgardo Lander (Buenos Aires: CLACSO, 2005), 126.

[24] Walter D. Mignolo, "Epistemic Disobedience: The De-colonial Option and the Meaning of Identity in Politics," *Niterói* 22 (2007): 14.

[25] The term *Amazon* or *Amazonia* (*Amazônia*) in the singular also demands reflection. The vastness of the region is not just territorial. Samuel Benchimol identifies eight subregions: Eastern Amazon, Central Amazon, Northern Amazon, Guiano-Orinocense Amazon, Southern Amazon, Amazon of the Highlands, Western Amazon, and Pre-Andean Amazon, but here we limit ourselves to highlighting that in this term is embedded a diversity of lives, knowledges and practices, languages and idioms. In this regard, see Samuel Benchimol, *Amazônia: Um Pouco antes e além Depois* (Manaus: Editora da Universidade Federal do Amazonas, 2010), 608.

[26] See Pompa, *Religião Como Tradução*.

[27] Pompa will also show how the translation effort was not a one-way road: the native population also translated the European.

never been there, is in this permanent telling and retelling of a unique story, in the construction of an imaginary that includes the idea of an enchanted place that is full of riches and, at the same time, dangerous and backward, with a naive and dominable population. This unique story continued to be told by Flora's colleagues: "They thought that in Manaus it was all jungle and that we were all Indians." The Brazilian government's developmental policies from the 1960s to the 1980s reinforced the idea that the Amazon was basically a forest inhabited by Indians waiting for progress. This was the story that, in times of military dictatorship, they also read in textbooks, heard on the radio, and for those who had one, saw on television.

For Flora, who is now sixty-five years old, her memory of her school days was especially the memory of the violence experienced by being an Amazonian in São Paulo, because she is from a place where the natives of the land are viewed with suspicion and contempt. Coloniality's relations are also seen in the hierarchy established between being from São Paulo and being from Amazonas.[28] The predominant imagery in Flora's school days places her in an unequal relationship with the people of São Paulo City. It shows the colonial continuities in contemporary Brazil. Her classmates from São Paulo City, or perhaps not even from the city itself, learned the history of an Amazon full of mysteries, an almost impenetrable forest with dangerous waters, inhabited by "Indians," a generic term that hides the diversity of peoples, languages, knowledge, and powers existing in the region.

Índio (Indian) is here a colonial category, and the meanings it carries affirm an epidermal inferiority.[29] In Brazil, as in other Latin American countries, the word *índio* activates the reductionist and racist imagery of a society built on the basis of the dominant cultural grammar, a society that activates the "devices of raciality"[30] in order to forge the "Other" as nonbeing. The racialized process of producing the nonbeing is the strategy of affirmation and reaffirmation of being, as shown by Aparecida Sueli Carneiro.[31] Thus, the racial difference presents itself as a marker of power. The annulment of the "Other" guarantees the existence of the racially hegemonic; therefore, unlearning what has been learned about the Indigenous as nonbeings causes important fissures in the nurturing and updating process of coloniality.

---

[28] The city of São Paulo is known as the economic capital of Brazil and is considered one of the most modern and developed cities in the country, a fact that has produced, over the years, differentiations and hierarchies between those born in São Paulo and those born in other regions of Brazil.

[29] Here we take up Frantz Fanon's notion of "epidermization of inferiority." Frantz Fanon, *Pele Negra, Máscaras Brancas*, trans. Renato da Silveira (Salvador: EDUFBA, 2008), 28.

[30] Concept constructed by Aparecida Sueli Carneiro based on the Foucaultian notion of "device."

[31] Aparecida Sueli Carneiro, "A Construção Do Outro Como Não-Ser Como Fundamento Do Ser" (PhD diss., University of São Paulo, 2005), 99.

ON PLANTS, HERBS, AND PRAYERS: "THEY HAD TO HAVE FAITH. IT WASN'T JUST THE MEDICINE."

Flora's school trajectory was short. She left even before completing elementary school. For a long time, the shelving of books meant the shelving of other knowledge, especially that of her place of origin. Since Flora was from the Amazon, the "land of Indians," she was often reminded of her condition of "nonbeing." Hence she wished to move away from her roots and sought to "resemble" the people of São Paulo City, who, due to coloniality, understand themselves (and are understood by Brazilians from other regions) as a model of what it means to be "civilized" (and part of humanity). It is not about looking like any "Paulistanian" but about being with those whose biotype and way of life are close to the European. As Fanon states, referring to the relationship between Blacks and whites, "A black person wants to be white. A white person is encouraged to assume the condition of human being."[32]

During her adolescence and youth, Flora was not interested in food, music, customs, and other knowledge of the Amazon, including her mother's religious-medicinal knowledge, which was the object of constant family conflicts. The daughter of a Catholic mother and father, Flora converted to Pentecostalism at the age of seventeen. The new faith brought some instability to the family, as Flora and her younger sister, who is also Pentecostal, began to criticize their mother, Rosa, who prepared "bottled medicine"[33] for the neighborhood: "Before, I was only ashamed, but at church the pastor said that this was witchcraft, that it was not from God. So we kept fighting with our mother to stop making the bottled medicines. We were afraid."

The association of knowledge and manipulation of medicinal herbs with witchcraft is another story learned and perpetuated over time. The abjection of popular healing practices has marked the history of Brazil since colonial times, with a long record of persecution of people accused of witchcraft and even of inquisitorial visits with the purpose of identifying and punishing such practitioners.[34] During the beginnings of Brazil's republic at the end of the nineteenth century, this became a topic to be addressed also by the new political order. For some decades, there was a debate within different sectors of society on the legitimacy of practices until then considered witchcraft. As Paula

---

[32] Fanon, *Pele Negra, Máscaras Brancas*, 27.

[33] A *garrafada* (literally "bottled") is a liquid that mixes some sort of drink, alcoholic or not, with different medicinal plants, and that is used to treat various diseases. Some types of bottled medicine are administered orally, and others are for external use. The preparation is artisanal and not regulated by Brazilian health legislation. Even so, the bottled medicine is quite popular in our society.

[34] See Laura de Mello e Souza, *O Diabo e a Terra de Santa Cruz: Feitiçaria e Religiosidade Popular No Brasil Colonial* (São Paulo: Companhia das Letras, 1986).

Montero indicates, in addition to physicians, this debate involved different professionals, including representatives of the Catholic Church, whose task it was to arrive at a decision about the criminalization of these practices, because "at that moment, it was widely-considered self-evident that 'religion' . . . was only the Catholic religion. The status of these other practices, which evidently did not fit this model, was the subject of medico-legal controversies."[35] The denial and repression of the practice of popular medicine served the interests of affirming a given religion (Catholicism) and a paradigmatic scientific model for republican ordination. Under the argument of Catholic morality and an aseptic science, free from "beliefs," popular medicine was stigmatized.

The knowledge that involves the practice of blessing and the medicinal use of plants is knowledge resulting from amalgamated traditions—more specifically the traditions of the autochthonous peoples, quilombola traditions, and singular and relatively autonomous appropriations and resignifications of European Catholicism.[36] The stigmatization of the wisdom of women healers and root herbalists[37] by the hegemonic knowledge, whether religious or scientific, highlights the process of the racialization of such knowledge. Modern Western science and Christianity in its Eurocentric version are the measure of medical and religious knowledge and are sustained in the production and reproduction of colonial difference, disqualifying and denying the medical-religious status of the practices of those healers and root herbalists.

Affected by secular medical discourse and by the idea that this is "greater" knowledge, the knowledge that involves healing by blessing and the preparation of bottled medicines and other healing practices was and is still today considered superstition. Stigmatization is often of a religious nature, and popular healing practices, involving more than the materiality of the formula and evoking a complex system of beliefs, have been identified as witchcraft based on a highly negative notion of what witchcraft would be. When affirming that "the pastor said that this was witchcraft," Flora reconfirms what women who are healers and root herbalists from different regions of Brazil report in different testimonies. According to them, three insults are very frequent when they are confronted by religious leaders or their followers: they are called sorceress,

---

[35] Paula Montero, "Secularização e Espaço Público: A Reinvenção Do Pluralismo Religioso No Brasil," *Etnográfica* 13, no. 1 (May 2, 2009): 11.

[36] On this issue, see Raymundo Heraldo Maués, "Medicinas populares e pajelança cabocla na Amazônia," in *Saúde e Doença: Um olhar antropológico*, ed. Paulo César Alves and Maria Cecília de Souza Minayo (Rio de Janeiro: Fiocruz, 1994), 73–81; Giselda Shirley da Silva, "Um cotidiano partilhado entre práticas e representações de benzedeiros e raizeiros: Remanescentes de quilombo de Santana da Caatinga—MG/1999–2007" (master's thesis, University of Brasília, 2007); and Souza, *O Diabo*.

[37] Original term: *raizeiras*—women who use *raizes*, roots, for cures in traditional medicine.

witch, and *macumbeira*. These words are used as a way of producing fear, disqualifying the work of these women, and questioning their medical and spiritual authority. Male healers are also stigmatized, but due to gender issues, their authority is less questioned.

The resistance to healing by blessing and to the free exercise of popular medicine occurs both from agents of medical-scientific institutions who insist on the affirmation of their scientific authority in the handling of plants and from religious institutions that claim for themselves the title of exclusive mediators of the sacred. Melvina Araújo sums up this tension well: "The performance of the agents of magical-religious healing has, on the one hand, aggravated the concern of religions to control mediation with the divine and, on the other, the efforts of scientific medicine professionals to eliminate any magical-religious character from the healing processes."[38]

The use of medicinal plants is reported in different societies. In Brazil, the colonizers documented the use that the native population made of some herbs to heal wounds and diseases. European travelers, missionaries, and naturalists were also interested in botany and the healing power of plants. Knowledge about natural medicine also increased with the presence, due to slavery, of Africans in Brazil. Despite the existence of the intense scientific work of cataloging Brazilian flora, it was only very recently that people sought to work in a more systematic way with popular knowledge about plants. However, this is still done from a salvationist perspective, which, despite being well intentioned, bears the mark of the superiority of scientific knowledge, which aims to "teach the right way" to prepare natural remedies. The point is that when we refer to medicine practiced by healers, we are dealing with a more complex universe. It is not just about knowledge of the properties of each plant that is used. The cure is possible because healers promote the intermediation between the human and the sacred world. By disconnecting the knowledge about the healing properties of plants from the cosmologies that surround this knowledge, people break with the harmony of the healing process, which is directly related to the supernatural authority of the healer, her knowledge of the secrets of plants, and the faith of those who seek her help. In Flora's words, "People came to our home because they knew that my mother was spiritual. . . . They had to have faith. It wasn't just the medicine."

Rosa was a native of Lábrea. She was a Catholic, a midwife, and a healer. Lábrea is a city in the interior of the Amazon with a strong Catholic presence since its founding in 1881. Rosa's mother was also a midwife and a healer and

---

[38] Melvina A. M. (Melvina Afra Mendes de) Araújo, *Das Ervas Medicinais à Fitoterapia* (Cotia: Ateliê Editorial, 2002), 126.

passed her knowledge on to her daughter, who learned how to deliver babies and make prayers, teas, and bottled medicines. According to Flora, the public health system in the region where they lived was very precarious, and people turned to Rosa to take care of everything from small injuries to the delivery of babies. In addition, the natural resources available for the collection of plants for teas and bottled medicines favored the elaboration of a great diversity of medicines. When they moved to Manaus, the capital of the state of Amazônia, everything changed. The city was bigger, the neighborhood was unknown, the work of midwives was no longer in demand, and the natural resources were no longer at hand as in Lábrea.

Rosa had to adapt herself. The preparation of bottled medicines did not involve exclusively the manipulation of herbs. Rosa was a healer. The whole process, from the choice of plants to the consumption of the bottle, involved a whole ritual that needed to be observed, thus guaranteeing the effectiveness of the medicine. Flora says her mother was "one of those who prayed every day.... She was a midwife and praying woman, but when she went to live in Manaus with my father, she did not deliver anymore. . . . She just prayed and made a few bottled medicines." Flora has some memory fragments from that time in Manaus. She was still a child, but she remembers that the house was always busy.

The big change in the family's life occurred when her father decided to look for work in São Paulo in 1965: "Then everyone came here, my father, my mother, me and my sister. . . . At that time there were only the two of us. Then here in São Paulo, my brother was born." The decision to move to São Paulo was related to the fact that Flora's uncle, her father's brother, had already lived in the city for some years. The family lived for a certain period in that relative's house and then rented a house in the same neighborhood. Once again, Rosa had to reinvent herself. Among the few belongings she had brought from the Amazon, a bag of plants was her most precious treasure. This is the memory that she made a point of telling her daughters, her son, and later her grandchildren: "She always said that she had carried her pharmacy from Manaus to São Paulo. My mother never tired of telling that."

The medicinal plants would be the great link between Flora's family and the neighborhood. In São Paulo, people from certain Brazilian regions are concentrated in certain neighborhoods. This is because an important network of solidarity is created among people from the same region that facilitates facing the difficulties resulting from change. Mutual support among people from the same region not only was essential for the first months of adaptation for Flora's family but, as she reports, is so today. After some time, the neighbors realized that Rosa was a healer and began looking for her to ask for prayers and also recipes for teas and other remedies. As the demand increased, she started preparing bottled medicines again. Initially, she donated the medicine. People just had to bring a bottle to fill with the medicinal drink. Later, more people began to appear interested in her bottled medicines, and she started to receive gifts in exchange for the medicines and also money, since the plants she had in the small backyard of her house were no longer enough to meet the demand of the neighborhood. It was necessary to purchase some ingredients at the fair or at the market. The medicines were intended for the treatment of several problems: "Mother used to make bottled medicines for coughs, for urine infection, for worms, for the uterus, even to get pregnant. . . . I only remember her treating women and children."

Rosa's medical-religious authority was recognized by the people who sought her, but this did not save her from being called a witch and a *macumbeira* by other people in the surrounding areas, especially by some evangelicals. In the case in question, *sorceress* and *macumbeira* were words that activated the colonial imagery of Rosa's accusers and that they used as resources for disqualification, accusation, and association with demonic forces. The enemy's production takes place once again on a colonial basis. Rosa was an Amazonian woman with medical power that was a fit neither for modern science nor for religious power subject to indoctrination and discipline by the leaders of Christian churches (Catholic or Protestant). This meant that in the persistence of her existence as a woman in a patriarchal society, in the affirmation of her geographic-cultural origin, in the insistence on maintaining her medical-religious practices, she broke with the colonial logic that sums up the medical/scientific and religious power in the generic, monochromatic, and monotheistic figure of the white Christian man.

Flora, who had already suffered the violence of being stigmatized at school for being an Amazonian, also lived with the dilemma of being the daughter of a healer and all that this means in people's imaginations. When her daughters decided to become Pentecostals, Rosa did not try to stop them; she just asked them to respect what she did. According to Flora, "She didn't like it very much. She was sad but did not scold us. She only asked [us] to respect her gift, that she only did good things. But we kept asking her to stop doing these things."

Flora married a young man from her church, and this caused her to withdraw from her mother. When she became pregnant for the first time, she started to have serious blood pressure problems, and the doctor prescribed absolute rest, as it was a risky pregnancy. The fear of eclampsia and of losing the baby led her to seek her mother's help without her husband knowing. Rosa took care of her daughter with teas and some prayers: "I was afraid. I didn't want to lose

134

the baby. Mother said she was not going to give me a bottled medicine because I was taking medicine, but I had to drink a lot of tea made from horsetail, garlic, and other plants. She also did her prayers . . . until I was feeling better and the baby was born well, without any problem."

This situation dramatically changed the course of Flora's life. According to her, her mother was adamant in saying that now she was prepared to learn, that now she was "open." Flora had to unlearn to learn. Little by little, she started to get to know medicinal plants and formulas for preparing bottled medicine but always hid this from her husband and the church.

THEY DON'T FIT IN THE CHURCH: "MY GIFT IS FOR EVERYONE"

The coloniality of power constitutes a permanent process of subordination of different forms of knowledge in the silencing of local histories. The trajectories of Rosa and, later, of Flora are marked by this colonial insistence to deny and disqualify knowledge that does not align with the dominant knowledge, which is validated by science and institutional religion. The hidden practice, the insults, the repression at school, the threats from the church, and the disapproval of her husband are just some of the desperate manifestations of a coloniality that depends on its reproduction to continue to exist and that does not find that continuity in these root herbalists.

Rosa, despite claiming to be Catholic, did not go to church. According to Flora, she said that "priests do not understand spirits and plants." It would have been an honor to meet this woman who questioned the dominant understandings by saying that her daughter's schoolmates "don't understand anything" and the priests "don't understand spirits and plants."[39] The pastor of the church attended by Flora and her husband also did not understand. After many tensions, she stopped attending church, and over the years, her marriage broke up. Rosa and Flora resist the fractures of a coloniality that constitutes scientific and religious knowledge. These two Amazonians in São Paulo had to deal with the colonial difference of being "from the jungle" in a "stone jungle," as São Paulo City is known. Two women who have had to deal with the colonial difference of being women. Two root herbalists, one that claimed to be Catholic and another that claims to be Pentecostal, questioning the logic of these religious systems.

Today Flora claims to be a root herbalist. According to her, being a root herbalist "is not the same thing as a healer. A healer (*benzedeira*) has the orisons (prayers) of the Catholic Church. I don't pray! . . . Yes, yes, I say my prayers for

---

[39] Dona Rosa died in 2017 at age eighty-one. She never got back to the Amazon.

the person to be healed, but it is not an orison." For Flora, this demarcation is important but not exclusive to her healing practice: "I attend [to] everyone. I don't ask if you are a Pentecostal, if you are a Catholic, if you are an Umbanda. My gift is for everyone." She calls herself a Pentecostal even though she does not fit in the church. Her insistence on asserting herself as a Pentecostal and her mother's insistence on asserting herself as a Catholic cause embarrassment for those religious institutions that do not see in these women the expected obedience to their authority. In fact, disobeying was a fundamental movement in Flora's process, for only thus could she unlearn to learn and weave new and disobedient narratives.

PART III

PEACE AND RECONCILIATION INITIATIVES

CHAPTER 8

RESISTING THE LORD'S RESISTANCE ARMY

HOW WAS INTERFAITH PEACE ACTIVISM POSSIBLE IN NORTHERN UGANDA?

David A. Hoekema

*We had to build trust, and we did not take sides. We tried to be
completely neutral in talking to both sides, first the government
and then the rebels. You know when two elephants are fighting,
it is the grass that suffers. The government and the LRA
[Lord's Resistance Army], of course, are the two elephants,
and the people are the grass. And the grass is crying out, "I am
innocent! I am innocent!" And we are the voice of this grass.*

—Monsignor Matthew Odong, vicar general, Diocese of
Northern Uganda (interview by the author, January 31, 2020)

Many civil wars pit one ethnic group against another. The Lord's Resistance
Army (LRA) occupation of northern Uganda from 1987 to 2006, in contrast,
was a conflict in which an Acholi rebel movement terrorized and victimized the
Acholi population of the region. An alliance of religious leaders came together,
however, as the war was raging around them. It played a critical role in negotiating its resolution and continues to assist today with postwar rebuilding.

I have recounted the history and the work of this organization, the Acholi
Religious Leaders Peace Initiative (ARLPI), in a recent study that placed it in
the context of Uganda's tumultuous history since achieving independence from
Great Britain in 1962 and the earlier history of the region before and during

European colonization.[1] In this essay, supplementing that study, I highlight the importance of ARLPI as a remarkable convergence among the leaders of northern Ugandan religious communities whose relationship over the previous century had been marked by mutual indifference at best and open hostility at worst.

The significance of this aspect of Ugandan peacemaking initiatives became clearer to me during a recent visit to three countries in the Middle East and East Africa, with the goal of learning more about, and participating in, initiatives for better Muslim-Christian understanding in each. In Oman, a Muslim sultanate that has been ruled by the same family since the eighteenth century, the small Christian minority is not merely tolerated but assured of freedom to worship, land to build churches, and a voice in shaping national policies. (Proselytizing is illegal, however, as is conversion to Christianity.) In the second Muslim-majority country I visited, Egypt, a vigorous Christian community has been present since the apostolic era, and yet Muslim-Christian relations are tense and volatile, with periodic outbreaks of violence.

In Uganda, my third stop, with a large Christian majority and a Muslim minority, one finds neither the respect and openness of Oman nor the simmering conflict of Egypt. Christian and Muslim communities regard each other with a cautious tolerance, but cooperation and even mutual understanding are the exception rather than the rule. Traditional African religion still shapes some family and community rituals and practices, but very few Ugandans consider these central to their religious identity.

Geographic and demographic factors play a role in this. In rural Uganda, Muslim villages, Catholic villages, and Protestant villages carry on their lives independently. In cities, the populations are diverse, but religious communities often cluster together in distinct neighborhoods. Interreligious violence, thankfully, has been rare in Uganda. The only major Islamist attacks in recent decades were two Kampala suicide bombings staged by al-Shabaab, an al-Qaeda affiliate from Somalia, in 2010.

But interreligious cooperation and understanding have not been much in evidence, either, in the 150 years since European missionaries arrived in the interior regions of East Africa. They sent home glowing reports of churches, schools, and hospitals they were building and of hundreds of new believers they had baptized. But their reports and journals also complained of Catholic priests kidnapping young Protestant catechumens to inflate their numbers and vice versa. Relations were muddied, too, by Catholic ties to France and Belgium and Protestant

---

[1] David A. Hoekema, *We Are the Voice of the Grass: Interfaith Peace Activism in Northern Uganda* (New York: Oxford University Press, 2019).

links to Britain and Germany. Willingly or unwillingly, the mission communities became pawns in the colonizers' competition for influence and exports.

CHIEFS, MISSIONARIES, AND COLONIZERS IN COMPETITION

Protestant missions began in earnest after journalist and explorer Henry Morton Stanley visited the Buganda court on the north shore of Lake Victoria in 1875 and reported that *kabaka* Muteesa, paramount chief of the ethnic group that had come to dominate the region, received him warmly and would welcome British missionaries. In the same period, the "White Fathers," Catholic priests who wore distinctive white vestments, were expanding their mission work. Far from trying to resolve the conflicts that arose between them, the Buganda ruler cannily played the missionaries against each other to obtain concessions from the European powers that supported them.

In the 1880s, under *kabaka* Muteesa's son and successor, Mwanga, conflicts and intrigues abounded, fueling religious mistrust. An Anglican bishop was killed as a (falsely) suspected German sympathizer, two hundred Christian royal attendants and young pages were massacred for displeasing the king, and for a short time, the Buganda kingdom became a Muslim state.[2] By the end of the decade, British forces had driven the *kabaka* into exile, sidelined the Catholic and Muslim communities, and secured the region for the Crown—and the archbishop. Catholics received grudging permission to continue their work.

The Muslim presence in East Africa dates back far longer. In the centuries following the death of the Prophet Mohammed, his Arab followers dominated trade routes along the Swahili Coast of East Africa. Some settlements and mosques in coastal Kenya date back a thousand years. In the eighteenth and nineteenth centuries, a Muslim sultanate stretched from Muscat in Oman, on the Persian Gulf, to Zanzibar. By the turn of the twentieth century, Oman and Zanzibar had become separate kingdoms, while Britain and Germany claimed the interior regions south of never-colonized Ethiopia. Kenya became a British colony with large settler communities, Germany ruled Tanzania until its African holdings were distributed to other powers in 1918, and Uganda became a British protectorate, governed from Whitehall but closed to settlers. Located in a zone of transition between people groups and languages, its climate and soils are well suited to agriculture.

The birth of the Republic of Uganda in 1962 was relatively peaceful, free from the widespread violence that afflicted Kenya. After independence, however, the new nation endured a succession of rapacious autocrats. The first of them,

---

[2] Hoekema, 107–10; Kevin Ward, "A History of Christianity in Uganda," in *From Mission to Church: A Handbook of Christianity in East Africa*, ed. Zablon Nthamburi (Nairobi, Kenya: Uzima, 1991).

Milton Obote, was overthrown by the notorious Idi Amin, a military commander who could not read or write and yet granted himself dictatorial powers
over the nation. After Amin's overthrow, Obote returned to power, heading a
regime whose violence and repression equaled his predecessor's but were less visible to the outside world. Yoweri Museveni came to power at the head of a rebel
army in 1986, and ten years later he was elected to a five-year term as president.
Under Uganda's constitution, he was eligible to serve only two five-year terms,
but he persuaded parliament to remove that limit and remains Uganda's president today. To no one's surprise, his party, the National Resistance Movement,
has asked him to stand for another term in 2021. The outcome is not in doubt.

THE ROOTS OF THE NORTHERN UGANDA CONFLICT

Created soon after Museveni's rise to power, the LRA promised to protect the
Acholi people of northern Uganda from neglect and abuse by the Kampala
government. At first, it enjoyed considerable popular support, both among
the residents of the region and among northern Ugandans residing in Europe
and North America. While the Kampala government boasted of the rapid economic development it had brought to Uganda, eliciting lavish rewards in foreign aid, little money and few benefits crossed the Victoria Nile. Government
neglect fed northerners' resentment.

Joseph Kony identified himself as both a military commander and a
religious reformer, emulating the teachings and the military tactics of Alice
Lakwena's Holy Spirit Movement, which had staged an unsuccessful campaign
to oust the Museveni regime in 1986–87. Like Lakwena—his aunt, claimed
Kony, though this is disputed—the leader of the LRA claimed to receive messages from several spirits directing the people of Acholiland to repent of their
evil ways and follow God. They must observe the Ten Commandments, must
rest from work on both the Friday Muslim sabbath and the Sunday Christian
one, must not smoke or drink, and must never kill bees or snakes, who would be
their allies in combat. Before battles, LRA soldiers would sprinkle holy water
on the ground, spend hours in prayer and singing, and coat their bodies with
shea butter so that enemy bullets could not harm them.[3]

In the 1990s, from its remote military camps, the LRA turned to more brutal
tactics to augment its power and challenge government authority. Raids on rural
villages now seized not just crops but people. Tens of thousands of children were
abducted, crops and livestock were either stolen or destroyed, and villages that
put up any sort of resistance were burned. Suspected government collaborators
were killed or maimed.

---

[3] Hoekema, *We Are the Voice*, 60–98.

Government troops moved into the region from the south to put down the rebellion, employing tactics no less brutal than the rebels'. Survivors of this period whom I interviewed recalled the terror they felt whenever uniformed men approached their villages: whether they were soldiers of the LRA or the national army, devastation was sure to result. LRA reprisals against any villagers suspected of government contact were matched by government punishment of those they believed had helped the rebels. When elephants fight, says the Acholi proverb, it is the grass that suffers.

In 1997, LRA violence was at its height. Nearly all of the rural population had been forcibly relocated to camps for internally displaced persons (IDP camps), where they had no access to farmland, disease was rampant, and the soldiers who protected them sometimes fled when they saw rebels approaching. It was at this dark time that Catholic, Protestant, and Muslim leaders in the Gulu region came together to create ARLPI.

Reaching across religious divisions in this way was a bold move in light of long-standing rivalry and conflict not just between Christians and Muslims but also between Protestant and Catholic communities. Gaining trust both within and across these communities was a slow and difficult undertaking. But the founders understood that the only hope for peace, as elusive a goal as ever after a decade of fruitless military campaigns by the Ugandan government and its allies, lay in collaboration and courageous direct action on behalf of all of the people of the region.

ARLPI's work drew little notice, in Uganda or outside. The Ugandan government pressed on with its military campaigns and insisted that LRA defeat was imminent. Donor nations, lacking any basis for challenging these reports, sent food to the camps for displaced persons and arms to the Ugandan military. But the grass was still being trampled, and the people's suffering continued.

My previous study was based on extensive interviews, conducted in 2014 and 2016, with those who had lived through the conflict.[4] When I visited Uganda in 2020, I was able to conduct follow-up interviews with several key players in ARLPI, bringing my picture of its work up to date. I will recount some of the

---

[4] These visits, and my research project, arose initially from January interim courses that I taught for students from Calvin College, studying the work of church-assisted development in Kenya and Uganda. My interviews in 2014 and 2016 were arranged by Dr. Lucy Dora Akello, senior lecturer in education at Uganda Martyrs University (UMU). She was a resourceful and effective assistant in arranging my interviews and, in one case, translating to and from Luo, the language of the Acholi. I benefited also from the insights of her colleagues at UMU when my students and I visited its campus in Nkozi in southwestern Uganda. Partial support for my research in 2014 was generously provided by the Nagel Institute for the Study of World Christianity and in 2016 by the Calvin Center for Christian Scholarship. Staff members of the development organization World Renew also provided valuable insights and suggestions.

accomplishments and challenges they related below and discuss the factors that made cooperation possible in the difficult circumstances of a protracted civil war. To provide context, I will begin by recounting some of the experiences of those who lived through the conflict. The narratives taken together provide an instructive example of how different sorts of alliances and different modes of collective action can work for good or ill. On the one hand, ethnic identity and mistrust among ethnic groups helped exacerbate the suffering caused by the rebellion. On the other, an alliance among leaders of several religious communities, overcoming centuries of mistrust, contributed in critical ways to the resolution of the conflict.

THE STORY OF PAUL: ESCAPING AN AMBUSH

"You see, I keep a bullet-proof vest here in my office," said Paul Rubangakene, director of the Justice and Peace Commission of the Gulu Archdiocese.[5] "But it has been many years since I felt any need to wear it while traveling to villages in the region." In the late 1990s, when he began working with residents of rural villages frequently attacked by LRA forces, the situation was very different. "At that time the government had control of the towns and trading centers," he said, "but the LRA did whatever it wanted in the countryside and in isolated villages."[6]

On one trip to Patiko, a village north of Gulu, Paul encountered an LRA ambush along the main road. He managed to abandon his vehicle and flee into the bush, where he remained in hiding for two weeks and then took a safer route back to Gulu. Today, a roadside monument honors fifty-nine residents massacred in another incident at the same site, and memorial services are held there each year. "These victims were fortunate simply to be shot dead and left behind," said Paul. "At Patongo, a town farther to the east, LRA soldiers cooked the bodies of their victims and forced new abductees to eat them."

There were two periods of especially widespread LRA violence, Paul told me: from 1996 to 1998, when LRA troops were in frequent battle with government forces, and then from 2001 to 2003, after LRA forces that had been trained in Sudan returned to Uganda and intensified their campaigns of looting and abduction. For two years, Paul and his family were "night commuters" fleeing nighttime raids on their village by rebel soldiers: they walked several miles to Gulu each night to sleep on the grounds of the Catholic cathedral there.

---

[5] Paul Rubangakene, interview by the author, January 28, 2020.

[6] This and the quotations in subsequent sections are drawn from interviews that I conducted in Gulu, Uganda, in January 2014 and November 2016. More excerpts and more context are provided in Hoekema, *We Are the Voice*.

Catholic Relief Services provided bedding, food, and other aid to all who needed it, whether Catholic, Protestant, or Muslim, during this period.

After LRA withdrawal from Uganda in 2006, Paul worked with former LRA soldiers in rehabilitation camps, where he heard stories that defied belief. One former commander recognized an abducted boy on the basis of Paul's description and told him, "Yes, I knew him—he was a very clever boy. So I beat him to death." The boy was Paul's nephew. His parents know that he was killed in an LRA camp, but Paul has not told them what he learned about the circumstances of his death.[7]

THE STORY OF PATIENCE: KIDNAPPED AS A SEX PARTNER

At twelve years of age, fearing that, like other girls of her age, she might be swept up in an LRA raid, Patience took refuge in her older sister's compound. There were no school-age children there, and Patience believed she would be safe. She was mistaken. LRA soldiers swept through the village, found Patience's hiding place, and took her captive, together with other children in the village. They looted village compounds for food and other supplies. Children older than Patience, old enough to resist indoctrination, were not abducted.[8]

Patience spent seven years as an LRA abductee in the bush, moving frequently from camp to camp in northern Uganda and across the Sudanese border. "Our main job was to carry looted goods," she said, "and if we became tired and stopped to rest, the soldiers would beat us. Sometimes they told us to go into a village and ask for money. If you did not succeed, they might kill you." Each time government troops began to close in on an LRA camp, the soldiers would move into nearby villages to terrorize their residents and abduct more children, warning that anyone who cooperated with the government after they left would pay a heavy price.

At age thirteen, Patience was assigned as the sexual partner to a much older LRA officer, one of Kony's bodyguards. The man already had three other wives, some of whose children were older than Patience. As the youngest wife, she was resented and mistreated by the other wives, she told me, and she was frequently beaten by her husband if he took offense at anything she did or said. Nevertheless, she bore two children, a boy and a girl.

After seven years in captivity, Patience escaped with one of her children. She was reunited with the other child three years later, after he made his own escape.

---

[7] Rubangakene, interview.

[8] "Patience" is a pseudonym. Unlike the others whom I interviewed and whose accounts I include here, she asked that I not use her actual name. Patience, interview by the author, January 28, 2014.

Employed as a maid in a hospital, Patience met the man who is now her husband. They have two children, aged six and four. Her older children "from the bush," now aged fifteen and thirteen, are part of the family also. Her husband has accepted them fully as his own children, she said, but they still have many painful memories.

"The prayers of those who asked God to help us escape were very powerful," Patience told me. "Please keep praying for those who have not yet been released."[9]

The Story of Moses: Sole Survivor of a Raid on a School

Moses Rubanbageyo Okello was abducted at age sixteen with thirty-nine other students at his secondary school. They were taken across the border to Sudan. Only twenty-five survived that journey. Moses's two brothers, taken at the same time, died soon afterward in the bush. Today, Moses is the only survivor of the abductees. In our interview, he described the horrors of being beaten, forced to assist in other abductions, and even forced to kill captives.

After he had survived these ordeals, he was given higher and higher levels of responsibility in the LRA camps, eventually rising to the level of second lieutenant, in charge of a brigade of soldiers. Among them were the soldiers who had kidnapped him:

> I was leading those who had abducted me. Some of them were under my direct control. But I was not seeking revenge. I took the Bible point of view because I realized that they were forced to do what they did, against their will. So I cannot blame them for what they have done because they were ordered to do so. . . . At one point, the same commander who led the soldiers who abducted me was under my direct control, and his wife was the one cooking my food, because he was a junior officer, and I was the highest-ranking officer. I don't know how he was feeling! It is very funny that someone whom you abducted can become like your father who keeps you.[10]

Another prisoner placed under his care for a time was an abducted UN worker, and Paul's humane treatment paid a rich dividend several years later. When Paul was injured in a firefight and decided to try to escape and seek treatment, the same UN officer learned of his escape and arranged to airlift him to a hospital. Moses still bears the wounds of four bullets that struck him, one so deeply lodged in his chest that it cannot be removed.

---

[9] Patience, interview.

[10] Moses Rubangangeye Okello, interview by the author, January 29, 2014.

Today, Moses is the administrator of the Northern Uganda Initiative for Affected Youth, which provides counseling, training, and job search assistance to more than two thousand young men and women in the areas that were most affected by the war.[11]

THE STORY OF ARLPI: LEADERS OVERCOMING MISTRUST FROM THEIR COMMUNITIES

Joseph Kony claimed to be a spiritual reformer and a spokesman for divine spirits, as has been noted, but no one I spoke to in Uganda accepted his claim to be a Christian prophet. Those who lived in constant fear of LRA raids did not regard Kony as having any legitimate spiritual authority. All the same, many feared that he was able to invoke malignant spiritual forces. Kony's claim to speak for a purified Christianity was not taken seriously, but the reports filtering in from LRA camps seemed to provide evidence that his army was directed and assisted by forces more powerful than guns.

Nevertheless, in the late 1990s, leaders of the Catholic, Protestant, and Muslim communities came together and resolved that despite very little contact and less cooperation over many decades, they would work together for three essential purposes: to assist those suffering from LRA kidnapping and raids, to bring the situation to the attention of national and international observers, and to facilitate negotiations that would bring an end to the conflict. In the decade that followed, they were able to facilitate the accomplishment of goals that relentless military pressure had utterly failed to achieve: the end of LRA occupation and the cessation of the civil war.

In order to work toward these ends, the founders of ARLPI had to win the trust of their own congregations, and they also had to convince both the Ugandan government and the rebel movement of their good faith and their readiness to seek a resolution of the conflict. These were daunting tasks. Members of Protestant congregations, especially the Pentecostals and other evangelicals, were reluctant to collaborate with Catholics, let alone Muslims. Muslims in turn saw members of the Christian majority in Uganda as unsympathetic, if not openly hostile, to their religious beliefs and practices.

Even more difficult was gaining the trust of the opposing sides in the conflict. Government representatives regarded the Acholi ethnicity of ARLPI leaders as implying complicity with the rebels. Kony's followers, learning that the religious leaders were meeting with army officers, suspected that their claimed neutrality was only a ruse for helping the government destroy their movement.

---

[11] Okello.

147

Gradually, by small step after small step, these obstacles were overcome, and the group's efforts began to bear fruit. Time and time again, I was told by ARLPI leaders, small groups of bishops, pastors, and imams allowed themselves to be driven far into the bush, blindfolded, for meetings with LRA commanders. They were never certain that they would return alive, but rebel leaders insisted that such secrecy was necessary to prevent government troops from learning the location of their hideouts. At the same time, ARLPI's pursuit of negotiations with the LRA heightened the suspicions of government representatives that the religious leaders were rebel sympathizers. But they pressed on with their work in several channels: arranging safe sleeping spaces in town for thousands of "night commuters" from rural villages, contacting Christian and Muslim communities and foreign governments, and pleading with each side to respect innocent lives and seek an end to the violence.

Sheik Musa Khalil, the *khadhi* of the Muslim community in Gulu and a longtime member of the ARLPI board, told me,

> We sustained the community with the one important weapon of forgiveness. We preached this seriously from subcounty to subcounty, from community to community. And we preached forgiveness from both the Bible and the Qur'an. We started working with the cultural institutions and the local leaders, and members of Parliament became involved. We organized seminars that included all stakeholders, including the international community.
>
> What we have done is a lesson to the whole world in peaceful coexistence. We are trying our level best as religious leaders to show the world that we can live together, and this we would like to consolidate and continue. . . . What is taking place in Nigeria [conflict between Muslims and Christians], what is spilling over to other countries like Algeria and Mali—as ARLPI we want to be one of the world's advocates joining hands with other interfaith, interreligious bodies in the world so that we can continue educating children in the schools. We want to teach coexistence and tolerance despite our different faith.[12]

The comments above are from our conversation in 2014. When I visited the *khadhi* again in 2020, he described a wide range of activities through which this mission of reconciliation is being advanced today, more than a decade after the shooting stopped. Land disputes remain a contentious issue, he said, often pitting those who cultivated the land for generations against newcomers who found the fields untended because the population had been relocated to IDP camps. "We have helped establish commissions to resolve the disputes, and we are planting trees to mark property lines," he told me, and he added,

---

[12] Muza Khalil, Khadhi of Gulu Muslim Community, interview by the author, January 30, 2014.

"Climate change is making agriculture more difficult, and we are research-ing and distributing traditional seed varieties that cope better with heat and drought." ARLPI workers are also encouraging farmers to replace European cattle varieties with zebu cattle, a South Asian strain more suited to the tropics. HIV/AIDS remains a pervasive problem: with assistance from UNICEF, the staff of ARLPI and community volunteers focus on prevention and treatment. "We encourage changes in lifestyle, but we do not point fingers," he said. In these ways and many more, ARLPI is acting on the understanding that the end of open conflict is only the first step toward lasting peace.

THE CONFLICT IS RESOLVED AND THE LRA WITHDRAWS

A civil war that had raged for nearly three decades, with devastating disruption of lives and livelihood, at last came to an end as a result of negotiations between government and rebels that ARLPI helped put into motion. In 2006, Kony's forces ceased attacking villages, permitted both abductees and voluntary recruits to return to their families, and withdrew from Uganda. By 2008, the region was at peace.

Since the 1990s, ARLPI had been the most patient and most effective advocate of a negotiated settlement, but as the two sides began drawing up terms for the cessation of violence, other interested parties played a more public role. In Juba, in the region (now the nation) of South Sudan, government and LRA representatives met to discuss a settlement. Members of the Catholic lay community of Sant'Egidio, which had recently helped end a bloody civil war in Mozambique, offered their advice and assistance. Having helped bring the two parties to the negotiating table, ARLPI now retreated into the background.

Deadlines for approving a peace agreement were repeatedly missed, and dis-cussions broke off each time provisional cease-fires were violated. Moreover, with the threat of arrest and extradition to the International Criminal Court now hanging over their heads as a result of 2005 indictments, Kony and his senior advisors sent only lower-level representatives to the peace talks, whose author-ity to speak for their commander was dubious. No formal agreement was ever signed in the end, but both parties honored the proposed terms all the same.

After most of Kony's followers had returned home, a small band of loy-alists followed him across the Ugandan border into hiding elsewhere. One of ARLPI's most challenging tasks, several people told me, was providing safe passage for them—protecting those who had terrorized the entire region from angry villagers eager for revenge.

A small LRA remnant remains in the bush today, perhaps a hundred in all, probably in the Democratic Republic of Congo (DRC) or the Central African

Republic. After its departure, the Museveni government pulled back its troops and invested in reconstruction—better roads, more schools, even a new university at Gulu. "Today the infrastructure is better than in most of the areas where there was no war," an ARLPI staff member told me: "Northern Uganda now has the best roads, the best water systems, and the best primary schools in Uganda."[13]

What Made the Interfaith Initiative of ARLPI Possible, and What Were Its Goals?

Against the background of long-standing conflict among religious communities and in an environment where the claims of purported prophets had launched a decade of kidnapping, rape, and murder, how was it possible for an organization to arise from the cooperative efforts of religious leaders? Why did the appeals of the priests, pastors, and imams of the Acholi region elicit support and cooperation from their respective communities, overcoming past indifference, even hostility?

For answers to this question, let us review what brought the founders of ARLPI together in 1997 and what they sought to achieve. They saw four major obstacles to peace, they told me: first, continuing fear of violence from both rebel and government forces; second, isolation of the region leading to lack of awareness of the situation both in Uganda and abroad; third, disruption of agriculture and other means of livelihood; and fourth, high levels of mistrust in communities and families divided by the conflict. They made it their goal to address all of these issues in a coordinated way. And all four, they realized, afflicted all the people of the northern region, whatever their ethnic identity and religious affiliation.

In its first decade, ARLPI focused on four major areas: first, assisting families divided or displaced by the conflict; second, preparing the groundwork for negotiations between LRA and government representatives; third, seeking greater national and international awareness of the suffering of the region; and fourth, working alongside nongovernmental organization (NGOs) and international actors to prepare for peace talks.

After LRA withdrawal, ARLPI priorities shifted to postconflict recovery. Working with local governments and international NGOs, it sought to help returning LRA camp residents reconcile with their families and communities. It also promoted grassroots economic development programs such as village

---

[13] Abdala Latif Nasur, Project Officer, Acholi Religious Leaders Peace Initiative, interview by the author, January 30, 2014.

savings groups, community road building, agricultural assistance, and vocational training. In all its programs, ARLPI sought to advance understanding and collaboration among religious communities, facilitating the creation of interfaith councils in each town and district of the region. Only when this foundation is in place, leaders of the group told me, will development initiatives be responsive to the needs and priorities of all.

Mistrust both within and between religious communities threw up many obstacles along the way. Some ARLPI founders faced hostility from both above and below: their congregations saw them as meddling in politics and possibly becoming agents for the Kampala government, while their supervisors in the church and the mosque feared that any contact with the LRA would arouse the anger of the government and army. Yet it is evident, looking back on more than two decades of patient peacemaking efforts, that the position that ARLPI leaders held in their respective religious communities was indispensable to their many achievements.

POLITICAL, RELIGIOUS, AND CULTURAL AUTHORITY IN A TIME OF CRISIS

The story of ARLPI illuminates the complex relationship among different modes of authority in a community. Traditional religious responses to extreme suffering—providing comfort, praying for relief, and offering assurance of God's presence—lack effectiveness and credibility without accompanying practical measures. Throughout the civil war, religious leaders continued to lead public worship, comfort broken families, and offer words of hope to the war's victims. But they also sought, at great personal risk, to bring the Ugandan military and the LRA to the negotiating table, knowing that each side feared that they were allies of its enemies. They pressed on all the same, and in doing so, ARLPI earned a degree of credibility and authority that the national government had lost through the brutality of its anti-LRA tactics.

Courageous efforts to build a practical interfaith alliance, the work of ARLPI has shown, can overcome centuries of hostility and mistrust. In nineteenth-century East Africa, Catholics kidnapped Protestant converts and vice versa, and both sought to isolate and exclude Muslims. More recently, there has been less hostility but still very little cooperation. As religious leaders struggled to cope with the brutality of the war, they overcame their mistrust, realizing that they could achieve far more by working together. Eventually, the communities that the leaders served—communities that held them in high esteem—understood that the trauma of civil war, which had only been exacerbated by military campaigns, could be allayed far more effectively by coordinated grassroots initiatives.

Those who guided them on this path, holding no public office and aligned with no political faction, sought to resolve a seemingly intractable conflict and heal broken families and communities.

From the distance of Europe and North America, it often appears that Africa's most urgent problems can be resolved only with the expertise—and the dollars and euros—of experts from afar. ARLPI has also shown that local resources and local wisdom can be far more effective. Donor nations provided the weapons that made ineffective military campaigns ever more destructive—and many of the guns ended up in LRA hands. NGOs and international development agencies provided essential food aid that kept those confined in displaced persons camps alive, but they did little to restore satisfactory lives or ensure adequate means of livelihood. Residents of the Acholi region remained under a heavy cloud of poverty and recurrent violence. But when religious leaders undertook not only to provide temporary relief but also to work toward a resolution of the conflict, through many channels and on several levels, a path to peace at last opened.

CONVERGENCE ON GOALS WITHOUT CONSENSUS ON DOCTRINE

ARLPI's work of reconciliation and healing has drawn support from several traditions without denying their differences. This is another key to the effectiveness of interfaith collaboration in Uganda. Too many European and North American ecumenical enterprises have sought to formulate a common set of doctrines as the foundation for collaborative action. We can seek peace and justice together, on this view, only when we set aside our disagreements on matters of theology as unimportant. But the differences among Protestants, Catholics, and Muslims—and Hindus and Buddhists and adherents of traditional African religion—are not incidental but integral to each system of belief and practice. For that reason, a common enterprise built on the presumption of unanimity is likely to be limited in its accomplishments and vulnerable to fragmentation.

By contrast, the leaders of ARLPI called on their communities to respect and learn from one another while holding to their own faiths and their own religious practices. Then they could find common ground and pursue common goals by drawing on the ideals and teachings of their respective traditions. The theology of the Qur'an and the theology of the New Testament are far removed in many ways, but each supports the call for forgiveness as an essential element in righting wrongs.

Sheik Musa Khalil, leader of the Gulu Muslim community, emphasized how critical it was that all of the religious communities join together after the LRA withdrawal to say, "It is time now to forgive." To the representatives of government, foreign NGO staff, and members of their own communities, the leaders of ARLPI urged, "We must forgive ninety times, or is it one hundred times?" Are you thinking of the saying of Jesus, I asked, that we should forgive seventy times seven? He responded, "Yes! That is it! In the Qur'an, it is ninety times, and in the Bible it is seventy times seven." Listening to a Muslim leader trying to remember whether he was quoting the New Testament or the Qur'an was a startling confirmation of the remarkable collaboration that has emerged among formerly divided religious communities as they work together to heal the wounds of war.[14]

GENDER, JUSTICE, AND PEACE

Two recent analyses of the LRA conflict and its resolution have called attention to the ways in which adherence to traditional gender roles impeded progress in resolving the northern Ugandan conflict. Sidonia Angom's 2018 analysis of women's role in northern Uganda peace efforts draws on both published and unpublished reports by government agencies and international organizations, and also on extensive personal interviews, to understand the perspectives and the contributions of women. Angom, a faculty member at Gulu University, finds that in nearly every instance, women's role was minimal. Government and NGO officers claimed to be placing a high priority on the welfare of women and children, but their actions and policies often prolonged and exacerbated their suffering. Angom concludes, "Efforts taken by various actors can be argued to have contributed fundamentally to the achievements of peacemaking and peacebuilding processes in northern Uganda. It could be argued that where success did not materialise, it could be partly attributed to lack of women's involvement in the peace processes. Peacemaking efforts with the LRA could have been facilitated if women had been recognised and involved as equal partners, especially during the Juba peace talks."[15]

A political scientist with appointments in both Uganda and the United States has offered a very different perspective on gender roles in relation to Acholi traditions and international agents. In a 2014 journal article, Adam Branch challenges the claim that traditional processes and rituals of conflict resolution can heal the wounds of Acholi communities more effectively than Western modes of criminal justice. Recommendations for traditional adjudication—for "ethnojustice," in Branch's coinage, in parallel with "ethnophilosophy"—have come from international observers, from survivors of the conflict, and especially

---

[14] Khalil, interview.

[15] Sidonia Angom, *Women in Peacemaking and Peacebuilding Processes in Northern Uganda* (Cham: Springer International, 2018), 142.

loudly from Acholi living abroad. In support, they cite the slow pace of formal court proceedings, the insensitivity of Western laws and procedures to African communal values, and the rich local heritage of healing practices and rituals.[16]

Branch is critical of this recommendation in many ways. Its characterization of traditional Acholi culture, he argues, ignores the distortions of the colonial period and the differences among many subgroups. Moreover, focusing on traditional community healing for rebels guilty of atrocities overlooks the equally heinous actions of government troops.

Worse yet, Branch argues, the demand for "ethnojustice" serves the personal interests of those who claim to be the legitimate elders of the Acholi people. Their claims, he observes, are questionable. Invoking the support of expats, they misrepresent Acholi traditions, which are more egalitarian than hierarchical, and many use their position to help friends and punish enemies. The elders are invariably older men, rightly respected in their families but lacking any legitimate authority to judge and punish.

The call to resort to traditional modes of conflict resolution, in short, serves as a means to perpetuate patriarchal systems and deprive women of any role in bringing justice and seeking reconciliation. Women suffered the brunt of the brutality coming from both sides in the conflict—kidnapped and assigned as sex partners, raped in their villages, forced to watch as children were killed or abducted—and yet their voices have no place in the supposed traditional rituals of healing. Relying on those who claim the authority of Acholi elders may pervert rather than advance justice:

> It is unreasonable to assume that women would agree to male elders deciding what justice means for them, or to assume that women would be satisfied with men deciding that the perpetrators of violence against women should simply be forgiven, as male elders may very well do under the mantle of tradition. Men may be satisfied with a negotiated, ritualized solution among themselves that does not involve punishment or compensation, whereas women may not be willing to accept that as a just solution at all. The imposition of such justice could create a peace among men built on a reinforced regime of gendered violence.[17]

In my study of the LRA conflict and its resolution, I took note of the way in which rituals of reconciliation helped overcome hostility between returning LRA soldiers and their communities, but I also voiced my own misgivings—substantive but not as grave as Branch's—about the dangers of

---

[16] Adam Branch, "The Violence of Peace: Ethnojustice in Northern Uganda," *Development and Change* 45, no. 3 (May 2014): 608–30.

[17] Branch, 626–27.

exaggerating their importance and efficacy.[18] In highlighting the ambiguity and the malleability of "Acholi tradition," Branch sounds a necessary caution. Perhaps it can be overcome if traditional reconciliation rites are a supplement to, and not a substitute for, processes and institutions that demand accountability for wartime atrocities—on both sides, not only that of the rebels.

GENDER ISSUES IN ARLPI

Issues of gender justice and male privilege were deeply implicated both in the unfolding of the LRA conflict and in the responses of ARLPI and other agencies. Spiritual authority in a traditional African context is by no means restricted to men. In every community, some women are recognized for their wisdom and insight into matters that bridge the visible and spiritual worlds. Most use their abilities to benefit others, helping with life choices and family relations; others use their gifts in less salutary ways, as did Kony's predecessor, Alice Lakwena. The formal structure of established religious communities, on the other hand, is almost entirely male dominated. Women are ineligible for leadership positions in mosques or Catholic parishes, and female Protestant pastors, most of them in independent churches, are usually supervised by male bishops or other superiors.

The composition of the early leadership of ARLPI, accordingly, was entirely male. Even today, women hold relatively few positions on its small staff and even fewer on its board. But one of the repeating themes in all of my follow-up interviews in 2020 was the critical need to address issues of equity for women and gender justice in a war-damaged society. ARLPI staff member Abdala Latif Nasur set out a long list of current programs and projects, describing how each has changed in recent years in response to community requests and reduced outside funding, and then he added that most of the persisting problems in northern Uganda are at the root essentially "problems of gender balancing and women's empowerment." Every ARLPI initiative, he said, makes these issues a priority.[19] Defying the impression of many Western observers that Islam is oppressive to women, both Nasur and the head of the local Muslim community, Sheik Khalil, placed gender equality in law and society high on their list of goals. There is a continuing problem of domestic violence in families, they observed, which both Muslim and Christian leaders condemn and seek to prevent. But gender justice requires far more than no longer condoning abuse: it requires active efforts to provide equal education, equal opportunities, and equal respect for women.

---

[18] Hoekema, *We Are the Voice*, 206–11.

[19] Abdala Latif Nasur, Project Officer, Acholi Religious Leaders Peace Initiative, interview by the author, February 3, 2020.

Another of the individuals I interviewed in 2020, not affiliated with ARLPI, put this point even more strongly. As the regional director in northern Uganda for the US-based relief agency World Renew, Joseph Mutebi now spends a great deal of his time in the camps that house vast numbers of refugees fleeing violence in the DRC to the west and in South Sudan to the north, and he also coordinates self-help and sustainable agriculture initiatives in villages throughout the northern region. "Our goal," Mutebi told me, "is promoting practical literacy in agriculture—and transforming lives." A key to food sustainability, he added, is gender equality. Weeding is traditionally women's work, for example, because it requires stooping; but when crops are planted in raised rows, yields are higher—and men help with weeding. Use of mulch, the planting of nitrogen-fixing cover crops and complementary crops, and water management practices all become more widely practiced when a community engages in gender justice education. "Harmony in the home is critical for food sustainability," he emphasized.

Some Concluding Thoughts

We should be careful not to exaggerate the accomplishments of the Acholi Religious Leaders Peace Initiative in Uganda. It played an indispensable role in bringing about the resolution of a wantonly destructive rebel movement that had effectively dominated the life of the region for more than twenty years while national armed forces not only failed to defeat the rebels but also compounded the suffering of the population. But the road that led from initial and extremely risky overtures to the two sides to the Juba accords was rocky and circuitous. At crucial junctures along the way, the government of Sudan, the community of international allies and donors, and the Community of Sant'Egidio each played a vital role. As the formal negotiations moved slowly forward, ARLPI representatives served as observers more than negotiators.

Furthermore, the end of the northern Uganda rebellion was not the end of civil conflict in the Great Lakes region of East Africa. It was not even the end of the LRA as a guerrilla militia, as we have noted, with a band of perhaps a hundred still loyal to Kony in his remote hideout. The absence of effective central government control in the eastern DRC, where competing warlords command private armies and plunder natural resources, has created an environment in which an LRA remnant may evade capture indefinitely.

Yet we can find many reasons for optimism in the story of an organization formed during a dark period of a civil war that has remained steadfast in seeking a sustainable peace for more than two decades. Against a history of inter-religious rivalry and conflict, leaders of diverse communities came together to diminish the suffering being inflicted on their congregations and to work with patience and courage for a resolution of the conflict. Out of the public eye, little known even to other Ugandans, let alone to the outside world, ARLPI leaders have pursued peace on several parallel paths: convening public peace marches and prayer meetings to bring their communities together; carrying on risky negotiating sessions with two sides, each of which suspected them of treachery; and as the war at last came to an end, creating local committees and programs to make their work both more accountable to those served and more effective in repairing the wounds to family and society.

If the relationship that the Acholi religious leaders have established and sustained among diverse faith communities during and after one of the world's bloodiest and most brutal internal wars could become a pattern for interreligious cooperation everywhere, we would be living in a far more just and peaceful world today.

CHAPTER 9

"JOS IS THE EPICENTER OF CHRISTIANITY"

ANCESTRAL LAND RIGHTS AND THE DESPATIALIZING OF IDENTITY IN JOS NORTH, NIGERIA

Amidu Elabo

I am a seed
Even in burial, I shall germinate
I am JOS like Jesus, Our Savior
When I die, I shall resurrect?

—"I Am Plateau," stanza of a poem written by
an unknown group of Plateau indigenes

For most Indigenous Christians in Jos and Plateau State, the creation of Jos North, Nigeria, as a local government area (LGA) in 1991 represented a spatial transition and strategy by Hausa-Fulani Muslims to wield power in order to redefine the identity of the city.[1] Currently, such anxieties are being exacerbated by (1) over four decades of interethnic and interreligious tensions and hostilities between Hausa-Fulani Muslims and the Anaguta, Berom, and Afezere ethnic groups, who are mainly Christians; and (2) the current Fulani herdsmen's perpetual "sneak" attacks on "Christian" villages, which have left thousands of Christians dead, most surrounding villages destroyed, and many churches burned down, leading to the internal displacement of Indigenous people whose land was alleged to be *appropriated* by the aggressors.

---

[1] Umar H. D. Danfulani, "The Jos Peace Conference and the Indigene/Settler Question in Nigerian Politics," unpublished lecture, African Studies Center, University of Leiden, March 2, 2006, p. 4.

This chapter explores how Christians imagined the spatial identity of Jos North as *Christian* and how they deploy such spatiality, *simultaneously* fused with ancestral privileges, in a way that connotes a deep sense of *inalienability*. If we accept that inalienability can be defined as a "restriction on the transferability, ownership, or use of an entitlement,"[2] it then implies that imagining Jos as the "epicenter of Christianity," by virtue of its grounding in the ancestral definition of land, organically correlates the *preservation* of land with the perpetuity of Christianity. In other words, any sort of infringement on such land not only is inherently immoral and disempowering but represents a form of despatialization that undermines Christian identities and cosmologies. Thus, the current *threat* to its territorial integrity by the predatory invasions of Fulani militias and their (alleged) audacity of "grabbing"[3] ancestral lands has created anxieties about the implicit demise of the *sense of the Indigenous* as well as the *death* of Christianity among the Christian populations. This chapter, therefore, argues that both the (re)affirmation of ancestral spatial rights and the Hausa-Fulani monolithic reconfiguration of place are inconsistent with the spatiality of "simultaneity" espoused by critical spatial theories.[4]

Accordingly, I use a combination of ethnographic data and quantitative cartographical software methodologies to achieve my aims. On the one hand, I draw on data collected during fieldwork (November 2014 to July 2019) in Nigeria, where I conducted unstructured interviews and made nonparticipant observations. On the other hand, I also utilize ESRI ArcGIS cartographical software along with Google Earth Pro (version 7.3.2.5776) to represent and analyze the various settlements that were attacked, their inhabitants evicted, and how efforts were made by the aggressors to erase the spatial presence (in some cases completely) of the Other. This work also gleans data from media sources like YouTube, WhatsApp posts, and secondary data collected from Jos.

HAUSA ETHNIC MIGRATION AND SPATIAL VISIBILITY IN JOS NORTH

Hausa-Fulani migration to the Jos area started before the colonial invasion, mostly through economic transactions, slave raids, and jihadic expeditions.

---

[2] Susan Rose-Ackerman, "Inalienability and the Theory of Property Rights," *Columbia Law Review* 85, no. 5 (January 1, 1985): 931–69.

[3] In Defense of Christians, "IDC Press Conference on Genocide of Nigerian Christians," YouTube video, June 25, 2020, https://www.youtube.com/watch?v=8s0t4Z2pg4k.

[4] Kim Knott, *The Location of Religion: A Spatial Analysis* (Abingdon, UK: Routledge, 2014); Doreen Massey, "Politics and Space/Time," in *Place and the Politics of Identity*, ed. Michael Keith and Steve Pile (London: Routledge, 1993), 139–59; Michel Foucault, "Of Other Spaces (1967)," in *Heterotopia and the City: Public Space in a Postcivil Society*, ed. Michiel Dehaene and Lieven De Cauter (London: Routledge, 2008), 13–30.

The exact time that the first batch of Hausa-Fulani came to the Jos area is not known, but academic literature places their presence around the Plateau area in the seventeenth century.[5] While it is on record that the Indigenous polities of Jos and their lands were never subjugated under the caliphate of Uthman dan Fodio, these polities, however, entered a nonaggression pact (*Amana*) with Ibrahim dan Yakubu, the jihad flag bearer of Bauchi.[6] Bauchi is one of the thirty-six states that share a boundary with Jos North to the north. Such political configurations and spatial proximity encouraged Hausa migration to satellite villages and settlements close to the city of Jos North. Ultimately, one of these satellite settlements, Naraguta, became the place where the British mining engineer C. H. Law of the Royal Niger Company set up his first head-quarters in 1903.[7]

Law's discovery of high-quality tin ore at Ibi in 1902 triggered the second and most significant wave of Hausa migration as well as the migration of other ethnic groups from different parts of the country to the Jos area. The prospects of substantial commercial mining activity also created the need for a significant labor force, in which the Indigenous polities were hardly interested, in contrast to the Hausas, who were more than willing to meet the demand. The Indigenous tried to resist the economic ambition of the colonialists but were brutally subdued by the combined army of Hausa and Yoruba led by Law with the use of sophisticated weaponry.[8] This so-called *pacification* of the Indigenous groups resulted in major mining expeditions and the birth of Jos's urban center. According to economic historian Bill Freund,

> The rapid growth of a laboring population on the Plateau that was willing to work for the money wage was absolutely essential. Most of this labor came from a great distance. In order to expand operations from Jos in 1906 Col. Law brought up labor from Lokoja—Yorubas, Hausas, and Nupes—who were then trained in pick-and-shovel work. In 1906–1907 Naraguta market began to develop and attract traders and men looking for work. From this time on, labor began to appear on the Plateau from the central Hausa-speaking areas of Northern Nigeria: Kano, Zaria, Bauchi, followed by Kanuri from Borno. By 1909, the mines were said to have attracted a "floating mining population

---

[5] John Nengel, "The Polities and Cultures of Plateau State," in *Centenary History of Plateau State 1914–2014*, ed. Monday Y. Mangvwat and Chris M. A. Kwaja (Jos, Nigeria: Vis Art Nigeria, 2015), 21–66.

[6] Nengel, 47.

[7] Monday Y. Mangvwat, Timothy B. Parlong, and Fidelis M. Longban, "From Colonial Conquest to 1926," in Mangvwat and Kwaja, *Centenary History*, 77.

[8] Leonard Plotnicov, *Strangers to the City: Urban Man in Jos, Nigeria* (Pittsburgh: University of Pittsburgh Press, 1971), 33.

of 9,000." In 1914, the "floating mines population" was estimated at 9,570, together with a Hausa immigrant community of 2,250.[9]

This constant influx of Hausa migrants to the Jos area and the economic significance of the growing tin industry eventually led to the birth of the city of Jos North. The Indigenous polities, however, resented working in the tin mines; they saw it not only as the inversion of their ancestral territory but also as a distraction from their normal life of subsistence farming. The Hausa-Fulani Muslim migrants, on the other hand, by cooperating with the British colonialists, successfully populated the geographical space that now constitutes the heart of the city and other places beyond the city boundaries. Consequently, their spatial presence gave the Hausa-Fulani the privilege of partly configuring the landscape of the city by inscribing their unique spatial forms on it as well as creating significant memories that tie them to the city.

The sociospatial configurations of most Hausa-Fulani settlements in Jos North are saturated with all kinds of Islamic religious markers and spatial practices. Major places in the city were named after accomplished Hausa-Fulani personalities, like Ali Kazure, Ibrahim Kashim, Balarabe, and Turaki, among others. Other places were given Hausa names, like Angwan Rogo, Layin Zana, Farin Wata, and Dogon Karfe, thereby replacing their Indigenous names and identity. The landscapes of most Hausa-Fulani settlements are replete with the histories of Islamic activities so profoundly that they tend to elicit spatial identities objectified by the iconic presence of Islamic clothing styles (especially for women and elderly males); incense and perfume brought from the Middle East; the religious names of primary and secondary schools and private business enterprises; Islamic medicine stores; the sounds of *tafsir* or *warzi* (preaching) and the call to prayer from numerous mosques' loudspeakers; ad hoc prayer moments and points (*musallah*) by the roadside, in front of business centers, under the shade of trees, and at official roadside demarcations in the city; the daily sights and sounds of children reciting the Qur'an at *makaratan alo* (qur'anic schools); and the public use and display of Islamic prayer rosaries (*tisbi*) and pictures of revered Sufi figures, among others. Such spatial configurations of these settlements significantly highlight the social and spatial visibility of the Hausa-Fulani as well as their Islamic identity.

In contrast, the history of missionary activities and Christianity in Jos is not only profound but defining. For most Christians, the name of the city is synonymous with Christianity to such an extent that the letters that constitute "Jos" are interpreted as *Jesus Our Savior*. Among other things, to objectify such a signification, Christians refer to the presence of prominent theological institutions:

---

[9] Bill Freund, *Capital and Labour in the Nigerian Tin Mines* (London: Longman, 1981), 50–53.

the headquarters of big Christian churches that have a significant influence in northern Nigeria and beyond; the missionary agencies that have a significant presence of Americans and Europeans; the Christian population, which stands at 85 percent in the city and across the state;[10] the presence of Christian book-shops, Christian publishing companies, and Christian music studios; and of course, the vivid presence of Pentecostal churches dotting every interstice of its urban landscape.[11]

To complicate such contrasting spatialities of the city of Jos, the impact of over four decades of repeated conflict has become a force that drives and is driven by the spatial transitioning of the city along religious lines. According to Danfulani and Gaiya, "Conflict has produced and left in its wake the culture of religious everything," where religious communities are ramped up with the passion for spatially labeling and permeating the urban space with religious symbols.[12] To them, this has led to the strong (re)assertion and (re)inser-tions of religious identities in urban centers in northern Nigeria. They argue that repeated conflict in the region has led to "aggressive competition for religious space and territory" and "has dramatically and drastically changed the religious geography and landscape of Nigeria."[13] As a result, Danfulani and Gaiya note how the "geography of religious expression [is] important in understanding the new face of religion in Nigeria."[14] In other words, the chang-ing reality of the complex relationships of religious adherents with the spatial dimensions of urban centers in the region needs a holistic and critical investi-gation. To address this concern, I explore in-depth the anxieties of Christians in Jos North about the predatory invasions of Fulani militias and their alleged audacity of "grabbing" ancestral lands by focusing on their efforts to eliminate the spatiality of the Other from the physical geographies of different localities in Jos South, Barkin Ladi, and Riyom. Suffice it to say that such phenomena are prevalent in many places within Plateau State and across Middle Belt states such as Kaduna, Benue, and Nasarawa, among others. Focusing on Jos North, it is germane to clarify the larger context of the struggle over its identity and ownership.

---

[10] Plotnicov, *Strangers to the City*, 31.

[11] Umar H. D. Danfulani, "Religious Exclusivism & Religious Space," *Exchange* 27, no. 4 (1998): 342–59.

[12] Umar H. D. Danfulani and Ahmadu Barnabas Musa Gaiya, "The Interplay between Art and Religious Metaphors: Popular Christianity in Nigeria's Religious Space," unpublished paper, n.d., p. 2.

[13] Danfulani and Gaiya, 2.

[14] Danfulani and Gaiya, 2.

HAUSA AND FULANI NARRATIVES OF JOS

The Hausa and Fulani narratives of Jos North are built around four core propositions. First, they argue that they found and occupied the Jos area as virgin land. Second, the Hausa-Fulani maintain that they have the population size that justifies their ownership of the city.[15] Third, they argue that they have existed in the area much longer and, above all, have labored more by contributing to the social and economic configuration of the city.[16] Fourth, they further state that eleven of their people (*Sarki*) have served as chiefs of Jos's native town from 1902 to 1947. Nevertheless, imperial powers in the middle of the nineteenth century subjugated them under the chieftaincy of Berom, Gbong Gwom Jos. For them, this was not just an act of injustice but also an act that diminished their capacity for territorial influence.[17] With such a historical contribution to the growth of the city, the Hausa-Fulani assume that this should be sufficient grounds for them to be accepted equally not only as autochthonous to the area but as legitimate owners (as it were) of the city.

THE "INDIGENOUS" NARRATIVE
AND LOCAL SCHOLARSHIP OF JOS

Rather than look at the narrative of Jos North by the three "Indigenous groups" (Anaguta, Berom, and Afezere) of the area separately, this section will examine them together. I do this because when it comes to challenging the Hausa-Fulani claims, all three share a number of things in common, differing mainly with respect to where the exact limits of boundaries to their territories start and end. Also, there is a consensus among these groups of having a common ancestry, shared cultural values, and some language similarities. Suffice it to say here that among the many works written by Indigenous people of Plateau State, the one that most eloquently captures their argument is the book published by the Plateau Indigenous Development Association Network (PIDAN). PIDAN is an association of the ethnic groups of Plateau State that brings under its auspices all ethnic groups from parts of the Plateau beyond the boundary of Jos North.

The arguments of the "Indigenous groups" represented by PIDAN against the Hausa-Fulani claim of ownership of Jos are built on four core premises. First, they maintain that the early Hausa-Fulani settlers were migrant ethnic

---

[15] Shedrack Gaya Best, *Conflict and Peace Building in Plateau State, Nigeria* (Ibadan, Nigeria: Spectrum Books, 2007), 24.

[16] *The Truth about the Hausa of Jos*, vol. 1 (Jos, Nigeria: Coalition of Jasawa Community Development Association, 2013), 28–29.

[17] *Truth about the Hausa of Jos*, 28.

laborers who came to Jos to work in the tin mines.[18] Unlike the Hausa-Fulani narrative, PIDAN argues that the presence of Anaguta, Berom, and Afezere Indigenous groups in the current site of the city goes beyond recent memories. They draw on archival, colonial, anthropological, and archaeological documents to assert their ancestral rights to the area. From this evidence, they insist that the current site of the Jos Plateau has been inhabited by prehistoric polities dating back to 37,000 BCE.[19] For instance, PIDAN has noted that the Nok civilization (250 BCE to 1000 CE), renowned for terracotta head sculpture and iron smelting, is regarded as the earliest in a large area, which also includes the city of Jos.[20] The second premise of the PIDAN argument is that Jos was never a conquered territory; thus, it cannot be claimed by any other group. Third, the Indigenous groups resent the idea that because some of the place names are in Hausa, that means the city belongs to them. For them, under colonial subjugation, the original native place names were changed and tactfully perverted through faulty pronunciations by the Hausa and Fulani immigrants. Finally, they argue that while the Hausa and Fulani are not willing to accommodate other people's cultures, they nevertheless demand that others should embrace theirs.[21] PIDAN sees this antiassimilation posture as a form of cultural arrogance and imperialism that is bent on destroying their cultural heritage and identity.[22]

JOS NORTH AND ITS ENVIRONS

At the battle of Naraguta in 1873, the allied forces of all the Indigenous ethnic groups of Jos fought and defeated the Islamic jihadists of Uthman dan Fodio to avert subjugation and secure their ancestral land against forced appropriations.[23] The memory of this victory, combined with other arguments, is drawn upon by the area's current Indigenous polities (who are mostly Christians) to undermine any real or imagined ambitions by the Hausa-Fulani Muslims to assert themselves as owners of the city. The sense of invincibility that this historical act creates and the perpetual quest for territorial freedom handed down by

---

[18] PIDAN, *Effects of the Jos/Plateau Conflicts and Crises, and Their Implications on Nigeria's National Security: The PIDAN Perspective*, vol. 2, no. 1 (Jos, Nigeria: La'Suk Publications, 2013), 14–20.

[19] PIDAN, *The History, Ownership, Establishment of Jos and Misconceptions about the Recurrent Jos Conflicts*, vol. 1, no. 1 (Jos, Nigeria: DAN-SiL, 2010), 1–3.

[20] See also Thurstan Shaw, "The Nok Sculptures of Nigeria," *Scientific American* 244, no. 2 (1981): 154–67.

[21] PIDAN, *History, Ownership, Establishment*, 31.

[22] Danfulani, "Jos Peace Conference."

[23] Anthony Dung Bingel, *Jos, Origins and Growth of the Town, 1900 to 1972* (Jos, Nigeria: Dept. of Geography, University of Jos, 1978), 2.

their ancestors continue to frame how the Christian population in Jos North now imagines the intentions of Hausa-Fulani Muslims.

Furthermore, not willing to lose the geopolitical agencies bequeathed to them by their ancestors, the current Indigenous residents of the cities tend to deploy specific forms of *spatial hermeneutics* that help them understand and navigate the political landscapes of the northern region as well as those of the nation. For instance, the call for Sharia implementation in 1999 in twelve states by Muslims in northern Nigeria not only triggered conflict but also intensified the anxieties of non-Muslims in the region and probably the nation as well. This situation was exacerbated by the emergence of the terrorist group Boko Haram and the growth of the Muslim population, driven mostly by a high birth rate.[24] This has led to Christians feeling spatially threatened and ideologically uncertain about the future of their identity in the region.

This predisposition was complicated even further when such spatial sensibilities, rooted in Indigenous cosmology, became central to Christian spatial imaginations in ways that now lead them to (re)secure the ideological identity of place against the fear of despatialization by the Other in an era of seismic spatial shifts. Christian residents of the city see it as their mission to obey the "will of God" in ways that play a significant role in (re)shaping the spatial identity of the city. Thus, their allegiance to a "higher power" plays a significant role in the process of space production (physical, social, and cognitive) in Jos North. Whether it accelerates or slows the process, the obligation to adhere to divine dictates demonstrates an effort to ensure the preservation of space in order to sustain an ideological hegemony. Presently, this has led to efforts among Indigenous Christian landowners to make it difficult for Muslims to have access to available land.[25] In the past, they were criticized by other Christian immigrants to the city for being careless with their land. For example, one informant noted, "The local Anaguta, especially Berom, to some extent, the Afezere on the eastern side are seriously criticized by the Igbos and the Yoruba [ethnic migrants from eastern and western Nigeria] for selling their lands. You know, if you interact with especially the outsiders, they will seriously blame them; they complain about the encroachment of Islam, but they are very eager to sell their lands and get money out of it."[26]

One of the reasons for such criticism is the implicit assumption that when Hausa-Fulani Muslims seek and acquire land as immigrants in the diaspora for

---

[24] Interview with Janet A. Olubunmi, Jos North, January 20, 2015.

[25] Philip Ostien, "Jonah Jang and the Jasawa: Ethno-religious Conflict in Jos, Nigeria" (SSRN research paper, Social Science Research Network, Rochester, NY, August 2009), https://ssrn.com/abstract=1456372.

[26] Interview with Danny McCain, Jos North, January 6, 2015.

business or residential purposes, they will then proceed to invite more of their kith and kin to join them.[27] The suspicion here is that by using this strategy, the Hausa-Fulani grow their population to the point where they can politically assert themselves and claim ownership of their host land. Thus, the refusal to sell land, according to an informant, is "to stop the advance of Islam by holding on to those properties that were traditional Christian areas; at least, it gives some kind of self-satisfaction that we are doing our little part by not selling that property."[28] With such a way of imagining the Other, the current predatorial invasion of villages outside the city of Jos by Fulani militia is interpreted as not only genocidal but the "grabbing" of ancestral land and the permanent displacement of their original inhabitants.

Suffice it to say here that the ideological and cultural configuration of other spatial entities beyond the city borders and what happens in them affects the stability of Jos North as well as shapes how Christians perceive religious interaction in the city. The attempt to isolate the urban center and examine it alone without regard to other spatial units outside its boundary provides a limited understanding of the forces that feed into its spatial identity. For instance, Jos North, as one of the seventeen LGAs of Plateau State, is made up of over twenty electoral wards as well as eighteen localities. While the Anaguta, Afezere, and Berom are the immediate *Indigenous* residents of Jos, their ability to wield spatial significance in Jos North is also a function of the city's spatial ties with other places outside its domain. In other words, out of the remaining sixteen LGAs, fourteen are nonemirate geopolitical entities and are significantly dominated by Christians and adherents of Indigenous religions. The mixed membership of people from all the LGAs in Plateau State in churches such as the Evangelical Church Winning All (ECWA) and the Church of Christ in Nations (COCIN), among others, demonstrate the nuances and spatiality of such inter- and intralocal ties.[29] Such spatial ecumenicity forged from multiple localities and framed by the boundary of the church and Plateau State gives birth to the imagery of the seed that one sees in the poem quoted at the beginning of this essay, about the identity of Jos as Christian.

The Despatialization of Jos North
and the Spatiality of Simultaneity

After the first major violence broke out in 2001, conflicts continued to plague Jos and its environs down to the present. As these conflicts spread to villages

---

[27] Interview with Janet A. Olubunmi, Jos North, January 20, 2015.

[28] Interview with John Soemlat, Jos North, August 31, 2015.

[29] The complexity of these intra- and interlocal ties that are vivified by the boundaries of the Christian church is outside the scope of this essay.

and towns beyond the city borders, they took on a different dimension, with the aggressors on both sides using a significant amount of force to despatialize the presence of the Other from the physical landscape of Jos North, Jos South, Barkin Ladi, and Riyom. In other words, houses, religious buildings, and any material traces of the imagined *enemy* were selected, targeted, and destroyed. In some cases, these acts of spatial derepresentation of the Other were partial, but in other cases, they were total to the point that when nature reclaimed most of these lands, it became almost impossible to think that settlements had once existed at those sites. From 2010 to the present, Fulani predatorial militias have systematically invaded and obliterated villages mostly dominated by Christians. Out of the many Christian villages[30] attacked by Fulani militias and destroyed completely are Gashish, Rantis, Ruku, Shonong, Razat, Zim, Sagas, Dajak, and Kampwas in Jos South, Barkin Ladi, and Riyom. On the other hand, Kuru Karama and Kuru Babba are two Hausa-Fulani settlements (products of the history of colonial tin mining) in Jos South that were attacked, their residents killed, and the entire settlement despatialized.[31]

In retaliation, the Hausa-Fulani settlements of Kuru Karama and Kuru Babba were invaded and destroyed in January 2010 by angry Berom youths bent on preserving the territorial integrity of their ancestral land. The atrocities inflicted on these settlements were quite disturbing. On the nineteenth of that month, Kuru Babba, a settlement of about 0.1 square kilometers (15.8 acres) in size, about 29 kilometers from the city of Jos, was destroyed entirely. Currently, there is little or no visible evidence of its existence until that time (see figs. 1 and 2). And in Kuru Karama, over 150 residents were killed and their bodies dumped in a well. About 22.9 acres of the built residential area of Kuru Karama were destroyed (see figs. 3 and 4),[32] making one wonder why such pulverizing aggression was used on these communities.

As Adam Higazi has noted, the Fulani and Berom people had once lived together in peace, depending on each other for their social and economic existence.[33] While the Berom as farmers would allow the cows belonging to Fulani herdsmen to graze on their corn stalks after harvest, the manure of cows belonging

---

[30] It is important to mention here that the use of the phrase *Christian villages* refers to villages with a significant population of Christians. This important caveat avoids an essentialist depiction of these villages. In such villages, there is still a significant number of practitioners of indigenous religions.

[31] For more on this, see Human Rights Watch, *"Leave Everything to God": Accountability for Inter-communal Violence in Plateau and Kaduna States, Nigeria* (New York: Human Rights Watch, 2013); and Adam Higazi, "Farmer-Pastoralist Conflicts on the Jos Plateau, Central Nigeria: Security Responses of Local Vigilantes and the Nigerian State," *Conflict, Security & Development* 16, no. 4 (July 3, 2016): 365–85.

[32] Another version of these images (figs. 3 and 4) was presented in Human Rights Watch, *"Leave Everything to God,"* 50–51.

[33] Higazi, "Farmer-Pastoralist Conflicts," 371.

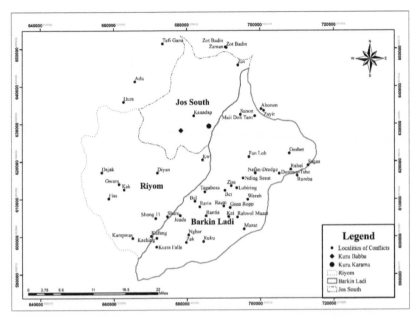

MAP 1: Localities of conflicts in Jos South, Riyom, and Barkin Ladi

to the Fulani would, in turn, fertilize the Berom farmlands for the future planting season.[34] One of the drawbacks of their relationship in the past was in the area of inter-ethno-religious marriage. This is because Fulani men were able to marry Berom women, but it was virtually impossible for Berom men to marry Fulani women.[35] With this said, the Berom and the Fulani had a history of mutual civility. In the event of any disputes, they had had recourse to nonviolent solutions.[36] However, this relationship began to deteriorate when the Berom, doubting the Nigerian government's ability to provide for their security or to retaliate to the extent they wanted,[37] turned to violence to "defend" themselves and their ancestral land.[38]

While Kuru Karama and Kuru Babba were destroyed in 2010, from 2012 Christian villages have been invaded down to the present and their inhabitants massacred by the Fulani-Muslim militia. However, with some academics interpreting the whole saga in terms of farmer-herder clashes, Christians are beginning to object to such a categorization. Given the pattern, the identities of their

---

[34] Higazi, 371.

[35] Danfulani, "Jos Peace Conference."

[36] World Watch Monitor, "Rev. Gideon Para-Mallam," YouTube video, June 28, 2018, https://www.youtube.com/watch?v=9A2Rmy5U67E.

[37] "Nigeria: Unfolding Genocide? New APPG Report Launched," APPG for International Freedom of Religion or Belief, June 15, 2020, 8, https://appgfreedomofreligionorbelief.org/nigeria-unfolding-genocide-new-appg-report-launched/.

[38] Interview with Gyang Da, August 9, 2020.

FIGURE 1: Kuru Babba, February 14, 2011, before destruction

FIGURE 2: Kuru Babba, January 3, 2012, after destruction

FIGURE 3: Kuru Karama, March 27, 2009, before destruction

FIGURE 4: Kuru Karama, December 7, 2011, after destruction

targets, and the ferocity of the force employed by the militias, Christians are convinced that Fulani aggressions are a genocidal mission to Islamize Jos and the lands beyond its borders. In the words of Benjamin Kwashi, "[Academics] have always explained it away as farmer-and-herders clashes." For him, this is "an evil cover-up." He emphasizes that "these are calculated, systematic, intentional killing of people and driving them away from their land."[39] Another prominent clergyman in Jos could hardly imagine how "the same Fulani people that had been living peacefully with the farmers" could suddenly "change from using sticks to rear their cows" to a highly militarized outfit armed with sophisticated weapons.[40] He contemplated further how "all of a sudden" Fulani militiamen were "going to the farmlands, killing farmers, surrounding whole villages wiping out Christian farmers, killing their wives, killing their children, burning their homes, displacing them."[41] His explanation for such aggression is that "very clearly, an agenda is emerging. Why Jos? For the simple reason that these attacks began in Jos, spread to other parts of Nigeria particularly, the Middle Belt, and it is now coming back to Jos with horrible mass killings in large numbers taking place, and dozens of villages wiped out within days. It is a pointer; it is a reality. *Because Jos is the epicenter of Christianity, Plateau state is the epic center [sic] of Christianity in the North, in the middle belt, and significantly in Nigeria.*"[42]

While this seems to be a substantive interpretation with a definite theological-spiritual dimension to it, the observation about how "dozens of villages [are] wiped out" has a level of empirical validity. By relying on a list of localities with their geographical coordinates, sourced from my fieldwork in Jos, I scanned the satellite images of these locations on Google Earth by utilizing its "historical imagery tool." From my search of these locations, I examined the level of destruction wreaked upon them. It was an exercise that involved going back to past satellite images in the Google Earth geodatabase to the sites of the settlements before they were attacked and scrolling forward to the years after their destruction. After scanning for their locations on Google Earth, I discovered that more than fifteen of them were either partially destroyed or despatialized completely in Barkin Ladi and Riyom LGAs (see figs. 1–6). Suffice it to say that the tracking of these villages was not exhaustive. However, there is a growing consensus among Christians that some of these villages are currently occupied by Fulani, while their original residents either had to flee to other villages or are now in internally displaced camps (IDC) in Jos.[43]

---

39 World Watch Monitor, "Rev. Gideon Para-Mallam."
40 World Watch Monitor.
41 World Watch Monitor.
42 World Watch Monitor (italics mine).
43 Interview with Gyang Da, August 9, 2020.

FIGURE 5: Dajak settlement, March 27, 2011, before destruction

FIGURE 6: Dajak settlement, January 15, 2014, after destruction

FIGURE 7: Sharus settlement, March 27, 2011, before destruction

FIGURE 8: Sharus settlement, January 8, 2014, after destruction

FIGURE 9: Kufang settlement, January 12, 2012, before destruction

FIGURE 10: Kufang settlement, January 8, 2014, after destruction

FIGURE 11: Zim settlement, November 10, 2010, before destruction

FIGURE 12: Zim settlement, October 21, 2016, after destruction

The constant contestations over the identity and ownership of the city of Jos and lands beyond its borders have led to the politicization of historical, anthropological, and archaeological data in order to serve particular group interests and to advance a specific spatial ideology. It has been difficult for most studies to avoid becoming platforms that advance the spatial sentiments, ideological missions, or territorial aspirations of a particular group. While this seems to be the case, most academic studies have interpreted the predatorial invasions of Christian villages by Fulani militia from a materialistic-functional perspective. First, some argue that the invasion of villages and eviction of ethnic inhabitants from their ancestral land by Fulani militia and their subsequent occupation of these lands are rooted in climate change. According to the International Crisis Group, "As drought and desertification have dried up springs and streams across Nigeria's far northern Sahelian belt, large numbers of herders have had to search for alternative pastures and sources of water for their cattle."[44] They argue that the combination of such migrations and population growth in the regions where the Fulani have become resident immigrants has resulted in competition for scarce resources and the demand for land.[45] Second, other studies explain the nature of the aggression between the Fulani and the Jos ethnic groups in terms of the existing political framework and the weak security approach of the current government of Muhammadu Buhari. This approach sees the framing of the Nigerian constitution in terms of indigenes who enjoy certain privileges and nonindigenes who are excluded as discriminatory and in dire need of rectification.[46] Also, some observers have argued that the government's inadequate security response and failure to apprehend offenders have emboldened the aggressors to constantly be on the rampage in the region's villages.[47] These perspectives, among others, are the various ways that herder-farmer clashes have been explained. However, little has been said about how the (re)affirmation of ancestral spatial rights by the Jos ethnic groups and the Hausa-Fulani monolithic reconfiguration of place are inconsistent with the spatiality of "simultaneity" espoused by critical spatial theories.

Drawing on the works of Henri Lefebvre, Michel Foucault, Doreen Massey, and other scholars of religious and secular studies, Kim Knott has developed

---

[44] "Stopping Nigeria's Spiralling Farmer-Herder Violence," International Crisis Group, July 26, 2018, https://www.crisisgroup.org/africa/west-africa/nigeria/262-stopping-nigerias-spiralling-farmer-herder-violence.

[45] "Stopping Nigeria's Spiralling."

[46] See Ostien, "Jonah Jang"; and Johan Andersson, Joanna Sadgrove, and Gill Valentine, "Consuming Campus: Geographies of Encounter at a British University," *Social & Cultural Geography* 13, no. 5 (August 2012): 501–15.

[47] World Watch Monitor, "Rev. Gideon Para-Mallam."

spatial tools for examining contested spaces, whether religious or nonreligious.[48] While such an analytical framework helps "constitute an aide mémoire for spatially interrogating a place in all its complexity,"[49] this essay will only utilize aspects of the spatial method[50] to examine the "multiple shifting spatial nodes of powers" embedded in the African religious landscape.[51] The aspects that are of interest to my argument here involve what Knott refers to as the properties of space: configuration, extension, simultaneity, and power.[52] For Knott, the spatial concept of configuration has the capacity to bring all things into a "closure in which other things . . . are brought together, gathered or configured."[53] In the words of Massey, "Space is the sphere of the possibility of the existence of multiplicity; that is space 'as the sphere in which distinct trajectories co-exist; as the sphere therefore of co-existing heterogeneity.'"[54] The second quality, according to Massey, is "a sphere of dynamic simultaneity, constantly disconnected by new arrivals, constantly waiting to be determined (and therefore always undetermined) by the construction of new relations."[55] Extension as the third quality of space represents how "synchronous spaces contain the past within them."[56] This means that the current existing spaces are the extensions of those in the past. "All intersections and configurations," therefore, "are the fluid outworkings of earlier occurrences or causes. They extend from those, in the past, to other events and consequences in the future."[57] Finally, while space is not ahistorical, it is the manifestation of social relations, which implies the existence of power dynamics. For Knott, "it is the capacity of space to be shot through with ideology that makes it power-full."[58] She argues that space can be "used to contain, even obliterate others. Spaces through construction and manipulation of boundaries are used to include and exclude."[59]

The efforts to obliterate the settlement of the ethnic Other on the basis of religious and ethnic identities in order to fine-tune the spatiality of Jos to

---

[48] Kim Knott, "Spatial Theory and Method for the Study of Religion," *Temenos—Nordic Journal of Comparative Religion* 41, no. 2 (September 1, 2005): 153–84.

[49] Kim Knott, "Spatial Methods," in *The Routledge Handbook of Research Methods in the Study of Religion*, ed. Michael Stausberg and Steven Engler (London: Routledge, 2011), 496.

[50] For a detailed understanding of the spatial method, see Knott, *Location of Religion*, 2014.

[51] Doreen Massey and Pat Jess, "The Conceptualization of Place," in *A Place in the World? Places, Cultures and Globalization*, ed. Doreen Massey and Pat Jess (New York: Oxford University Press, 1995), 45–75.

[52] Kim Knott, *The Location of Religion: A Spatial Analysis* (London: Equinox, 2005), 20–28.

[53] Knott, "Spatial Theory," 9.

[54] Doreen B. Massey, *For Space* (London: SAGE, 2005), 9.

[55] Massey, 107.

[56] Knott, *Location of Religion*, 2014, 21.

[57] Knott, 22.

[58] Knott, 25.

[59] Knott, 27.

resonate with a way of being tend to undermine the spatial quality of simultaneity as defined above by Massey. Self-evidently, while simultaneity is a spatial fact, a religious adherent's cognitive perceptions of space may be homogeneously idealistic. That is to say, religious believers tend to prefer utopian homogeneity as an inoculation against what I refer to as spatial proselytization in order to eliminate contradictions that challenge the dominant narrative. In other words, the existence of a rival religious spatial form acts as a provocateur of critical questioning and the driver of self-reflection that may undermine the authority of the dominant religious worldview in a given place.

The answer to the question raised earlier about the extreme aggression perpetrated by the Berom on the spatialities of Kuru Karama and Kuru Babba might seem simple, but a closer look reveals specific nuances and subtleties. As it appears, the audacity to assert *ownership* and possession of lands that are deemed as ancestral, a privilege reserved for the Indigenous, amounts to a violation that is not only inherently immoral; it also represents a form of despatialization that undermines Indigenous identities and cosmologies. In their submission to the Center for Humanitarian Dialogue, the Berom argued that "northern Muslim incursions into our traditional spaces are being driven by a specifically religious intention—namely, as part of a jihad, to take control first of Jos North." For them, "this is a strategic political and economic onslaught to Islamize, colonize and annihilate Berom."[60] However, one wonders whether the despatializations of Kuru Karama and Kuru Babba are acts of pure anger, acts of revenge, or efforts at erasing the material visibilities of the Other with the aim of asserting ethnic homogeneity. If the latter is the case, it then implies that such spatial defaulting of land is a way of reversing and (re)securing ancestral lands and their significations against the supposed tides of Islamization or caliphization. As Yusufu Turaki notes,

> Today, what are the motivating factors for the Fulani Headsmen killings of indigenes? It is land. During the caliphate period, it [was] land. Today, it is land; the Fulani wants land. And therefore, they come to kill; they come to occupy and destroy, so they have the land. So, these are the motivating factors. The Fulani are an ethnic group, the Fulani, the majority of them are Moslems and so they use Islamic values. They use ethnic values in order to entrench their position in Nigeria. And that is what is inflaming the situation, while the other groups are saying, hay! Why are you coming to take our land? Why are you imposing yourself upon our ancestral land?[61]

---

[60] Unpublished document, "Progress Report: On HD/Jos Peace Dialogue Forum, Achievements and the Way Forward, Submitted to Mr. Paul Rushton (Programme Analyst Africa, Ottawa Office), Thursday, 5th March, 2015."

[61] World Watch Monitor, "Rev. Gideon Para-Mallam."

Such a way of imagining and the unremitting predatorial invasions of Christian villages by Fulani militias and their alleged audacity of "grabbing"[62] ancestral lands have created anxieties about the implicit demise of the *sense of the Indigenous* as well as the *death* of Christianity among the Christian populations. Thus, there is now a growing patriotic aspiration among Christians/ Indigenous that is leading to the (re)affirmation of ancestral spatial rights that engenders conditions conducive to the ethnic spatialization of Christianity and its territorialization. In the poem quoted at the beginning of this essay, Plateau State represents the "seed" that will "germinate" regardless of all the attempts to bury it. The significance of such a way of imagining the spatiality of Plateau State comes out in the same stanza of the poem, which reconstrues the real meaning of Jos as "JOS" ("Jesus Our Savior"), making any and all attempts at subjugating Jos eternally impossible. Thus, the sense of the Indigenous and Christianity intersect to ignite a patriotic passion for land that catalyzes the spatial transitioning of place along the lines of a specific ideology.

ANCESTRAL LAND RIGHTS AND THE CONCERNS OF DESPATIALIZING THE IDENTITY OF JOS NORTH

In most African folk societies, the convictions about ancestors and the centrality of their powers in the sociocultural existence of most ethnic groups are very profound, Nigeria included. Members of the Niki Tobi commission drew extensively on such African spatial understandings of Indigeneity to deliver their verdict in favor of the Indigenous ethnic groups of Jos. The final verdict of the commission was as follows:

> The [Hausa] elders owe posterity the duty to tell the youth the truth that the Hausa was not the founder of Jos and, therefore, not the owner of the city. They should alas tell the youth where they came from so that the youth may know their *ancestral homes* or roots. . . . Mere rhetoric, which has no relationship with the past, cannot pass the test of valid and authentic history. It will be tantamount to selling or disgracing history if tin mine workers are said to be the owner of the *town Jos* when there is clear evidence that they came for tin mining labor and met the natives, the owners of Jos.[63]

The verdict of the Niki Tobi commission quoted above assumes that the criterion of ancestral ties to place is sufficient spatial evidence to vest the right

---

[62] In Defense of Christians, "IDC Press Conference."

[63] *Government White Paper Report of the Judicial Commission of Inquiry into the Civil Disturbances in Jos and Its Environs September 2001* (Jos, Nigeria: Plateau State Government, 2009), 51–57 (italics mine).

of ownership to a group of people.[64] However, one wonders how such a position is sustainable in the era of hypermobilities and "superdiversity."[65] The question that comes to mind is how the ancestral sensibilities of Indigenous communities in Jos are being (re)shaped by the seismic spatial shift engendered by globalization and hypermobility. It seems the fusion of Christian and Indigenous cosmologies is forging a sense of rootedness that transforms the ethnicity of its practitioners and imbues it with inexhaustible passion for controlling the transitioning of place under the hegemony of a specific ideology. In this era of seismic spatial change, ancestral privileges continue to fuel the African imaginations in ways that engender a bounded sense of place and territoriality and spatialization of Christianity. It appears that it is hard to erase ancestral footprints. That is, beneath the visible landscape and topology of an African land are layers of spatial stories, memories and forms of entombment that vivify Indigenous ways of being. These are not just spatial references and footnotes that validate microcosmic ties but the underpinnings that sustain a collective group identity through space and time.

CONCLUSION

As my research has shown, the contemporaneous existence of different spatial formations on the physical landscape of the city of Jos and in the different LGAs of Plateau State seems to be testing African capacity for spatial pluralism, both for intra- and interfaith relations. Thus, unpacking the significance of accepting and respecting the visible and critical spatial presence of the Other in the city and across the state appears to be essential in order to engage religious differences at the most basic level. This essay, on the one hand, has argued that the (re)affirmation of ancestral spatial rights also engenders the conditions in which Christianity's ethnic spatialization and territorialization begin to occur. On the other hand, the Hausa-Fulani aggressive reconfiguration of place is inconsistent with the spatiality of "simultaneity" espoused by critical spatial theories. Foucault argues that "our era, on the other hand, seems to be of space. We are in the age of the simultaneous, of juxtaposition, the near and the far, the side by side and the scattered."[66]

Foucault's point brings us to the question previously raised: namely, "whether it is possible to reverse the process of spatial transitioning configured to serve a capitalist ideology and modernistic agenda in an era of simultaneity

---

[64] See also page 37, section 3:14 of the same report and the *Government White Paper Report of the Judicial Commission of Inquiry into the Riot of 12th April 1994 in Jos Metropolis* (Jos, Nigeria: Plateau State Government, 2009), 23.

[65] Andersson, Sadgrove, and Valentine, "Consuming Campus."

[66] Foucault, "Of Other Spaces (1967)," 14.

of space." On the face of it, the present era of human history appears to be corrosive to any project that pursues fixed boundary formations (even if the plan is to build walls) and ultimately tends to engender fading boundaries. Thus, is the agitation of the Indigenous Christians in Jos North a romantic and utopian spatial idealism or an ideological quest rooted in a premodern moral order and cosmologies that are diminishing in their capacity to shape social behaviors as cosmopolitanism and globalism advance?

CHAPTER 10

"BAD OMEN!"

NAKED AGENCY AND BODY POLITICS IN PUBLIC DISCOURSE AND CONTEMPORARY WORLD CHRISTIANITY

Ruth Vida Amwe

On July 23, 2020, hundreds of women, mostly Christian adherents, stormed the streets of Samaru Kataf in Atyap kingdom, located in the southern part of Kaduna, a state in northwestern Nigeria. In a year marked by a series of protests, this stood in juxtaposition to the unfolding realities of the coronavirus (Covid-19) global pandemic, which necessitated reduced human contact and the popularization of terms such as *social distancing* and *quarantine*, among others. Like many other countries—such as the United States, Hong Kong, Peru, and Chile—Nigeria witnessed its own share of mass demonstrations, including the #EndSARS protest in October of the same year, which attracted thousands of people to numerous rallies in major cities across the country and reverberated among Nigeria's diasporic population.[1] A prominent feature of the orchestration and execution of these protests was the centrality of the role of women as key instigators. Reporting for BBC News, Azeezat Olaoluwa chronicled the activism of women in the series of protests and captured the words of Aisha Yesufu, cofounder of the Bring Back Our Girls movement, whose image

---

[1] See Allwell Uwazuruike, "#EndSARS: The Movement against Police Brutality in Nigeria," *Harvard Human Rights Journal*, 2021, https://harvardhrj.com/2020/11/endsars-the-movement -against-police-brutality-in-nigeria/; Halima Gikandi, "Nigerians in the Diaspora Join #EndSARS Protests," World from PRX, accessed September 26, 2021, https://www.pri.org/stories/2020 -10-23/nigerians-diaspora-join-endsars-protests; "People of Faith in the USA Denounce the Shooting of Peaceful Protestors in Nigeria," Medium, accessed July 5, 2021, https://medium .com/@savviors/people-of-faith-in-the-usa-denounce-the-shooting-of-peaceful-protestors-in -nigeria-752793c606c7.

during the #EndSARS protest went viral, drawing both national and international attention. Affirming the notion that women formed the backbone of the #EndSARS protest, Yesufu declared, "Women have always been the ones who get things done. Any protest that led to change has always been women-led. . . . The EndSARS protest went as far as it did because of the role women played."[2]

However, in comparison to the #EndSARS protest, the event that took place on the streets of Samaru Kataf on July 23, 2020—the feelings it evoked as well as the natural and supranatural elements employed and deployed in and through the actions of its executants—ensured that it stood in distinction to the #EndSARS protest, complexifying the use of the word *protest* in describing the events.[3] By focusing on this event, which was arguably distinct in its cause, its purpose, its executants, and its significance, this chapter attempts to examine the resilience and deployment of Indigenous religious understandings of women's bodies in engaging public discourse. Using Laura Grillo's idea of female genital power and Naminata Diabate's concept of naked agency, I seek to explore how evangelical Christian women in northwestern Nigeria continue to employ their ritual power in moral critique while simultaneously entering into public discourse as critics. Primarily, this chapter seeks to do so in light of world Christianity and against the backdrop of the shift in the center of Christianity from the Global North to the Global South and the current status of Nigerian women as the typical representatives of the Christian faith today. It will draw out some implications for engaging gender and women's participation in public discourse and world Christianity discourse. I seek to engage how Indigenous and Christian religious identities are renegotiated, redeployed, and contested in African Christian women's cosmologies, worldviews, and lived experiences.

LOCATING ATYAP KINGDOM IN THE CONTEXT OF CONFLICT AND PUBLIC DISCOURSE

The Atyap society is located in the southeastern portion of the present-day Zangon Kataf local government area of Kaduna State in northeastern Nigeria. It forms part of the Nok culture complex in the upper river valley and shares linguistic, cultural, social, and religious affinities with other ethnic groups within the region, including the Bajju, Chawai, Bakulu, Kagoro, Ikulu, and Ham. They speak a language in the Kwa group of the Benue-Congo language family. In addition to the designation Atyap, they are also known as Kataf or Katab. The

---

[2] Azeezat Olaoluwa, "End Sars Protests: The Nigerian Women Leading the Fight for Change," *BBC News*, December 1, 2020, sec. Africa, https://www.bbc.com/news/world-africa-55104025.

[3] The use of the word *protest* in this chapter, particularly in relation to women's action of baring their naked bodies in public spaces, is to be understood in view of its inadequacy and its use only for lack of a better word.

designation Atyap is a derivative of *Tyap*, meaning "the people who speak Tyap."[4] In an analysis of the migratory experiences of their forebears prior to settling in their current location, Yoila Kimbers recounts that there exists a variety of oral accounts and mythologies about them, which speaks of their migratory movements as having begun from a source not far from their current location.[5]

Alongside other ethnic groups in the region of southern Kaduna, the Atyap community is predominantly Christian. This follows from a long history of Christian missionary presence and activity within the area. By the 1930s, four Christian missions—Sudan Interior Mission (SIM), the Roman Catholic Church Mission, the Church Missionary Society (CMS), and the Sudan United Mission (SUM)—had solidified their presence and were fully functional in southern Kaduna. These mission agencies worked throughout the area and had an enormous influence that included education, commerce, and religious and other social institutions. SIM was the largest and most established mission organization in this region. Its administrative headquarters of operation within Nigeria and other West African countries was located in Jos, in the neighboring state of Plateau, and was only a few hundred kilometers from southern Kaduna. As expected, Indigenous people in the vicinity became the majority in SIM missionary ventures.[6] In the 1950s, on the cusp of nationalism and independence movements, Indigenous Christians and SIM churches were incorporated into the denomination now known as the Evangelical Churches of West Africa (renamed Evangelical Church Winning All, or ECWA) with millions of members.[7]

The vibrancy of Christianity within the region is interspersed with the proliferation of Islam as well. Caught between the Islamic missionary movement emanating from majority-Arab North Africa, which was prevalent in the upper northern region of Nigeria, and Western Christian missionary movements radiating from the coastal regions of West Africa and making their way into the hinterlands from the southern part of the country, the Northwest/Middle Belt region of Nigeria therefore forms a key site of religious contestation.[8]

---

[4] See Achi Bala, "Local History in Post-Independent Africa," in *Writing African History*, ed. John Edward Philips (Rochester, NY: University of Rochester Press, 2007), 374–80.

[5] Yoila Yakubu Kimbers, "A Reconsideration of the Origin and Migrations of the Atyap People of Zangon Kataf Local Government Area of Kaduna State, Nigeria," *Journal of Tourism and Heritage Studies* 2, no. 2 (2013): 71–76.

[6] See Yusufu Turaki, *An Introduction to the History of SIM/ECWA in Nigeria, 1893–1993* (Jos, Nigeria: Challenge, 1993); and Samuel Waje Kunhiyop, *Christian Conversion in Africa: The Bajju Experience* (Jos, Nigeria: ECWA Productions, 2005).

[7] See Turaki, *Introduction to the History*.

[8] Northwest and North-Central Nigeria include Benue, Kogi, Kwara, Nasarawa, Niger, Plateau, Abuja, Jigawa, Kaduna, Kano, Katsina, Kebbi, Sokoto, Zamfara States. North-Central Nigeria is also loosely referred to as the Middle-Belt region.

In addition to religious differences, these regions are the most diverse in terms of languages and cultural expression. The consequent melding of religions, cultures, and ethnic groups ensures the region's rich diversity. In recent times, however, such differences—accentuated by harsh economic realities and the rise of religious extremists, among other factors characterizing the instability of colonized societies—have effectively catalyzed civil unrest.

While introducing the recent volume *Fighting in God's Name: Religion and Conflict in Local-Global Perspectives*, Afe Adogame, Olufunke Adeboye, and Corey Williams observe that the upsurge of conflicts poses a crucial security threat that challenges both local and global society.[9] In 2011, the country had witnessed a series of such conflicts, including sporadic bombings in various states and central locations, such as the Nigerian Police headquarters and the United Nations headquarters.[10] Reporting for the International Peace Institute, Alice Debarre suggests that since the emergence of Boko Haram religious extremists, over twenty thousand people have been killed, about two million have been internally displaced, and another two hundred thousand have fled the country into the neighboring countries of Cameroon, Niger, and Chad.[11] Although these numbers are subject to statistical error, they do offer a glimpse into the scope and intensity of the problem at hand.

It is within this sociopolitical and socioreligious landscape that the Atyap community experiences its own instances of conflict. Like many other communities in Northwest/Central Nigeria, they have increasingly become the victims of wanton attacks and killings of loved ones as well as the destruction of properties in rural villages. The causative agents have been identified variously, such as banditry, interethnic disputes, farmer-herder rivalries, and—the most popular—militarized Fulani herdsmen and the Islamic extremist group Boko Haram, for reasons relating to land grabbing, indigene-settler controversies, and the effects of climate change, among others. The immediate trigger leading to the July 23 event was a mass murder just the night before in surrounding villages of the Atyap community. After a series of such massacres throughout the months of June and July, the communities in question came face-to-face with arguably some of the most traumatic incidents that have plagued the country since its post–civil war history. I shall now turn to the actions and reactions of Atyap women in response to this series of occurrences.

---

[9] Afe Adogame, Olufunke Adeboye, and Corey L. Williams, eds., *Fighting in God's Name: Religion and Conflict in Local-Global Perspectives* (Lanham, MD: Lexington Books, 2020), vii.

[10] Adogame, Adeboye, and Williams, viii.

[11] Alice Debarre, "Providing Healthcare in Armed Conflict: The Case of Nigeria," International Peace Institute, January 31, 2019, https://www.ipinst.org/2019/01/providing-healthcare-in-armed-conflict-nigeria.

"THE KILLINGS ARE ENOUGH!" GENDER, RELIGION, AND PUBLIC DISCOURSE

On July 23, Atyap kingdom was brought to a standstill. Hundreds of women stormed the streets in a manner that was uncanny, eerie, and indicative of a grave situation. In the pictures and video clips that circulated via different media outlets, including social media and news reports, the women were mostly older and postmenopausal, with a sizable portion of younger women of childbearing age in their midst. Most of them wore black clothing. A considerable number were partially clothed, while another undeniably significant number were naked, exposing various parts of their bodies, including their breasts and buttocks. Their faces were marked with black, ash, or blue paint. With them were an ample collection of leaves, all fresh and green and strategically placed on various parts of their bodies, such as on their heads, in their hands, or on their genitals. They were also wielding various objects, including sticks, pestles, diggers, and pans. Including the leaves, these objects were forced to touch the ground as the women willed. A few of them held up paper banners saying, for example, "Enough Is Enough," "Mr Southern Kaduna Leaders Where Are You?" "Our Land Is a Promised Land," and "El-Rufai Where Are You?" referring to Nasir El-Rufai, the governor of Kaduna State.

Among numerous media and news outlets that covered the event, Mohammad Sabiu of the *Nigerian Tribune* reported the women's grievances to include the incessant killings in the community by gunmen. In their words to the paramount ruler, the women's leader submitted, "The killings were enough. . . . Many women were turned to widows and their children into orphans. We can no longer farm because of the insecurity in our area. Hunger is looming and people are gradually leaving their ancestral homes."[12] In describing their actions, one of the women, Judith Simon, stated, "Usually, when women come out naked, it is a sign of [a] bad omen. The leaders understand that. We are hopeful that the gods will be appeased in order for peace to be restored in the community."[13]

With these words, the women grounded their actions in deeply religious ritual practices that transcend mere civil or political protest. Thus, it becomes essential to recognize the vitality and functionality of the "third religion" in this same ambience, African Indigenous religions. Simon laid claim to their actions as those that were equally necessitated by a breach of moral and societal ethics, which, consequently, required such a gesture in order for adverse consequences to be evaded and for harmony to be restored to the community. In corroboration, Esther

---

[12] Muhammad Sabiu, "Southern Kaduna: Why We Protested Naked—Kaduna Women," Nigerian Tribune Online, July 25, 2020, https://tribuneonlineng.com/southern-kaduna-why-we-protested-naked-kaduna-women/.

[13] Sabiu.

Monday identified the women's actions using the Indigenous terms *byanfwo* and *kagbang*, which literally mean "aggressive anger" and "nakedness or nudity," respectively. She explained that such acts have deep historical roots in Atyap kingdom and have come to signify one of the major ways in which women assert their position, often in criticism of happenings in their communities. Supporting this claim and establishing its long history in Atyap kingdom, John Asake, president of the Southern Kaduna Peoples Union, in an interview with PlusTV Africa, submitted that "symbolically and culturally too, when a woman—not just a woman, a mother—decides to go naked to protest a situation, it is the extremity of the gravity of the situation and the frustration that comes with it. The woman is the mother of the nation. The woman is the mother of everybody, whether you are president, governor, member of the house. That is the mother of everybody. . . . The protest was spontaneous. It was not even planned. If it was planned, it would have been hundreds of thousands of people."[14]

The women sang, chanted, and vocalized words and songs of dissatisfaction, anger, and discontent as they journeyed along the streets. They performed violent stunts and gestures as they forcefully annexed the streets to themselves. Others assumed a state of lament, rolling on the ground and striking their fists on the ground once they arrived at their destination, the doorstep of the palace of the paramount ruler of the Atyap kingdom, Sir Dominic Gambo Yahaya, the Agwam Atyap of Zangon Kataf in the Atak Njei area. In a short video that enjoyed multiple views on social media, the women were seen in a moment of simultaneous wailing, singing, and lamenting. Quite interestingly, however, was the deployment of overtly Christian practices, including vocalized Pentecostal-style prayers and the rendition of hymns and Christian songs amid loud reverberations of "Amen" and "in Jesus's name," mostly rendered in local languages.[15] The scene revealed a seamless blending of the overt expression of a ritual practice that finds its legitimacy within Indigenous religions in a face-to-face encounter with what may easily be described as a typical Christian revival or awakening church service. Drawing on various religious elements and justifications, these women entered the public arena in a way that was simultaneously private. Bearing their naked bodies as a mode of capital and an entry point into public discourse on the state of insecurity in the country, Atyap women orchestrated a scene that held multiple elements in the ambivalent state of contestation and synergy, vulnerability and invulnerability, all of which complexify notions of power, agency, and religious capital in public discourse.

[14] Plus TV Africa, "Women Protest Naked, Demand End to Killings," YouTube video, July 27, 2020, https://www.youtube.com/watch?v=UBMxWgZF89g.

[15] See Anthonia Sheyin, "Oh Lord Arise and the Enemies Be Scattered," YouTube video, July 23, 2020, https://www.facebook.com/anthonia.sheyin.77/videos/988272118295926/.

Women's Bodies, Religion, and Public Discourse

The deployment of bodies, African women's bodies, as instruments of critique in public discourse has a long history in Nigeria, across West Africa, and in Africa at large. The Atyap women's ritual practice emerges as one of the most recent and contemporary enactments of such critique.[16] Other examples include the 1929 Aba Women's War against British colonial entities in southeastern Nigeria; the 1930s Abeokuta Women's Union's naked protest against the Alake of Abeokuta's political actions; the 2002 naked protest against Chevron, Texaco, and other foreign oil companies in the Niger-Delta region of Nigeria; the 2013 naked protest against the military siege in Delta State; and the 2017 naked protest by women of the Indigenous People of Biafra movement in Abia State. Women's naked bodies in public spaces, both large and small in scale, are increasingly becoming an important aspect of scholarly interest. Although the practice of women baring their naked bodies in public as an act of defiance is not restricted to Africa alone, the religious, social, and cultural elements that validate its enactment and reception make its occurrences in Africa unique.[17] Scholars have approached this phenomenon with an interest in understanding its historical roots, its impelling worldview and causative circumstances, its meaning, and its consequent effect on immediate and distant contexts from sociological, historical, political science, and anthropological lenses. Recently, scholars have sought to revisit the subject in light of postcolonial theories, media studies, and feminist theories and in view of modernization and globalization. These approaches are evident in the most recent works on this subject by Laura Grillo in *Intimate Rebuke* and Naminata Diabate in *Naked Agency*. With an emphasis on such a scenario as played out among Ivorian women in 2011, both scholars approach the subject of women's bodies from different yet complementary perspectives, providing a rich context for understanding its meaning, contemporary relevance, and efficacy. I shall now turn to an examination of Grillo's and Diabate's analyses, as they offer important theoretical and conceptual insights for engaging the deployment of women's bodies in public discourse in light of world Christianity.

---

[16] In 2016, there was another similar ritual practice also in Southern Kaduna region. See news reports by Sahara Reporters, for example, "Naked Women Protest against Gov. El-Rufai, Destroy Cars in Governor's Entourage in Southern Kaduna," Sahara Reporters, December 20, 2016, http://saharareporters.com/2016/12/20/naked-women-protest-against-gov-el-rufai-destroy-cars-governors-entourage-southern-kaduna.

[17] It is also important to note that although this phenomenon is not limited to Africa alone, this chapter pays close attention to its expression by African women.

Grillo: Matri-archive of Female Genital Power and Matrifocal Morality

In *Intimate Rebuke*, Grillo examines the practices of *Dipri* and *Egbiki* in Côte d'Ivoire. Following an extended period of ethnographic research spanning the length of three decades, she provides a rich description of the ritual processes and the material symbols and culture that accompany them, as well as the Indigenous religious and cosmological underpinnings and institutions that sanction their emergent and continued practice. By juxtaposing the deportment of young men in *Dipri* with that of postmenopausal women in *Egbiki*, she theorizes and distills the logic of power, spirituality, and gender in African cosmology and social construction and defends the claim that "at the foundation of West African civilization is the widespread and deeply rooted conception that Woman is the innate bearer of spiritual power, the seat of moral authority, and the provenance of legitimacy for worldly rulership."[18] Reckoning with the long history and proliferation of practices such as *Egbiki* across the continent of Africa and specifically in West Africa, Grillo asserts that the site of this power is located in women's genitalia. According to Grillo, it was a man among her interlocutors who most forcefully articulated the extent and meaning of this power and its expression in the practice of *Egbiki*. He explained to Grillo, "The women do a rite but it is dangerous. Woman comes out when it is really serious because Woman holds power in her hands. . . . Women here are God. When God arrives, witches flee, because *Woman represents God. . . . So when they see the women naked and that thing [their genitalia], it is like seeing God.*"[19] Typically characterized by naked women wielding branches, pestles, and other objects as they slap their breasts and genitals, the deployment of their bodies in this form and the logic of power it emanates from and exerts is what Grillo has termed female genital power (FGP).

Building on Cheik Anta Diop and Ifi Amadiume's ideas of the origin of African matriarchy and the idea that West African societies have been founded on a strong ideology of motherhood and a general principle of maternal love, Grillo deviates from this trajectory by insisting that in the expression of FGP, the empowerment of women is not founded on motherhood and the ability to conceive life nor on the understanding of love as the warm sentiment of care that Westerners often associate with maternity. Instead, she postulates that "it is the principles of justice and respect for the most intimate social bonds for which the women stand and fiercely defend with ruthless righteousness. These bonds are rooted in the primacy of the mother-child unit and matrilineal

---

[18] Laura S. Grillo, *An Intimate Rebuke: Female Genital Power in Ritual and Politics in West Africa*, Religious Cultures of African and African Diaspora People (Durham, NC: Duke University Press, 2018), 55.

[19] Grillo, 44 (italics in the original).

kinship. It is the *moral principle* and not the social structure that is most vigorously enforced. The most compelling articulation of these principles and their most potent sanction is the terrible curse imposed through FGP."[20] With that, she introduces the idea that it is not matriarchy—which she interprets as the structural organization of society that privileges female authority—that undergirds African societies. Rather, it is matrifocal morality. Coining the term in opposition to matrifocality as advocated by Wendy James, which signals the moral primacy of biological motherhood in the definition of relations, Grillo contends that matrifocal morality removes the mother's position and the structure of matrilineal descent or rulership from the primary locus.[21] Instead, the "moral position that informs the ethical relations in all societies, regardless of the system of descent or the sex of the ruler," assumes centrality.[22] With that, Grillo establishes the grounds for validating the expression of FGP even in patriarchal and patrilineal societies such as the Atyap of Kaduna. A ritual embodiment of moral authority, such as in *Egbiki*, therefore, becomes the ultimate sanction that performs the dual role of authorizing both rulership and otherworldly powers as well as chastising the abuse of such powers.

Diabate: Naked Agency and the Paradox of Legibility and Illegibility

In her book, Diabate seeks to employ a multidisciplinary approach to the deployment of women's bodies in African public spaces, paying close attention to biopolitics and media representation by means of documentaries, social media, literary fiction, and narrative film. Diabate situates and engages such occurrences in Africa as one of many other forms of similar expression in other parts of the globe. Thus, she draws on African cosmogonies and theories of agency as well as biopolitics to examine how forms of political participation can inhabit the ambivalence of legibility and illegibility in the contemporary era. With her background in comparative literature, gender and sexuality studies, and media studies, Diabate, like Grillo, approaches the context of Côte d'Ivoire and the practice of *Egbiki* in both similar and dissimilar ways.

Like Grillo, Diabate seeks to examine the sociopolitical conditions that call for such actions. Of particular interest in her research, which arguably forms a departure from Grillo's anthropological and ethnographic approach, is her focus on how acts such as *Egbiki* and their potency are perceived or understood by their targets and other stakeholders. At the same time, she differentiates between

---

[20] Grillo, 76.
[21] Wendy James, "Matrifocus on African Women," in *Defining Females: The Nature of Women in Society*, ed. Shirley Ardener, Cross-Cultural Perspectives on Women (New York: Wiley-Blackwell, 1978).
[22] Grillo, *Intimate Rebuke*, 77.

the deployment of women's naked bodies in public spaces in Africa, which she thinks of as a solemn ritual, and the often festive disposition toward public nakedness in the United States, resulting in the ambiguity between vulnerability and celebration. Hence by incorporating both biopolitics and postcolonial approaches to agency into her assessment of political agency in the context of desperation and assertion of power, Diabate seeks to contribute to earlier discussions by highlighting what she believes is missing in Western discussions and undervalued in African studies on women's ritual practices such as *Egbiki*.

Diabate deviates from earlier taxonomies of these ritual practices as FGP,[23] bottom power,[24] punitive delegation,[25] genital power,[26] genital cursing,[27] women's mobbing,[28] sexual insult,[29] and shaming parties.[30] Instead, she coins the term *naked agency*, which she uses interchangeably with others, such as defiant disrobing, assaultive nakedness, intentional nudity, and naked self-exposure. As descriptive terminology, *naked agency* holds in tandem the dynamics of power and vulnerability revolving around women and their targets.[31] According to Diabate, *naked agency* suggests the complexity and unstable nature of the gesture, unlike other taxonomies that, she claims, are suggestive of "fixity, localization, the ethnic, and freedom from effects of historical and social variations."[32] She critiques what she calls the "cosmological" approach employed by previous scholars, including Grillo, and its tendency to "romanticize" women while failing to account for the opinions of spectators or the often futile outcomes of such practices, particularly in contemporary times. Her idea of naked agency takes seriously the negotiation of power among women, their targets, and other stakeholders. As such, she propounds that "in one sense, defiant disrobing is not

---

[23] Grillo.

[24] Linda Day, "'Bottom Power': Theorizing Feminism and the Women's Movement in Sierra Leone (1981–2007)," *African and Asian Studies* 7, no. 4 (2008): 491–513.

[25] Aud Talle, "'Serious Games': Licences and Prohibitions in Maasai Sexual Life," *Africa* 77, no. 3 (2007): 351–70.

[26] Phillips Stevens Jr., "Women's Aggressive Use of Genital Power in Africa," *Transcultural Psychiatry* 43, no. 4 (December 2006): 592–99, https://doi.org/10.1177/1363461506070784.

[27] Misty Bastian, "The Naked and the Nude: Historically Multiple Meanings of Oto (Undress) in Southeastern Nigeria," in *Dirt, Undress, and Difference: Critical Perspectives on the Body's Surface*, ed. Adeline Marie Masquelier (Bloomington: Indiana University Press, 2005), 35–60.

[28] Paul Spencer, *The Maasai of Matapato: A Study of Rituals of Rebellion*, International African Library 3 (Manchester: Manchester University Press, 1988).

[29] Shirley G. Ardener, "Sexual Insult and Female Militancy," *Man* 8, no. 3 (September 1973): 422–40, https://doi.org/10.2307/2800319.

[30] Robert B. Edgerton and Francis P. Conant, "Kilipat: The 'Shaming Party' among the Pokot of East Africa," *Southwestern Journal of Anthropology* 20, no. 4 (1964): 204–18.

[31] Naminata Diabate, *Naked Agency: Genital Cursing and Biopolitics in Africa*, Theory in Forms (Durham, NC: Duke University Press, 2020), 3.

[32] Diabate, 17.

fundamentally antipatriarchal; rather, it works in tandem with patriarchy. The gesture derives its power effects from the patriarchal parameters of anatomical determinism—worth emphasizing in light of interpretations of these gestures as implying safety, freedom, and success for the women."[33]

Grillo and Diabate: On Religion and Agency

Grillo and Diabate offer us important and pertinent perspectives on the phenomenon earlier elaborated that occurred in the Atyap community on July 23, 2020. Their insights allow us to situate this conversation amid the long line of its historical expression and scholarly analysis. Through Grillo, we have a rich understanding of the cosmological underpinnings of the women's actions as well as possible postulations of what the phenomena mean for both the actors and the communities in which they are performed. On the other hand, Diabate invites us to take seriously the perception of these actions by onlookers both within and outside of these contexts as well as the important question of their efficacy, particularly in light of the onslaught of globalization, mass media, and similar developments in other parts of the world.

Through their explication, Grillo and Diabate both touch on the subject of religion, particularly Christianity and Islam. By privileging a cosmological and ethnographic approach, Grillo provides a more thorough engagement with the important subject of Indigenous religiosity, cosmologies, and worldviews in the practice of FGP. According to Grillo, the onslaught of Christianity and colonialism, accompanied by its Western ideas of gender, social structure, and political organization, challenged and, in some cases, forcefully eradicated African notions of the same as embedded in Indigenous religions and cosmologies. Particularly impacted were women and their social, political, and ritual agency.[34] Regardless, Grillo affirms the survival of this practice and its deployment by both Christian and Muslim women across the continent.[35] For Grillo, these women's agency is based on a distinctive local and Indigenous understanding of their gender that bears currency even in its contemporary dispensation.

Examining religion in tandem with the perception of onlookers or the targets of naked agency in the context of secularization, Diabate observes that "given that secular governance supposedly shuns religiosity, indigenous religious practices and their spirits, of which genital cursing is a constitutive part, are thought to have no space within postcolonial biopolitical circumstances."[36]

---

[33] Diabate, 17.

[34] Grillo, *Intimate Rebuke*, 103–6.

[35] Grillo, 114.

[36] Diabate, *Naked Agency*, 132.

She argues that the often contradictory responses of religious and political onlookers or targets to naked protests speak to the complexity surrounding secularizing effects on these ritual practices.[37] Early on in her book, Diabate advocates that women's capacity to exercise agency through these ritual practices is located in their ability to occupy liminal spaces, which curtails the simple dichotomy between victimhood and sovereignty as well as women's ability to act or react intentionally and unintentionally in both punishing offending males and signaling vulnerability.[38]

However, neither one of these scholars engages the subject with special attention to Christianity and its vibrancy in sub-Saharan Africa. Thorough attention to the impact of Christianity is essential in light of the fact that one sees an interconnectedness between the overt expression of Christianity in a ritual practice and its rootedness in African Indigenous religions. At the same time, engaging in this subject in Northwest/Central Nigeria is especially important, since there is a scarcity of research on the deployment of women's bodies within that region. Until now, the focus has been on women from majority ethnic groups from the eastern or western parts of the country. Remedying this lacuna is especially important because of the rise of Protestant Christianity and the centrality of the ECWA within this region. In addition, the melding of cultures and religions, as well as the sociopolitical climate within Northwest/Central Nigeria, shifts the conversation as a result of women deploying their bodies in acts of public critique in ways that could potentially offer new insights into and shift the previous conversation on agency.

World Christianity: Engendering the Field

For the first time in the greater history of Christianity, the typical face of the faith is nonwhite, non-Western, and nonmale. The contemporary representation of Christianity is a Black woman[39]—to be precise, a Black Christian woman on the streets of Nigeria or in the favelas of Brazil.[40] This is in keeping with the recorded demographic shift in the center of gravity of Christianity from the Global North (GN) to the Global South (GS).[41] This shift was popularized by the release of Philip Jenkins's *The Next Christendom* in 2002. He reveals

---

[37] Diabate, 132–47.

[38] Diabate, 19, 46.

[39] Dana L. Robert, "Shifting Southward: Global Christianity since 1945," *International Bulletin of Missionary Research* 24, no. 2 (April 2000): 50.

[40] Philip Jenkins, *The Next Christendom: The Coming of Global Christianity* (Oxford: Oxford University Press, 2002), 2.

[41] *Global North* and *Global South* are used in this chapter and widely in world Christianity discourse to refer to the continents of Europe and North America and those of Africa, Asia, South America, and Oceania, respectively.

that over the course of the twentieth century, Christianity had witnessed two major demographic realities within the regions of the GN and GS. On the one hand, there had been a steady demographic increase in the population of the GS and, on the other, a steady decline in the GN.[42] In 2011, the Pew Research Forum revealed that between 1910 and 2010, the geographical location of most Christians had changed. Europe and the Americas, which accounted for 93 percent of the world's Christian population in 1910, had shrunk to 63 percent of the world's Christian population by 2010. Interestingly, however, was the fact that Christianity in regions of the GS had increased exponentially. For example, Africa had shifted from a Christian population of 1.4 percent in 1910 to 23.6 percent in 2010.[43] In 2020, the Protestant population on the continent represented 44 percent of the entire world Protestant population. By 2050, it is estimated that nearly half of all Protestants will emerge from Africa. In their 2015 analysis, Todd Johnson and Gina Zurlo revealed that Nigeria recorded the largest Protestant population in the world, second only to the United States. At the same time, the ECWA has emerged as the tenth largest Protestant congregation in the world and the second largest in Nigeria after the Anglican Church of Nigeria.[44] Scholars of world Christianity are consequently interested in engaging deeply with what this shift means for Christian history, theology, and the fate of the faith as a whole.

According to Dale Irvin, the field of world Christianity seeks to investigate and understand Christian communities, their faith, and their practices as expressed in diverse ecclesial traditions and informed by the multitude of historical and cultural experiences found on the six continents and in a world transformed by globalization.[45] Irvin adds that this kind of study of Christianity is concerned with "both the diversity of local expressions of Christian life and faith throughout the world, and the variety of ways these interact with one another critically and constructively across time and space."[46] As a field of study, world Christianity has its roots in missions, ecumenics, and world religions and thus "pursues a three-fold conversation, across borders of culture (historically the domain of mission studies); across borders of confession or communion (historically the domain of ecumenics); and across borders with religious

---

[42] Jenkins, *Next Christendom*, 1–15.

[43] "The Global Religious Landscape," Pew Research Center's Religion & Public Life Project, December 18, 2012, https://www.pewforum.org/2012/12/18/global-religious-landscape-exec/.

[44] Gina A. Zurlo and Todd M. Johnson, eds., *World Christian Database* (Boston: Brill, 2016).

[45] Dale Irvin, "What Is World Christianity?," in *World Christianity: Perspectives and Insights: Essays in Honor of Peter C. Phan*, ed. Peter C. Phan and Jonathan Y. Tan (Maryknoll, NY: Orbis Books, 2016), 4.

[46] Irvin, 4.

studies (historically the domain of world religions)."[47] Concurrently, it seeks to identify and engage new and different theories, methods, and practices by embracing local and translocal ways of knowing and doing by employing an interdisciplinary approach.[48]

While these statistics and Irvin's insights into the academic study of world Christianity continue to provide the underpinnings for important conceptual, theoretical, and methodological discussions, I argue that they could also provide important markers for conceiving of gender within world Christianity. In addition to the threefold frontiers earmarked by Irvin and against the backdrop of the overt presence and active participation of women in world Christianity—especially in view of the representative demographic image of the faith as an African woman—I suggest a fourth frontier: gender. To better situate my argument, I will rephrase Irvin's remarks and redraw the borders and boundaries of world Christianity by submitting that *world Christianity pursues a fourfold conversation across borders of culture (historically the domain of mission studies), across borders of confession or communion (historically the domain of ecumenics), across borders with religious studies (historically the domain of world religions), and across borders of gender in the historical and contemporary domain of culture, confession or communion, and religious studies.* Embracing gender not just as an appendage but as a formative element of the scope of Christianity could potentially allow us to reflect more deeply not only on how non-Western contexts experience and express Christianity but also on how women in these regions—for instance, the Atyap women of Nigeria—embody and engage Christianity as a lived religion.

There is a deficiency of research on gender and women's religious experiences in current world Christianity discourse. In accentuating this claim, Dana Robert submits that the shift in world Christianity should be analyzed as a women's movement. Robert's work offers an important critique of the omission of women in the historiography of world Christianity, particularly in terms of Western women's efforts in helping catalyze the shift in the center of Christianity through their role as missionaries and the high rate of conversion as well as the ways in which they engage cross-cultural interactions. She argues that although men tend to occupy formal and ordained positions as religious leaders, women constitute the majority of active participants.[49] Consequently, I suggest that since, for the first time in the history of Christianity, the representative face of

---

[47] Dale Irvin, "World Christianity: An Introduction," *Journal of World Christianity* 1, no. 1 (2008): 2.

[48] Irvin, 3–5.

[49] Dana L. Robert, "World Christianity as a Women's Movement," *International Bulletin of Missionary Research* 30, no. 4 (October 2006): 180.

the faith is now that of an African woman, one can see more clearly new parameters for (re)conceptualizing gender in Christian history, in world Christianity, and in the broader discourse about women's spirituality and the role of religion in society. It also suggests that the majority status of African women within Christianity should be conceived beyond mere demographics but also in terms of their influence. Thus, as the new faces of the faith, their experiences and expressions of Christianity carry within them the possible shape of the future of world Christianity. It therefore becomes pertinent to ask, What does it mean for world Christianity that such a deeply Indigenous religious ritual is alive in the memory and worldview of those characterized as the ideal representation of the faith? What does it mean to grapple with the realities of what happens when Christian women, by employing such overt expressions as FGP, refuse to be ashamed of their nakedness but rather use their nakedness to shame wrongful action? What might we postulate about the nature of agency and the public role of world Christianity through their actions?

CENTERING BLACK WOMEN'S BODIES, EMBRACING NEW METHODOLOGIES

Here it is important to preview subsequent comments with the observation that African women do not enter into the position of the majority from a point of privilege in the same way as their Western counterparts had historically. Taking gender seriously and privileging African women's religiosity in world Christianity requires a transdisciplinary approach that reckons with the historical and contemporary subjugation and oppression of their bodies within and outside of the continent of Africa. It also suggests the need for a robust reassessment of the historical and contemporary demonization of their religions and religious expressions.[50] Note, too, that African women do not approach this role from a position of subjectivity. In Grillo's exploration of *Egbiki* and its centrality in the religious cosmos and social organization, the very ideas of sovereignty and divinity are constructed in feminine terms. As mentioned earlier, Sahuye explains, "Woman holds power in her hands. . . . Women here are God. When God arrives, witches flee, because *Woman represents God. . . . So when they see the women naked . . . it is like seeing God*."[51] Jacob Olupona opines that "while men in principle hold political authority and power, women control the

---

[50] See Jan Platvoet, James Leland Cox, and Jacob K. Olupona, eds., *The Study of Religions in Africa—Past, Present and Prospects*, Religions of Africa 1 (Cambridge: Roots & Branches, 1996); Afeosemime U. Adogame, Ezra Chitando, and Bolaji Bateye, eds., *African Traditions in the Study of Religion in Africa: Emerging Trends, Indigenous Spirituality and the Interface with Other Religions* (New York: Routledge, 2016).

[51] Grillo, *Intimate Rebuke*, 44 (italics in the original).

ritual power that makes political rule possible."[52] The vitality of such sentiments even in contemporary times is worthy of further exploration, as doing so simultaneously engages possible (re)construction processes that emanate from the spread of Christianity and colonialism.[53] This apparent contradiction carries important implications for engaging gender and African women's new roles and experiences within world Christianity and within womanist and feminist discourse.[54]

Revisiting current approaches, employing a transdisciplinary lens, and embracing both historical and contemporary ambiances underscore the fact that the fundamental claim is not only that "women" are the majority population of world Christianity. Rather, the pivot is that for the first time in the history of the faith, the face of Christianity is not a Western, white male but a Black woman in the streets of Jos, Nigeria, or in the favelas of Bahia, Brazil. Such a realization could engineer new entry points for engendering creative approaches to world Christianity scholarship. However, by centering on Black women's bodies, we are compelled to wrestle with the seeming contradiction of how the vilified, objectified, commodified, primitivized, brutalized, dehumanized, debeautified, and "Othered" bodies of Black women can simultaneously form the site of the present and possible future of the Christian faith. As postcolonial bodies living in the trenches of the afterlives of slavery and colonization and in the predicament of empire and globalization, this seeming contradiction—being both a demographic majority and a still largely voiceless majority—therefore raises important implications for engaging African women's spirituality within world Christianity discourse.

Considered concurrently with the deployment of female bodies in public critique, as in the case of the Atyap women and their expression of *byanfwo* and *kagbang* on July 23, Diabate's insistence on the need to consider African women's social position in terms of both power and vulnerability becomes essential. This is especially pertinent as contemporary studies on African women tend to sway toward both extremes of the pendulum. Rather than pose an

---

[52] Jacob K. Olupona, "Women's Rituals, Kingship and Power among the Ondo-Yoruba of Nigeria," in *Queens, Queen Mothers, Priestesses, and Power*, ed. Flora Kaplan, vol. 810 (New York: New York Academy of Sciences, 1997), 319.

[53] See Oyèrónké Oyěwùmí, *The Invention of Women: Making an African Sense of Western Gender Discourses* (Minneapolis: University of Minnesota Press, 1997); and Ifi Amadiume, *Male Daughters, Female Husbands: Gender and Sex in an African Society* (London: Zed Books, 2015).

[54] See Mercy Odoyuye, "Reflections on Geneva 1966 and Liberation Theology from the South," *Ecumenical Review* 59, no. 1 (January 2007): 60–67; Chandra Talpade Mohanty, Ann Russo, and Lourdes Torres, eds., *Third World Women and the Politics of Feminism* (Bloomington: Indiana University Press, 1991); and Teresia M. Hinga, *African, Christian, Feminist: The Enduring Search for What Matters* (Maryknoll, NY: Orbis Books, 2017).

irreconcilable dilemma resulting in the problematic conclusion in favor of one at the expense of the other, holding both power and vulnerability in tandem, dialectically, draws attention to the ways biblical interpretations of women and women's nakedness have been used to both empower and disempower. Hence, through their actions, Atyap women's agency can also be conceived in Grillo's terms, which pay attention to self-representation rooted in a cosmological orientation. At the same time, Diabate's terms take seriously the contradiction between power and vulnerability in tandem with the efficacy and inefficacy of their actions. Additionally, we can situate women's agency in terms of their ability to draw on multiple religions and religious elements—Christianity or Islam and African Indigenous religions—for the sake of legitimizing their entry into public discourse and validating their public critique. Although here I have paid particular attention to the deployment of this ritual power in relation to Christianity, I submit that exploring this relationship with respect to Islam might generate further notable nuances.

WORLD CHRISTIANITY AND THE PUBLIC FACE
OF AFRICAN WOMEN'S SPIRITUALITY

In their introduction to *World Christianity as Public Religion*, the editors (Barreto, Cavalcante, and da Rosa) propose that Christianity has always been shaped by its contact with other religions. Consequently, issues such as intercultural communications and theologies, interfaith dialogue, hybridity, liminality, border thinking, and contact zones are central to world Christianity discourse.[55] As such, making sense of and reckoning with the multiplicity of ways in which Christian religious identities and their Indigenous religious underpinnings are renegotiated, redeployed, and contested in African Christian women's cosmologies, worldviews, and lived experiences are crucial. In the case of the Atyap, their invocation of both female power and Christianity in their fervent prayers and songs entails many important consequences for the emerging face of Christianity. This is because their deployment is no longer necessarily restricted to African Indigenous religions alone but now has a newfound legitimacy in their Christian faith. This legitimacy cannot be located within precolonial frameworks alone. Rather, its continuing relevance must be conceived locally in consideration of their cosmological and religious frameworks and also globally with respect to the new discourse emanating from the field of world Christianity and the impact of the shift of the center of Christianity. As a field that takes perspectives emerging from the Global South seriously, the

---

[55] Wanderley Pereira da Rosa, Ronaldo Cavalcante, and Raimundo Barreto, *World Christianity as Public Religion* (Vitoria: Editora Unida, 2016), 27–43.

efficacy of women's actions could be interpreted as transcending their success or the perception of onlookers. It also becomes inadequate to simply locate Atyap women's naked assertion and public critique through *byanfwo* and *kagbang* through the lens of traditions solely grounded in African Indigenous religions. They come across as postcolonial Christian women who now represent the face of an erstwhile Western faith and whose actions are grounded in both Christianity and Indigenous religious understandings of femininity, power, and sovereignty. Their performance invokes not just a (re)reading of their actions but also a (re)reading of dominant Christian accounts of nakedness as signs of poverty and shame.

Jenkins suggests that the new center of Christianity tends to be conservative, traditional, charismatic, visionary, and apocalyptic. According to him, what the Christian world is witnessing is the emergence of a new Christendom that will play a decisive role in global affairs and in defining the future shape of the faith.[56] While such postulations can be apt on several counts, the disposition of Atyap women suggests important nuances as well. Rather than inhabiting the shape of a next "Christendom" as Jenkins suggests, the reverberations of African women's religiosity, their continuing renegotiation of religious capital, and the deployment of their embodied spirituality in both religious/nonreligious spaces and private/public discourse render a perpetual critique of the historical and contemporary legacies of Christendom as well as its residual elements in Western hegemony, theological and otherwise. The persistence of rituals performed on and by the Black postcolonial naked bodies of the Atyap in the globalized twenty-first century reflects the ways in which those bodies, though living within the memories of their Othered and vilified history, are able to call into question neocolonial legacies. Not only that, but they also question the apathy of the nation and state within which they are located as well as the extremist actions of other religions that threaten the harmony and moral cohesiveness of their location. The resilience of these blatant deployments of female power does not allow women to succumb to pressure to conform to evangelical standards of piety and pushes them to complexify the meaning of these standards with this form of unconcealed public action. At the same time, the deployment of their ritual power does not allow them to be restricted by state-sanctioned modes and modalities of public discourse. Thus, these women are empowered to reject the postcolonial subjugation thrust upon them by society and the state, thereby allowing them multiple entry points into public discourse.

---

[56] Jenkins, *Next Christendom*, 1–14.

PART IV

NORTH-SOUTH/SOUTH-NORTH AND SOUTH-SOUTH INITIATIVES IN GRASSROOTS AND PARTICIPATORY ECUMENISM

CHAPTER 11

EMBODYING TRANSNATIONAL CHRISTIAN-MUSLIM SOLIDARITIES IN INDIA AND CANADA

Sunder John Boopalan

Focusing on transnational moving and meeting of bodies across real and perceived religious and social differences, this chapter privileges the need for embodied interfaith solidarity. As a Dalit Christian from India, I recognize an organic solidarity between Christians and Muslims in India owing to a common oppression experienced in a majoritarian state that does not eschew empty rhetoric. When I think through my location in the Canadian context, however, the solidarity that I otherwise naturally recognize also needs to name a certain complicity in that it is Christian ethno-nationalism that marginalizes Muslim communities.[1] It is impossible for Indian Christians to speak of interfaith solidarity with Muslims without naming this complicity that distributes benefits to those who do not self-identify as Muslims and steer away from physical and other markers of commonly recognized Muslim identity. Thus, even though I derive inspiration and direction from experiences and realities in the Global North, it is vital to view "Asia and America not as two separate entities but as ones that are constantly influencing each other."[2] This is a major reason for making connections between Indian and Canadian contexts in this essay.

This chapter begins by using a 2021 Pew Research Center report, "Religion in India: Tolerance and Segregation," as a launching point to describe identity crises in modern nation-states. The next section builds on this to note the

---

[1] I am grateful to critical Muslim studies scholar Shaista Patel's reminder that sparked this essay, that in the Indian context, while Muslims and Dalits suffer marginalization by the Indian national state, the logics that inform their marginalization are related *and* different.

[2] Helen Jin Kim, "Asian American Women's History Is American Religious History," in *Asian and Asian American Women in Theology and Religion: Embodying Knowledge*, ed. Kwok Pui-lan (Cham: Palgrave Macmillan, 2020), 91.

connections between the concepts of secularism and multiculturalism in Indian and Canadian contexts while simultaneously highlighting the contradictions in those concepts. After using the lens of religious ethnonationalism to analyze the contradictions of secularism and multiculturalism, I make the case for eschewing empty rhetorical strategies and embracing embodied interfaith boundary crossings.

Identity Crises in Modern Nation-States: Moving Away from the Majoritarian Gaze

A 2021 Pew Research Center report, "Religion in India: Tolerance and Segregation," notes that "Indians' concept of religious tolerance does not necessarily involve the mixing of religious communities. While people in some countries may aspire to create a 'melting pot' of different religious identities, many Indians seem to prefer a country more like a patchwork fabric, with clear lines between groups."[3] This chapter does not argue for the melting pot model, nor does it propose that boundary lines between groups should collapse in pursuit of some abstract notion of unity. What is concerning is simply how the impulse for maintaining boundaries works itself into a societal life in which "Indians generally stick to their own religious group when it comes to their friends."[4] People seem to be laissez-faire about other religions in the abstract but disinclined to welcome them as next-door neighbors. The report refers to more than one religious group in India. While such developments are concerning and inform the essay's boundary-crossing goals, I am also cognizant of the identity crises brought about by the constituting and governing processes of nation-states.

Modern nation-states often seek to unite their diverse populations under the broader label of *nation*. This causes identity crises that can be classified under two major categories—the crises of those who do the governing and the crises of those who fall under the purview of government. As they reflect on *what* or *who* is a "nation," governing bodies need to find the basis upon which a nation can be united. If the nation consists of diverse people, whose traditions and worldviews will they privilege? This causes the first set of crises because dominant traditions often "win," and other marginalized traditions, consequently, are left on the periphery. Relatedly, a second set of crises arises among the diverse people that inhabit the nation. This is simply because specific ethnic and religious communities may not find their culture and ethos represented in the dominant articulation and, consequently, feel alienated by the nations that

---

3 "Religion in India: Tolerance and Segregation," Pew Research Center's Religion & Public Life Project, June 29, 2021, https://www.pewforum.org/2021/06/29/religion-in-india-tolerance -and-segregation/.

4 "Religion in India."

claim to represent them.[5] Identity crises frequently erupt in modern nation-states simply because of the fundamentally flawed pursuit of hegemonic unity.

India, the country of my birth and current citizenship, has one of the most religiously and ethnically diverse populations in the world (on which, more below). Whether such diversity leads to hospitality and peace or increasing antagonism continues to be a much-debated point with concrete on-the-ground implications. In terms of religion, Hindus (over 80 percent of the population) are the country's majority. Although there are other religious minorities, such as Sikhs, Buddhists, Jains, and so on, Christians (conservatively estimated as a little over 2 percent) and Muslims (a little over 13 percent) merit special mention, as they are often treated in the dominant national imagination as being adherents of "foreign" religions and therefore, intentionally or otherwise, forced into a position where they have to constantly prove their Indianness to secure their belonging in the body politic. To offer an example of this predicament, I quote from Peniel Rajkumar's essay "Christian-Muslim Engagement in Contemporary India": "In January 2015 the police department in Gujarat state (the home state of Prime Minister Narendra Modi, which had earlier in 2002 witnessed one of the worst massacres of Muslims) conducted mock security drills in which fake 'militants' were dressed as Muslims in long tunics and skull caps and were made to shout 'Islam Zindabad' (long live Islam) reiterating the Hindu fundamentalist's preferred stereotyping of Muslims as 'terrorists.' While the terrorist tag is attached to Muslims, Christians are branded with an 'imperial tag'—as foreign agents out to destabilise and divide the Indian nation."[6]

The sort of normalized Othering that Rajkumar refers to is part of a larger coercive force that marginalized communities feel under the nation-state. Although nation-states refer to the identity assertion of marginalized communities as fault lines, as Rajkumar notes, the real fault lines are majoritarian, and minorities get "caught in" them.[7]

Minorities in majoritarian states often feel what Arkotong Longkumer, in his book *Greater India Experiment*, calls a "totalizing force" that usurps diverse identities into a totalizing unity that erases particularity. A quote from Longkumer

---

[5] Arkotong Longkumer's *The Greater India Experiment: Hindutva and the Northeast*, South Asia in Motion (Stanford, CA: Stanford University Press, 2021); and Glen Sean Coulthard's *Red Skin, White Masks: Rejecting the Colonial Politics of Recognition*, Indigenous Americas (Minneapolis: University of Minnesota Press, 2014) are good descriptions of these crises in the Indian and Canadian contexts, respectively.

[6] Peniel Rajkumar, "Christian-Muslim Engagement in Contemporary India: Minority Irruptions of Majoritarian Faultlines," in *The Character of Christian-Muslim Encounter: Essays in Honour of David Thomas*, ed. Douglas Pratt et al., History of Christian-Muslim Relations 25 (Boston: Brill, 2015), 330.

[7] Rajkumar, 326.

is helpful to make sense of how such totalizing forces affect predominantly Christian northeastern states in India:

> When I visited many of these Vishwa Hindu Parishad / Vidya Bharati / Janjati Vikas Samiti (VHP/VB/JVS) schools all over the Northeast, providing sanctuary to tribal children, I was unprepared for the scale of their involvement, and I often wondered at what price. Looking at the visual material in these schools—ranging from quotes from eminent figures, maps, painted images of deities to pictures of the goddess Lakshmi (goddess of wealth), Bharat Mata (Mother India), or even a cross-stitch decoration of the Sanskrit syllable Om—reminded me of a quote in one of the classrooms of the Zeliangrong Heraka School in Tening, Nagaland, run with the help of Janjati Vikas Samiti. The quote by Ramakrishna reads: "Knowledge leads to unity; ignorance to diversity." In this quote, these Sanskritized forms of messages make a presence and form mental maps in an attempt to organize, to forge a certain route through which knowledge is gained, and to simplify diverse and rich narratives to a story of oneness, a gradual but seemingly inevitable process of creating a totalizing force.[8]

The totalizing force that Longkumer refers to is strengthened through mechanisms of majoritarian nationalistic rationalization. The saying by Ramakrishna in the above quote—"Knowledge leads to unity; ignorance to diversity"—is telling in this regard. Rejecting the idea that "ignorance leads to diversity," historically marginalized communities and persons are increasingly reclaiming and asserting their identities. Yet the kind of (Vedantic or neo-Vedantic) logic in the saying from Ramakrishna that is used in totalizing strategies is a cause for concern.

Getting caught in the fault lines of majoritarian impulses means that minoritized communities are often busy navigating how to position themselves vis-à-vis the majoritarian gaze. Writing as a Dalit Christian seeking to be in hospitable interfaith solidarity with Muslims, I ask, What might it mean for minoritized communities to move away from the majoritarian gaze? Before fleshing that out, however, I turn to the geographical and national context of Canada, where I am currently situated.

INDIA AND CANADA: CONTRADICTIONS OF SECULARISM AND MULTICULTURALISM

Before highlighting the contradictions of secularism and multiculturalism in Indian and Canadian contexts, it might be helpful to get a basic sense of these concepts that seem to have positive national resonances. As readers will notice,

---

[8] Longkumer, *Greater India Experiment*, 19.

even though the nomenclature differs, secularism in the Indian context and multiculturalism in the Canadian context are more similar than dissimilar, thus making for interesting points of comparison.

"Secularism" in the Indian context, as Anna Bigelow rightly notes, "refers not to the separation of religion and state based on a post-Enlightenment model of the relations between state and citizen, public and private, but to the equality of distribution of state services to all religious communities and equal representation and respect in the public sphere."[9] The concept of secularism intends for religious communities to be treated equally. In other words, minority religions and communities are not to be minoritized. The identity crises outlined in the above section highlight, nevertheless, how majoritarian impulses continue to minoritize communities, thus leading to a contradiction between governmental intention and action. In intention, however, the notion of secularism is written into the preamble of India's constitution.

In the Canadian context, the concept of multiculturalism is the equivalent of India's secularism. Canada passed the Canadian Multiculturalism Act in 1988, recognizing that multiculturalism is simply a sociological fact and that policy should flow from that basic recognition. The diverse cultures and religions of Canada are thus intended to be on equal footing. In the Canadian national imagination, comparisons to their southern neighbor, the United States, often mean lifting up the Canadian social context as not being "as politically or ethnoracially charged."[10] Despite such comparative national imaginations, evidence points to a different reality. In Canada—my current geographical location—the bodies of 215 children were discovered in May 2021 in just one location at Kamloops in British Columbia at the site of a former residential school.[11] Residential schools in Canada existed from the seventeenth century all the way to the 1990s as part of a violent assimilation effort to remove Indigenous children from their traditional homes and cultures and destroy their ways of life. Many of these residential schools were run by Christian churches, and assimilation efforts simply kept moving and were federally funded.[12]

Although these brutal realities have been described and evidenced by Indigenous communities over the years, the magnitude of this finding, and now

---

[9] Anna Bigelow, *Sharing the Sacred: Practicing Pluralism in Muslim North India* (New York: Oxford University Press, 2010), 7.

[10] Néstor Medina and Becca Whitla, "(An)Other Canada Is Possible: Rethinking Canada's Colonial Legacy," *Horizontes Decoloniales / Decolonial Horizons* 5 (September 2019): 15.

[11] "First Nations in Central B.C. Honour Children Discovered at Kamloops Residential School," *CBC News*, June 20, 2021, https://www.cbc.ca/news/canada/british-columbia/first-nations-in-central-b-c-honour-children-discovered-at-kamloops-residential-school-1.6072828.

[12] "The Residential School System," Government of Canada, September 1, 2020, https://www.canada.ca/en/parks-canada/news/2020/09/the-residential-school-system.html.

several others, points to how the Canadian context *is* politically and ethno-racially charged. This is the conundrum that Nestor Medina and Becca Whitla note when they say,

> By perpetuating the myth of multiculturalism and its attending politics of recognition, attempts at unmasking ongoing realities of racism, xenophobia, and white supremacy are seen as social maladies which Canadians have already overcome. As a result, people who raise concerns about these realities are stigmatized as disgruntled and are accused of unearthing issues that are part of a time long gone. Multiculturalism, then, functions as the governing social imaginary which promotes the idea that it is possible to construct a society where ethnocultural differences are welcome as long as minoritized people learn to function within the scope of the dominant "white" Euro Canadian (English- and French-speaking) culture(s), including Indigenous peoples and all other "others." Whiteness remains the ubiquitous feature, framework, and point of reference—though it is absent from the official rhetoric—and is "synthesized into a national we," which decides "on the terms of multiculturalism and the degree to which multicultural others should be tolerated or accommodated."[13]

This quote allows readers to decipher how Canada's racialized substratum informs its multiculturalism. Though "absent from the official rhetoric," it is whiteness that "remains the ubiquitous feature." When we compare this to secularism in India, we discover comparable absent-from-the-official-rhetoric substrata that inform India's multiculturalism. Such absent presences are the major reason for the contradictions of secularism and multiculturalism.

RELIGIOUS ETHNONATIONALISM

The language of secularism and multiculturalism can hide deep divides. Oftentimes, such language becomes a "façade" claiming to "celebrate diversity without prejudice when in fact it actually excludes those who do not fit the dominant/normative."[14] At the time of this writing, a white mass murderer killed a family of Muslims by running them down with his truck in London, Ontario. Such terroristic killings are often motivated by what Justice François Huot, referring to the 2017 mass murder of Muslims in a Quebec mosque, calls a "visceral hatred toward Muslims."[15] The next section focuses on such "visceral hatred" to make some constructive proposals.

---

[13] Medina and Whitla, "(An)Other Canada," 24.

[14] Medina and Whitla, 19.

[15] Amanda Coletta, "Four Muslim Family Members in Canada Killed in 'Targeted' Attack, Police Say," *Washington Post*, June 8, 2021, https://www.washingtonpost.com/world/2021/06/07/canada-london-vehicle-attack-hate-veltman/.

Religious ethnonationalism complicates the contradictions of secularism and multiculturalism. Consider this example from India in Muthuraj Swamy's book *The Problem with Interreligious Dialogue*, on which I'll offer more commentary below: "There was a dispute between a Hindu man and a Muslim woman about a neem tree which was on the border of their lands. The dispute was about to whom it belongs, but in the course of dispute, it became a quarrel. Then the Hindu man threatened the woman saying that he would complain to the police that this woman belongs to 'Al-Umma Muslim terrorist group.'"[16]

Reflecting on this incident, Swamy notes this is "a problem which has nothing to do with religion or religious identity, but for personal reasons the difference in religious identity is misused."[17] I agree with Swamy here that religious identity was misused. The fact remains that the threat was seen as serious enough to merit use by the Hindu man. A Muslim could be accused of being a terrorist and their whole life could take a downward spiral because governmental structures are prejudiced against them.

In 2010, Bashir Ahmed Baba, a Muslim man from Kashmir, was arrested in the state of Gujarat by India's Anti-Terrorism Squad (ATS). Baba's arrest was celebrated by the nation-state's officials. Gujarat's ATS chief Ajay Tomar claimed that Baba was responsible for identifying, brainwashing, and recruiting vulnerable youths to send them to Pakistan for training in terroristic activities and that Baba had done this already with three thousand youths. Baba was also nicknamed the "Pepsi Bomber" for his alleged skill and past involvement in making explosives with empty Pepsi cans.[18] Baba was interrogated, beaten, and kept in prison for twelve years. He was cleared of all charges and released from prison in June 2021.[19]

In the dominant Indian national imagination, the association of Muslims with terroristic activities is so strong that visible markers such as names, beards, hats worn by Muslim men, or burkas worn by Muslim women take on twisted imaginary meanings in the dominant imagination. Such an imagination causes what Justice Huot terms "visceral hatred toward Muslims."

---

[16] Fatima, recounting the experience of one of her relatives, cited in Muthuraj Swamy, *The Problem with Interreligious Dialogue: Plurality, Conflict and Elitism in Hindu-Christian-Muslim Relations* (London: Bloomsbury, 2016), 172.

[17] Swamy, 172–73.

[18] "Gujarat: Hizbul Mujahideen's 'Pepsi Bomber' Arrested," NDTV, March 10, 2010, https://www.ndtv.com/india-news/gujarat-hizbul-mujahideens-pepsi-bomber-arrested-412718.

[19] Azaan Javaid, "'Twelve Years in Jail, I Never Lost Faith,' Says Kashmiri Man Cleared of All Terror Charges," Wire, accessed July 2, 2021, https://thewire.in/rights/i-never-lost-faith-after-12-years-in-prison-kashmiri-man-cleared-of-all-terror-charges.

This hatred is furthered by ethno-religious nationalistic impulses. As Shaista Patel observes, "Each nation is founded on narratives or mythologies that glorify the magnanimity of those belonging within its ideological borders. These national narratives are socially and historically constructed rather than being a consequence of any natural or even real course of events. The vocabulary of myths is part of the 'imagined community' and is based on those national stories that give its members spaces for imagining themselves as part of a homogeneous community, while simultaneously foreclosing the borders of the nation to the racial Others."[20] Such mythologies allow for the dominant nationalist imagination to think of itself as civilizing. Such sinister imaginations tend to think that they need to protect the land against Other(ed) forces that threaten such civilization.

Patel notes how myths can have very concrete consequences. After 9/11, Mohammed Attiah, a Muslim engineer in a nuclear plant, was interrogated by the Canadian Security Intelligence Service and the Royal Canadian Mounted Police. He was subsequently fired from his job because "it was feared that he 'might' have been making bombs for the terrorists."[21] Similar to Bashir Ahmed Baba's case mentioned above, Attiah was cleared of charges and was offered his job back. Getting the job back and being reunited with family cannot, however, become the plot of the story. The truth of the matter is that Attiah's Muslim identity became a liability. He was treated as guilty by association because of his religious identity. If Attiah were named John and worked in a nuclear plant, this simply would not have been the case.

INTERFAITH SOLIDARITY WITH MUSLIMS: ESCHEWING EMPTY RHETORIC IN FAVOR OF EMBODIED ENCOUNTERS

I write as a Dalit Indian Christian theologian currently located in Canada seeking to be in hospitable interfaith solidarity with Muslims there and here. As mentioned before, however, it is impossible for me as an Indian Christian to speak of interfaith solidarity with Muslims without naming a certain complicity that distributes benefits to those who do not self-identify as Muslims and who steer away from physical and other commonly recognized markers of Muslim identity.

Christians are not immune from xenophobic contradictions present in empty rhetoric that characterizes the language of secularism and multiculturalism that otherwise associates Muslim identity with violence. Elsewhere, I have observed how "despite a globalized world in which people live in closer

---

[20] Shaista Patel, "The Anti-terrorism Act and National Security: Safeguarding the Nation against Uncivilized Muslims," in *Islam in the Hinterlands: Exploring Muslim Cultural Politics in Canada*, ed. Jasmin Zine (Vancouver: University of British Columbia Press, 2012), 274–75.
[21] Patel, 281.

proximity and with more sophisticated degrees of interconnectedness than ever before, deep-seated prejudice and misunderstandings often go uncorrected."[22]

With major violent events such as the demolition of Babri Masjid in 1992 in India or the 9/11 attacks on the World Trade Center in 2001, there is, as Swamy notes, a dominant assumption that conflicts arise because of a "misunderstanding of religions."[23] According to Swamy, this assumption leads to two major shortcomings. The first is the "uncritical acceptance" that religion(s) "contribute to violence (directly or indirectly)."[24] Even if such a notion were true, it is, as the above section has shown, unequally applied to Muslims, thus pointing to the empty rhetoric of secularism and multiculturalism. A second major shortcoming is the dominant proposed solution to the "misunderstanding of religions," which is intellectual dialogue to facilitate greater understanding. This is a major shortcoming because of the dominant belief that interreligious encounters are best done intellectually through rational educational gatherings across various differences. My proposal, then, is that interfaith encounters are to be bodily, transcending mere intellectual positions and investing in embodied reciprocal relationships.

The concern that needs to be allayed before this chapter moves further might be stated via a question: Isn't interreligious dialogue, despite its privileging of belief and intellectual encounter, a bodily encounter between people of different faiths? In responding to this question, I find Joshua Samuel's description of the problem enlightening. Samuel argues that interfaith encounters are beset by the problem of "text-centrism."[25] Text-centrism is the privileging of texts and codified beliefs as the locus for interfaith encounters. "Dialogue," then, "is not an intellectual pursuit towards understanding dogmas and doctrines of other religions."[26] Samuel's proposal is for a "body-centered" approach to interfaith dialogue.

Body-centered approaches still need to eschew empty rhetoric. I recall reciting the "National Pledge" (different from India's national anthem) several times in Indian public and private schools.[27] One line stuck with me—not in

---

[22] Sunder John Boopalan, "Holy Proximity," in *One Nation, Indivisible: Seeking Liberty and Justice from the Pulpit to the Streets*, ed. Celene Ibrahaim (Eugene, OR: Wipf & Stock, 2019), 15.

[23] Swamy, *Problem with Interreligious Dialogue*, 7.

[24] Swamy, 8.

[25] Joshua Samuel, *Untouchable Bodies, Resistance, and Liberation: A Comparative Theology of Divine Possessions* (Leiden, Netherlands: Brill, 2020), 34–37.

[26] Joshua Samuel and Samuel Mall, *Church and Religious Diversity* (Delhi: ISPCK/CWM, 2020), 93.

[27] "The 'Pledge,' Now 50, Is the Pride of Telugus!," *Hindu*, September 14, 2012, https://www.thehindu.com/news/cities/Visakhapatnam/the-pledge-now-50-is-the-pride-of-telugus/article3896153.ece.

the sense of leaving a lasting impression but simply *stuck* in my memory by virtue of repeating it several times: "All Indians are my brothers and sisters." Samuel argues that "it is necessary for theologians of religions and dialogists to be aware of and candid about the systems and structures that surround them, either bestowing them with privileges or rendering them vulnerable, and (thereby) influence their respective theological positions of religious plurality."[28] In what Samuel notes about interfaith relations, there is a connection to the reciters of the pledge. One can call *Othered* (read Muslim) Indians "brothers and sisters" and yet treat them with contempt in private and public embodied life. This happens because of Indians' dishonesty about "the systems and structures that surround them" such that it allows them to recite seemingly inclusive pledges without ever having to think about how privilege of various kinds unequally distributes vulnerability.

For these reasons, boundary crossings are to first begin by eschewing empty rhetoric. This means, among other things, the embracing of a consciousness that is "able to recognise one's minor status and being perceptive of the manifold manifestations of domination."[29] In my case, for instance, I need to be mindful that while I may not enjoy a dominant-community advantage in India by virtue of being a Christian, I do enjoy an advantage in Canada by virtue of not being Muslim. Identifying these nuances and being honest about privileges and complicities when and where they exist is part of the effort in undoing domination and eschewing empty rhetoric.

Our collective survival depends on using these embodied encounters as opportunities to employ "our collective full-bodied intelligence toward collaboration."[30] As Sharon A. Suh notes astutely, "It is not enough to just study and theorize about bodies; we need to practice settling into them and accessing their hard-earned wisdom and truths they have been privy to over the ever-evolving iterations of who we are."[31] In describing ourselves vis-à-vis world Christianity today, every community, it seems to me, has to honestly face the question of interreligious encounters and how that can vary transnationally when we take our embodiment seriously in the particular local contexts in which we may find ourselves.

---

[28] Joshua Samuel, "Re-viewing Christian Theologies of Religious Diversity: Some Lessons at/from the Margins," *Ecumenical Review* 71, no. 5 (December 2019): 754.

[29] Rajkumar, "Christian-Muslim Engagement," 331.

[30] Adrienne Maree Brown, cited in Sharon A. Suh, "Taking Refuge in the Body to Know the Self Anew: Buddhism, Race, and Embodiment," in *Asian and Asian American Women in Theology and Religion: Embodying Knowledge*, ed. Kwok Pui-lan, Asian Christianity in the Diaspora (Cham: Palgrave Macmillan, 2020), 56.

[31] Suh, 56.

CHAPTER 12

"NO ONE CAN SERVE CHRIST AND CASTE"

INDIAN ECUMENICAL INITIATIVES TO COMBAT CASTE

Peniel Jesudason Rufus Rajkumar

In October 2010, the National Council of Churches in India (NCCI), in partnership with the World Council of Churches (WCC), Geneva, convened a National Ecumenical Conference on Justice for Dalits, communities that were previously pejoratively known as "untouchables" and are even today considered outcasts under the caste system. This conference, which took place in New Delhi, was a follow-up to the Global Ecumenical Conference on Justice for Dalits held March 21–24, 2009, in Bangkok. It highlighted the question of caste as an ecumenical issue that the ecumenical movement worldwide and in India could not afford to bypass. A joint affirmation of faith produced by participants of the conference unequivocally affirmed, "As Christians we claim to reflect the mind of Christ but we are vested in the logic of caste. Jesus says 'no one can serve two masters, for a slave will either love the one and hate the other, or be devoted to one and despise the other' (Matthew 6:24). In a context of caste division, caste discrimination and caste violence we announce from the rooftop: 'No one can serve Christ and caste!'"[1]

What the New Delhi conference unequivocally affirmed was the incompatibility between the practice of caste and service to Christ. Having attended both the New Delhi and Bangkok conferences, what struck me about these conferences was the reiteration of the need for the church, both local and global, to address the question of caste-based discrimination anew as a question of "ortho-praxis" (right practice). This chapter seeks to document the shape and scope of such ortho-praxis by focusing on the efforts that happened at the interstices

---

[1] "Affirmation of Faith on Justice for Dalits," World Council of Churches, accessed April 12, 2021, https://www.oikoumene.org/resources/documents/affirmation-of-faith-on-justice-for-dalits.

of (1) the ecumenical movement (local and global); (2) the various human rights movements; and (3) Dalit theological discourses. However, in seeking to document the various sites of the Indian church's engagement in combatting caste, I will highlight how these various impulses toward resisting caste-based discrimination were shaped around questions of identity. This will throw light on the different forms of ecumenical cooperation that characterized the struggles for Dalit liberation in India, paying specific attention to the shifting shapes of this focus on Dalit identity vis-à-vis non-Dalit Others. Due to constraints of time and space, I will focus on two dominant areas of Christian engagement with Dalit realities—namely, (1) Dalit theology, which emerged as an ecumenical theology, and (2) the broad ecumenical focus on Dalit human rights.[2]

DALIT THEOLOGY AND THE SEARCH FOR A NEW IDENTITY

Dalit theology is arguably one of the earliest ecumenical expressions of the Indian church's engagement with the question of caste discrimination. This new theological development could be attributed to the critical consciousness of a few theologically educated Dalits who strived to systematically articulate Christian faith in interaction with the emerging Dalit aspiration for liberation.[3] These pioneers organized consultations that brought together Indian Christians from different church traditions for reflection on the identity of Christian Dalits, their existential struggles for justice and equality, and the role of the Indian churches in responding to these struggles.

A joint national consultation of Roman Catholic and Protestant Christians, focusing on the theme "Christians of Scheduled Caste Origin," was held in 1978 in Bangalore and was one of the earliest of these ecumenical initiatives. It is known for the interventions of Masilamani Azariah (who would later go on to become the bishop in Madras of the Church of South India) concerning the need for the Indian church to ally itself with the Dalits' struggle for justice.[4] The United Theological College (UTC) in Bangalore, an ecumenical theological institution, functioned as a wellspring for the emergence of what later came

---

[2] Some of the materials used in this chapter are drawn from a few of my previous writings, including Peniel J. Rufus Rajkumar, *Dalit Theology and Dalit Liberation: Problems, Paradigms and Possibilities*, Ashgate New Critical Thinking in Religion, Theology, and Biblical Studies (Surrey, UK: Ashgate, 2010); Peniel J. Rufus Rajkumar, "Christian-Muslim Engagement in Contemporary India: Minority Irruptions of Majoritarian Faultlines," in *The Character of Christian-Muslim Encounter: Essays in Honour of David Thomas*, ed. Douglas Pratt et al. (Leiden, Netherlands: Brill, 2015), 326–42, https://doi.org/10.1163/9789004297210; and Peniel J. Rufus Rajkumar, "In Witness to God's 'With-ness': Dalit Theology, the God of Life, and the Path towards Justice and Peace," *Ecumenical Review* 64, no. 4 (December 2012): 546–59.

[3] Rasquinha Dionysius, "A Brief Historical Analysis of the Emergence of Dalit Christian Theology," *Vidyajyothi Journal of Theological Reflection* 66, no. 5 (2002): 353–54.

[4] John C. B. Webster, *The Dalit Christians: A History* (Delhi: ISPCK, 2000), 231–32.

to be known as Dalit theology. The widely acknowledged watershed event was Arvind P. Nirmal's address at UTC in March 1981. Despite not mentioning the word *Dalit*, the paper "Towards a Sudra Theology" proved to be a clarion call to the Dalits "to shun theological passivity and sociological camouflage" and pick up the gauntlet of "reclaiming the liberative ends of theology."[5] This paved the way for a theological orientation that pushed the Indian church to acknowledge its overwhelmingly Dalit social base and construct theologies that contained good news for Dalits.[6] Among the several lay contributions to Dalit theology, one can mention Kothapalli Wilson's work *The Twice-Alienated: Culture of Dalit Christians* (1982). Understanding Christianity as a renascent cultural movement committed to humanization, Wilson called for a shift from Christianity's supernatural and soteriological concern to involvement in humanizing struggles.[7] Wilson's stringent critique that the "salvation theology" paradigm of Christian missions promoted "psychological dependency, political passivity and communal exclusiveness among Dalit Christians" in some ways contributed to more liberation-focused paradigms of theological articulation.[8]

The gradual emergence of grassroots Christian Dalit movements like the Christian Dalit Liberation Movement (CDLM) in 1984 and the Dalit Liberation Education Trust (DLET) in 1985 facilitated the change in the theological orientation. The national conventions of the CDLM and the subsequent collaboration with the Christian Institute for the Study of Religion and Society (CISRS) fostered an increased attention to the predominantly Dalit context of Indian churches. The establishment of the Department of Dalit Theology in the Gurukul Lutheran Theological College and Research Institute in Chennai in 1987 was an important sign of institutional interest in Dalit theology among Indian theological institutions. Gradually, the Indian theological scene in the 1980s and '90s was inundated with some of the earliest publications on Dalit theology.[9] Therefore, one can say that Dalit theology was the fruit of a confluence of commitments to liberation by church leaders, theological institutions,

---

[5] Sathianathan Clarke, *Dalits and Christianity: Subaltern Religion and Liberation Theology in India* (New Delhi: Oxford University Press, 1998), 45.

[6] Webster, *Dalit Christians*, 233.

[7] Kothapalli Wilson, *Twice Alienated: Culture of Dalit Christians* (Hyderabad: Booklinks, 1982), 59.

[8] Webster, *Dalit Christians*, 235.

[9] Prominent among these were K. Wilson, "An Approach to Christian Dalit Theology," in *Towards a Dalit Theology*, ed. M. E Prabhakar (Delhi: ISPCK, 1988), 48–56; Xavier Irudayaraj, ed., *Emerging Dalit Theology* (Madras: Jesuit Theological Secretariat, 1990); M. E. Prabhakar, "The Search for a Dalit Theology," in *A Reader in Dalit Theology*, ed. Arvind P. Nirmal and V. Devasahayam (Madras: Gurukul Lutheran Theological College and Research Institute, 1991), 2–13; and James Massey, ed., *Indigenous People: Dalits; Dalit Issues in Today's Theological Debate*, ISPCK Contextual Theological Education Series 5 (Delhi: Indian Society for Promoting Christian Knowledge, 1998).

and liberation movements. It is important to recognize a triple dynamic within Dalit theology where advocacy for Dalit issues, accompaniment of Dalit communities, and accountability of the church and theological institutions are interwoven into its fabric in critical and constructive ways. Inherent to this dynamic is a particular identity focus wherein the category *Dalit* was reinterpreted in a particular way.

1. Countertheological Re-membering

Dalit theology emerged as a "countertheology" to the existing Indian Christian theologies of the day that failed to take into account the true identity of predominantly Dalit Indian Christian and articulated Christian theologies using idioms and frameworks from dominant caste cultures. Sathianathan Clarke accuses Indian Christian theology of functioning as an instrument of ideological co-option. He points out that the metanarrative of Indian Christian theology that has been woven by combining the Christian story with the tradition of caste Hindus "has tended to serve hegemonic purposes."[10] What is inherent in the process of "combining" these two stories is the elevation of the cultural and religious traditions of one dominant group of Christians to serve as the overall framework within which Christian theology is articulated. From the perspective of the caste communities, they were presented with an opportunity "to configure a normative master-narrative" that combined the heritage of their Hindu ancestors and the Christian story.[11] However, for the Dalit communities, this only provided temporal and "short-term benefits," as they were now "given an opening to mask their real identity and live with illusory conviction that they were truly part of the overall Hindu society and heritage."[12] The subtle reinforcement inherent in such an articulation—that Dalits were inferior because of their Dalitness and caste communities were superior and hence their worldview should be accepted as the normative worldview—did very little to remove the stigma associated with the Dalit communities. Against this background, grasping the political potential of theological symbolization, Dalit theology sought to effectively expose and rupture the prevailing, sometimes theologically sustained hegemony and subvert the political dividends of theology to serve the oppressed and challenge the oppressors.[13] It did so by reimagining God in close resonance with Dalitness and in a way that sought to interrupt the unflourishing

---

[10] Clarke, *Dalits and Christianity*, 43.
[11] Clarke, 43.
[12] Clarke, 43.
[13] Peniel J. Rufus Rajkumar, "Christian Ethics in Asia," in *The Cambridge Companion to Christian Ethics*, ed. Robin Gill, Cambridge Companions to Religion (Cambridge: Cambridge University Press, 2011), 139.

status of Dalits and herald the flourishing of all those under the restraint of caste-based discrimination. Let me explain.

When we consider the question of the symbolization of God in the Indian context through the association of the divine with the holy and the pure, there was an inordinate inclination to co-opt the divine into the same semiotic domain that proved to be foundational for the oppressively hierarchical and debilitatingly hegemonic caste system—namely, the notions of purity and pollution. Such symbolization of the divine inadvertently, yet invariably and irrevocably, projected the Dalits (who were considered to be the polluted and polluting ones) as the very antithesis of the pristinely pure divine being. Such a "pure" God ceased to be a God of life and instead proved to be the God of death for the Dalit communities. In such a context, the Dalit communities reconfigured God as a God of life by focusing on God's "with-ness" or God's solidarity with the Dalit communities. Jesus Christ was reimagined as the Dalit Christ, who became one of the Dalits. In one of the most provocative reconfigurations of God, Nirmal spoke of God as a servant God, a *bhangi* (a manual scavenger), and a *dhobi* (a person who washes clothes)—all professions considered to be polluting—and raised the challenging question, "Are we prepared to say that my house-maid, my sweeper, my bhangi (scavenger) is my God?"[14]

Such a radical reidentification of the divine set in motion a theology that broke the debilitating process of demonizing the Dalits. Theological imagination became a process of furthering life for those to whom life was denied in the name of God. Such a reimagination of the divine has a polysemic significance that is perceptively brought out by Joseph Prabhakar Dayam, who points out, "In the ritual practices of the dominant religions, anything polluted and polluting distances the human from the divine. Inversely, in the Dalit imagination of the divine and the practice of the ritual, the dichotomy of purity and pollution is not only dismantled, but pollution is privileged as the necessity in the divine human interaction and the life-giving and life-saving acts of the divine. To be divine is to be polluted."[15]

As a counterintuitive symbol, the Dalit resymbolization of God as one who unambiguously identifies with the Dalits is a God of life for the Dalits. According to Clarke, such a view of God bridges the gap between God and Dalit experience in a way that promotes human flourishing. In this theological reconstruction of God "into one who serves human society," Clarke finds a

---

[14] Prabhakar, "Search," 224.

[15] Joseph Prabhakar Dayam, "Gonthemma Korika: Reimagining the Divine Feminine in Dalit Christian Theo/Alogy," in *Dalit Theology in the Twenty-First Century: Discordant Voices, Discerning Pathways*, ed. Sathianathan Clarke et al., Kolkata Symposium on "Dalit Theology in the Twenty-First Century" (New Delhi: Oxford University Press, 2010), 145.

resolve within Dalit theology "to remove the distance and aloofness of God from the toiling people and bring the divine close to what was thought to be polluting locations." Through this process, "God becomes so identified with 'polluting' professions (that is, scavengers and the washerman . . .) that encountering God and embracing Dalits become synonymous."[16] Thus, it can be stated that the liberative processes of *decentering* the power of theologies and the *ideological dismantling* of those theological themes that have the potential to obfuscate injustice and oppression were inherent in and intrinsic to the process of Dalit theological imagination. In many ways, Dalit theology became a corrective process of the insertion of Dalit experiences and culture in the reimagining of God. In granting epistemological primacy to Dalit experiences and culture, Dalit theology reinscribed what constitutes acceptable or appropriate resources for theological imagination. Its subversiveness lay in systematically recalling and creatively remembering what had long been silenced and sidelined.

2. Liberation in Collaboration

Alongside the aforementioned identity-affirming focus, Dalit theology also had a deep concern to enlist the non-Dalit church as a partner in the task of Dalit liberation. An important outcome of this advocacy-accompaniment-accountability dynamic of Dalit theology was the quest for a theological language that addressed dominant-caste Christians who were often complicit in caste-based discrimination.

It is interesting to note that some of the strongest affirmations of the need for the non-Dalit church to be in solidarity with Dalit Christians came from two non-Dalit theologians, Samuel Rayan and Dhyanchand Carr. Rayan, a Jesuit priest, used Hebrews 13:11–13 as a biblical paradigm for the church to engage in the Dalit issue.[17] According to Rayan, this biblical passage recounts the story of Jesus, and in him God, immersing themselves in "the Dalitness of the oppressed in order to rescue its victims and plant them in the realm of freedom, dignity and creative living."[18] The praxis of Jesus made it clear that "discipleship and churchhood did not consist in sharing his throne of glory, but in sharing his cup of suffering, the baptism of his humiliation and the distress of his passion in an act of befriending and participating in their condition and giving our life for their liberation."[19] Appropriating the invitation to follow Jesus

---

[16] Sathianathan Clarke, "Dalit Theology: An Introductory and Interpretive Theological Exposition," in Clarke et al., *Dalit Theology*, 30.

[17] Samuel Rayan, *The Challenge of the Dalit Issue*, ed. V. Devasahayam, Gurukul Summer Institute (Madras: Gurukul Lutheran Theological College and Research Institute, 1992), 117–37.

[18] Rayan, 121.

[19] Rayan, 121.

in Hebrews in service of the Dalit situation, Rayan says, "Hebrews 13 urges us and the church to go outside the camp and share the degradation of Jesus and his friends, the Jobs and the suffering servants of our times. Not in order to romanticize Dalitness, but to subvert it by loving the oppressed, rebuilding their pride, and enabling them to struggle to equality and freedom."[20] According to Rayan, "The invitation of Hebrews to share Jesus' degradation outside the gate implies a socio-cultural revolution, however tiny or fragmentary, that would liberate the Dalits and make them heirs to a world of new relationships where everyone's dignity and rights are honoured and upheld."[21]

Carr, another non-Dalit theologian, proposes the need for incorporation of what he calls "ecumenical" and "evangelical" concerns if the gospel is to become relevant to the oppressed groups. According to Carr, "Contextual theologies which seek to confront situations of oppression can at the same time hold together the ecumenical concern for one human community as well as the evangelical concern that God accepts everyone on the basis of genuine repentance. In other words, by being open to Dalit theology, the non-Dalits also can feel included within the pale of salvation through conscious repentance of their past participation either directly or indirectly in the unjust structures, practices and attitudes produced and nurtured by the caste system."[22]

Alongside these non-Dalit theologians, several Dalit theologians have consistently emphasized that in the task of Dalit liberation, multilateral alliances are forged with like-minded movements and groups—both Dalit and non-Dalit—whether religious or secular.[23] The idea that Dalit theology was a countertheology was held in creative tension with the understanding that Dalit theology was also a collaborative theology. An approach of mutuality was emphasized across the caste divide within Christianity, where the middle and the upper strata of the church had the obligation to "[extend] their solidarity and actions with Dalits in achieving their liberation" and the Dalits actively "[sought] alliances with and solidarity of the non-Dalits in trust, friendliness and on an equal basis."[24] There was also a call to "join hands and work in cooperation with secular humanizing forces."[25] Interreligious appeals were also

---

[20] Rayan, 131.

[21] Rayan, 123.

[22] Dhyanchand Carr, "A Biblical Basis for Dalit Theology," in Massey, *Indigenous People*, 231.

[23] Shiri Godwin, "People's Movements: An Introspection as We Enter the 21st Century," *Religion and Society* 43, no. 1–2 (June 1996): 129.

[24] M. E. Prabhakar, *Missions in a Dalit Perspective*, ed. V. Devasahayam, Gurukul Summer Institute (Madras: Gurukul Lutheran Theological College and Research Institute, 1992), 86–87.

[25] Kothapalli Wilson, "A Dalit Theology of Human Self Development," in Massey, *Indigenous People*, 269. See also Kothapalli Wilson, "Towards a Humane Culture," in Nirmal and Devasahayam, *Reader in Dalit Theology*, 161.

made to various religious traditions and ideologies like Christianity, Buddhism, Hinduism, and humanism to "bring together the liberative visions and values from their scriptures and to share their spiritualities towards building a new humanity knit together by God's love, justice and peace."[26] Therefore, one can say that Dalit theology, by its posture of radical hospitality, which embraces non-Dalits as partners in the project of human flourishing, offers them the possibility of redemption from their past complicity with caste-based discrimination and opens up a new way of moving toward justice and peace.

Alongside this enlisting of non-Dalit communities as partners in liberation, Dalit theologians also emphasized that it was imperative for Dalit theology to have a "universal appeal" that encompassed the concerns of other oppressed groups who were "linked in a chain of oppression created by the same set of theological-ideological presumptions of the dominant sections of society."[27] The category of *Dalit* was expanded as a reference to "the broken human condition, on the basis of which unity and solidarity can be fostered with other oppressed sections."[28]

3. Troubling the Still Waters of Dalit Identity

Some theologians have problematized the very manner in which Dalit theology has focused on identity questions. The most systematic of such problematizing can be found in *Dalit Theology in the Twenty-First Century*. This collection of essays, which emerged out of a consultation organized by the WCC, acknowledged the need for Dalit theology to "move beyond parochial identity politics" and explore "broader identifications that are shaped by missiological commitments to bring God's reign of freedom and justice among the poor and oppressed."[29] In a more recent article, Philip Peacock makes a point that "the implicit location of Dalit theology as a theology of identity does a disservice to Dalit theology itself" and goes on to argue for rethinking Dalit identity as a "fluid identity . . . that can be both a destabilising identity and an identity that allows for the assemblage of alliances among all afflicted."[30] Peacock uses insights from queer studies that contend that binary identities "simplify the

---

[26] M. E. Prabhakar, "Women and Gender Equality: Towards an Authentic Spirituality—Theologising with Poet Joshua," *Religion and Society* 42, no. 1 (March 1995): 47.

[27] Prabhakar, "Search," 203.

[28] See Dionysius Rasquinha, "A Critical Reflection on the Meaning of Dalit Christian Theology," *Vidyajyothi Journal of Theological Reflection* 66 (April 2002): 256. See also Wilson, "Approach."

[29] See Clarke, "Interpretive Theological Exposition"; and Clarke et al., eds., introduction to *Dalit Theology*, 12.

[30] Philip Vinod Peacock, "'Now We Will Have the Dalit Perspective': Dissecting the Politics of Identity," *Ecumenical Review* 72, no. 1 (January 2020): 120.

complexity of identities and fix them rather than account for the slipperiness and fuzziness of identity itself."[31] He goes on to claim that the Dalit existential reality of "being outcaste and outside caste" demands an "identity that is informed not only by an 'as-againstness' but also by a 'non-belongingness' to fixed space."[32] This understanding of Dalit identity as fluid helps us understand the category of *Dalit* as a "destabilising identity" that "exposes all power relations while imagining an alternative reality of justice and equality."[33] Positing Dalit identity as fluid also helps Dalits forge alliances with other afflicted groups without falling into the trap of relating to these groups as the Other.[34] Peacock's nudge toward the fluidity of Dalit identity is also in line with sociological thinking that has increasingly recognized the category of *Dalit* as "a perspective that performs a foundational role in defining a world view for political action and everyday life."[35]

DALIT HUMAN RIGHTS AND THE ECUMENICAL QUEST FOR JUST AND INCLUSIVE COMMUNITIES

The need for "trans-global solidarities among oppressed communities" has been a recurrent feature of ecumenical efforts toward Dalit liberation.[36] Forming transglobal solidarities requires a shift in discourse to what Asian American feminist theologian Namsoon Kang calls a "with-discourse"—a politics of solidarity that is founded on "the radical realization" of mutual interconnectedness, "the need for solidarity for the common good," and that does not "overlook the interactive mediations between differences."[37]

Within the Dalit movement, the "with-discourse" of self-identification alongside other oppressed communities has served both to strengthen solidarity and also to galvanize wider attention to the discrimination faced by Dalits. This has particularly been the case in the translation of "caste discrimination" into an international discourse in which global Christian organizations such as the WCC and the Lutheran World Federation partnered in the India-based

---

[31] Peacock, 122.

[32] Peacock, 122.

[33] Peacock, 122, 123.

[34] Peacock, 123, 124.

[35] Ramnarayan S. Rawat, "The Making of a Dalit Perspective: The 1940s and the Chamars of Uttar Pradesh," in *Claiming Power from Below: Dalits and the Subaltern Question of India*, ed. Manu Belur Bhagavan and Anne Feldhaus, Oxford India Paperbacks (New Delhi: Oxford University Press, 2009), 38.

[36] Samuel, *Untouchable Bodies*, 243.

[37] Namsoon Kang, "Re-constructing Asian Feminist Theology: Toward a Glocal Feminist Theology in an Era of Neo-empire(s)," in *Christian Theology in Asia*, ed. Sebastian C. H. Kim (Cambridge: Cambridge University Press, 2008), 214–15.

National Campaign on Dalit Human Rights (NCDHR) in facilitating the internationalization of the Dalit issue through their global networks.[38]

One of the most high-profile examples of the internationalizing of the Dalit issue was during the United Nations World Conference against Racism, Racial Discrimination, Xenophobia and Related Intolerance, which took place in Durban, South Africa, in 2001. Though the Dalit movement's original goal of including caste-based discrimination in the conference's Declaration and Programme of Action wasn't successful, the issue of caste-based discrimination gained unprecedented international attention during and following the conference. It was acknowledged that "key to the internationalizing of the issue of Caste-based discrimination successfully" is the recognition of caste-based discrimination "as a human rights problem of global significance" and analysis of the Dalit situation analogously with the struggles of other marginalized groups, such as the Burakumin in Japan.[39]

Two interrelated issues that have persistently called attention to questions of identity and have been a recurrent feature of Dalit human rights discourses are the question of religious conversions and the question of reservations (affirmative action) for Dalit Christians and Muslims. Both issues call attention to the question of Dalit Christian identity in a distinctive way.

1. Dalit Conversions and the Issue of Dalit Identity

The question of the religious conversions of Dalit communities to Christianity has been a contentious issue in India and has, over the past few decades, led to the justification of violence against the Christian communities in India. A submission made by a delegation of the NCCI to the Universal Periodic Review process of 2016 recognized how allegations of conversion have been used to rationalize the gravity of religious violence against Christians. It particularly referred to the murder of Graham Staines, an Australian missionary who was burnt alive with his two young sons in the state of Orissa in 1999: "Violence, mainly against Christians is associated with allegations of religious conversions. The perception that Christians are congenital proselytizers is widely prevalent in India. This view is shared not only by legislators and administrators but also the Indian judiciary. This is evident in the Graham Staines murder case. The judgement of the case referred to the murder as an instance of reaction

---

[38] Eva-Maria Hardtmann, *The Dalit Movement in India: Local Practices, Global Connections* (New Delhi: Oxford University Press, 2009), 184.

[39] Peter N. Prove, "Caste at the World Conference against Racism," in *Caste, Race, and Discrimination: Discourses in International Context*, ed. Sukhadeo Thorat Umakant (New Delhi: Indian Institute of Dalit Studies; Jaipur: Rawat, 2004), 324.

by the Hindu community because of fraudulent proselytisation practiced by Graham Staines."[40]

In the context of the resurgence of majoritarian nationalism in India, the curbing of conversions is recognized as a veiled attack on Christianity.[41] As Nandini Chatterjee says, the most pervasive legal threat faced by Indian Christians today is "the aspersion that they are either victims or perpetrators of forced or fraudulent religious conversions."[42]

The question of conversions has particular implications for Dalit Christians in India, as conversion constitutes the primary social imaginary through which Dalit Christians are identified in contemporary India. Ironically, in the present discourses of Hindutva (literally "Hinduness," a nationalist ideology based on Hindu majoritarianism), even a fourth-generation Christian is a convert in the sense of an apostate who potentially needs to be reconverted to a monolithic pan-Hindu identity through *ghar-wapsi*—a ritual process of "righting" the presumed historical "wrong" of conversion.

The issue of Dalit conversions to Christianity calls attention to the question of identity in a special way vis-à-vis questions of Dalit agency and self-determination. The dialogical manner in which Dalit Christians reconfigure their identities vis-à-vis conversions, in terms of being multiply constructed and constituted, challenges the majoritarian fault lines that Hindu nationalism seeks to perpetuate in India today and can constitute a resistance to majoritarianism. Therefore, ecumenical solidarity with Dalits on the question of religious conversions is an important feature of contemporary ecumenical with-ness.

What seems to be a particularly relevant framework for understanding Dalit conversions is Victor Turner's classic understanding of liminality as being applicable "to all phases of decisive cultural change, in which previous orderings of thought and behaviour are subject to revision and criticism, when hitherto unprecedented modes of ordering relations between ideas and people become

---

[40] "Annexure I—a Study on Discrimination and Violence against Christians and Muslims in India (2013–15)," National Council of Churches in India (NCCI), September 2016, https://uprdoc.ohchr.org/uprweb/downloadfile.aspx?filename=3682&file=Annexe1.

[41] We need to recognize that the question of conversions is the necessary foundation to sustain an anti-Christian campaign in India because Hindu-Christian relations do not have other issues—like the memories of communal violence or partition or "go-korbani" (cow slaughter)—that have affected Hindu-Muslim relationships. See Gauri Viswanathan, "Literacy and Conversion in the Discourse of Hindu Nationalism," *Race & Class* 42, no. 1 (2000): 1.

[42] Nandini Chatterjee, *The Making of Indian Secularism: Empire, Law and Christianity, 1830–1960* (London: Palgrave Macmillan, 2011), 242.

possible and desirable."[43] This is because Dalit conversions are widely acknowledged as attempts to break free from the stranglehold of the caste system and gain a new self-understanding. Particularly, what is more appropriate in the context of Dalit conversions is Turner's observation that "liminality is not only *transition* but also *potentiality*, not only 'going to be' but also 'what may be.'"[44] It is this *potentiality* of Dalit conversions to Christianity that renders Dalit conversions dangerous in the context of a Hindu nationalism that aims to "straitjacket and to chain the potential assertion of the subalterns" by reinforcing the caste system.[45] In a context where conversions outside the caste system could pose a real threat to people with a vested interest in poverty, this potentiality has economic dimensions.[46] In a context of vote-bank politics—where communities are treated as vote banks and appeased on the basis of their caste or religious identities—the potentiality of conversions has political dimensions.[47]

The liminality of conversions is counterintuitive to the Hindutva agenda of cultural nationalism that thrives on the perpetuation of binary notions of identity. Dalit conversions contest nationalism's recourse to watertight conceptualizations of identity by demonstrating how porous these reifications of identity are. They demonstrate that identity can be formulated and reformulated at will, thereby making it particularly threatening to cultural nationalism, which resorts to positivist ways of conceptualizing difference through such essentializing markers as race, religion, color, ethnicity, and nationality. As Viswanathan states, "When identity is destabilised by boundaries that are so porous that movement from one world view to another takes place with the regularity of actual border-crossings, a challenge is posed to the fixed categories that act as an empirical grid for interpreting human behaviour and action."[48] Against this

---

[43] See Robin Gill's introductory comments on the excerpt from Victor Turner's "Pilgrimage as a Liminoid Phenomenon," in *Theology and Sociology: A Reader*, ed. Robin Gill, new and enlarged ed. (New York: Cassell, 1996), 384. "Liminality may perhaps be regarded as the Nay to all positive structural assertions, but as in some sense the source of them all, and, more than that, as a realm of pure possibility whence novel configurations of ideas and relations may arise." Victor W. Turner, *The Forest of Symbols: Aspects of Ndembu Ritual* (Ithaca, NY: Cornell University Press, 1967), 97.

[44] Gill, *Theology and Sociology*, 386 (italics in the original).

[45] P. R. Ram, "Left Ideology, Ends and Means and Hindutva," *Economic and Political Weekly* 32, no. 24 (1997): 1428.

[46] Walter Fernandes points out how in the state of Uttar Pradesh, for example, dominant castes make it a point to send their own children to school while ensuring that no schools are built in the villages, "lest their labourers gain access to it and then leave either the village or demand better wages and working conditions." Walter Fernandes, "Attacks on Minorities and a National Debate on Conversions," *Economic and Political Weekly* 34, no. 3/4 (1999): 82.

[47] For more on this, see Martand Jha, "Vote-Bank Politics Is Not Such a Bad Thing," *Hindu Business Line*, March 30, 2019, https://www.thehindubusinessline.com/opinion/vote-bank-politics -is-not-such-a-bad-thing/article26685400.ece.

[48] Viswanathan, "Literacy and Conversion," 6.

background, one can understand why Hindutva aggressively resists the conversion of Dalits to Christianity by discounting these conversions as fraudulent.

One of the ecumenical challenges for the Indian church is to be in solidarity with Dalit communities as they exercise their fundamental right to profess and follow a religion of their choice. However, because of casteist attitudes, Dalit Christian communities are treated in a pejorative manner by dominant-caste communities, even within the churches. This is primarily because of the captivity of many "elite" Christians to two dominant narratives surrounding Dalit-Christian conversions.

It can be argued that many Christians who are not familiar with the Dalit Christian context are entangled in the twin narratives of what can be called "rice-conversions" and "rights-conversions." The framework of "rice-conversions" follows the line of thought of Gandhi, who in his infamous 1936 conversation with John Mott said that "harijans" (Gandhi's preferred term for Dalits) "can no more distinguish between relative merits of Islam, Hinduism and Christianity than a cow."[49] This narrative adopts an elitist view of freewill and autonomy and essentializes India's marginalized communities, such as the Dalits and Adivasis (tribals), as "essentially disabled, incapable of distinguishing motives and inexperienced in the exercise of their own judgement" and considers them "vulnerable to the inducements of converting to another religion."[50]

Against this narrative, another narrative of Dalit conversions has emerged that can be loosely termed "rights-conversions." This narrative accentuates the agency and autonomy of the converts in a very modernist approach, where ideas of rationality and autonomy are lifted up in an exclusively secularized sense. This has been particularly the case in studies that have examined Babasaheb B. R. Ambedkar's conversion to Buddhism, in which conversion is described as a modernist project anchored in and embracing the values of the French Revolution—liberty, equality, and fraternity.[51] Understood in a postcolonial sense, such depictions of Dalit conversions often are founded on an "invisible" and often unarticulated subtext that Shane P. Ganon terms a "thematic site" in which there is a valuation of the rational "West" as positive and the traditional

---

[49] M. K. Gandhi, *Christian Missions*, 2nd ed. (Ahmedabad: Navjivan, 1960), cited in S. M. Michael, "Dalit Encounters with Christianity: Change and Continuity," in *Margins of Faith: Dalit and Tribal Christianity in India*, ed. Rowena Robinson and Josepha Mariyānusa Kujūra (New Delhi: SAGE India, 2010), 66. Gandhi is supposed to have said, "Would you Dr. Mott, preach the gospel to a cow? Well, some of these untouchables are worse than cows in understanding. I mean they can no more distinguish between relative merits of Islam, Hinduism and Christianity than a cow."

[50] Viswanathan, "Literacy and Conversion," 4.

[51] Debjani Ganguly, "Buddha, Bhakti, and Superstition: A Post-secular Reading of Dalit Conversion," *Postcolonial Studies* 7, no. 1 (April 2004): 50.

"East" as negative.[52] It is important to discern the colonial investments in such singular narratives of Dalit conversions as exercises of rationality as they accentuate the "West" at the expense of the "East."

The problem with "rights-conversion" narratives is that they leave out the faith dimension of conversions from the picture. The clash is between what can be called "emic" (intrinsic/insider) and "etic" (extrinsic/outsider) theoretical conceptualizations. In the context of Dalit conversions to Christianity, the "rights-conversion" narrative is partial, incomplete, and empirically untenable. Dalit Christian conversion experiences are much more dialogical. Here the rhetorically compartmentalized aspects of the religious and secular are brought into creative coalescence to promote a conscious self-identity of the Dalit-Christian as being multiply constituted and constructed. Let me at this point indulge in a personal story to illustrate how I myself failed to understand this element of Dalit Christian conversions:

> While I was in university doing my master's in English literature, I had a friend who had secured admission into his MA program under the Scheduled Caste (the constitutional term for Dalits that entitled Dalits of Hindu, Sikh, and Buddhist religions to positive discrimination) category. In my limited Christian understanding, my friend was a "Hindu" Dalit. This was confirmed to me on the cricket field, where he often loudly invoked the Dalit goddess Matangi amma while bowling and usually after securing a wicket. What pleasantly surprised me a few weeks later was that he joined me in worshipping at the local Lutheran church on Sundays. In all naivety, I was thrilled at my "success" (as a potential priest) in leading a "Hindu" friend to the church. He was perplexingly regular in his attendance, and soon it dawned on me that he *was* a Christian.

My friend's revelation that he attended his local Baptist church regularly duly punctured my newly overinflated ego as someone "who had led a Hindu to Christ." It brought home a basic truth about Dalit Christianity—as being multiply constituted, where one sought "to live abundantly from their own particular religious heritage, while also living partially, but intently, from the richness of another or other religious tradition(s)."[53] One perplexity that it did not solve, however, I have to confess, was his preference for his native goddess Matangi amma over Jesus on the cricket ground when playing a colonial sport!

My experience also helped me understand that for Dalits, conversion to Christianity was not just a symbolic political leap but a change of significant

---

[52] Shane P. Gannon, "Conversion as a Thematic Site: Academic Representations of Ambedkar's Buddhist Turn," *Method & Theory in the Study of Religion* 23, no. 1 (2011): 19.

[53] Sathianathan Clarke, "Religious Liberty in Contemporary India: The Human Right to Be Religiously Different," *Ecumenical Review* 52, no. 4 (2000): 487.

spiritual relevance. Describing Dalit conversions to Christianity as "Christ-founded identifications," Clarke and Peacock affirm that "humanization founded on God-in-Christ is at the heart of religious conversion of Dalits to Christianity," thus attesting to the spiritual dimensions of conversion.[54] It is this dialectical aspect of Dalit conversion experiences, where the realms of the "secular" and "sacred" coalesce, that needs to foreground dominant Christian understandings of Dalit conversions. Therefore, in the face of a clash of perspectives—between "rice-conversions" (which reduce Dalits to passive objects of conversions) and "rights-conversions" (a parochial "rational" interpretation that reduces Christianity to a mere ideology)—we need to take seriously Ankur Barua's suggestion. Barua stresses the need to move beyond "a one-sided emphasis either on the passivity of the converts who can easily be deceived through fraudulent means and are determined by forces beyond their control or on the quasi-economic rationality of the convert who is quarantined from the surrounding environment" and emphasize the need to recognize the dialectical nature of the encounter between the subaltern converts and their "thick" contexts.[55]

2. Ecumenical Accompaniment on the Issue of Affirmative Action

In February 2014, the NCCI organized a meeting between the erstwhile United Nations Special Rapporteur on Freedom of Religion or Belief, Dr. Heiner Bielefeldt, and an ecumenical and interreligious delegation comprising church leaders, human rights activists, lawyers, academics, leaders of the Muslim community, and representatives of the Catholic Bishops Conference of India.[56] One of the important issues they discussed was the long-standing issue of the denial of Scheduled Caste status to Dalit Christians and Muslims, which excludes them from availing themselves of the protective and affirmative measures provided by the Indian state to Dalits belonging to the Hindu, Buddhist, and Sikh faith traditions.

In a context of religious nationalism that believes that Christians and Muslims should be accorded second-class citizenship, this discrimination on the basis of religion is seen by Christians as a move to both curtail religious conversions to Christianity and Islam and deny full citizenship rights to these

---

[54] Sathianathan Clarke and Philip Vinod Peacock, "Dalits and Religious Conversions: Slippery Identities and Shrewd Identifications," in Clarke et al., *Dalit Theology*, 191.

[55] Barua makes a case for employing a Weberian perspective, "which sees religious responses as guided by complex sets of relationships between religious ideas, the world images that are systematically formed out of these ideas, and interests which can be both material or ideal." Ankur Barua, *Debating "Conversion" in Hinduism and Christianity* (London: Routledge, 2015), 109–10.

[56] "Indian Churches Speak against Discrimination Faced by Dalits," World Council of Churches, accessed May 21, 2021, https://www.oikoumene.org/news/indian-churches-speak-against-discrimination-faced-by-dalits.

two minority religious communities. As a resistance to this discrimination on the basis of religion, several Dalit Christians hold on to a dual religious identity, where they identify themselves as both Dalit and Christian.

This holding of multiple identities by Dalit Christians, as well as concerted efforts to secure Scheduled Caste status for Dalits of Muslim and Christian origin, is very important in a context where Hindu nationalists seek to undermine the egalitarian potential of citizenship through the invocation of "primary citizenship" status for "Hindus" over against Christians and Muslims.[57] Noted sociologist Dipankar Gupta has brought out this conflict between "primary" and "secondary" citizenship perceptively in his 2005 Paul Hanly Furfey Lecture entitled "Citizens versus People: The Politics of Majoritarianism and Marginalization in Democratic India." Gupta argues that the politics of majoritarianism in democratic India has thrown up two categories of self-understanding—namely, as "people" by the majoritarians and as "citizens" by minorities. For Gupta, "With minority inspired multicultural politics, the emphasis is clearly on inclusive citizenship, whereas with majoritarianism, there is the contrary emphasis on exclusivity as a 'people.'"[58] According to him,

> The tension clearly is between citizens and people. Under nationalism, being "a People" means more than an aggregation of citizens. In a liberal democracy, however, it is not the people but citizens that take precedence. A nation-state is thus faced with two options: to be liberal democratic or nationalist. Either it delves into memories of blood and soil, or it moves on to a different form of national identity that is based on citizenship. In the latter case, the focus is on delivering education, health, employment, and other essential public goods to citizens across social strata, classes and communities. Affirmative action policies and developmental initiatives belong to this genre of interventions for creating substantive citizenship.[59]

In such a context, the assertion that Dalit Christians are "Christians" and "converts" who deserve the same privileges as other Dalit converts (to Sikhism and Buddhism) is at the same time a reassertion of their rights as "citizens." At this point, it needs to be mentioned that the Indian church's participation in the struggle to achieve special Scheduled Caste status for Dalit Christians as a claiming of Dalit identity and rights as "citizens" is very different from the

---

[57] This attitude only mirrors the convictions expressed by an erstwhile leader of the Rashtriya Swayamsevak Sangh (RSS), Madhav Sadashiv Golwalkar, who in 1939 declared, "The non-Hindu peoples in Hindustan ... must ... stay in the country wholly subordinated to the Hindu Nation, claiming nothing, deserving no privileges, far less any preferential treatment—not even citizen's rights." M. S. Golwalkar, *We, Our Nationhood Defined* (Nagpur: Bharat Prakashan, 1939), 48–49.

[58] Dipankar Gupta, "Citizens versus People: The Politics of Majoritarianism and Marginalization in Democratic India," *Sociology of Religion* 68, no. 1 (2007): 31.

[59] Gupta, 32.

earlier Indian Christian assertions of "citizenship," which were done through "indigenization" and inculturation, adopting dominant-caste Hindu idioms and frameworks of meaning. Therefore, one can say that the Indian church has come full circle in self-identifying its "citizenry" in solidarity with a majority of its members who hail from Dalit backgrounds rather than its previous self-identification with "dominant-caste" backgrounds.

Today, both the NCCI and the Catholic Bishops Conference of India are passionately involved in the struggle for Scheduled Caste status for Christians and Muslims of Dalit origin. On August 10, 2020, Dalit Christians and Dalit Muslims came together to "highlight and protest the denial of the fundamental constitutional rights to them for the last seventy years!"[60] One sign of progress in this issue was when the Supreme Court of India agreed on January 7, 2020, to examine the plea filed by advocate Franklin Caesar Thomas, a tireless Dalit legal activist, that Dalit Christians should enjoy the same affirmative benefits reserved for Scheduled Caste communities (a constitutional term for Dalits) from Hindu, Buddhist, and Sikh backgrounds. A notification was issued to the central government to make reservations of government jobs and admissions to educational institutions "religion neutral."

However, all this progress still does not mean that the self-identification of Dalit Christians as Dalit Hindus in public (in order to be eligible for affirmative action) and Christians in private (as a matter of faith) is not without its problems. Paul Divakar, a prominent Dalit activist, calls into question the "value judgement that many priests and pastors inflict upon the [Dalit] church members" who employ multiple identities as a means of resistance. Divakar questions the reluctance of the church in accepting a "Dalit Christian's multiple layers of identity as long as the law itself discriminates on the basis of faith or religion."[61] This is one area of church engagement where the sparks of hope need to be nurtured into a flame of liberation.

Conclusion

This chapter has examined the various ways in which the global and local ecumenical movements have enlisted themselves as allies in the Dalit struggle for liberation. It paid particular attention to how questions of identity vis-à-vis the

---

[60] Priscilla Jebaraj, "70-Year Wait for Dalit Christians, Muslims on SC Verdict over Caste Status," *Hindu*, August 10, 2020, https://www.thehindu.com/news/national/70-year-wait-for-dalit-christians-muslims-on-sc-verdict-over-caste-status/article32312331.ece.

[61] Paul N. Divakar, "Afterword: Can We Reimagine a Public Witness Imagining Caste in India and Our Church?," in *Dalitekklesia: A Church from Below*, ed. Raj Bharath Patta, Reimagining Church as Event: Perspectives from the Margins (New Delhi: Indian Society for Promoting Christian Knowledge; Council for World Mission, 2020), 159.

Other were an integral aspect of such engagement. This interweaving of identity questions meant that Dalit theology engaged the ecumenical movement not only in the language of the imperative (what we ought to do) but also in the language of the indicative (who we are and are to become).[62] It drew churches across the world into a new pattern of discipleship "empowered by a deep faith in God, who binds us into communion, who frees us for justice and who heals us towards wholeness"—to use the words of the New Delhi affirmation of faith. More importantly, it bound Christians across the globe into a new bond of solidarity, as members of the broken body of Christ, and helped them reaffirm with renewed commitment the words of the Global Ecumenical Conference on Justice for Dalits held in Bangkok: "Today, regardless of where we come from, which church we represent, we all become Dalits. Not only for today . . . but also for life until Dalits are liberated, we all become Dalits."[63]

---

[62] Patrick J. Wilson, "Who We Are: Luke 10:25–37," *Christian Century*, June 26, 2007, https://www.christiancentury.org/article/2007-06/who-we-are-0.

[63] World Council of Churches, "Bangkok Declaration: Introduction," accessed April 25, 2022, https://www.oikoumene.org/resources/documents/the-bangkok-declaration-and-call.

CHAPTER 13

SHIFTING THEOLOGICAL BOUNDARIES

THE ENCOUNTER BETWEEN WESTERN CHRISTIANITY AND AFRICAN CULTURES AND RELIGIONS IN SOUTHERN AFRICA

Henry Mbaya

Theology has no boundaries, knows no colour, class or creed. The AICs [African Instituted Churches] are the spiritual base for Africans experiencing a spiritual crisis and loss of identity in the so-called mainline churches, which are desperately seeking theological transformation in the form of enculturation and Africanization. They [the Africans] must begin to voluntarily liberate from the bondage of dependency on the higher authorities beyond the [borders] of Africa, and learn to transform themselves into real African Christians.

—N. H. Ngada, "Transformation of Theology
in the African Indigenous Churches"

In 1999, explaining the reasons for the establishment of the African Instituted Churches, Archbishop N. H. Ngada pointed out a number of areas that he said the Africans protested against in South Africa. The first concerned a Western theological system that centered on theology, spirituality, and confessional statements. The second entailed issues revolving around "colour"—that is, racism—and "class," which were embedded in the institutions and structures in society and church. In his address, he asserted that Africans in the African

Initiated Churches[1] had traversed the boundaries that existed within Western theology and church structures to develop an African Christianity that they believed was authentically African.

In other words, for Ngada, Western Instituted Churches had monopolized knowledge of the "Christian" Bible, theology, and spirituality given that race (and by implication, Western cultures and traditions) had become a criterion for inclusion and exclusion. Ngada's analysis suggests that these systems acted as "borders" of Western "knowledge systems" and seemed to act as a standard of "truth" differentiating between the missionary churches and Africans.

As Walter Mignolo notes, borders are constitutive of, and arise from, the processes of "coloniality of power" and "knowledge" in the modern period. He describes a border as the "line that divides and unites modernity/coloniality and materialises in actual new walls."[2] Within the Western colonial project, Mignolo describes the manner in which boundaries came to exist and function. He asserts that European "management of knowledge" influenced and went along with the drawing of boundaries. In this respect, "knowledge" and "coloniality of power" and creation of boundaries functioned in a continuum. Mignolo links the concept of border and colonial epistemology. "These borders," he asserts, "are re-enforced by colonial projects that manage knowledge—for they operate in reciprocal relationships. . . . Both the political and economic expansion of the Western civilisation have gone hand in hand with the management of all spheres of knowledge."[3] Knowledge then defines the configuration of political and economic spheres. More significantly, Mignolo argues that global schemes also suppress local histories from which they themselves have evolved. He goes on to state, "There is no contradiction here, either, between local histories and global designs: global designs respond to the logic of coloniality, but they are described and promoted in the image of progress and development for the local histories whose actors and institutions benefit from global designs."[4]

Similarly, Mary I. Hayle, Anne Marie Dalton, and Nancie Erhard argue that not only do borders demarcate spaces, but more importantly, they also *define* them. In their words, "Borders separate and define places, all kinds of places

---

[1] Western scholars have also identified these types of churches *inter alia* as African Independent Churches or African Indigenous Churches. See, for instance, Dawid Venter, "Concepts and Theories in the Study of African Independent Churches," in *Engaging Modernity: Methods and Cases for Studying African Independent Churches in South Africa*, ed. Dawid Venter (Westport, CT: Praeger, 2004), 15.

[2] Walter Mignolo, *Local Histories/Global Designs: Coloniality, Subaltern Knowledges, and Border Thinking*, Princeton Studies in Culture/Power/History (Princeton, NJ: Princeton University Press, 2012), xvi.

[3] Mignolo, x.

[4] Mignolo, xvi.

whether these are physical or psychological or philosophical. The very emergence of abilities to order life, involves the creation of borders around things." Specifically speaking about borders in religion, they go on to assert, "The borders among religions and among variations of the same religion have always been porous."[5]

This last point is critical for this study. The act of defining borders is an issue that entails power relations precisely because those who presume to have knowledge tend to assume the "right" to determine who must be "inside" and who must remain "outside," who ought to be "included" and "excluded." Mignolo further argues that coloniality demarcated two forms of borders, interior and exterior. Accordingly, one European displacing another border in colonial hegemony entailed an interior border. This contrasted with European colonial power in the interface with, say, African culture or territory, which entailed exteriority.[6] Africans (and others) existed on the margins of the Western powers. It is the latter with which this study is primarily concerned.

These borders, namely, of Western knowledge—Western Christian faith/ spirituality and teaching (doctrine/theology)—not only operated on several tiers, levels, and frontiers of the encounters between Western colonial order and traditional African systems and beliefs but also coalesced. This essay argues that borders that apparently had been erected or projected between the Western Instituted Church and African Indigenous Churches (AICs), seemingly impenetrably, continued to gradually shift in, and through, the processes of the complex encounters within Western colonial knowledge systems. This happened even more specifically between Western missionary Christianity and African knowledge systems, culture, and religions in twentieth-century southern Africa.

COLONIZATION IN SOUTHERN AFRICA, 1700–1900

The Protestant missionaries arrived in southern Africa in the seventeenth century from a European context that had been profoundly influenced by the principles, teachings, and values of the sixteenth-century Reformation but more immediately by those of the Enlightenment and the evangelical revival of the eighteenth century. These perspectives were to determine the nature and extent of their encounter with African religions and cultures in southern Africa. They were to define the extent and limits within which dialogue with the African religions was to take place.

---

[5] Mary I. Hale, Anne Marie Dalton, and Nancie Erhard, "Crossing Borders: Eco-theology in the Shadowlands; Christian Faith and the Earth," *Scriptura: International Journal of Bible, Religion and Theology in Southern Africa* 111, no. 3 (2012): 364–65.

[6] Mignolo, *Local Histories/Global Designs*, xvi.

For Protestant missionaries, the Bible was the key religious symbol of missionary authority and legitimacy; it was the embodiment of *the word of God*, the whole truth, of which the church was the custodian and interpreter. In their view, the Bible defined what was true and what was false. However, particular parts of the Bible drove specific missionary ideologies. According to J. N. J. Kritzinger, the theological teaching that defined and characterized the Protestant Reformation was based on the Pauline theology of *sola gratia, solo Christo, sola fide*, which categorized humans into two groups: the saved and the damned.[7] The three *solae* defined the truth as conceived by the missionaries; it delineated the terms on which this theology would enter into dialogue with African religions and cultures. "Universalizing" and "absolutizing," this view did not countenance alternative perspectives.

Operating within the logic of the Enlightenment, *the Word*, the Bible, could be unveiled only through the magic of literacy—as education was pivotal to the whole missionary enterprise. In this respect, knowledge was almost synonymous with biblical knowledge; being Christian was identified with school attendance.

Kritzinger has highlighted the influence of prominent European missionaries such as Nikolaus Zinzendorf, a Moravian in South Africa, and Dwight L. Moody, Donald McGavran, and John Mott in ecumenical circles in promoting missiological and anthropological perspectives that stressed personal or individual salvation and moral regeneration, a concept that ran counter to African worldviews and cultures that stressed communality and corporality. This theological-missiological perspective stressed what the missionaries perceived as their obligation as the "saved ones" to go out and save lost souls, "to win the souls for Christ." The dichotomization of a person into soul and body, Kritzinger asserts, "devalued human life and the human body which made not only the Christian message difficult for the Africans to understand but also caused an intrapersonal rift in the lives of those who became Christians." Kritzinger asserts that a gap existed in the missionaries' approach to the question of salvation; the missionaries stressed the salvation of the soul almost to the neglect of the body. In his view, the neglect of the body in "spiritual" matters was a result of the missionaries' inability to integrate biomedical science and faith. In his view, the lack of integration between biomedical science and faith meant the Bible did not play any significant role in their ministry of healing.[8]

From another perspective, Klaus Nurnberger, a Lutheran missionary and academic, argues that the "spiritualised concept of salvation," a doctrine that

---

[7] J. N. J. Kritzinger, "The Functioning of the Bible in Protestant Mission," *Missionalia* 31, no. 3 (2003): 542–67.

[8] In the section above, the quoted material comes from Kritzinger, 553–54.

presented Jesus as far removed from the Africans, highlighted the critical issue of authority.[9] Nurnberger argues that the missionaries proclaimed "the historical Jesus and the dogmatic Christ," depicted as "sitting at the right hand of the Father."[10] It was "knowledge" that was framed within the paradigm of the key Enlightenment principle of rationalism: "truth" to be acquired through biblical inquiry. It was knowledge defined within the European boundaries of reason and belief systems. In a similar vein, Ben Knighton notes that theology was defined by "a highly Germanic approach to Biblical studies, with international discussion conveniently skipping over the Atlantic and the rest of the continent in an insecure search for academic respectability."[11] This knowledge system set borders of "truth" and "falsehood"; it sealed European theological orthodoxy.

Moreover, the Reformation maxim "No salvation outside the Church," which was first asserted by the Roman Catholic Church and that the Protestant churches would soon arrogate to themselves against their rivals, was naturally transferred to their attitude toward the African religions.[12] Fundamentally, access to "salvation" actually implied access to "truth." It was truth versus falsehood, purity versus impurity. As A. N. Mushete notes, "This conservative position led to a position like staunchly loyal to the adage *extra ecclesiam nulla salus*, the theology of the salvation of souls logically leads its partisans to an across-the-board rejection of the cultural and religious traditions of the African peoples."[13]

The Christian concept of "salvation" as embodied in the Bible, whose access was solely through the acquisition of literary knowledge, was taught and projected as the "truth" or "objective" reality, symbolically portrayed as the "light" of "knowledge" to the African people, whom they assumed dwelt in darkness. For this reason, the missionaries tended to consider Christianity as "civilization" and were mostly unable to distinguish the kernel of the gospel (Jesus) from European culture and traditions. In stark contrast to this approach, they saw African culture as an obstacle to Christianity and civilization, so it had to be extirpated.[14] In both respects, cultural values either became a vehicle through which theological symbols and concepts could be disseminated or acted as a barrier against entry into salvation, which was closely identified with Western culture. To put it in

---

[9] See Klaus Nurnberger, "Ancestor Veneration in the Church of Christ?," *Journal of Theology for Southern Africa* 129 (2007): 54–69.

[10] Nurnberger, 64.

[11] Ben Knighton, "Issues of African Theology at the Turn of the Millennium," *Transformation: An International Journal of Holistic Mission Studies* 21, no. 3 (July 2004): 148.

[12] C. A. Njoku, "The Missionary Factor in African Christianity, 1884–1914," in *African Christianity: An African Story*, ed. Ogbu Kalu (Trenton, NJ: Africa World, 2007), 195.

[13] A. N. Mushete, "An Overview of African Theology," cited in Knighton, "Issues of African Theology," 148.

[14] Knighton, 160.

other words, the interface of Western cultures and African cultures entailed cultural frontiers between two theological systems or religion systems.

The Word (Bible), Salvation, and Sacraments as Theological Borders

On April 6, 1652, Jan van Riebeeck of the Dutch East India Company landed at the Cape of Good Hope and established a settlement. The company declared "the need for the 'Reformed Christian religion' to be promoted in the settlement."[15] Accordingly, van Riebeeck officially opened "the first meeting of the Council of Policy with a prayer that echoed the Company's stipulation, namely that the 'true Reformed Christian Doctrine' be spread among 'these wild insolent people.'"[16] In their view, African (Khoisan) religions and culture were nonnegotiable; theological boundaries were firmly drawn between the Reformed faith and Khoisan religion and culture.

However, the Dutch Reformed Church (and others) soon stressed that the borders separating them from the Khoisan were not only theological but also racial, as these were intertwined. For the Dutch at the cape in the seventeenth century, Christianity was equated with European identity and "civilization."[17] What is more, equating Christianity with "civilization" and with Europe, the Dutch community saw it as unwise to evangelize the Khoisan, as their entry into Christianity seemed to imply a degree of racial equality with Europeans. Likewise, the Dutch considered the Khoikhoi as falling outside the European "covenant" community of believers,[18] justifying their exclusion on the basis of a wrong interpretation of the word "nation" in the Dutch State Bible that denigrated all non-Europeans as "heathens." Baptism and Holy Communion became badges of European identity, which the Dutch guarded from the Khoikhoi. Richard Elphick notes that in the seventeenth and eighteenth centuries at the cape, "The Dutch Reformed sacraments of baptism and communion provided a social boundary that reinforced the emerging identity of white settlers as 'Christians,' and excluded most 'heathen' slaves, Khoisan, and free people of color."[19] The Dutch found security in their common identity as the "elect" versus

---

[15] Charles Villa-Vicencio, John W. de Gruchy, and Peter Grassow, *Christianity and the Colonisation of South Africa, 1487–1883: A Documentary History*, Hidden Histories Series, vol. 1 (Pretoria: Unisa, 2009), 4–5.

[16] Villa-Vicencio, de Gruchy, and Grassow, 4–5.

[17] Jonathan N. Gerstner, "A Christian Monopoly: The Reformed Church and Colonial Society under Dutch Rule," in *Christianity in South Africa: A Political, Social & Cultural History*, ed. Richard Elphick and T. R. H. Davenport (Cape Town: David Philip, 1997), 24–25.

[18] Gerstner, 24–25.

[19] Richard Elphick, *The Equality of Believers: Protestant Missionaries and the Racial Politics of South Africa*, Reconsiderations in Southern African History (Charlottesville: University of Virginia Press, 2012), 39.

the "heathen." For missionaries, the Word was powerful because it was logically predetermined by the light of knowledge, the Spirit.

Borders as a Contested Arena of Struggle

Meanwhile, the nineteenth century marked a watershed in the relations among Africa, Europe, and America. Studies done by Edward Tylor in his *Primitive Culture* (1871) relegated African religions to the categories of "animism," "paganism," "savage," "tribal," and "pagan."[20] James Frazer (1854–1941), a Scot, asserted that religion, including African varieties, developed from magic, from which modern people had graduated to science. Hence the disparagement of African religious beliefs remained one of the long-lasting legacies of the nineteenth-century Euro-American mentality, which projected Africa as devoid of the light of Christ and therefore "dark." In his Brampton Lecture at Oxford in 1843, a divine in the Church of England, Anthony Grant, who had never been to Africa, described African religion as a "religion . . . of barbarism, of the primaeval tradition run to its very dregs, varying its form according to the state of the savage understanding."[21] For Grant, African religion was the very antithesis of European religion: it was false, idolatrous, debased, and degenerate. The core tenet of this view was the primacy of reason (rationalism), "mind" over "heart," the "intellect" as opposed to emotions, and the sacred as opposed to the secular. In contrast, European religion boasted of possessing a systematic doctrine. Its God was a God defined by doctrine, understood as the Trinity of Father, Son, and Holy Spirit framed in the creeds. In the view of the missionaries, this was a universalizing theology, which sought to absolutize "truth." Education and modes of socializing would play a critical role not only in making Africans accept the teaching but also in the view that their religions and cultures were inferior. Thus, N. M. Nyaundi notes that "when Christian missionaries arrived, the mood was already strongly opposed to [African Traditional Religion]."[22]

At the eastern frontier of South Africa in the nineteenth century, John Brownlee, a missionary of the Glasgow Mission, described the Xhosa as a people who were "the slaves of sin and the children of wrath."[23] For Brownlee,

---

[20] Edward Burnett Tylor, *Primitive Culture: Researches into the Development of Mythology, Philosophy, Religion, Language, Art, and Custom*, 6th ed. (London: Murray, 1920).

[21] Anthony Grant, *The Past and Prospective Extension of the Gospel by Missions to the Heathen: Considered in Eight Lectures, Delivered before the University of Oxford* (London: F. & J. Rivington, 1845), 95.

[22] N. M. Nyaundi, "African Traditional Religion in Pluralistic Africa: A Case of Relevance, Resilience and Pragmatism," in *Traditional African Religions in South African Law*, ed. T. W. Bennett (Cape Town: University of Cape Town Press, 2011), 5.

[23] Brownlee to Walker, August 3, 1822, Report of the GMS, 1823, p. 21, cited in J. Hodgson, "Ntsikana: History and Symbol Studies in a Process of Religious Change among Xhosa-Speaking People" (PhD diss., University of Cape Town, 1985).

possession of "true" knowledge of God marked a clear border distinguishing Europeans from the Xhosa. In his view, for the Xhosa to cross the boundary of social status, they needed "the light of the gospel and civilization," which could raise them to the "true dignity of human nature." These theological borderlines existed in the form of metaphorical symbols; the whites saw themselves as a "liberated" people of the "light" in contrast to the Xhosa, who lived in "bondage" (in darkness).[24] However, this boundary not only existed on religious and cultural levels; it also had intellectual dimensions: to "know" God (Jesus) was to acquire the Word, or knowledge of Scriptures, for which the Xhosa had to master the "magic" of literacy. Because symbols and metaphors entailed powerful boundaries, which the missionaries monopolized, they became a focal point of power struggles with Blacks.

In the nineteenth century, the rise of the prophets Ntsikana and Nxele among the Xhosa shows the critical role that Christian symbols played as definers and markers of identity. As noted, the two critical missionary symbols hitherto considered as border posts between the "saved" and "lost" were loose, most notably Jesus, the Lamb of God, the Savior, and blood of the Lamb.[25] Being grounded in Xhosa culture and tradition, Ntsikana seized these symbols and reframed them within his worldview and cultural values, giving them new Xhosa meaning and interpretation. In Xhosa culture, blood symbolizes life and health, and the imagery of the lamb is not unfamiliar, since a lamb is slaughtered for ancestral rites. Consequently, this would mean that salvation was no longer a white prerogative but accessible to the Xhosa. Ntsikana used them as resources that his society could employ to cope with colonial dispossession. In his prophecy, the doctrine of salvation is central. Jesus, the Lamb of God, would, at the appointed time, intervene and usher in a period of peace. While some in the Xhosa community accepted this message, the whites despised Ntsikana's pretensions. In their view, Ntsikana was only marginally Christian. His borrowing of symbols demonstrates his ability to negotiate the liminal boundaries of colonial Christianity and African culture, just as his appropriation of Christian symbols represents resistance to, and acquiescence in, missionary Christianity and colonialism. The missionaries' negative attitude toward Nxele and Ntsikana's Christian "prophetic roles" during the Xhosa and colonial conflicts in 1819 highlights their unwillingness to enter into dialogue with Xhosa spirituality and culture.

---

[24] Elphick, *Equality of Believers*, 336.

[25] Janet Hodgson, "A Battle for Sacred Power: Christian Beginnings among the Xhosa," in Elphick and Davenport, *Christianity in South Africa*, 70–73.

Ethiopianism: A Challenge to Ecclesiological Borders

In his study about the interface between Western Christianity and African culture in South Africa, Luvuyo Ntombana notes that from 1900, an African consciousness and identity started to emerge that sought to challenge missionary hegemony. He notes that this was to accelerate and gain momentum in the twentieth century.[26] The first major challenge to missionary hegemony was the emergence of Ethiopianism. As a major missiological theme in African Christianity—in this particular case, southern Africa in the late nineteenth and early twentieth centuries—Ethiopianism deserves special consideration precisely for its theological imperatives. Richard Elphick has argued that central to Ethiopianism was the quest for racial "equality" and "justice" in ecclesiastical matters.[27] The African leaders created churches where they experienced equality, which they found lacking in the missionary churches. Underlying this movement were critical theological issues, God's universal love and Christian brotherhood/sisterhood in the church as the family of God.[28] Thus, Elphick asserts, "the Ethiopians' political stance was a natural extension of their religious commitment; they demanded of the British Empire what they demanded of the mission churches: that it live up to the promise of racial equality evident in its rhetoric and its proclaimed ideals."[29] This was the key issue for the Ethiopians. Africans were challenging the mission churches to live up to their ideals. Moreover, Elphick asserts, "the missionaries . . . had to concede that Ethiopian rebels, in their demand for Africanisation, were aligning themselves with the official mission policies the missionaries in the field had so often resisted."[30]

However, in the twentieth century, beginning in the landmark year of 1902, a more enduring challenge to institutional missionary churches emanated from the emergence and development of the Zionist Pentecostal churches in South Africa.[31] Through the American Pentecostal link, Pentecostalism started in South Africa, a movement that would transform the country's religious landscape for the next century.[32] Piet Le Roux, a Dutch Reformed minister, was baptized by the Pentecostals, an event that started the Zionist church movement. Theologically, this movement challenged the mainline churches on

---

[26] Luvuyo Ntombana, "The Trajectories of Christianity and African Ritual Practices: The Public Silence and the Dilemma of Mainline or Mission Churches," *Acta Theologica* 35, no. 2 (October 17, 2016): 119.

[27] Elphick, *Equality of Believers*, 85, 92.

[28] Elphick, 85, 92.

[29] Elphick, 85, 92.

[30] Elphick, 85, 92.

[31] Henry Mbaya, "Dordt and Pentecostal Traditions: African 'Spiritual' Churches in South Africa Today," *In Die Skriflig / In Luce Verbi* 53, no. 3 (September 30, 2019): a2469.

[32] Mbaya.

issues of African identity right around the time that the South African General Missionary Council met in 1904. At the council, Edouard Jacottet of the Paris Evangelical Mission spoke as follows: "In its professed aims and theory, the Ethiopian movement is certainly in the right direction, viz., the organisation of a purely native church, the formation of an authentic African Christianity, but it has come too soon. It has been started, and is being engineered by men not always of good repute; it has assumed a hostile form, and has often become quite antinomian. . . . But, bad as it undoubtedly is, we must nevertheless welcome it as an indication that the time is ripe for giving the native element a larger scope and influence in our churches."[33] At the same conference, Frederick Bridgman of the American Board, echoing similar sentiments, introduced a resolution that Ethiopianism required "not so much repression as careful guidance," and the resolution was adopted.[34]

Ecclesiastical and theological shifts had occurred. African Christianity was now accepted, albeit grudgingly, on the terms of the missionaries. There was a recognition that African forms of Christianity would remain a permanent feature of the South African religious landscape. In the aftermath, a few attempts were made to try to reconcile some Ethiopians within the mainline churches. In 1899, one branch of Ethiopianism, under James Dwane, was accommodated within the Anglican Church as "The Order of Ethiopia."[35] Ogbu Kalu evaluates the movement as "an early expression of the interior of African spirituality. It operated within the church, to promote Christianity of a different kind. One that was sensitive to the African environment and the dignity of people."[36] It was in the same vein that Norman Etherington asserted that it was "an independent spirituality not really attributable to any missionary."[37] This accommodating but paternalistic spirit must be seen within the broader scope of events.

BORDERLINES IN FLUX? 1950s–1970s

In my abbreviated historical overview, a crucial development occurs in the aftermath of decolonization and the emergence of the African states. Africans faced the critical question of African and Christian identity: How can I be authentically African and Christian? The call for a moratorium on missionaries by John Gatu in 1971 characterized this quest and the resulting shift of

---

[33] Quoted in Elphick, *Equality of Believers*, 93.

[34] Quoted in Elphick, 93.

[35] Elphick, 93.

[36] Ogbu Kalu et al., *Christian Missions in Africa: Success, Ferment, and Trauma*, The Collected Essays of Ogbu Uke Kalu, vol. 2 (Trenton, NJ: Africa World, 2010), 339.

[37] Norman Etherington, "Kingdoms of This World and the Next: Christian Beginnings among Zulu and Swazi," in Elphick and Davenport, *Christianity in South Africa*, 100.

theological thinking, which took place in an era of increasing global communication.[38] Africans were highly critical of the perceptions of the superiority of Western rule and institutions. Scholarly debate on the value of African religions, traditions, and culture escalated. Among others, John Mbiti and Bolaji Idowu positively evaluated African Traditional Religion (ATR) and argued that ATR prepared Africans to receive the gospel brought by the missionaries, while others such as Byang Kato took an opposite stance. In the same period, Vatican II (1962–65) ushered in a spirit of openness to the relationship between Western Christianity and other religions, including African religions. On a visit to Uganda in 1969, Pope Paul VI appealed to Catholics: "You must have an African Christianity. Indeed, you possess human values and characteristic forms of culture which can rise up to be capable of a richness of expression of its own, and genuinely African."[39]

The pope's positive affirmation of African culture seemed to characterize a spirit of openness toward non-Christian cultures and religions. To accommodate some aspects of African religious spirituality, many mainline Christian denominations have, since the 1970s, engaged in the processes of inculturation, the effort to make the Christian faith respond to local contexts in expression. However, Laurenti Magesa notes the weakness of this initiative when he observes that "the process seems to be very much controlled from the Christian centre, as yet allowing little room for popular, African cultural imagination and innovation."[40] Thus, in spite of progress, the central authority in the church still controlled the extent of inculturation on the ground. Good intentions were undermined by bad faith.

The same year that Pope Paul VI appeared to affirm African culture in relation to the gospel, John Mbiti published his book *African Religions and Philosophy*, in which he responded to the commonplace conception disseminated by the missionaries that Africans have no notion of God, that they do not know God, and that their religions and cultures have no value. Mbiti showed that that was not the case. By 1970, he was in a position to critique the missionaries' tendency of mixing up the gospel with Christianity, stating, "We can add nothing to the Gospel, for this is an eternal gift of God; but Christianity is always a beggar seeking food and drink, cover and shelter from the cultures it encounters in its never-ending journeys and wanderings."[41]

---

[38] Kalu et al., *Christian Missions in Africa*, 6.

[39] In *Gaba Pastoral Letter* 7 (1969): 50–51.

[40] Laurenti Magesa, "Christianity and African Religion," in *The Routledge Companion to Christianity in Africa*, ed. E. K. Bongmba (New York: Routledge, 2016), 264.

[41] John S. Mbiti, *African Religions and Philosophy* (Garden City, NY: Anchor Books Doubleday, 1970), 438.

Mbiti affirmed two critical dimensions at the core of missionary Christianity—namely, the gospel was the kernel of Christianity, the latter was its husk, and the two were not one and the same. For Mbiti, it was as if the problem with Western Christianity was that it had mixed the husk with the kernel. As Mbiti, a Protestant, called for meaningful indigenization, so also did the Roman Catholic Church increasingly shift toward the language of inculturation.[42]

SOUTHERN AFRICA IN THE TWENTIETH AND TWENTY-FIRST CENTURIES

Throughout the twentieth century, Africans in southern Africa, as was the case with the rest of the continent, were going through social upheavals with regard to the issue of identity. The question of what it meant to be a Christian and an African became more urgent, and a growing social consciousness led to a process of recovering African symbols of worship. This process was taking place during the time when the African Initiated Churches, which had begun to emerge in 1902, were flourishing. Central to the quest of the elite was the issue of African symbols of worship. They asserted that contrary to the missionaries' claims that Africans never worshipped but venerated their ancestors, they in fact worshipped uThixo ("God" in Xhosa) or Nkulunkulu ("the highest being" in Zulu) or Modimo ("God" in Sesuthu). Increasingly, the issue of ancestors came to the center of African spirituality. From the 1960s to the 1980s, "mainstream Christianity" faced a formidable challenge from the Zionist and Pentecostal churches on one critical issue—how these churches were taking African identity issues more seriously.[43] However, in spite of the attempts to enter into some form of dialogue with African culture, the general attitude of the mainline missionary churches was negative. John de Gruchy notes, "Opinions have varied about the significance of this rapidly growing movement. Sundkler first regarded it negatively as a bridge across which black Africans would return from Christianity to heathenism. He discerned the danger of syncretism, the confusion of culture and Christ. This was the view of most missionaries and the mainline churches until the sixties."[44]

Generally speaking, missionaries believed that there could be no dialogue between Western Christianity and African culture; for them, African cultures and traditions were incompatible with Christian principles. As a consequence, the forms of indigenization that missionaries initiated fell short of meeting the aspirations and needs of Africans who yearned for an African church that

---

[42] Kalu et al., *Christian Missions in Africa*, 310.

[43] Ntombana, "Trajectories of Christianity," 112–14.

[44] John W. de Gruchy, *The Church Struggle in South Africa* (Grand Rapids, MI: W. B. Eerdmans, 1979), 46.

reflected an African spirituality, ethos, and idioms.[45] Africans needed an African church that reflected African patterns of worship, leadership, and church structures that spoke to African idioms and ethos. Partly, this movement and consciousness found expression in Kenyan John Gatu's call for a moratorium on missionaries from Europe and America for a definite period.

FROM ACCOMMODATION TO INCULTURATION, 1980s–2000s

The increasing numerical strength of the AICs in southern Africa was noticeable in the 1970s and throughout the 1980s. Ogbu Kalu noted that some of the energy of the blossoming African Independent Churches, Pentecostal churches, and charismatic churches in the 1980s and 1990s found its way into the mainline churches.[46] Thus, by the 1990s, theological and spiritual borders between mainline theological thought on some aspects of African religions had shifted considerably. In 1994, a synod of the Roman Catholic Church meeting at the Vatican gave official impetus to indigenization. And in 2003, the Episcopal News Service reported, "The [Roman Catholic church in South Africa] is growing fast with new places of worship being built every year." This phenomenon was partly attributed to the "'Africanization' of the church—the incorporation of African culture and style into a formerly very European style of liturgy." It asserted that "inculturation was taking place on several aspects: There was dancing, singing, music and robes and dresses which reflected 'African feel.'"[47] This was a far cry from the colonial missionary era; no longer were Africans barred from practicing their traditional cultures. However, for Africans, healing (and well-being) in relation to the role of Jesus Christ versus Christ in salvation remained the most critical issue of daily concern. Missionaries had always preached that the ancestors (and African culture in general) were the chief barrier to Africans attaining salvation. Jesus was the border through which an African would be either admitted into or barred from entry into God's household associated with Christendom.

A "THIN" BOUNDARY BETWEEN JESUS AND THE ANCESTORS?

The critical importance of the role of the ancestors in African life is evident in the way in which mainline churches have embraced African tradition and culture within their doctrinal and ecclesiastical systems. Again, to quote from the Episcopal News Service, the Roman Catholic Church took note of similarities

---

[45] Kalu, *African Christianity*, 309.

[46] Kalu, 309.

[47] Quotations in this paragraph are from "African Traditions Help Catholic Church Grow in South Africa," Episcopal News Service, June 13, 2003, https://www.episcopalarchives.org/cgi-bin/ENS/ENSpress_release.pl?pr_number=2003-139E.

between the Catholic tradition of saints and the African ancestors among African Catholics for an enhanced understanding of the mass. "We find in some of our liturgies that people kneel down at the beginning of mass and invite the ancestors to be present," George Daniel, the archbishop of Pretoria observed. "I have even, on occasion, invited the ancestors of the Catholic church in Pretoria, the former bishops and archbishops, to be present at a ceremony. It's a close link with African culture, and since we allowed that, people have been flocking to mass."[48] The African ancestors were no longer considered as a "barrier" but rather as a bridge to understanding the Catholic doctrine of the communion of the saints. Doctrinal boundaries had shifted—namely, from condemnation to embrace and from intolerance to accommodation.

A more reconciliatory approach toward the veneration of ancestors has been embraced more openly by some Protestant churches. Luvuyo Ntombana, who conducted a study among the Pentecostals and mainline churches on this issue, notes that there was no difference between these religious groups with regard to African rituals.[49] He asserts that the African Independent Churches and the mainline churches allowed their members to practice male initiation with accompanying ceremonies. Further, he observed that while the mainline churches drew a distinction between "church life" and "cultural traditional life," the AICs took the opposite view, which affirmed integration of life. Ntombana observed that the mainline churches allow their members to observe these rituals only outside church spaces, while the AICs permit them to take place within the sacred spaces. There are cases involving an *igqirha* (a traditional healer) where individuals or family members can perform their rituals at home as long as the secret remains in the family. Those who are called to become traditional healers (*sangomas*) are allowed to enter and participate in a service but practice only outside the church.[50]

Meanwhile, in the late 1980s, an array of African theologians, notably Desmond Tutu, Gabriel Setiloane, and Itumeleng Mosala, espoused a Christian theology that took African cultures and traditions more seriously. It was, however, Siqgibo Dwane, a Xhosa theologian and Anglican bishop for the Order of Ethiopia, who represented the more radical stream. For Dwane, theology and the churches had to completely open up to African cultures and religious belief systems. He called for the Western churches to embrace critical elements of African religions, such as ancestors and *sangomas*.[51] Dwane practiced what

[48] "African Traditions Help Catholic."
[49] Ntombana, "Trajectories of Christianity."
[50] Ntombana.
[51] S. Dwane, "Christianity in Relation to Xhosa Religion" (PhD diss., King's College London, 1979), 10.

he preached, and his Order of Ethiopia was one of the first to indigenize by replacing the Anglican liturgy with Xhosa symbols and idioms.[52] According to P. T. Mtuze, "The new liturgy ushered in a number of extrinsic elements into the style of worship in the Order of Ethiopia. . . . This radical change of outlook comes out clearly [with regard to] the incorporation into the church of diviners or those who feel themselves called to divinership."[53] In this context, Western theology had traversed cultural and religious frontiers of Xhosa society. To put it bluntly, Dwane had crossed the line between what the missionaries would have considered "orthodoxy" to "syncretism."

Considering David Bosch's definition of mission as the church crossing frontiers, whether geographical, cultural, or religious,[54] it could then be argued that Dwane was legitimately involved in a form of missiological praxis—relating Western theological thought systems to Xhosa thought systems. Western theological systems had crossed Xhosa cultural boundaries in the Eastern Cape. Dwane's liturgical innovations, which aimed at incorporating diviners into the church, could have raised eyebrows among those who could not countenance diviners entering the church in their full regalia with the baggage of being seen as "idol worshippers."

However, the mainline churches' efforts to "indigenize" Western theology and ecclesiastical systems as practiced by Dwane and others have earned them criticism and ridicule from the AICs' Archbishop Ngada. To him, such churches are hypocritical and do despicable things, even using local beer (*umqombothi*) for Communion and allowing *sangomas* to lay hands on the faithful. In his view, they are still wearing European "masks." He goes on to assert, "Theology has no boundaries, knows no colour, class or creed. The AICs are the spiritual base for Africans experiencing a spiritual crisis and loss of identity in the so-called mainline churches, which are deeply seeking theological transformation in the form of enculturation and Africanisation."[55] The implication here is that theology cannot be confined to a particular race; it defies borders and limitations. This implies that theological borders in Western theology are never completely impenetrable; they are open to negotiation and hence can shift due to pressure

---

[52] P. T. Mtuze, "Bishop Dr. S. Dwane and the Rise of Xhosa Spirituality in the Ethiopian Episcopal Church (Formerly the Order of Ethiopia)" (PhD diss., University of South Africa, 2008), 113–14.

[53] Mtuze, 207.

[54] David Jacobus Bosch, *Transforming Mission: Paradigm Shifts in Theology of Mission*, American Society of Missiology Series, no. 16 (Maryknoll, NY: Orbis Books, 2011), 282.

[55] N. H. Ngada, "Transformation of Theology in the African Indigenous Churches," in Hearing the AIC-Voice: Proceedings of a Conference Held by the Research Institute for Theology and Religion at Unisa on 2 & 3 September 1998, ed. C. W. Du Toit and N. H. Ngada (Pretoria, South Africa: Research Institute for Theology and Religion, 1999), 3.

from other cultural forces. As Mignolo puts it, "Porous borders represent an important and often an overlooked dimension of Western theology."[56] For Mignolo, the porousness of borders in Western theology is inherent. It is also contingent on the dynamics of the context in which it is practiced, as observed by Sibusiso Masondo: "The advent of new South Africa has provided space for African traditional religions and cultural expressions."[57] Traditional healers, notably *sangomas*, operating under the authority of the ancestors, appeared to "compete" with the authority of Jesus (of whom the missionaries were the agents).[58] Seeking integration in their lives, Africans would occasionally "cross over" to AICs seeking to experience healing and wholeness often associated with ancestral mediation. This had always appeared as a missing link in their spirituality.

To understand why Africans regularly crossed the boundaries of Western Christian spirituality and mainline church traditions to the AICs, it is important to understand the critical significance of the concepts of wholeness, healing (wellness), and salvation as critical borderline issues that define the African ontology and worldview. In African philosophy and religion, the term *salvation* was (and is) understood differently from the Western theological and philosophical framework. For Africans, the Christian notion of "salvation" approximates what is understood as the life force or life energy, and although its dimensions have been critiqued in recent years, nevertheless, it explains life as spirit-centered or "power-centered" in the form of the spirit. William Dyrness and Oscar García-Johnson describe it as "viable life" or "a life of total wholeness."[59] This notion tends to stress material abundance (financial and economic progress, etc.), "but it must also include justice and morality" and is a salvation "mainly achieved through a spiritual battle between good and evil forces," making power "the hermeneutic for interpreting African religiousness."[60] In their perception, Jesus Christ is no longer an "immovable" boundary or a "fixed frontier" but rather a "window" through whom you can see the ancestors. Jesus is a proto-ancestor.

CONCLUSION

This chapter has established that from the seventeenth to the twenty-first centuries, Western theological systems and values that presumably held an absolutist

---

[56] Mignolo, *Local Histories/Global Designs*, 28.

[57] Sibusiso Masondo, "The Practice of African Traditional Religion in Contemporary South Africa," in Bennett, *Traditional African Religions*, 95.

[58] Masondo, 95.

[59] William A. Dyrness and Oscar García-Johnson, *Theology without Borders: An Introduction to Global Conversations* (Grand Rapids, MI: Baker Academic, 2015), 112.

[60] Dyrness and García-Johnson, 112.

position on doctrinal matters have in fact been shifting in South Africa through their encounter with African cultures and systems. The intransigent position that Western missionary theology once projected in its encounter with African cultures and religion, specifically with regard to the Bible, salvation, God, and Jesus as borderlines in theology, has gradually loosened. Correlatively, African cultural systems and values started to challenge the former. The challenge entailed offering alternative ways of perceiving truth, knowledge, and reality as conceived in African cultural and religious worldviews, most critically the notions of ancestors, healing, and salvation. These shifts demonstrate that after all, Western theological systems did not have "fixed" boundaries of "truth" and "knowledge" as Africans had been made to believe over the years; rather, they entailed theological boundaries that were fluid.

CHAPTER 14

A NEW PENTECOST?

THE STORY OF PEOPLES IN THE HISTORY OF THE GLOBAL CHRISTIAN FORUM AND ITS CONTRIBUTION TO WORLD CHRISTIANITY

Casely Baiden Essamuah

When the Global Christian Forum (GCF)[1] held its first Global Gathering in 2007, veteran Pentecostal scholar and eminent ecumenist Cecil "Mel" Robeck applauded the event with these words: "We have here what might be described as a new Pentecost."[2]

The original day of Pentecost, the birthday of the church, is a magnificent chapter in Christian history. It marked not only a day of new beginnings but a combination of strange, otherworldly incidents. The report of that first Global Gathering invokes Acts 2:2–4, where it speaks of nature conspiring with Spirit to affect newness: "Suddenly a sound like the blowing of a violent wind came from heaven and filled the whole house where they were sitting. They saw what seemed to be tongues of fire that separated and came to rest on each of them. All of them were filled with the Holy Spirit and began to speak in other tongues as the Spirit enabled them."

Since 1900, modern experiences of a similar nature have given birth to a Christian movement that is arguably the second-largest Christian family outside

---

[1] The author accepts responsibility for the views and opinions expressed in this chapter, and they should not be considered as expressing or implying endorsement by any of the church families that constitute the Global Christian Forum.

[2] Blurb for Huibert van Beek, ed., *Revisioning Christian Unity: The Global Christian Forum*, Studies in Global Christianity, Global Christian Forum (Oxford: Regnum Books International, 2009).

Roman Catholicism.[3] For a Pentecostal as eminent as Robeck to assert that the Global Christian Forum's emergence merits comparison to the original Pentecost is a remarkable claim worthy of careful scrutiny.

PERCEPTIONS

Others share this outlook as well. For instance, the memorandum governing the relationship between the World Council of Churches and the GCF asserts that "the . . . development of GCF has shown that at this stage in history the calling for Christian unity requires more than one expression of ecumenical commitment and cooperation."[4] Huibert van Beek, the founding GCF secretary, used the title *Revisioning Christian Unity* for the report on the first GCF Global Gathering. The immediate past secretary general of the World Evangelical Alliance (WEA), Bishop Efraim Tendero, has called the GCF "a precious gift from God to all of us at the WEA," and his recently installed replacement, Dr. Thomas Schirrmacher, has said that if the GCF had not already been established, we would have needed to form it. Dr. Richard Howell, a longtime GCF committee member and former general secretary of the Asia Evangelical Alliance, has written a book with the subtitle *Transforming Ecumenism*.[5]

The Very Rev. Dr. Sarah Rowland Jones, dean of St. David's Cathedral, Wales, writes that she overheard one church leader describe the GCF as "the-best-value-for money-ecumenism anywhere in the world."[6] In a 2011 article, Domenic Marbaniang, a theologian at Hong Kong Baptist University, argues, "The GCF brought in two advantages: historical freshness and postmodern approach. In its historical freshness, it differed in its autonomous nature and separation from the older ecumenism that had historically accrued suspicion among many groups. It did succeed in carving a new space. In its postmodern approach, it forwarded a transformed ecumenism that emphasized mutual cooperation and fellowship rather than structural unity and

---

[3] There are currently 644,260,095 Pentecostals/charismatics in the world as of 2020. Of these, 123,681,629 are Pentecostals; 268,307,218 are charismatics; and 252,271,248 are independent charismatics. "Pentecostals/Charismatics," World Christian Database, accessed July 12, 2021, https://worldchristiandatabase.org/wcd/#/results/306.

[4] "World Council of Churches and Global Christian Forum, Memorandum of Understanding between WCC and GCF," 2019, paragraph 7.

[5] Richard Howell, *Global Christian Forum: Transforming Ecumenism* (New Delhi: Evangelical Fellowship of India, 2007).

[6] Sarah Rowland Jones, "The Global Christian Forum, a Narrative History: 'Limuru, Manado and Onwards,'" in "The Global Christian Forum: Life Together in Jesus Christ, Empowered by the Spirit," ed. Larry Miller, special issue, *Transformation* 30, no. 4 (2013): 241.

doctrinal agreement. The emphasis is on narratives (Christian life) and networking (Christian fellowship)."[7]

In this chapter, I first highlight some of the internal and external dynamics that initiated the birth of the GCF in 1998. Since the raison d'être and unique calling of the GCF involves the sharing of faith stories toward building bridges for Christian unity, it is indeed the people and their stories that make the GCF exceptional. Finally, I will discuss highlights in the lives of the GCF's three secretaries as they reveal the organization's DNA.

SOURCES

Relevant historical documents and publicly available information on the GCF can be found on its website and in a few publications. The most useful sources are as follows:

1. Beek, Huibert van, ed. *Revisioning Christian Unity: The Global Christian Forum*. Studies in Global Christianity. Oxford: Regnum Books International, 2009.

2. Jones, Sarah Rowland. "The Global Christian Forum, a Narrative History: 'Limuru, Manado and Onwards.'" In "The Global Christian Forum: Life Together in Jesus Christ, Empowered by the Spirit," edited by Larry Miller. Special issue, *Transformation* 30, no. 4 (2013): 226–242.

3. van Beek, Huibert, and Larry Miller, eds. *Discrimination, Persecution, Martyrdom: Following Christ Together; Report of the International Consultation, Tirana, Albania, 2–4 November 2015*. Bonn, Germany: Verlag für Kultur und Wissenschaft, 2018.

4. Howell, Richard. *Faith Stories: A Methodology for Promoting Unity; Background Materials Compiled for the Bogotá World Gathering of the Global Christian Forum*. New Delhi: Caleb Institute, 2018.

5. Miller, Larry, ed. *Let Mutual Love Continue (Hebrews 13:1): Report of the Third Global Gathering of the Global Christian Forum, Bogotá, Colombia, 24–27 April 2018*. Bonn: Verlag für Kultur und Wissenschaft, 2021.

Some pertinent information can also be gleaned from the writings of Wesley Granberg-Michaelson, one of the GCF's earliest members, especially

---

[7] Domenic Marbaniang, "Unity in the Body: Ecumenical Attempts in the 21st Century," *Journal of the Contemporary Christian* (blog), July 16, 2014, https://marbaniang.wordpress.com/2014/07/16/unity-in-the-body-ecumenical-attempts-in-the-21st-century/.

Unexpected Destinations: An Evangelical Pilgrimage to World Christianity and *From Times Square to Timbuktu: The Post-Christian West Meets the Non-Western Church.*[8] In a sense, his books reflect the ethos and experience that he has gained through his involvement with global Christianity, in particular under the aegis of the GCF. See also his more recent *Future Faith: Ten Challenges Reshaping Christianity in the 21st Century*; "The Global Christian Forum: The Shape of Things to Come in an Ecumenical Future," in *Una Sancta*; and "Crossing Boundaries of Faith," in *How to Heal Our Divides*, edited by Brian Allain.[9]

Since the GCF is the only known forum for formal encounters between the two streams of contemporary Christianity that are commonly (albeit inadequately) labeled as "ecumenical" and "evangelical," I will also highlight some of the ways that the latter have conceptualized and become engaged in interchurch relations.

THE GCF'S BIRTH

At the turn of the twenty-first century, experts were forecasting a series of global catastrophes that would completely reshape the world as we knew it. Churches and global ecumenical bodies were not immune from the need to undergo self-examination and assess whether they were well placed to meet the challenges of the new century. Led by a visionary ecumenical leader, Konrad Raiser, the World Council of Churches (WCC), together with its member churches, engaged in a wide self-study of its relevance and mission for the new age. Raiser questioned whether the ecumenical movement was suffering stagnation. Instead of succumbing to a sense of helplessness, he pointed to a paradigm shift that could possibly lead to fresh approaches to the issues at hand.[10]

After nearly a decade of self-study, the WCC produced *Towards a Common Understanding and Vision of the World Council of Churches*, in which it acknowledged the following changes in the global landscape of Christianity:

---

[8] See Wesley Granberg-Michaelson, *Unexpected Destinations: An Evangelical Pilgrimage to World Christianity* (Grand Rapids, MI: W. B. Eerdmans, 2011); and Wesley Granberg-Michaelson, *From Times Square to Timbuktu: The Post-Christian West Meets the Non-Western Church* (Grand Rapids, MI: W. B. Eerdmans, 2013).

[9] See Wesley Granberg-Michaelson, *Future Faith: Ten Challenges Reshaping Christianity in the 21st Century*, Word & World Books: Theology for Christian Ministry (Minneapolis: Fortress, 2018); Wesley Granberg-Michaelson, "The Global Christian Forum: The Shape of Things to Come in an Ecumenical Future," *Una Sancta* 76, no. 1 (2021): 50–61; and Wesley Granberg-Michaelson, "Crossing Boundaries of Faith," in *How to Heal Our Divides: A Practical Guide*, ed. Brian Allain (independently published, 2001), 182–89.

[10] Konrad Raiser, *Ecumenism in Transition: A Paradigm Shift in the Ecumenical Movement?* (Geneva: World Council of Churches, 1991).

Many churches and Christian communities, including some whose witness is vital and whose growth is rapid, have remained outside the fellowship of formal ecumenical bodies. New sources of division have appeared both within and among churches. In some churches, things which have been said or done ecumenically have proved so contentious that ecumenical commitment itself is rejected as heretical or even anti-Christian. At every level, from the local to the global, churches and ecumenical bodies have found themselves in competition with each other when they ought to have cooperated. These limitations, setbacks and failures call the ecumenical movement and the fellowship of churches in the World Council of Churches to repentance and conversion, renewal and reorientation as a new millennium approaches.[11]

General Developments in the Christian World

As the year 2000 approached, the global landscape of Christianity was affected by several critical, related developments. These included a notable shift of the demographic center of Christianity from the Global North to the Global South along with the increasing prominence of modern evangelical, Pentecostal, and charismatic variations of the faith. Other prominent factors reshaping global Christianity were the growth of the church in China, the dynamic reemergence of Christian churches in the former communist societies, and the continuing suffering of Christians in many parts of the world. Moreover, the beginning of the twenty-first century witnessed the emergence and multiplication of autonomous Christian fellowships, churches, and denominations. Migratory movements had also resulted in a growing awareness of religious pluralism, particularly in the West, at rates hitherto not experienced. All these events occurred in the shadow of increasing cultural and intellectual secularization in the West.

These developments led many to question the assumptions that undergirded some of the organizational manifestations of Christianity during the previous century and especially its quest for Christian unity. The so-called younger churches, many evangelical, Pentecostal, or charismatic, were experiencing burgeoning growth but had little appetite for intra-church relationships, except within their own genre. Many of these churches deliberately distinguished themselves from the mainline Protestant or Catholic churches that had preceded them in their locales. As a result, their vibrancy, spiritual fervor, and vitality were not bringing any positive influence to other churches. In some cases, mainline churches returned the favor by treating the newcomers as though they were not legitimate and credible. An article in the evangelical-based *Atlas of Global Christianity: 2009–2010* states,

---

[11] "Towards a Common Understanding and Vision of the WCC," World Council of Churches, accessed September 29, 2021, 7, https://archived.oikoumene.org/en/about-us/self-understanding -vision/cuv.

Christianity has become too fragmented.... The question for global Christianity over the next century is how to restore the theological and ecclesial unity within the Christian faith and the spirit of love and tolerance in Christ. The churches are intolerant towards each other and become exclusive and divisive over small differences.... Global Christianity will face internal battles.... Global Christianity will suffer from internal bleeding due to continued "regional battles" over the purity of Christian faith.... The major split between evangelical and ecumenical groups will be more difficult to reconcile, though it has significant bearing on the future of global Christianity. The ugly ditch between these two camps seems deep and wide.... The polarization of the Christian world between evangelical and ecumenical groups will not be easily healed, and the battle between these two sides over the integrity of the Christian faith will continue and will damage global Christianity, draining much of the energy and resources of the global churches.[12]

Although normative ecumenism had made considerable achievements in its quest for Christian unity, producing closer cooperation and more engaged collaboration among churches belonging mainly to the mainline Protestant fraternity and the Orthodox churches, its modus operandi revolved around these three arenas:

1. Dialogue around theological differences, searching for points of convergence and agreement

2. Cooperation around common challenges in society and the world, such as immigration, climate change, economic injustice, and public health

3. Dialogue and potential cooperation around engagement in God's mission and evangelism

A significant part of the global and active Christian family was left out of this mode of engagement in ecumenism. This extremely significant mode of engagement prominently involved the Global North, where the Christian church was on the whole undergoing attrition. Evangelical and Pentecostal growth—mostly in but not limited to the Global South—was outside the confines of these conciliar and intellectual ecumenical engagements.

It thus became imperative to consider a different model of engagement. As the memorandum governing the relationship between the WCC and the GCF

---

[12] Lee Moonjang, "Future of Global Christianity," in *Atlas of Global Christianity: 2009–2010*, ed. Todd M. Johnson, Kenneth R. Ross, and Sandra S. K. Lee (Edinburgh: Edinburgh University Press, 2009), 104–5.

stated, "At this stage in history the calling for Christian unity requires more than one expression of ecumenical commitment and cooperation."[13]

Why a Forum?

The idea behind establishing a *forum* instead of an organization was to ensure that participation would be more important than membership. The GCF was to be open to all bodies and organizations that confess Jesus Christ as Lord and Savior and seek to be obedient to God's call. It was intended to create space for genuine exchange about challenges facing the churches and where possible cooperation could flourish. From the beginning, it was asserted that the GCF should not become another institution with administrative and bureaucratic structures, nor should it be a framework where decisions would be made or resolutions passed. Instead, the forum was designed to shape a network of relationships that would transcend the limitations of existing arrangements. Finally, and quite magnanimously, the WCC, while lending significant support to the project, would participate in the forum alongside other partners without claiming any privileged place.

Thus, the GCF's 2002 Guiding Purpose Statement stated that the GCF existed "to create an open space wherein representatives from a broad range of Christian churches and interchurch organizations, which confess the triune God and Jesus Christ as perfect in His divinity and humanity, can gather to foster mutual respect, to explore and address common challenges."

WHAT'S UNIQUE ABOUT THE GCF?

Over the years, the GCF has taken on a life of its own, characterized by an expansive vision that is carried out with five distinctives.

First, it has introduced a new method of engagement in ecumenical relationships. Whereas previous models started with theological differences, common denominators, or a desire to do things together, the GCF model of engagement starts with relationships. We prioritize and put a high premium on knowing one another well.

Second, the GCF's operation system ensures a sense of parity and distinction between historic churches and younger churches. It always aspires to bring to the table an equal balance between participants from the traditionally ecumenical bodies (WCC members and the Roman Catholic Church) and

---

[13] Memorandum of Understanding, WCC and GCF, paragraph 8, 2013, 2019. The first paragraph states, "This MOU is a timely marker of the relationship between the WCC and the GCF, celebrating all that has been achieved, and affirming their distinct and complementary roles in the quest for Christian unity."

church traditions not previously engaged in formal ecumenism beyond their own families.

Third, for administrative purposes, the GCF has established a common table where what we call the "four pillars" meet together. The Roman Catholic Church (through its Pontifical Council for Promoting Christian Unity), the WEA, the WCC, and the Pentecostal World Fellowship sit together, commonly and equally, and in some instances for the very first time, as happened under the auspices of the GCF in 2017. The Orthodox churches (Eastern and Oriental) are also represented at this table.

Fourth, the GCF model is based on participation rather than membership. In this way, we broaden the range of who can participate so that it is not limited to the four pillars, recognizing that the circumference of global Christianity is even larger. We are always asking, "Who is not at this table?"

Lastly, and most importantly, the GCF has opened up remarkable new avenues for interchurch relationships through the sharing of faith stories. Indeed, this has been the GCF's special charism. As American Lutheran and longtime GCF Committee member Dr. Kathryn Johnson puts it, "Every Christian has his or her relationship with Jesus Christ, every Christian life is a journey with Jesus. Telling that story is a way of introducing ourselves to each other, Christian to Christian." The beauty of sharing faith stories is that it enriches both the one telling the story and the one listening. Dr. Johnson continues, "We are invited at this gathering to listen as if we do not already know, to listen generously with open hearts, minds and spirits; to listen with our theological disquiets momentarily set aside; to listen for the surprising work of the Spirit of God. . . . We each listen with our ears open to the faithfulness which that perspective expresses, listening for Christ's presence where it was not expected to be."[14]

Robert Gribben, an Australian Methodist clergyman, recounts his own first experience of listening to faith stories: "When you give an honest account of how your life was encountered by Jesus Christ, and how that encounter has brought you to your present vocation and ministry, the witness of a Sri Lankan Catholic Bishop, a Pentecostal pastor from Peru, a bearded Coptic monk from Los Angeles, a Bolivian Baptist catechist and a Methodist nurse from Norway, or an Anglican woman bishop from Canada, sound remarkably the same."[15]

---

[14] Kathryn Johnson, "Why Do We Tell Each Other Our Faith Stories?," in *Let Mutual Love Continue (Hebrews 13:1): Report of the Third Global Gathering of the Global Christian Forum, Bogotá, Colombia, 24–27 April 2018*, ed. Larry Miller (Bonn, Germany: Verlag für Kultur und Wissenschaft, 2021), 47–50.

[15] Robert W. Gribben, "The Future of Christianity?," Academia.edu, accessed May 13, 2021, https://www.academia.edu/5002563/The_Future_of_Christianity.

That spontaneous testimony or recall of a church's story is remarkable when heard in a group setting. Indeed, its untapped transformational potential can be revealing. Brian Stiller, global ambassador for the WEA, describes his faith-story sharing group at the GCF's Bogotá Global Gathering:

> Rosalee, raised in Brazil, educated and now living with her husband and children in the UK, walked us through her early coming to faith. She now heads up the global office of the Theological Commission of the WEA. Said, living in the unrest and struggle of Lebanon, told us how he and his family survived and thrived in the midst of gun battles and Syrian refugees. Paolo, serving in the Taizé community in France, through worship led us in their plaintive and inspiring music. Stefan from Moscow (we had met at the 500th anniversary service of the Protestant Reformation last October in Moscow) told of his early knowing of God's presence. Joseph from Ghana learned of the Gospel as a child. We learned from Rauli, a Finlander, of his early adventures into the former Soviet community. We laughed and prayed as we learned the ways of the Spirit.[16]

Likewise, Wesley Granberg-Michaelson, GCF committee member and former general secretary of the Reformed Church of America, offers this recollection:

> My group in Bogotá reflected the mix of the whole gathering, with several evangelicals and Pentecostals, and others who were Catholic, Orthodox, and versions of Protestantism, from diverse regions. Some of the stories still haunt me, spiritually. A Pentecostal described reluctantly attending a revival as a young man when an unknown preacher powerfully prophesied that he would be called into ministry and travel the world to build unity in the body of Christ. Decades later that has described his life. An Anglican priest told of being strangely overcome by an experience of God's love, like John Wesley, while in an economics class. A Vatican official shared how as a boy he was stunned when a non-Catholic friend told him he wasn't allowed to come into a Catholic church for a funeral. God spoke, and he works globally for Christian unity.[17]

Sharing faith stories is thus the distinguishing characteristic of GCF ecumenical activity.

---

[16] Brian Stiller, "June 2018," dispatchesfrombrian, accessed June 29, 2021, https://dispatchesfrombrian.com/2018/06/.

[17] Wesley Granberg-Michaelson, "An Open Window on a Mutilated Body," Sojourners, May 2, 2018, https://sojo.net/articles/open-window-mutilated-body.

A Timeline of GCF Meetings

Since its inception, the GCF has hosted three Global Gatherings: in 2007 in Limuru, Kenya; in 2011 in Manado, Indonesia; and in 2018 in Bogotá, Colombia. Global Gatherings, other committee meetings, and consultations are listed below with the date, venue, and (in some cases) approximate number of participants.[18]

1998, August 26–29, Chateau de Bossey, Switzerland, 28 participants

2000, September 9–11, Fuller Theological Seminary, Pasadena, CA, 38 participants

2002, June 15–20, Fuller Theological Seminary, Pasadena, CA, 60 participants

2004, Apr 30–May 4, Hong Kong, Asia and Pacific, 60 participants

2005, August 9–13, Lusaka, Zambia, Africa Consultation, 59 participants

2006, June 19–22, Warburg, Germany, Europe Consultation, 51 participants

2007, June 26–29, Santiago, Chile, Latin America and Caribbean Consultation

2007, November 6–9, First Global Gathering, Limuru, Kenya, 230 participants

2008, November 8–11, New Delhi, India, Consultation on Three-Year Program, 50 participants

2009, June 20–30, Middle East Team Visits to Egypt, Lebanon, and Syria

2009, November 16–20, Accra, Ghana, Africa Regional Meeting, 70 participants

2010, September 28–30, Lathi, Finland, Baltic and Nordic Countries, 40 participants

2010, November 12–16, Seoul, South Korea, Asia Regional Meeting, 70 participants

2010, November 23–25, San José, Costa Rica, Latin America Regional Meeting, 40 participants

2010, November 30–December 2, Beirut, Lebanon, Middle East Team Visit Follow-Up

2011, January 27–28, Istanbul, Turkey Committee Meeting

---

[18] Magali Moreno Sancho, a Mennonite Christian from Asunción, Paraguay, serves the GCF as an events coordinator and works closely with the only full-time employee of the GCF, the secretary. I am indebted to Sancho for diligently compiling this timeline of GCF meetings with available facts in our archives. Some of the numbers of participants may be either more or less by a few numbers, taking into account double counting as church representatives or stewards.

2011, August 8–11, Lima, Peru, Launch of Pentecostal Forum of Latin America, 35 participants

2011, October 4–7, Second Global Gathering, Manado, Indonesia, 287 participants

2012, January 27–28, Rome, Italy, Committee Meeting

2012, November 13–15, Pentecostal Forum of Latin America, Santiago, Chile (Southern Cone), 31 participants

2013, April 8–9, Amman, Jordan, Middle East Consultation, 21 participants

2013, May 20–23, Tunapuna, Trinidad, Caribbean Consultation, 30 participants

2013, October 15–17, Pentecostal Forum of Latin America, Bogotá, Colombia (Andean Region), 17 participants

2014, September 30–October 2, Pentecostal Forum of Latin America, Pachuca, Mexico (Central America), 31 participants

2015, May 27–29, Pentecostal Forum of Latin America, São Paolo, Brazil, 64 participants

2015, November 2–4, Tirana, Albania, *Discrimination, Persecution, Martyrdom: Following Christ Together*, 140 participants

2016, May 25–28, near Beirut, Lebanon, Second Middle East Consultation, 26 participants

2016, November 21–23, Pentecostal Forum of Latin America, Panama City, Panama, 50 participants

2017, May 22–23, Chateau de Bossey, Switzerland, *Complementary Roles on the Way to Greater Oneness in Christ*, 25 participants

2017, June 8–11, Accra, Ghana, *Call to Mission and Perceptions of Proselytism*, 30 participants

2018, April, 24–27, Bogotá, Colombia, Third Global Gathering, Let Mutual Love Continue, 250 participants

2018, September 18–21, Thessaloniki, Greece, Enlarged Facilitation Group Meeting

2019, February 10–13, Kuala Lumpur, Malaysia, Committee Meeting

2019, October 10–13, Christiansfeld, Denmark, Enlarged Facilitation Group Meeting with Youth Representatives

2019, October 24–25, Bogotá, Colombia, Latin America Exploratory Meeting

2020, January 21, Nairobi, Kenya, Africa Regional Leaders Exploratory Meeting

2020, April 23–September 3, Committee Meeting by Zoom

2021, February 22–23, Committee Meeting by Zoom

2021, April 27, Bogotá, Colombia, Virtual Reunion and Published Report Launch

Over the years, the membership of the committees overseeing the work of the GCF has evolved, and the earliest membership lists the following:[19]

1. Msgr. Jean-Claude Périsset, Pontifical Council for Promoting Christian Unity

2. Rev. Dr. Hilarion Alfeyev, Moscow Patriarchate

3. Dr. Musimbi Kanyoro, World Young Women's Christian Association

4. Metropolitan Mor Gregorios Yohanna Ibrahim, Syrian Orthodox Patriarchate of Antioch

5. Rev. Canon David Perry, Episcopal Church Center

6. Dr. Cecil M. Robeck, Assemblies of God (USA)

7. Rev. Majiza McKinty, South African Council of Churches

8. Rev. Canon David Hammid, Anglican Communion

9. Msgr. John Radano, Pontifical Council for Promoting Christian Unity

10. Dr. George Vandervelde, Institute for Christian Studies

11. Rev. Fr. Mikhail Goundiaev, Moscow Patriarchate

12. Rev. Dr. David Sang-Ehil Han, Church of God (Cleveland, USA)

13. Rev. Dr. Richard Howell, Evangelical Fellowship of India

14. Rev. Dr. John Graz, General Conference Seventh-day Adventists

15. Rev. Kuzipa Nalwamba, United Church of Zambia

16. Rev. Sarah Rowland Jones, Anglican Communion

17. Rev. Wesley Granberg-Michaelson, World Council of Churches

18. Rev. Dr. Fausto Vasconcelos, Baptist World Alliance

The current International Committee comprises the following:

1. Anglican Communion—Rev. Canon Dr. William Adam

---

[19] This was referred to in the literature as Continuation Committee, presumably to continue the efforts that had been made by the ecumenical bodies to explore closer cooperation and collaboration. As GCF became more established, we have tended to use International Committee to reflect the nature of the oversight body.

2. Association of Evangelicals in Africa—Rev. Dr. Aiah Foday-Khabenje

3. Baptist World Alliance—Rev. Everton Jackson

4. Catholic Church (Pontifical Council for Promoting Christian Unity) Fr. Andrzej Choromanski

5. Church of God (Cleveland)—Rev. Dr. David Sang-Ehil Han

6. Ecumenical Patriarchate—H. E. Metr Gennadios of Sassima

7. Latin America Evangelical—Dr. Ruth Padilla DeBorst

8. Lutheran World Federation—Dr. Dirk Lange

9. Megachurches—Rev. Dr. Hana Kim

10. Mennonite World Conference—Dr. Anne-Cathy Graber

11. Moscow Patriarchate—Fr. Mikhail Goundiaev

12. Organization of African Instituted Churches—Rev. Nicta Lubaale

13. Pentecostal World Fellowship—Dr. William Wilson

14. Pentecostal World Fellowship—Dr. David Wells

15. Pentecostals—Dr. Cecil M. Robeck Jr.

16. Salvation Army International—Commissioner Elizabeth Matear

17. Seventh-Day Adventist Church General Conference—Rev. Dr. Ganoune Diop

18. Syrian Orthodox Patriarchate of Antioch—H. E. Archbishop Mor Chrysostomos Michael Chamoun

19. World Communion of Reformed Churches—Rev. Dr. Chris Ferguson

20. World Council of Churches—Dr. Dimitra Koukoura

21. World Evangelical Alliance—Dr. Yassir Eric

22. World Evangelical Alliance—Dr. Thomas Schirrmacher

23. World Methodist Council—Bishop Rosemarie Wenner

24. World Vision International—Rev. Christo Greyling[20]

25. Global Christian Forum Foundation—Rev. Wesley Granberg-Michaelson

26. Fondation du Forum Chrétien Mondial—Dr. Jean-Daniel Plüss

---

[20] As of May 2021, there are vacancies to be filled by additional members from the Pontifical Council for Promoting Christian Unity, the World Council of Churches, the World Student Christian Fellowship, and the World Young Women's Christian Association.

Larry Miller, the GCF's second secretary, identifies the following as the distinctive outcomes of the GCF experience:

1. It prioritizes experience of unity rather than producing texts about unity.

2. It is a journey of those who set out together in spite of different and sometimes conflicting visions of the church and of Christian unity, and without knowing in advance what unity they will experience and can even seek.

3. Its purpose is faithfulness in both unity and mission, love both for one another and for the world.

4. A sufficient basis for undertaking the journey is faith in God and Jesus Christ, both divine and human—a faith that can be confessed together by both older churches and younger churches.

5. On the journey, equal space is given to the older churches and the younger churches, according to the GCF's 50/50 principle.

6. On the journey, participants bear witness to one another, sharing the stories of their own and their church's faith journey with Christ.

7. The journey consists of both being together and doing together.

8. There is also the acknowledgment that there need to be other journeys.

9. Thus, there is generally a relational and testimonial culture rather than an analytical and doctrinal one focusing on theological differences or ethical challenges.[21]

THE GCF'S SECRETARIES

Dana Robert, reflecting on the relationship between mission and Christian unity since the Edinburgh missionary conference of 1910, identifies several factors in current missiology and describes contemporary frameworks for mission and Christian unity since the Edinburgh 2010 centennial event. One of these frameworks, described as common witness through global networking, is the GCF, about which Robert quips that "there is no commitment to an organization, a headquarters, or permanent staff."[22]

In fact, though, the GCF does have one permanent staff member, its secretary. The story of the GCF is reflected in the lives, faith stories, and convictions of the three people who have had the privilege of serving as its secretaries. I will

---

[21] Larry Miller, "Responding to the Transformed Landscape of World Christianity: The Global Christian Forum," in *A History of the Desire for Christian Unity: Ecumenism in the Churches (19th–21st Century)*, ed. Alberto Melloni and Luca Ferracci, vol. 3 (Boston: Brill, forthcoming).

[22] Dana L. Robert, "One Christ—Many Witnesses: Visions of Mission and Unity, Edinburgh and Beyond," *Transformation: An International Journal of Holistic Mission Studies* 33, no. 4 (October 2016): 276.

briefly summarize their faith stories and show how they dovetail with the DNA of the GCF.

Huibert van Beek

Huibert van Beek, the GCF's founding secretary and a Dutch native, was born into a "very strict environment of exclusive Plymouth Brethren."[23] His exposure to a Bible study meeting of the Student Christian Movement (SCM) and his subsequent involvement in the Dutch Student Christian Association marked a return to faith at a time when he had decided to "discover the world" while in college. Relating personal faith to issues of society, culture, and politics, which is the hallmark of the SCM, was pivotal in his life and career afterward. The second decisive moment in his life was turning down a potentially lucrative career offer so that he could instead volunteer for international service through Service Abroad, a program of the Dutch Protestant churches for young people seeking to work in mission, development, and interchurch aid.

After a stint at the Paris Missionary Society, van Beek was sent, in June 1965, to Madagascar to teach at a Protestant secondary school, Paul Minault in Antananarivo. After several years of teaching and youth work, van Beek was invited in September 1969, by the general secretary of the newly formed United Church of Jesus Christ in Madagascar, Victor Rakotoarimanana, to be his assistant at the head office of the church. He thus had extensive interaction with all the segments of the church and even served as deputy on behalf of the General Secretary in his absence. One of his legacies was to set up a department of development to oversee all the church's projects.

After several stints, van Beek left Madagascar in July 1978 to take up a one-year position as a consultant at the WCC's Africa desk. This entailed extensive travel and also led to different positions within the WCC. Eventually, in 1992, van Beek was appointed executive secretary of the newly established Office of Church and Ecumenical Relations. In this role, he was in charge of relations with WCC member churches, national councils of churches, regional ecumenical organizations, and ecumenical officers of member churches and was assigned to develop relations with evangelical and Pentecostal nonmember churches, movements, and groups. The assignment came in the wake of the 1991 Canberra WCC Assembly, which had the theme of "Come Holy Spirit, Renew the Whole Creation." This theme indicated that the world's foremost ecumenical organization was beginning to take seriously the burgeoning Pentecostal and evangelical movements within global Christianity. In this environment, the 1998 discussions on the feasibility of forming the GCF were born.

---

[23] Huibert van Beek, email to the author, March 25, 2021.

Arguably the best preparation van Beek had for serving the global Christian family beyond the ecumenical confines of the WCC was his compilation of the authoritative 2006 *Handbook of Churches and Councils*, which listed all the ecclesial families and their regional and national configurations.[24] The completion of this encyclopedic work required a degree of diligence and unrivaled attention to detail.

Larry Miller

Larry Miller also had extensive global ecumenical experience before responding to the call to serve as GCF Secretary. He grew up in a strong Mennonite family in the United States, and one of his first tests of faith was when attempting to follow Jesus's word to the "rich young man," he decided to give away an early inheritance from his parents. Growing up in the 1960s, Miller was greatly impacted by dramatic events such as the Vietnam War, racial strife, and the starvation of Biafrans during the Nigerian Civil War. For Mennonites committed to conscientious objection and peacemaking, it was a very trying period.

Just before he concluded his doctoral studies at the University of Strasbourg (France), Miller had another formative experience: "I was working in the library on my dissertation, and I looked up and noticed a book by one of my professors on a shelf. I pulled it down. It was dusty, and no one had ever checked it out. I suddenly realized that I was poised to write those kinds of books!"[25]

That awareness motivated him to accept instead of university teaching a calling to serve the global fraternity of Mennonites, a position he held for twenty-two years. In this role, Miller sought, among other things, to amplify the voice of the Global South and to facilitate its capacity building. In so doing, he successfully organized a first world conference in Calcutta (now Kolkata, India) in 1997, along with subsequent ones in Bulawayo, Zimbabwe (2003), and Asunción, Paraguay (2009). These events, unlike previous ones held in fancy surroundings in the Global North, were equally memorable and took place without any discernible hitches.

Miller testifies that his ecumenical journey has been quite transformational in that "walking with Christians of other churches [has] brought many moments of revelation and conversion." Continuing, he elaborates,

---

[24] Huibert van Beek, ed., *A Handbook of Churches and Councils: Profiles of Ecumenical Relationships* (Geneva: World Council of Churches, 2006).

[25] Larry Miller, "A Journey with Jesus Christ: Moments of Revelation and Conversion," in *Sharing of Faith Stories: A Methodology for Promoting Unity*, ed. Richard Howell and Thomas Schirrmacher (Bonn, Germany: Verlag für Kultur und Wissenschaft, forthcoming).

Thanks to Lutherans, I came to understand that it is not enough to be baptized one day as an adult believer; our vocation is to live out our baptism every day. From Baptists, I learned that it is insufficient to follow Christ daily; our calling is to invite others to do so. Reformed Christians helped me see more clearly that not only is Jesus Christ the Lord of the Church, he is also the Lord of history. Relating to Pentecostals, I sensed in a new way the importance of experiencing transcendence personally and frequently. From Orthodox Christians, I learned that every act of the believer should be a spiritual act. The stories of African Instituted Churches demonstrated strikingly that the body of Christ is and always must be incarnated in very specific cultural contexts. In the Taizé Community, I found a place of rest for my spiritual heart. Thanks to Catholics, I came to believe that when we fracture the Church, we wound the body of Christ and Christ himself suffers the pain. Lord have mercy![26]

Casely Baiden Essamuah

Born in Ghana, West Africa, to a distinguished Christian family (his father, Samuel Benyarku Essamuah, was the presiding bishop of the Methodist Church from 1979 to 1983, and his mother, Ernestina Baiden Essamuah, was a women's ministry leader), Casely Essamuah (the author of this essay) had, by the time of his appointment as GCF secretary in 2018, spent half of his life on the East Coast of the United States. After studying at Harvard Divinity School (master's degree) and Boston University (doctorate), he served as global missions minister at two US evangelical churches with significant mission programs and budgets.

Even though he was raised in a Christian home, Essamuah credits Scripture Union for enabling him to make the faith his own. Serving in global missions exposed him to global Christianity and where the church can do evangelism and mission, whether explicitly or implicitly. During his educational career in the United States, he was impacted by Dana Robert, Rodney Petersen, and Harvey Cox, among others. While at Park Street Church in Boston, he led an effort to implement a "full support" policy for its missionaries. At Bay Area Community Church in Annapolis, Maryland, he led several short-term mission trips to different parts of the world. Opportunities for service in his homeland and also among the vast Ghanaian diaspora in North America opened up, and he has served in leadership roles there as well. And yet, as deeply rooted as he is in Ghanaian Methodism (the topic of his doctoral dissertation), he believes that the calling to serve US churches in global missions was a providential preparation for serving the GCF. In another publication, he reflects on his role as GCF secretary in this way:

---

[26] Miller.

My role therefore—as a bridge builder between the Global South and Global North—is even more significant given the demographic and numerical shift of the Christian faith to the Global South, and the continuing economic ascendancy of the church based in the Global North. The following questions are always with me: How do Westerners whose Christianity is based primarily on rationalistic interpretations co-exist peacefully with Global South Christians whose Christian pilgrimage is more experiential? How can churches that are growing rapidly in the Global South and among immigrants in the Global North meaningfully engage churches in the Global North, some of whom are in decline and yet with a lot of church history, global engagement and financial resources? What is the next step in ecumenism that GCF is suitably positioned to provide?

Essamuah considers himself an accidental missionary, called to build bridges for the mission of the church.[27]

The GCF's Secretaries and the Organization's DNA

In each of the life histories of those called to serve as GCF secretary, we find that they have come from a distinctive spiritual background and heritage, but not one that led them to take a divisive stance. Instead, standing firmly on the solid rock of their convictions, they have facilitated outreach to other spiritual families, transcending church, geographical, and sociocultural boundaries. Having been bridge builders and orchestra conductors, they have demonstrated servant leadership that ensures that all voices are heard at the table.

Returning to the theme of this chapter, the GCF is a new Pentecost as it reveals God's power to create something new out of our own distinctives. The spectators on the day of Pentecost had this experience, according to Acts 2:7–12: "Utterly amazed, they asked: 'Aren't all these who are speaking Galileans? Then how is it that each of us hears them in our native language? Parthians, Medes and Elamites; residents of Mesopotamia, Judea and Cappadocia, Pontus and Asia, Phrygia and Pamphylia, Egypt and the parts of Libya near Cyrene; visitors from Rome (both Jews and converts to Judaism); Cretans and Arabs—we hear them declaring the wonders of God in our own tongues!' Amazed and perplexed, they asked one another, 'What does this mean?'" It was a recognition that those speaking were distinctive and yet unified in "declaring the wonders of God."

---

[27] On the history of Boston's Park Street Church, see Garth M. Rosell, *The Surprising Work of God: Harold John Ockenga, Billy Graham, and the Rebirth of Evangelicalism* (Grand Rapids, MI: Baker Academic, 2008). And on my own formation for evangelism and ecumenism, see Casely Baiden Essamuah, "Accidental Missionary: Called to a Life of Building Bridges for Christ and His Kingdom—an Interview with Casely Baiden Essamuah, Secretary, Global Christian Forum," ed. Michèle Miller Sigg, *Journal of African Christian Biography* 75, no. 4 (January 31, 2019): 53–67.

Pentecost was thus a dress rehearsal for Revelation 7:9–10, where we see also the distinctives of believers enveloped in oneness:

> After this I looked, and there before me was a great multitude that no one could count, from every nation, tribe, people and language, standing before the throne and before the Lamb. They were wearing white robes and were holding palm branches in their hands. And they cried out in a loud voice:
>
> *"Salvation belongs to our God,*
> *who sits on the throne,*
> *and to the Lamb."*

INDEX